21st-CENTURY OXFORD AUTHORS

21st-CENTURY OXFORD AUTHORS

Isaac Rosenberg

EDITED BY

VIVIEN NOAKES

OXFORD

UNIVERSITY PRESS

OXFORD
UNIVERSITY PRESS

Great Clarendon Street, Oxford OX2 6DP

Oxford University Press is a department of the University of Oxford.
It furthers the University's objective of excellence in research, scholarship,
and education by publishing worldwide in

Oxford New York

Auckland Cape Town Dar es Salaam Hong Kong Karachi
Kuala Lumpur Madrid Melbourne Mexico City Nairobi
New Delhi Shanghai Taipei Toronto

With offices in

Argentina Austria Brazil Chile Czech Republic France Greece
Guatemala Hungary Italy Japan Poland Portugal Singapore
South Korea Switzerland Thailand Turkey Ukraine Vietnam

Oxford is a registered trade mark of Oxford University Press
in the UK and in certain other countries

Published in the United States
by Oxford University Press Inc., New York

© Vivien Noakes 2008

The moral rights of the author have been asserted
Database right Oxford University Press (maker)

First published 2008

British Library Cataloguing in Publication Data

Data available

Library of Congress Cataloging in Publication Data

Data available

Typeset by SPI Publisher Services, Pondicherry, India
Printed in Great Britain
on acid-free paper by
CPI Antony Rowe, Chippenham, Wiltshire

ISBN 978-0-19-955340-2

1 3 5 7 9 10 8 6 4 2

ACKNOWLEDGEMENTS

THE family of Isaac Rosenberg have been consistently supportive during the preparation of this book. Rosenberg's sister, the late Annie Wynick, championed her brother's work during the years when his reputation was at its lowest, and protected his surviving manuscripts. Any scholar of his work owes her an immense debt. I am most grateful for the help and encouragement given to me by her son, Bernard Wynick, Rosenberg's literary executor.

The Principal and Fellows of Somerville College, Oxford, offered invaluable support and generous hospitality during the early years of my working on this edition. In particular I would like to thank Professor Katherine Duncan-Jones and Dr Fiona Stafford. I would also like to express my warm thanks to Professor Jon Stallworthy. To the Revd Ralph Waller, Gillian Carey and Ann Mann of Harris Manchester College, Oxford, I owe an immense debt.

Most of Rosenberg's manuscripts are housed in the Department of Documents in the Imperial War Museum. Work on this project would have been immeasurably more complicated but for the astonishing generosity of the Rosenberg family, and of the late Patric Dickson, Ian Parsons, and Roger Lancelyn Green, who arranged for Rosenberg's papers to be deposited in the museum. During the years that I worked there I received much help from Roderick Suddaby, Keeper of the Department of Documents, and from Nigel Steel, Simon Robbins, Stephen Walton, Anthony Richards, Amanda Mason, Wendy Lutterloch, Simon Offord, and the late David Shaw. I thank them all.

For help in various ways, I am most grateful to Richard Andersen, Tom Chandler, Professor Joseph Cohen, Dr Steve Crook, Mrs Mignon Franks, Ruth Freestone King, Luke Gertler, Leofranc Holford-Strevens, David J. Holmes, the late Isaac Horvitch, Jonathan Legg, Jean Liddiard, Dr Jean Moorcroft Wilson, Bernard O'Donoghue, Professor Patrick Quinn, Dennis Silk, the late Jon Silkin, Mrs Betty Silver, Isambard Thomas, the late Frank R. Waley (at one time Rosenberg's commanding officer on the Western Front).

The staffs of the following have been most co-operative in assisting me and answering my queries: Ben Uri, The London Jewish Museum of Art (Sarah MacDougall and Rachel Dickson in particular for their help with the illustrations); the Bodleian Library, Oxford; Benthams University Library, University of Bristol (Hannah Lowery, Archivist,

Special Collections); University of Cape Town Libraries; Special Collections Research Center, the Joseph Regenstein Library, the University of Chicago Library (Paula Y. Lee and Sandy Roscoe); Eton College Library (Michael Meredith, Librarian); the Jewish Chronicle (Sue Greenberg), Department of Manuscripts and Archives, the Jewish National & University Library, Jerusalem (Rivka Plesser); The National Archives, Kew; Henry W. and Albert A. Berg Collection of English and American Literature, The New York Public Library, Astor, Lenox and Tilden Foundations (Dr Steve Crook); The University of Reading (Michael Bott, Keeper of Archives and Manuscripts); The Society of Authors (Alison Watson); Hartley Library, University of Southampton (Jenny Ruthven, Special Collections Librarian); Rare Books & Special Collections, Thomas Cooper Library, University of South Carolina (Professor Patrick Scott, Associate University Librarian for Special Collections & Professor of English, and Maggie Vasterling); the Harry Ransom Humanities Research Center, The University of Texas at Austin (Dr Joseph Cahoon).

For permission to quote material in copyright I am grateful to: the Master and Fellows of Emmanuel College, Cambridge (Professor Denys Harding); David Higham Associates (Sir Edward Marsh); Scirard Lancelyn Green (Gordon Bottomley); New Directions Publishing Corporation (Ezra Pound).

For permission to reproduce illustrations, I would like to thank: Mrs Mignon Franks; Mrs Gerda Horvitch; the Imperial War Museum; the National Portrait Gallery, London; Joan Rodker; the Joseph Cohen Collection of World War I Literature, Rare Books and Special Collections, University of South Carolina; the Stern Pissarro Gallery, London; the Tullie House Museum & Art Gallery, Carlisle; Bernard Wynick.

I would also like to thank all those at the Oxford University Press with whom I have worked so happily in the production of this book, in particular Andrew McNeillie, Fiona Vlemmiks, and Jacqueline Baker.

Finally I would like to record my gratitude to the late Hermann Peschmann, who first introduced me to the work of Isaac Rosenberg nearly half a century ago. I dedicate this book to his memory.

CONTENTS

LIST OF ILLUSTRATIONS

FIGURES

PLATES

INTRODUCTION

WHEN Isaac Rosenberg died early in the morning of 1 April 1918, he left behind more than one hundred and fifty poems, four plays, three slight volumes of poems that he had published himself, a handful of prose works, and at least two hundred letters. He was 26, and had trained as a painter at the prestigious Slade School of Art in London. Enlisting in 1915, he spent two and a half years as a private in the British army, twenty-one months of which were on the Western Front. He was killed during the German spring offensive of 1918, which he had described three weeks before as 'this coming "earthquake"'.[1]

Rosenberg was born in Bristol on 25 November 1890. He was one of twins, the other of whom did not survive. His father, Dovber (who changed his name to Barnett) had been born in Lithuania into a family of scholars and rabbis. In his youth he had been a student of the Torah, preparing from the age of 10 for the rabbinate. However, following a decree of 1875, service in the Russian army was mandatory for Jewish men. By most, it was dreaded. Not only did the Jewish conscripts suffer bullying and humiliation, they also found it difficult to continue with the observation of their faith. Moreover, as Rosenberg wrote in 1916 after his own enlistment, 'my people are Tolstoyans and object to my being in khaki'.[2] After failed attempts to gain exemption, Dovber decided, in 1886, to leave his home, his wife and their small daughter, arranging that they would follow him when he was settled elsewhere. After various disastrous adventures, he arrived in Hull on a ship from Hamburg. His family followed in 1888, and by the time of Isaac's birth they were living in Bristol. Uprooted, unsettled, and unhappy, Barnett became a pedlar, living in poverty for the rest of his life. In 1897 they moved to London, and it was here, in Stepney and Whitechapel in the East End, that Isaac spent his boyhood.

There were eventually six children—three boys and three girls—of which Isaac was the oldest son and second child. His mother, Hacha, supplemented their meagre income by sewing, doing embroidery, and taking in lodgers. Her husband was away for six months every year, and she bore the burden of her children's upbringing.

[1] Letter to Gordon Bottomley, 7 March 1918.
[2] Letter to R. C. Trevelyan [last week of May 1916].

Unable to secure a place in the over-subscribed Jews' Free School in Whitechapel, Isaac went instead to the local board school where more than 90 per cent of the boys were Jewish. Their religious education took place after school hours, but Isaac found little reward in what he was taught, and consistently absented himself. This meant that, although he spoke Yiddish at home, he grew up without any real knowledge of Hebrew. He did, though, read the Old Testament with fascination, but in the authorized version rather than in Hebrew text. This, and the encouragement he received both in drawing and in the reading of English poets, established the course of his later life. By the time he was about 11 he knew that he wanted to be a poet and a painter, a decision from which he never wavered. Though strongly aware of his inheritance, he thought of himself as essentially an English, rather than a Jewish, poet. Both the power and the individual quality of his poetry grew from this double heritage.

In 1905, unable to go to art school as he would have wished, Rosenberg was apprenticed to an engraver, Carl Hentschel, in Fleet Street. It was soulless work which he came to hate, and in 1911 he was dismissed from his apprenticeship for slackness.

Meanwhile, he found himself part of the intellectually stimulating environment of pre-war Whitechapel. In 1892 the Whitechapel Library had opened and soon become a gathering place for young people, earning the nickname 'the university of the ghetto'. Nine years later, on the adjoining site, the Whitechapel Art Gallery was built. Its purpose was to 'bring great art to the people of the East End of London', showing the work of both old masters and young talent. At the Library Rosenberg met those of his own age, some of whom went on to become established artists and writers—including David Bomberg and Mark Gertler. He also became part of a group of four, all interested in poetry and in walking and talking into the night, who called themselves the Whitechapel Boys.

Unemployed after leaving Hertschel's, and with no immediate source of income, Rosenberg soon felt adrift and depressed. He had, for several years, been attending evening classes in drawing at the Arts and Crafts School in Stepney Green, and then at Birkbeck College, part of the University of London, where he won a number of prizes for his work, and he now applied to the Jewish Educational Aid Society for help in paying art school fees, but was turned down. Then, one day in 1911, as he was working in the National Gallery copying a portrait of Velàsquez's *Philip IV*, he realized that he was being watched. Mrs Lily Delissa Joseph, the sister of the painter Solomon J. Solomon and herself an artist, was fascinated with what he was doing. She invited him to visit her home, and here he met two other Jewish women—Mrs Henrietta Löwy and Mrs Herbert Cohen. Shortly after their meeting, Mrs Cohen agreed to fund one year's study for him at the Slade School of Art, one of the most prestigious London art colleges.

He enrolled there in October 1911. Among his contemporaries, as well as Mrs Löwy's daughter Ruth, were David Bomberg, Mark Gertler, Paul Nash, C. R. W. Nevinson, Stanley Spencer, William Roberts, and Dora Carrington. It was an exciting time to be a student there; new movements were developing as the whole basis of painting was questioned and explored. In his painting, as in his poetry, Rosenberg was an interested observer of what was going on in the contemporary scene, but he allied himself to no school, pursuing thoughts and ideas in his own way.

In 1912 he published a slim volume of poems, entitled *Night and Day*. With this to show them, he was now able to approach other poets, asking for their advice and help in publishing more widely. Laurence Binyon met him, and was impressed with the promise shown in his work; in 1922 he would write an Introductory Memoir for the first collected edition of Rosenberg's poems. The importance of his poetry was growing, so that in time he came to think of himself as a poet first and painter second.

Perhaps the most important meeting of his Slade years was with Edward Marsh, at that time Private Secretary to Winston Churchill. Marsh had inherited a part-share of a fund set up as compensation for the assassination in 1812 of his forebear, the English prime minister Spencer Perceval. The amount of money was not large, but it was enough to give him the freedom to support and encourage young painters and poets of promise. Bomberg introduced Rosenberg to Marsh at his favourite gathering place, the Café Royal in Regent Street. Marsh immediately bought some of Rosenberg's work, and for the rest of his life supported him both as patron and as critic.

Meanwhile, as the result of a misunderstanding with Mrs Cohen, the money for his studies came to an end. He applied again to the Jewish Educational Aid Society, and this time they agreed to pay his fees for a few more months, until March 1914.

During the winter of 1913–14 his health was not good. Fearing consumption, his doctor advised him to seek sunshine. The previous August his sister Minnie had married, and she and her husband, Wolf Horvitch, were now living in South Africa. Again with a grant, this time of £13 to cover the fare, Rosenberg sailed from Tilbury to Cape Town at the beginning of June 1914.

Initially excited by the beauty and the clarity of the light, he was soon frustrated by the cultural desert that he found. However, hoping to become known so that he might receive commissions, he delivered a lecture on art, which was published in two parts in the magazine *South African Women in Council.*[3] Meanwhile, Europe had erupted into the war that would decide his eventual fate. For a while, far from the conflict, he could stand back and observe, with sadness, what was happening, expressing his thoughts in his first war poem, 'On Receiving News of the War: Cape Town'.

In February 1915, he left South Africa, uncertain what he would find when he arrived back in England. The initial rush to the colours had abated, but he knew that he must decide whether to enlist or not. One of his first tasks was to prepare for publication a second slim volume of poems entitled *Youth*. Then he looked for work, but he could find nothing, and no work meant no income. Throughout the early autumn he vacillated. He thought about volunteering for the Royal Army Medical Corps, 'as the idea of killing upsets me a bit',[4] but, at little over five feet, he was too short. At one point he thought that he would enlist in the infantry, but then he decided against this, telling a friend: 'I have changed my mind again about joining the army. I feel about it that more men means more war,—besides the immorality of joining with no patriotic convictions.'[5] But with no money and no immediate prospects he had little choice, and in October he enlisted, saying that he had made the decision so that his mother could have the Separation Allowance that was given to dependants. He was sent to the Bantam Battalion of the 12th Suffolk Regiment stationed at Bury St Edmunds. These battalions had been set up in 1914 to take volunteers who were below the statutory height for military service but who were nevertheless fit. Some of those who were accepted into the Bantams were later weeded out, once it was realized that they were not strong enough to make good soldiers, but Rosenberg remained.

During his early days of training, which he found almost intolerably difficult, he worked on a play called *Moses* which he had begun in South Africa, and he gathered together a collection of poems for

---

[3] The text can be found on pp. 212–21.
[4] Letter to Mr Schiff [early Nov. 1915], p. 280.
[5] Letter to Mr Schiff [Oct. 1915], p. 278.

another small volume. In May they heard that their overseas posting was imminent. Before going he saw *Moses* (containing the play and nine poems) through the press; it was published shortly after he left for France at the beginning of June 1916. Within days of arriving in France he wrote his first trench poem, 'Break of Day in the Trenches'. Meanwhile, copies of *Moses* and his earlier volume, *Youth*, had been sent to the poet, R. C. Trevelyan, who responded with enthusiasm, forwarding copies to others of his friends, including Gordon Bottomley. Unable to believe the praise that he was receiving, Rosenberg suspected that he was having his leg pulled, but both poets believed that his was a new and exciting talent. He and Bottomley never met, but throughout his time in France they carried on a regular, and fascinating, correspondence. Edward Marsh, meanwhile, was concerned that Bottomley had given too much praise to *Moses*, a play that seemed to him to be magnificent in parts, but on the whole 'quite ridiculously bad', adding: 'I do want him to renounce the lawless and grotesque manner in which he usually writes and to pay a little attention to form and tradition.'[6]

Despite the very real encouragement that Marsh gave him, he never really understood what Rosenberg was trying to do. Bottomley, on the other hand, could see the vitality and power of the young poet's work, and their letters make delightful reading. It was Bottomley who proposed and carried through the publication of the first edition of his work in 1922. But Rosenberg had his own reason for publishing what he knew to be raw and unfinished work, replying to Marsh's criticism: 'You know the conditions I have always worked under, and particularly with this last lot of poems. You know how earnestly one must wait on ideas, (you cannot coax real ones to you) and let as it were, a skin grow naturally round and through them. If you are not free, you can only, when the ideas come hot, seize them with the skin in tatters raw, crude, in some parts beautiful in others monstrous. Why print it then? Because these rare parts must not be lost.'[7]

In France, Rosenberg settled into the routine of army life. He found it soulless and tedious, but he prided himself on being a good soldier. His otherwise empty mind was always occupied with his poetry, and he wrote to Binyon: 'I am determined that this war, with all its powers for devastation, shall not master my poetry—that is if I am lucky enough to come through all right. I will not leave a corner of my

---

[6] Letter from Marsh to Bottomley, quoted *JC* pp. 150–1.
[7] Letter to Marsh, 4 Aug. [1916], p. 308.

consciousness covered up, but saturate myself with the strange and extraordinary new conditions of this life and it will all refine itself into poetry later on'.[8]

As a private, Rosenberg confronted two particular problems: shortage of paper, and lack of opportunity to write. He had always been in the habit of composing his poems in his head, sometimes forgetting to write them down. Indeed, his friend, the artist John Amschewitz, recalled how Rosenberg came one day to his studio in a state of some excitement, proclaiming, ' "I have got a poem here,"—feeling in his pockets the while—"I think it is a good idea" (the search in his pockets getting more frantic) and then disappointedly, "I must have forgotten it somewhere"—and then he collapsed, shaking with laughter—"Great Snakes! but I have forgotten to write it!".'[9] When he was out of the line in France, he could use the paper given to the soldiers in rest areas by the YMCA and the Church Army. Otherwise he scribbled his thoughts on the backs of envelopes he had received, or on any scraps that he could find. These he carried round in his damp khaki pocket, creating considerable problems of legibility for his later editors. When I was cataloguing his papers at the Imperial War Museum the immediacy of the trench experience could be seen not only in the torn and muddy condition of many of the manuscripts, but also in the dustings of mud that fell from the creases as the papers were unfolded before being put into their transparent slip-cases.

He describes the problems of opportunity in a letter to Marsh in May 1917: 'Don't think [. . .] I've time to write. This last poem is only about 70 lines and I started it about October. It is only when we get a bit of rest and the others might be gambling or squabbling I add a line or two, and continue this way.'[10]

Having written the poem, he then sent it home for safekeeping or to be typed out and returned to him so that he could work on it further. At times this presented problems with censorship, as he told Marsh: 'I have been forbidden to send poems home, as the censor won't be bothered with going through such rubbish.'[11] Fortunately, other censors were not so squeamish, or few of his trench poems would have survived. As well as individual poems, he was working on a play which he initially called *The Amulet* and later, as he changed his plans

----

[8] Letter to Binyon [autumn 1916], p. 320.
[9] *The Zionist Record*, South Africa, 23 July 1937, p. 15.
[10] Letter to Marsh, postmarked 27 May 1917, p. 332.
[11] Letter to Marsh [Aug. 1916], p. 313.

for it, *The Unicorn*, telling a correspondent: 'If I am lucky, and come off undamaged, I mean to put all my innermost experiences into the "Unicorn". I want it to symbolize the war and all the devastating forces let loose by an ambitious and unscrupulous will.'[12]

By January 1917 he was feeling thoroughly run down and low, and Marsh wrote to a friend at the War Office, telling him of Rosenberg's talent and asking if he could be taken out of the line. As a result he was withdrawn from the front line and put into a Works Battalion. Though no longer exposed to constant danger and hardship, he had nevertheless to go up the line at night taking supplies, including rolls of barbed wire, in some ways a worse option. '[...] transport work was a veritable nightmare', says his Divisional history. 'All supplies of ammunition, water, rations, clothing, etc., had to be taken up on pack animals, as, owing to the mud, which for the greater part of the distance was seldom less than waist deep, vehicles became obviously impracticable. [...] Owing to the fact that the ground had been shelled so constantly during the Somme offensive, it was intersected with shell holes long since filled with mud, and when an unfortunate animal or man fell, it was a matter of the very greatest difficulty to extricate him alive [...] It soon became obvious that the majority of the men were physically unable to continue this nightly strain.'[13] As the line dried out in the early summer, limbers—the wheels and supporting structure taken from gun carriages—could be used as well as the mules. It was this experience that led to a poem thought by some to be the greatest poem of the war, 'Dead Man's Dump', written in the summer of 1917.

In September that year he had his only leave from active service in the twenty-one months he was in France. He was in England for ten days, in many ways a strange experience, as he told Bottomley: 'We have lived in such an elemental way so long, things here don't look quite right to me somehow; or it may be the consciousness of my so limited time here for freedom, so little time to do so many things— bewilders me.'[14]

He returned to France to face another winter. With talk of an impending German attack, he was once more back in the front line, telling Marsh in January: 'I am back in the trenches which are terrible now. We spend most of our time pulling each other out of the mud.

[12] Letter to Miss Seaton, 8 March 1918, p. 362.
[13] F. E. Whitton, *History of the 40th Division* (1926), pp. 43–4.
[14] Letter to GB, 21 Sept. 1917, p. 345.

I am not fit at all now and am more in the way than any use. You see I appear in excellent health and a doctor will make no distinction between health and strength. I am not strong. What is happening to me now is more tragic than the "passion play". Christ never endured what I endure. It is breaking me completely.'[15]

The expected attack burst upon the Western Front on the morning of 21 March 1918. The allied armies were not prepared for the ferocity of the onslaught, and their lines fell back. The old Somme battlefields were lost, the vital railhead of Amiens was threatened, and within days the Germans were only a few miles from Paris. On 11 April, Haig issued his famous Special Order of the Day: 'With our backs to the wall and believing in the justice of our cause each one of us must fight to the end.' For Rosenberg it was already over. He had been killed when the Germans raided their position early in the morning of 1 April.

His body was not immediately found. Without definite news, his family hoped that he might have been taken prisoner and that he would return. But then, as the battlefields were cleared after the war, the remains of a group of men belonging to his regiment were discovered. They could not be individually identified, but Rosenberg was known to be among them. They were reburied at Bailleul Road East British Cemetery, St-Laurent-Blagny, near Arras. As well as his details and the Star of David, the tombstone bears the words 'Artist and Poet', an extra for which the family had to pay 3s. 3d.[16]

The process of establishing Rosenberg's posthumous reputation was long and slow. Despite his huge talent, he was not a glamorous figure, and his work was known to only a few. The publication in 1922 of *Poems by Isaac Rosenberg*, edited by Bottomley and with an Introductory Memoir by Binyon, passed almost unnoticed.

The first full edition, *The Collected Works of Isaac Rosenberg: Poetry, Prose, Letters and Some Drawing*, ed. Gordon Bottomley and Denys Harding, with a Foreword by Siegfried Sassoon (1937),

[15] Letter to Marsh, postmarked 26 January 1918, p. 356.
[16] Letter from the Principal Assistant Secretary of the Imperial War Graves Commission to Barnett Rosenberg, 24 May 1927: 'I am to express regret that the Commission are unable to accede to your request to engrave the words "Artist and Poet" after the name of Private I. Rosenberg in the Military inscription on the headstone that is to be erected over his grave. | I am however, to say that they could be engraved at the foot of the stone as the personal inscription at your expense. The cost of engraving this inscription would be 3/3d.'

appeared at a time when a new war was threatened and there was little appetite for the old; again, it attracted sparse notice. Yet, ironically, it was a poet who was to die in that war who drew attention to his work: 'Rosenberg I only repeat what you were saying' wrote Keith Douglas in 'Desert Flowers' in 1943, a year before his own death.

By the mid-1970s, his collected works had been out of print for nearly forty years—the poems and fragments were reissued in a separate volume in 1949—and in 1976 they were published in an edition prepared by Ian Parsons. Since then, partly as a result of the ever-growing interest there is in the poetry of the Great War, Rosenberg has at last been recognized as an important poet. Although he is thought of as a war poet, the greatest part of his output has nothing to do with war; when he left for France in the summer of 1916 he had written 137 of the 158 poems that are known to have survived.

Meanwhile, there was the issue of what should happen to his papers, so carefully preserved by his sister Annie—these included most of the manuscripts and typescripts of his poems, plays, and prose—and by some of his correspondents. Many manuscripts have not survived. Apart from a few small scraps, 'Daughters of War', over which he worked for so many months, exists only in a single fair copy and a number of typescripts. Similarly, though there are typescripts, there are only two manuscript scraps for 'Dead Man's Dump', and three for his 370-line poem 'Night and Day'. We can only speculate on the loss of poems for which there is no record, but the number is likely to be considerable.

It was fortunate that two of those to whom he wrote his letters and often sent drafts of his poems—Bottomley and Marsh—realized the importance of what they had, and preserved his letters to them safely among their papers. Many of those to other correspondents have been lost, including, despite her careful custody of her brother's other papers, his letters to Annie.

In preparation for the 1922 edition, the surviving letters were sent to Binyon so that he could use them as the basis of his memoir. Most of these were then returned to their owners, but those to Bottomley were not. When he asked for their return, Binyon replied that he no longer had them. When Harding was preparing the 1937 edition he was again approached, but denied any knowledge of their whereabouts. In 1959, an exhibition of his work, including manuscripts, was mounted at Leeds University, and the curator wrote to Binyon's widow, asking once more if they were among his papers. Again the reply came that they were not. Then, in 1995, when the British

Library was preparing for its move from Bloomsbury to King's Cross, a brown paper package was found bearing a printed British Museum label inscribed 'Rosenberg Papers'. Binyon, who had been Keeper of the Department of Prints and Drawings in the British Museum, had apparently put them away safely and then forgotten them, and they had been lost for nearly seventy-five years. In 2007 they were published by Jean Liddiard in *Isaac Rosenberg: Poetry Out of My Head and Heart*, a volume that contains a number of misreadings which have been corrected in this edition.

In 1953, Annie decided to offer her papers as a gift to the British Museum. They declined the offer, but agreed to take the manuscript of *Moses* and 'a group of short poems as representative of your brother's literary work'[17]—his value was not yet recognized.

After her death in 1961, apart from Edward Marsh's papers which are in the Berg Collection in the New York Public Library, the manuscripts belonged substantially to two groups of people: those previously owned by Annie had been passed down to Patric Dickinson and Ian Parsons, and Roger Lancelyn Green had inherited the papers of Gordon Bottomley. These three, in a remarkable act of scholarship and generosity endorsed by Rosenberg's family, decided that all these papers should be deposited as a gift in one place where they could be made available to scholars. In 1979 they approached the Imperial War Museum in London, and that summer they were given into its safe-keeping.

Reviewing the 1922 edition, Edith Sitwell lamented how little critical attention Rosenberg's work had received: 'These poems are strong and rank as marvellous jungle animals', she wrote, 'they terrify by their crouch and spring; the fire in them is acrid and terrible. They have the real quality of greatness that is so rare in modern poetry. Sometimes, it is true, their strength is too much for the leash on which they are chained, but this is almost their only fault. [. . .] Isaac Rosenberg is one of the greatest poets we have had in this or the last generation, and I do not understand why the critics are preserving this strange silence on the subject [. . .] I do not dare to think what such a poet might have become, and what we have lost.'[18]

---

[17] Letter from A. J. Collins, Keeper of Manuscripts, to Annie Wynick, 5 Dec. 1953.
[18] *The New Age: A Weekly Review of Politics, Literature and Art*, vol. 31, no. 13, 27 July 1922, p. 161.

NOTE ON THE TEXT OF THE POEMS, FRAGMENTS, AND PLAYS

Only rarely did Rosenberg date his work. He kept no diary, at least none is known to have survived. One of his friends, Joseph Leftwich, kept a diary for 1911 which has provided some clues. His biographers give helpful biographical information for dating some of his early work. Most of the surviving pre-war letters say little about his poetry, although those written from France do speak directly of the composition of individual poems. Examining thematic and stylistic developments yields some evidence, but this is limited. Partly this is on the one hand because Rosenberg played with ideas over long periods, returning to themes, indeed to whole lines, that interested him, and on the other because his enjoyment of experimentation in form, which characterized his entire career as a poet, means that no formal preoccupation stands out at any time. For much of his work there is little to guide us but circumstantial evidence, and clues that arise from the actual manuscripts and typescripts.

The policy in dating and arranging the work has been to remove all previously given dates except those for which there is firm evidence; no date has been given to any poem for which there is only conjecture. Where there is evidence for such dating, these poems or fragments have been used as markers to which others might relate.

Such cross-referencing has often relied on manuscript evidence. For example, while staying with friends at Rondesbosch near Cape Town in 1914, Rosenberg wrote a letter to his family on distinctive blue writing-paper; a number of other manuscripts have survived using this same paper, suggesting that these poems were written out during the visit. We cannot assume that they were composed then, for they may be fair copies of poems he had already written. However, in the absence of evidence suggesting more precise dates for the composition of any of them, they have been placed together.

Some apparent evidence is deceptive. On the verso of a typescript of the poem 'If you are fire and I am fire', Rosenberg has written his London address in preparation for writing a letter. This immediately suggests the possibility of a London composition, but from other evidence it would appear that the poem was composed in South Africa.

Much of the manuscript evidence can establish no more than a date before which, or after which, a poem was written. For example, where an early pencil draft of one poem is written on the back of a completed typescript of another, it can be assumed that the typed poem pre-dates the draft; where a draft is written on the back of a letter which Rosenberg received, it can be assumed that the draft post-dates the letter.

Because of the inferior quality of most of the paper, there are few watermarks to yield clues; those that are watermarked are almost all typescripts which may have been prepared any time after the poem was written. Subject-matter can be useful but has to be handled with caution. The immediacy of 'Lusitania' combines with manuscript evidence to suggest that the poem was written shortly after the sinking of the passenger liner in May 1915, whereas what evidence there is suggests that 'August 1914' was written in France in the summer of 1916.

It was tempting to group together undated poems that share a common theme. However, where there was nothing but the theme to suggest contemporaneous composition, such grouping would suggest that Rosenberg was in the habit of working over a single theme before abandoning it and moving on to another. This may occasionally have happened—for example in his early poems reflecting his social awareness—but generally there is nothing to suggest that he worked in this way and so, in the absence of any other evidence, such grouping has been avoided.

Cross-referring paper or pencil types established links which in their turn yielded further links. On occasion, particular characteristics in the presentation of typescripts, such as a final flourish of distinctive asterisks, suggested a possible link between the copyings-out of different works, but evidence from this, or from particular typewriter-faces, is used only where there was no other evidence on which to place any possible connection. With those poems for which no manuscript or typescript has survived, there has been nothing on which a reliable dating, or even ordering, could be based.

In spite of these difficulties, however, an order slowly emerged to which most of the poems relate. Indeed, the considerations laid down above resulted in a sometimes radical reordering. The policy has been to avoid any definite decision that might distort scholarly analysis of the work.

Definite dates are given thus: 1914; probable but uncertain dates are given thus: ?1914.

There is no way of knowing what further work Rosenberg would have done on the poems had he survived, and many texts must be seen as provisional.

Where no manuscript or typescript has survived and the published poem is the only source, priority has been given to the text published by Rosenberg himself, e.g. 'The Dead Heroes'. Where he did not publish the poem, e.g. 'The Nun', the text has been taken from the 1937 edition, this being the most reliable published source.

In establishing the text, I soon realized that Rosenberg's own publications were not always reliable; they sometimes contain later handwritten alterations both to typographical mistakes and to punctuation. For example, in *Moses*, which he saw hurriedly through the printers before going to France in 1916, l. 7 of 'God' reads: 'He a lay bullying hulk to crush them more'. In his own copy, he has corrected the order of words and has added a pencil comma after 'hulk'. Similarly, in l. 85 of the play, he has crossed through the word 'Glitter' and replaced it in pencil with 'Glisten'. In the case of uncorrected typographical errors, the manuscript or typescript from which the published text was taken has been checked to establish the correct word, but where Rosenberg has made alterations to the published version, the amended version is used. Obvious spelling and typing mistakes have been tacitly corrected.

Where a poem is untitled, the complete first line is used as the title; this is enclosed in square brackets. In two cases—'[I did not pluck at all]' and '[Wan fragile faces of joy!]'—earlier editors gave titles to the poems where there are no titles in the surviving manuscripts or typescripts. It is possible that these came from a source that has since disappeared, but in the absence of this the titles have been dropped. However, since readers may search for these poems under their familiar title, they have been given in the Index.

Where there are alternative words, one written above the other and neither crossed through, a choice was made on aesthetic grounds, e.g. 'Louse Hunting' l. 19 where both 'Pluck' and 'Dug' have been cancelled and no alternative given. Readers wishing to know the full variants should consult *The Poems and Plays of Isaac Rosenberg* (2004).

Where lines that were later included in a longer poem or a play are known to have been written first as a separate poem, this poem is presented in its own right. For example, 'Song of Immortality', which became ll. 230–49 of the poem 'Night and Day', is described by Rosenberg as 'one of my first poems'.

Following the convention of earlier editors, two separate poems with the same title are named (I) and (II). Where these are undated, the designations [I] and [II] do not in themselves imply a definite order of composition.

In matters of syntax there has been a general policy of non-interference. Thus, for example, in 'On Receiving News of the War: Cape Town', ll. 2–3 have been left as

> No ice or frost
> Have asked of bud or bird [...]

In this case, to change 'Have' to 'Has' would have distorted the sibilant quality, and hence the rhythm, of the lines. However, in 'A Ballad of Whitechapel' l. 18, the word 'has' in 'What fearful land has my steps wandered to?' has been changed to 'have'; this change does not destroy the poetry and helps to eliminate the confusion of the original line.

Given the unfinished state of many of Rosenberg's poems, the distinction between a poem and a fragment is often difficult to define. 'Louse Hunting', for example, is fragmentary but can be read as a complete, if not completed, poem.

Because of the way in which Rosenberg worked—often composing single lines and then incorporating them into poems and plays, occasionally using them more than once—all fragmentary pieces have been given.

Rosenberg's often eccentric punctuation has presented a problem to all his editors. Writing to Harding on 16 April 1936, Bottomley said:

My own considered belief was that he was never literate enough to have grasped the ideas of English punctuation [...] I confess that in preparing my edition for press I punctuated it in order to make sure I understood it myself. When I began I found myself misunderstanding and tempted to revise the text with a view to clarity: but that is always dangerous, and it was also against my principles—and I found at last that I did always get some kind of sense when I had realised that his punctuation was casual and even sometimes misleading. I was also working, eventually, to convince people who did not think so much of Rosenberg's poetry as I did—which perhaps pushed me too much to desire superficial clarity! It was probably not a bad impulse in the preparation of a pioneer book of an unknown writer, so long as I preserved fidelity to him—which I feel he [sic] did'

In this present edition, Rosenberg's punctuation is given as he left it unless there are persuasive reasons for change. This policy of non-intervention allows the interpretation of sometimes difficult ideas to be left as fluid and open as possible; to alter the punctuation can sometimes be to suggest an immediately obvious interpretation and to remove the possibility of a less obvious one which Rosenberg may have intended. For example, in the first stanza of 'Twilight [III]', the manuscript reads:

> A sumptuous splendour of leaves
> Murmurously fanning the evening heaven
> And I hear
> In the soft living grey shadows
> In the brooding evanescent atmosphere
> The voice of impatient night.

Earlier editions have a semi-colon at the end of line 2, and commas after lines 4 and 5. This may be sensible, but it removes the possibility, which Rosenberg may have intended, of a growing sense of impatience.

In the only surviving source for the third stanza of '[A bird trilling its gay heart out]', the manuscript reads:

> I could not shut my spirit's doors
> I was so naked and alone
> I could not hide and it saw that
> I would not to myself have shown.

Earlier editions have introduced a comma at the end of the second line. If punctuation were to be introduced into this stanza, there could be as good a case for putting commas at the end of the first and in the middle of the third lines.

However, where Rosenberg's punctuation causes confusion and there is no risk of altering or distorting the sense, I have occasionally made an editorial intervention. For example, in 'Creation' ll. 97–9, Rosenberg has:

> And uncreated nothingness,
> Found, what creation laboured for
> The ultimate silence—[. . .]

Here I have removed the commas after 'nothingness' in l. 97 and 'found' in l. 98, and have introduced a comma after 'for' later in the lines. These lines now read:

> And uncreated nothingness
> Found what creation laboured for,
> The ultimate silence—[. . .]

An alternative could have been to remove the comma at the end of l. 97 but to keep that after 'found' in l. 98 and to introduce a comma at the end of l. 98, making it read:

> And uncreated nothingness
> Found, what creation laboured for,
> The ultimate silence—[...]

The Commentary gives the date of composition (if known); the publication history of the poem, fragment, or play; closely relevant historical, biographical, and textual contexts; and literary parallels, including Rosenberg's frequent use of similar ideas and phrases elsewhere in his writings.

The degree sign (°) indicates a note at the end of the book.

CHRONOLOGICAL SUMMARY
OF ISAAC ROSENBERG'S LIFE

1886   Dovber Rosenberg, Isaac's father and a native of Lithuania, is ordered
       to report as a conscript in the Russian army. As a Tolstoyan and
       student of the Torah, military service is against his moral principles
       and he crosses the border into Germany where he boards a boat at
       Hamburg which he believes is bound for the United States. He leaves
       behind a wife, Hacha, and baby daughter, Minnie. The boat docks at
       Hull on the north-east coast of England. Dovber settles briefly in
       Leeds and then moves to Bristol where he is joined by his wife and
       daughter. He begins to earn his living as a pedlar. His wife supple-
       ments their income with sewing and embroidery.

1890   November 25. Isaac is born, one of twins, the other of whom dies at
       birth.

1897   Urged on by his wife, Dovber (now known as Barnett or Barnard)
       finds a room for his family at 47 Cable Street, Stepney, in London's
       East End. He tries to enrol his son at the Jews' Free School but there
       are no vacancies; instead Isaac is sent to St Paul's School, Wellclose
       Square, St George's-in-the-East.

1899   Isaac moves to the Baker Street School in Stepney. Although an
       ordinary Board School, almost all the pupils are Jewish. At about
       the same time he joins after-school Jewish classes for instruction in
       Hebrew and the Scriptures. At home the family speaks Yiddish, but
       Isaac shows little interest in either this or the Hebrew language,
       although Jewish history, legend, and myth fascinate him. Barnett,
       financed by his sister, visits New York to see the possibility of moving
       his family there, but the plans are thwarted by the developing blind-
       ness of Isaac's oldest sister, Minnie, and he returns to London.

1900? The family moves to rooms in 58 Jubilee Street, Stepney; they will
       later move twice within Jubilee Street. Through her embroidery work,
       Hacha meets the Revd Asher Amschewitz whose son, the painter John
       H. Amschewitz, becomes a friend of Isaac. In Amschewitz's studio he
       meets Miss Winifreda Seaton with whom he corresponds about paint-
       ing, writing, and music until his death. She introduces him to a wider
       range of poets, including Donne, to whose work he does not immedi-
       ately respond, although he writes to her, 'I have certainly never come
       across anything so choke-full of profound meaningful ideas'.[1] Among
       those whose work he now particularly enjoys are Shelley, Keats, and
       Byron.

---

[1] Undated letter to Miss Seaton, p. 230.

1902   On 31 July, Isaac is awarded a school prize for good conduct. Encouraged by his headmaster, J. Usherwood, he begins to attend classes at the Arts and Crafts School in Stepney Green.

1904   On 14 May, he is awarded an RSPCA Certificate of Merit for an essay. He leaves the Baker Street School on 23 December.

1905   In January he is apprenticed to Carl Hentschel, a Fleet Street engraver. Some time before 26 September he writes his earliest surviving poem, 'Ode to David's Harp', a pastiche of Byron's 'The Harp the Monarch Minstrel Swept'. His sister Minnie writes to the Librarian of the Whitechapel Public Library, Morley Dainow, asking if he can help Isaac. Dainow invites him to come and see him, and IR sends him some of his poems, including 'Ode to David's Harp'. Dainow encourages his poetic ambitions and introduces him to the work of Browning, Tennyson, Dante Gabriel Rossetti, and Swinburne, but he cautions Rosenberg against writing too much, advising him: 'Only write when you feel inspired'.[2] Only three poems written between 1905 and 1909 are known to have survived.

1907   Encouraged by Amschewitz, he enrols for evening classes at Birkbeck College, London. Here he is instructed by Miss Alice Wright, who becomes a friend and correspondent and who introduces him to the work of William Blake. At the end of his first year he is awarded first prize for drawing from the antique and second prize for tonal drawing. The family moves to 159 Oxford Street, Mile End, East London.

1908   He enrols as an evening student at the London County Council School of Photo-Engraving and Lithography, known as the Bolt Court Art School, in Fleet Street, which he attends until 1910. In December the *Birkbeck College Students' Magazine* reports that 'In the National Competition an excellent head study in charcoal, by Isaac Rosenberg, was awarded a National book prize'. He also receives the Mason Prize for life drawing. The gathering place for aspiring young East End artists is the Whitechapel Library and Art Gallery, and here Rosenberg meets Mark Gertler, David Bomberg, and Mark Weiner.

1909   Rosenberg is apprenticed to a Mr Lascelles, a process engraver of Shoe Lane in the City of London, apparently still under the patronage of Hentschel.

1910   He wins the Birkbeck College Pocock Prize and a Certificate of Honour for timed life drawing. He meets Simon Weinstein who later, as Stephen Winsten, becomes a writer and editor, and the biographer of George Bernard Shaw.

1911   On 2 January, through Weinstein, Rosenberg is introduced to Joseph Leftowitz (later known as Joseph Leftwich) and John Rodker. Both will become established writers, Leftwich as a poet and anthologist

---

[2] Undated letter from Dainow to IR [Sept. 1905], quoted *JL* p. 39.

and Rodker as a novelist and publisher, particularly of important Modernist work. Rosenberg is invited to join this select group of friends, and they become known as the Whitechapel Boys. Amschewitz paints a full-length portrait of Rosenberg, which is exhibited in the Baillie Galleries in 1912 and later hangs for a time in Jews' College, London. In January 1911, Rosenberg stops working for Hentschel. An application to the Jewish Education Aid Society to pay for full-time studies at an art school is turned down. Early in the year he paints the self-portrait that now hangs in the National Portrait Gallery (see Plate 1). On 17 March, while copying Velàsquez's *Philip IV* in the National Gallery, he is observed at work by Lily Delissa Joseph, the sister of Solomon J. Solomon, the Royal Academician whom Rosenberg already knows. They discuss their painting methods, and Mrs Joseph invites him to call on her. In May he is taken on as art tutor to Mrs Joseph's son, and at her house he meets her sister, Mrs Henrietta Löwy, and Mrs Herbert Cohen.

Unemployed, and with no definite plans for the future, he becomes depressed and ill. In the autumn he hears that Mrs Cohen has arranged to pay the fees of £21 for him to study for one year at the Slade. On 13 October he registers as a student there.

1912   In the spring Rosenberg writes to, and subsequently meets, Laurence Binyon who will contribute an Introductory Memoir to the 1922 edition of his poetry. In this, Binyon writes of Rosenberg: 'Small in stature, dark, bright-eyed, thoroughly Jewish in type, he seemed a boy with an unusual mixture of self-reliance and modesty. Indeed, no one could have had a more independent nature. Obviously sensitive, he was not touchy or aggressive. Possessed of vivid enthusiasm, he was shy in speech. One found in talk how strangely little of second-hand (in one of his age) there was in his opinions, how fresh a mind he brought to what he saw and read. There was an odd kind of charm in his manner which came from his earnest, transparent sincerity.'[3] He then speaks of a 'sort of autobiography' that Rosenberg had sent to him, but this has not survived.

In May, Rosenberg's poem 'In the Workshop' is published in *A Piece of Mosaic*, a small private publication prepared for a Jewish bazaar. In the same month, *The Jewish Chronicle* publishes his review of an exhibition at the Baillie Galleries of the work of Amschewitz and Henry Ospovat. At about the same time, in the spring or early summer, he publishes his first book of poems entitled *Night and Day*. This 24-page, paper-bound pamphlet contains ten poems,[4] and is printed for him by his friend Reuben 'Crazy' Cohen at the works of

[3] *1922* pp. 3–4.
[4] For the contents and publication details see Appendix.

Israel Narodiczky in Mile End Road. Approximately fifty copies are printed as a cost of £2, money lent to him by Mrs Herbert Cohen.

By mid-July he has moved to 32 Carlingford Road, in the heart of Hampstead. Rosenberg receives the Slade School of Fine Arts First Class Certificate for the session 1911–12, but when the Slade reopens for the 1912–13 session, frictions develop with his patron, who mistakenly believes that he is not working hard enough. His allowance is reduced. In the autumn he is briefly at 40 Ampthill Square, Hampstead Road. In October he exhibits a drawing entitled 'Sanguine Drawing', at the New English Art Club; this sells for £4, and he is able to repay Mrs Cohen the £2 she had lent him. In November, unable to continue to pay rent, he returns home to 159 Oxford Street, Mile End. In December he hears that the Jewish Educational Aid Society has approved his application for funds so that he can stay at the Slade; they guarantee his fees until March 1914. During the winter his family moves to 87 Dempsey Street, Stepney, which remains their home during the rest of his life. By December, Rosenberg has moved back to north London where he rents a room at 1 St George's Square, Regent's Park.

1913   In the spring he submits work for the *Prix de Rome*, but fails to win the award. Bomberg paints a portrait of Rosenberg which he calls 'Head of a Poet' and for which he receives the Henry Tonks Prize for 1913.[5] He meets, and becomes involved with, a young music teacher named Annetta Raphael, but little is known of their relationship. His spirits and health begin to fail once more and he moves back to his family home. He is suffering from depression and has a stubborn cough, and during the summer he and Bomberg holiday together at Sandown on the Isle of Wight. Refreshed, he returns to London in time for the August wedding of his oldest sister, Minnie. In September she and her husband, Wolf Horvitch, leave for a new home in South Africa.

In November at the Café Royal, Mark Gertler introduces Rosenberg to T. E. Hulme and to Edward Marsh. Marsh, who is Private Secretary to Winston Churchill and the great champion of Georgian poetry, will buy his paintings and correspond with him for the rest of his life.

1914   During the winter, Rosenberg's health begins to decline again. His cough has returned, and at the end of February he spends a week in Bournemouth. When the Slade term finishes in early March, it is decided that he should go to stay with Minnie in South Africa. The Jewish Educational Aid Society agree to pay his fare. In May, Marsh buys his painting *Sacred Love*, and Rosenberg exhibits five works in

---

[5] The painting became part of the John Quinn Collection in New York, from which it was sold for ten dollars in 1927 to an unknown buyer.

'Twentieth Century Art: A Review of Modern Movements' at the Whitechapel Art Gallery.

At the beginning of June he sails from Tilbury for Cape Town, where he arrives at the end of the month. He goes to Minnie's house at 43 De Villiers Street. He is soon at work on commissions, but although he responds to the climate and the scenery he finds the people philistinic and dull. He decides to lecture on contemporary art, sending a copy of his proposed text to Marsh. In response to the events unfolding in Europe, he writes 'On Receiving News of the War: Cape Town'. In a letter to Marsh he says: 'By the time you get this things will only have just begun I'm afraid; Europe will have just stepped into its bath of blood. I will be waiting with beautiful drying towels of painted canvas, and precious ointments to smear and heal the soul; and lovely music and poems. But I really hope to have a nice lot of pictures and poems by the time all is settled again; and Europe is repenting of her savageries.'[6]

During the autumn he arranges for the publication of his lecture, entitled 'Art', and two of his poems, in the magazine *South African Women in Council*. Part I of the lecture and the poem 'The Dead Heroes' appears in the December 1914 edition; Part II and the poem 'Beauty'[7] in that for January 1915. Late in 1914 he stays with a Miss Molteno, sister of the Speaker of the South African Parliament, at Rondesbosch, near Cape Town.

1915   In February, Rosenberg leaves Cape Town to return to England. He loses a number of his paintings overboard in Cape Town harbour. He arrives in London in March, and shortly after his return sends three poems to the new magazine, *Colour*. They are accepted, and the first, 'Heart's First Word'[8] is published in the June issue, followed by 'A Girl's Thoughts' in July and 'Wedded'[9] in August. Meanwhile, he is assembling a second volume of his work, an eighteen-page pamphlet entitled *Youth*.[10] This is again printed at Narodiczky's printing works at the cost of £2 10s. The cost is met by the sale to Marsh of three life drawings. One hundred copies are printed, and of these Rosenberg sells ten at 2s. 6d. each; the other copies he gives away. At about this time, at the Café Royal he meets Sydney Schiff who, as Stephen Hudson, later becomes a successful novelist and with whom Rosenberg corresponds, sharing his thoughts on poetry. Early in June he tells him that he is working on a play, the

---

[6] Letter to Edward Marsh [Oct. or Nov. 1914], p. 262.
[7] Now known as 'Beauty [II]'.
[8] Now known as 'Heart's First Word [I]'.
[9] Now known as 'Wedded [II]'.
[10] For the contents and publication details see Appendix.

first direct reference to *Moses* on which he may have been working before he left Cape Town.

In the early summer he collaborates with Reuben Cohen in the production of a magazine, *The Jewish Standard*. The first issue is printed by Narodiczky and appears on 1 July; it includes extracts from Rosenberg's lectures, 'Art'. The venture is not a success, and after the first issue it ceases publication.

In June, Ezra Pound adds a postscript to a letter to Harriet Monroe, editor of the Chicago journal *Poetry: A Magazine of Verse*. He has apparently sent Monroe some of Rosenberg's work, and he now writes: 'Don't bother about Rosenberg, send the stuff back to him direct unless it amuses you.' Monroe keeps the material and writes back, asking for his advice. In his reply, Pound says: 'I think you may as well give this poor devil a show. Yeats called him to my attention last winter, but I have waited. I think you might do half a page review of his book, and that he is worth a page for verse. [. . .] He has something in him, horribly rough but then "Stepney, East" . . .'[11]

Unable to find work, in June he writes to Schiff : 'I am thinking of enlisting if they will have me, though it is against all my principles of justice—though I would be doing the most criminal thing a man can do.'[12] Instead he applies to Hentschel for a job, but is told that he needs further training. In September he enrols at evening classes in block-making, but does not pursue this. He again considers enlisting, but in October he tells Schiff, 'I have changed my mind again about joining the army. I feel about it that more men means more war,— beside the immorality of joining with no patriotic convictions.'[13] At the end of the month, however, he enlists. 'I wanted to join the R.A.M.C.', he tells Schiff, 'as the idea of killing upsets me a bit, but I was too small.'[14] He is sent to the Bantam Battalion of the 12th Suffolk Regiment, 40th Division, stationed at Bury St Edmunds. He later claims that he has enlisted so that his mother can receive the statutory Separation Allowance[15] but by the end of the year she has received nothing. She is distraught at the news that he has joined up.

Although the physical work in training represents a challenge to which he responds well, he is wretchedly unhappy. He has nothing in common with his companions, and is marked out as a Jew. In November he is in hospital after falling and cutting his hands; he takes with him Donne's poems and Browne's *Religio Medici*. Shortly before Christmas he receives a letter from Lascelles Abercrombie,

---

[11] Pound–Monroe, 28 June and [Sept.] 1915, Chicago, quoted *JC* p. 121.
[12] Letter to Schiff 8 June 1915, p. 274.
[13] Letter to Schiff [?Oct. 1915], p. 278.
[14] Letter to Schiff [early Nov. 1915], p. 280.
[15] Letter to Marsh [late Dec. 1915], p. 288.

whose work he much admires, praising his poetry. He is offered promotion to lance-corporal, but declines. He tells Marsh, 'I never joined the army for patriotic reasons. Nothing can justify war. I suppose we must all fight to get the trouble over.'[16] He writes 'Marching—as seen from the left file', the first poem he has written since joining the army. He returns home for four days' Christmas leave.

Two paintings and one drawing are accepted for the New English Art Club winter exhibition.

1916 Early in January he is transferred to the 12th South Lancashire Regiment in Alma Barracks, Blackdown Camp, Farnborough. He toys briefly with the possibility of applying for a commission. In March he writes to Abercrombie: 'Believe me the army is the most detestable invention on earth and nobody but a private in the army knows what it is to be a slave.'[17] He continues to work on *Moses*, and the distraction leads to his forgetting orders for which he receives 'a rotten and unjust punishment'.[18] His friend John Rodker sends a copy of 'Marching—as seen from the left file' to Harriet Monroe in Chicago, for possible publication in *Poetry: A Magazine of Verse*; she receives it on 22 April. He is again transferred, this time to the 11th Battalion of the King's Own Royal Lancaster Regiment, and given a new number—22311—that he will retain for the rest of his military service. He begins a correspondence with the poet R. C. Trevelyan.

In mid-May he receives news of posting to France, and is given six days' embarkation leave. In London, he arranges for the publication of his third book, *Moses: A Play*.[19] He is not happy with his resolution of the character of Moses, but wishes to get the work, and some of his poems, into print in case he should not return. Reuben Cohen again prints the work, using Narodiczky's press but now operating independently under the name of Paragon Printing Works. Rosenberg hopes to recoup the cost of printing by selling paperbound copies for 1*s*. and copies bound in cloth for 4*s*. 6*d*. (later reduced to 3*s*. 6*d*.). He has thoughts for a further play, this time about Adam and Lilith.

At the beginning of June he sails from Southampton, arriving in France on 3 June. His poem 'The Troop Ship' describes the passage over. Within a few days he is in the front line, writing to R. C. Trevelyan in an undated letter postmarked 15 June: 'We are in the trenches now and it's raining horribly.'[20] That month he writes 'Break of Day in the Trenches', the first of his trench poems.

---

[16] Letter to Marsh [late Dec. 1915], p. 288.
[17] Letter to Abercrombie dated 11 March 1916, p. 292.
[18] Letter to Miss Seaton [spring 1916], p. 293.
[19] For the contents and publication details see Appendix.
[20] Letter to R. C. Trevelyan postmarked 15 June 1916, p. 298.

At the beginning of July he begins a correspondence with the poet and dramatist Gordon Bottomley to whom R. C. Trevelyan has sent copies of *Youth* and *Moses*. Bottomley will later edit the first edition of his poetry, published in 1922, and will play a central part in establishing his post-war reputation. They never meet, but this becomes the most important and stimulating correspondence of Rosenberg's years in France. In an undated letter written towards the end of July he tells Bottomley of his ideal of 'Simple *poetry*—that is where an interesting complexity of thought is kept in tone and right value to the dominating idea so that it is understandable and still ungraspable'.[21] In August he complains to Marsh that he has been forbidden to send his poems home 'as the censor won't be bothered with going through such rubbish',[22] a ban that is soon lifted. In the same letter he asks Marsh about the possibility of his being transferred to a unit that specializes in painting camouflage under the leadership of Solomon J. Solomon, but nothing comes of the idea.

During the summer he writes to Mrs Cohen, 'I am thinking of a Jewish play with Judas Macabeas for hero. I can put a lot in I've learnt out here.'[23] A few weeks later he sends copies of 'Break of Day in the Trenches' and 'The Troop Ship' to Harriet Monroe;[24] 'Break of Day in the Trenches' is published in *Poetry Magazine* in December 1916, together with his earlier poem 'Marching—as seen from the left file'. In the autumn he writes to Laurence Binyon: 'I am determined that this war, with all its powers for devastation, shall not master my poetry; that is if I am lucky enough to come through all right. I will not leave a corner of my consciousness covered up, but saturate myself with the strange and extraordinary new conditions of this life and it will all refine itself into poetry later on. [. . .] it is impossible now to work and difficult even to think of poetry, one is so cramped intellectually.'[25] In October, after some weeks out of the line, he goes back into the trenches to face one of the coldest winters on record.

1917   In January, Rosenberg reports sick. His anxious family contact Marsh, asking if there is any chance of his being moved out of the line but, despite Marsh's intervention requesting that Rosenberg be given a clerical job, he is deemed fit enough to continue. In February he is transferred to the Fortieth Division Works Battalion; one of his tasks is to transport barbed wire up into the line. In early May, in a letter to Marsh, he mentions a new poem 'suggested by going out wiring, or

---

[21] Letter to Bottomley postmarked 23 July 1916, p. 305.
[22] Letter to Marsh [Aug. 1916], p. 313.
[23] Letter to Mrs Cohen, p. 304.
[24] The poems were enclosed with an undated letter of summer or autumn 1916, p. 319.
[25] Letter to Laurence Binyon [autumn 1916], p. 320.

rather carrying wire up the line on limbers and running over dead bodies lying about' ['Dead Man's Dump'].[26] Later in the month he tells Marsh that he is working on 'a much finer poem' ['Daughters of War'][27] and 'The Amulet' which he describes as a poem rather than a play.[28] In early June he is again transferred, this time to the 229 Field Company, Royal Engineers. In July, he writes to Marsh that he has completely changed his ideas for 'The Amulet'; it is now to be called 'The Unicorn'.

On 16 September, Rosenberg goes back to England for ten days' leave; it is his only leave during twenty-one months in France. He writes to Bottomley, 'I feel so restless here and unanchored. We have lived in such an elemental way so long things here don't look quite right to me somehow; or it may be the consciousness of my so limited time here for freedom, so little time to do so many things—bewilders me.'[29] On his return to France he is no longer attached to the Royal Engineers, but is sent back to his regiment. In late September his poem 'Ah Koelue' from *Moses* is published in *Georgian Poetry*, edited by Marsh.

On 10 October he reports sick, and is admitted to 51st General Hospital (see note to p. 349). His two soldier brothers—Dave and Elkon—are also in hospital. While there, he receives a letter from Leftwich inviting him to join the new Jewish Association of Arts and Sciences. In December he leaves hospital and rejoins his regiment, telling Bottomley, 'since I left the hosp[ital] all poetry has gone quite out of me. I seem even to forget words, and I believe if I met anybody with ideas I'd be dumb. No drug could be more stupefying than our work—(to me anyway) and this goes on like that old torture of water trickling drop by drop unendingly on one's helplessness.'[30]

1918   On 7 February he is transferred from the 11th to the 1st Battalion of the KORL. Early in March he writes to tell Marsh that he has applied for transfer to the Jewish Battalion serving in Mesopotamia. Amid rumours of an impending German attack, Rosenberg's battalion goes into training in Arras for a week, and on 19 March they move back to the Greenland Hill Sector near Arras. His brigade is holding the line south of Gavrelle but his company is at rest. On 21 March the Germans launch their massive spring offensive and on 28 March the front line is overrun and falls back to Fampoux. On 28 March Rosenberg writes to Edward Marsh enclosing his last poem, 'Through these pale cold days', and his company moves forward into the front line.

[26] Letter to Marsh postmarked 8 May 1917, p. 331.
[27] Letter to Marsh postmarked 27 May 1917, p. 332.
[28] Letter to Marsh postmarked 29 May 1917, p. 333.
[29] Letter to Bottomley dated by GB 21 Sept. 1917, *1937* pp. 77–8.
[30] Letter to Bottomley postmarked Feb. 24 1918, *1937* p. 359.

On 1 April Rosenberg is killed when the Germans raided the British lines.

1926   Eleven named soldiers of the KORL who were killed on the night of 1/2 April 1918, were buried together in Northumberland Cemetery, Fampoux. This cemetery was later moved, and the remains were disinterred and identified by their regimental insignia. Five of the bodies were identified but the remaining six, including that of Rosenberg, could not be individually named. They were reburied at Bailleul Road East British Cemetery, St-Laurent-Blagny, near Arras, each with an individual gravestone. That for Rosenberg has the words 'Buried near this spot', and beneath his name, dates, and regimental details are the Star of David and the words: 'Artist and Poet'.

POEMS

Ode to David's Harp

Awake! ye joyful strains, awake!
In silence sleep no more;
Disperse the gloom that ever lies
O'er Judah's barren shore;
Where are the hands that strung thy chords   5
With tender touch and true,
Whose silvery tone impassioned all?
Those hands are silenced too.

Those chords whose tender strains awoke
In hearts that throbbed for war,   10
The martial stir when glory calls,
Lies mute on Judah's shore.
One chord awake—one strain prolong,
To wake the zeal in Israel's breast,
O sacred lyre once more how long?   15
'Tis vain—alas in silence rest.

Many a minstrel fame's elated
Envies thee thy harp and fame.
Harp of David—Monarch minstrel
Bravely—bravely keep thy name.   20
Ay! every ear that listened
Was charmed—was thrilled—was bound,
Every eye with moisture glistened,
Thrilling to the harp's sweet sound.

Hark—the harp is pouring   25
Notes of burning fire,
And each soul o'erpowering
Melts the rousing ire,
Fiercer—shriller—wilder far
Than the brazen notes of war.   [NO BREAK   30

Accents sweet and echoes sweeter
Minstrel—minstrel, steeds fly fleeter,
Spurred on by thy magic strains,
Breasts are heaving—fate is weaving
Other bonds than slav'ry's chains,   35
For her chosen's blood are frozen
Icy fear in all their veins.

Tell me not the harp lies sleeping
Set not thus my heart aweeping,
In the muse's fairy dwelling   40
There thy magic notes are swelling.
But for list'ning mortals' ear
Vainly wait ye will not hear.
The chords are rent—for years have bent
Its living strings asunder.   45
But harp and name—shall life proclaim
In living voice of thunder.

[*In art's lone paths I wander deep*]

In art's lone paths I wander deep
And slowly, slowly onward creep.
I seek, I probe each deep recess
To reach the secret of success.
In vain, 'tis hidden from my gaze   5
I still must hail its glowing rays.

Cold time shall drag the weary hours
And slowly tint the blooming flowers;
The flowers shall fade, the flowers shall bloom,
Yes many a time shall fade to gloom,   10
Ere I can burst thro' the wild bounds
That the pure realm of art surrounds.

I see of art its dazzling star
In glorious splendour shining far;
It dims my eyes, but year by year   15
To enter in its flaming sphere

I wildly try; 'tis vainly tried
For e'en its drudgery I'm denied.

Zion

She stood—a hill-ensceptred Queen,
The glory streaming from her,
While Heaven flashed her rays between,
And shed eternal summer.

The gates of morning opened wide   5
On sunny dome and steeple,
Noon gleamed upon the mountain side
Throng'd with a happy people.

And twilight's drowsy, half closed eyes
Beheld that virgin splendour   10
Whose orbs were as her darkening skies,
And as her spirit, tender.

Girt with that strength first born of right,
Held fast by deeds of honour;
Her robe she wove with rays more bright   15
Than Heaven could rain upon her.

Where is that light—that citadel?
That robe with woof of glory?
She lost her virtue and she fell;
And only left her story.   20

Song of Immortality

Mortals—ancient syllables
Spoken of God's mouth,—
Do spirits them chronicle
So they be not lost?

Music, breathed ephemeral—   5
Fragrant maid and child:
Bellow, croak and droning—
Age and cumbrous man.

Music that the croaking hears:
Croak, to mate the music: 10
Do angels stand and throw their nets
From the banks Eterne?

Surely the speech of God's mouth
Shall not be for nought!
Music wrought of God's passion   15
Less than withered dew?

As the sea through cloud to sea,
Thought through deed to thought,
Each returneth as they were,
So man to God's mouth?   20

Dawn behind Night

Lips! bold, frenzied utterance, shape to the thoughts that are
    prompted by hate
Of the red streaming burden of wrong we have borne and still bear;
That wealth with its soul-crushing scourges placed into its hands
    by fate,
Hath made the cement of its towers, grim-girdled by our despair.

Should it die in the death that they make, in the silence that follows
    the sob;   5
In the voiceless depth of the waters that closes upon our grief;
Who shall know of the bleakness assigned us for the fruits that we
    reap and they rob?
To pour out the strong wine of pity, outstretch the kind hand in
    relief.

In the golden glare of the morning, in the solemn serene of the night,
We look on each other's faces, and we turn to our prison bar;   10

In pitiless travail of toil and outside the precious light,
What wonder we know not our manhood in the curse of the things
  that are?

In the life or the death they dole us from the rags and the bones of
  their store,
In the blood they feed but to drink of, in the pity they feign in their
  pride,
Lies the glimpse of a heaven behind it, for the ship hath left the
  shore,   15
That will find us and free us and take us where its portals are
  opened wide.

A Ballad of Whitechapel

God's mercy shines,
And our full hearts must make record of this.
For grief that burst from out its dark confines
Into strange sunlit bliss.

I stood where glowed   5
The merry glare of golden whirring lights
Above the monstrous mass that seethed and flowed
Through one of London's nights.

I watched the gleams
Of jagged warm lights on shrunk faces pale.   10
I heard mad laughter as one hears in dreams,
Or Hell's harsh lurid tale.

The traffic rolled.
A gliding chaos populous of din.
A steaming wail at doom the Lord had scrawled   15
For perilous loads of sin.

And my soul thought,
What fearful land have my steps wandered to?
God's love is everywhere, but here is naught
Save love His anger slew.   20

And as I stood
Lost in promiscuous bewilderment,
Which to my mazèd soul was wonder-food,
A girl in garments rent

Peered 'neath lids shamed,   25
And spoke to me and murmured to my blood.
My soul stopp'd dead, and all my horror flamed
At her forgot of God.

Her hungered eyes,
Craving and yet so sadly spiritual,   30
Shone like the unsmirched corner of a jewel
Where else foul blemish lies.

I walked with her
Because my heart thought here the soul is clean,
The fragrance of the frankincense and myrrh   35
Is lost in odours mean.

[She told me how
The shadow of black death had newly come
And touched her father, mother, even now
Grim-hovering in her home,   40

Where fevered lay
Her wasting brother in a cold bleak room,
Which theirs would be no longer than a day—
And then—the streets and doom.]

Lord! Lord! dear Lord!   45
I knew that life was bitter, but my soul
Recoiled, as anguish-smitten by sharp sword,
Grieving such body's dole.

Then grief gave place
To a strange pulsing rapture as she spoke,   50
For I could catch the glimpses of God's grace,
And a desire awoke

To take this trust,
And warm and gladden it with love's new fires,

Burning the past to ashes, and to dust 55
Thro' purified desires.

We walked our way.
One way hewn for us from the birth of Time.
For we had wandered into Love's strange clime
Through ways sin waits to slay. 60

Love's euphony
In Love's own temple that is our glad hearts,
Makes now long music wild deliciously,
Now Grief hath used his darts.

Love infinite, 65
Chastened by sorrow, hallowed by pure flame,
Not all the surging world can compass it,
Love—love—Oh! tremulous name.

God's mercy shines.
And my full heart hath made record of this. 70
Of grief that burst from out its dark confines
Into strange sunlit bliss.

Death

Death waits for me—ah! who shall kiss me first?
No lips of love glow red from out the gloom
That life spreads darkly like a living tomb
Around my path. Death's gift is best, not worst.
For even the honey on life's lips is curst. 5
And the worm cankers in the ripest bloom.
Yea, from Birth's gates to Death's, Life's travailed womb
Is big with Rest, for Death, her life, athirst.

Death waits, and when she has kissed Life's warm lips
With her pale mouth, and made him one with her; 10
Held to him Lethe's wine whereof he sips;
And stilled Time's wings, earth-shadowing sleepless whir;
Outside of strife, beyond the world's blood drips,
Shadowed by peace, Rest dwells and makes no stir.

A Ballad of Time, Life and Memory

Hold wide the door and watch who passes here
From dawn through day to dawn,
Bravely as though their journey but begun,
Through changèd still.
She, wild-eyed, runs and laughs, or walks and weeps;   5
But him, swift-footed, never can outrun,
Nor creep and he before.
And all she has and all she knows is his;
But not all his for her.

He gives her of the spices and the myrrh   10
And wonderful strange fruits,
He gives her more of tears, and girds her round
With yearning bitterness,
With fears that kill the hopes they feed upon,
With hopes that smile at fears and smile on her,   15
Till fears again prevail.
And as she goes the roses fall and die;
And as she goes she weeps.

But lo! behind, what dim processional?
What maiden sings and sighs?   20
And holds an urn, and as the roses fall,
And the wine pours and spills,
She gathers in her lap and breathes on them;
And in the urn the spilled wine glows again,
Lit by her eyes divine.   25
And all the roses at her touch revive,
And blush and bloom again.

And by her side, whose name is Memory,
The ghosts of all the hours,
Some smiling as they smiled within the sun.   30
Some, stained and wan with tears.
To those she gives the roses as they fall,
And bids them tune the praises of their prime.
To these their tears and dust.

And those are happy loves and wreathèd joys.　　35
And these are sorrows pale.

Even as she sings so Time himself makes pause,
Even Time, Death's conqueror.
And Life's reverted face grows tenderer,
While the soul dreams and yearns,　　40
Watching the risen faces of the hours,
And shrivelled Autumn change her face to June's,
And dead wine live again,
And dust discrowned know Life it knew before
Touched with a softened Light.　　45

There is no leaf upon the naked woods,
No bird upon the boughs;
And Time leads Life through many waste places,
And dreams and shapes of death.
Yet is the voice of Summer not quite dumb,　　50
Although her lips be still and silenter.
For Memory bids her rise
To sing within the palace of the soul,
And Life and Time are still.

In the Workshop

Dim, watery lights gleaming on gibbering faces.
Faces speechful, barren of soul, and sordid.
Huddled and chewing a jest, lewd, and gabbled insidious;
Laughter born of its dung, flashes and floods, like sunlight,
Filling the room with a sense of a soul lethargic and kindly,　　5
Touches my soul with a pathos, a hint of a wide desolation.

To J. H. Amschewitz

In the wide darkness of the shade of days
'Twixt days that were, and days that yet will be,
Making the days that are gloom'd mystery,

What starshine glimmers thro' the nighted ways
Uplifting? and through all vain hope's delays   5
What is it brings far joy's foretaste to me?
A savour of a ship-unsullied sea,
A glimpse of golden lands too high for praise.

Life holds the glass but gives us tears for wine.
But if at times he changes in his hand   10
The bitter goblet for the drink divine,
I stand upon the shore of a strange land.
And when mine eyes unblinded of the brine
See clear, lo! where he stood before, you stand.

[*In the heart of the forest*]

In the heart of the forest,
The shuddering forest,
The moaning and sobbing
Sad shuddering forest.—
The dark and the dismal   5
Persistent sad sobbing
Throughout the weird forest.—

Ah! God! they are voices—
Dim ghosts of the forest
Unrestfully sobbing   10
Through wistful pale voices,
Whose breath is the wind and whose lips the sad trees.
Whose yearning great eyes
Death haunted forever
Look from the dark waters,   15
And pale spirit faces
Wrought from the white lilies.

FIG. 1 '[In the heart of the forest]'. Illuminated fair copy, dated 1911 and presented to J. H. Amschewitz.

[*My days are but the tombs of buried hours*]

My days are but the tombs of buried hours;
Which tombs are hidden in the pilèd years;
But from the mounds there springeth up such flowers
Whose beauty well repays its cost of tears.
Time, like a sexton, pileth mould on mould,   5
Minutes on minutes till the tombs are high;
But from the dust there falleth grains of gold;
And the dead corpse leaves what will never die.
It may be but a thought, the nurseling seed
Of many thoughts, of many a high desire.   10
Some little act that stirs a noble deed,
Like breath rekindling a smouldering fire.
They only live who have not lived in vain,
For in their works their life returns again.

[*The world rumbles by me—can I heed?*]

The world rumbles by me—can I heed?
The rose it is crimson—and I bleed.

The rose of my heart glows deep afar;
And I grope in the darkness 'twixt star and star.

Only in night grows the flower of peace,   5
Spreading its odours of rest and ease.

It dies in the day like light in the night.
It revives like tears in the eyes of delight.

For the youth at my heart beats wild and loud;
And raves in my ear of a girl and a shroud.   10

Of a golden girl with the soul in her eyes,
To teach me love and to make me wise.

With the fire on her lips and the wine in her hands,
To bind me strong in her silken bands.

For time and fate are striding to meet   15
One unseen with soundless feet.

The world rustles by me—let me heed.
Clutched in its madness till I bleed.

For the rose of my heart glows deep afar.
If I stretch my hand, I may clasp a star.   20

Lines Written in an Album: To J.L.

The birds that sang in summer
Were silent till the spring;
For hidden were the flowers,
The flowers to whom they sing.
December's jewelled bosom—   5
Closed mouth—hill-hidden vale—
Held seed full soon to blossom;
Held song that would not fail.

I, silent all the winter,
No flower for me to praise,   10
For this rich wealth of roses
My song shall I not raise?
The lilies and the roses,
White hands and damask cheeks;
The eyes where love reposes   15
And laughs before he speaks.

Could this make music to thee,
The music of sweet thought;
Thy laughing eyes might hearken
To sounds sweet visions wrought,   20
Till the deep roses tingle
The cheeks they nestle in,
And music still would mingle,
And pleasure still begin.

Thus, hidden in these pages   25
My thoughts shall silent lie

Till gentle fingers find them
When idly bent to pry.
I see them fondly linger
And quicken with their breath 30
The music of the singer,
Whose silence was its death.

To Mr & Mrs Löwy, on their Silver Wedding

'Ye hearken as ye list' saith Time to all.
'Ye hear me as I pass or do not hear.
I gather all the fruits of all the year,
I hoard them when the barren seasons call.
Then, though I flew with Spring, with them I crawl. 5
To soothe their vacant eyes and feet of fear
I bid the Spring's sweet ghost rise from her bier,
And tender Memory come with light footfall.

'Then, when the seasons hang their heads in shame
And grief, I bring my store of hoarded fruit; 10
To warm the hands of age, youth's rosy flame;
And to old love the young love at the root,
Hallowed by me to silver sweet acclaim—
Hush—lo! the bride and bridegroom—hush—be mute.'

Summer in Winter: Six Thoughts

Before the winter's over
I know a way
The summer to recover,
The August and the May.

Before the month of blossoms 5
And sunny days,
I know that which unbosoms
Whate'er the summer says.

Ah! would you net the season?
And chain the sun? 10

For you will flowers do treason?
And how is treason done?

While still the land lies gleaming
And bare and dumb,
And love asleep is dreaming   15
Of the warm nights to come,

Catch these sweet thoughts in shadow,
Bring them to light,
At once the fragrant meadow
Will flash on sense and sight.   20

Six names of six sweet maidens,
Six honey flowers,
Name, and each name unladens
Its load of summer hours.

Ruth, joyous as a July   25
Song-throbbing noon,
And rosy as a newly
Flushed eager rose in June.

The August's dreamy languor
Is Maisy sweet,   30
Drowsed summer when she's sung her
Rich songs and rests her feet.

The stately smile and gracious
Of an April wood
[   ]   35
Is tall and fair Gertrude.

And like a clear May morning
When birds call clear
And quickly to each other,
Is little Lily dear.   40

And ripe as buxom Autumn
When she hold hands

With August, fruit enwroughten,
Fair sumptuous Ethel stands.

Sweet gleams of dawn and twilight,   45
Sunshine in shade,
Is Lena calm as starlight.
Now the six thoughts are said.

Fleet Street

From north and south, from east and west,
Here in one shrieking vortex meet
These streams of life, made manifest
Along the shaking quivering street.
Its pulse and heart that throbs and glows   5
As if its strife were its repose.

I shut my ear to such rude sounds
As reach a harsh discordant note,
Till melting into what surrounds
My soul doth with the current float,   10
And from the turmoil and the strife
Wakes all the melody of life.

The stony buildings blindly stare
Unconscious of the crime within,
While man returns his fellow's glare   15
The secrets of his soul to win.
And each man passes from his place,
None heed. A shadow leaves such trace.

Twilight [I]

A murmur of many waters, a moving maze of streams;
A doubtful voice of the silence from the ghosts of the shadows of
   dreams,

The far adieu of the day as it touches the fingers of night,
Makes all to the eye and ear but seem wings spread for the soul for flight.

Can we look behind or before us, can we look on the dreams that are
    done? 5
The lights gleam dim in the distance, the distance is dimmer when won.
Soon that shall fade dimmer behind us, and when the night before
    us is here,
Ah! who of us shall wait for the dawn, while the shadows of night
    disappear?

Birthday Song

To thy cradle at thy birth
Did not all the fairies come,
Genie of heaven and earth
While ogres stood afar and dumb,

And thy cradle to embower 5
Spun a roof of sun and flowers,
Gave thee for thy lifelong dower
Beauteous gifts and beauteous hours?

Time stood by, a gardener mild,
Watched the bud unfold to rose, 10
June's delight December's child,
Red rose of December snows.

Twenty years and one year more
Time here layeth at thy feet;
But thy friends bring twenty score 15
Wishes that the rest be sweet.

[Lady, you are my God]

Lady, you are my God—
Lady, you are my heaven.

If I am your God
Labour for your heaven.

Lady you are my God,   5
And shall not love win heaven?

If love made me God
Deeds must win my heaven.

If my love made you God,
What more can I for heaven?   10

Spiritual Isolation: Fragment

My Maker shunneth me.
Even as a wretch stricken with leprosy
So hold I pestilent supremacy.
Yea! He hath fled far as the uttermost star,
Beyond the unperturbed fastnesses of night,   5
And dreams that bastioned are
By fretted towers of sleep that scare His light.

Of wisdom writ, whereto
My burdened feet may best withouten rue,
I may not spell—and I am sore to do.   10
Yea! all seeing my Maker hath such dread,
Even mine own self-love wists not but to fly
To Him, and sore besped
Leaves me, its captain, in such mutiny.

Will, deemed incorporate   15
With me, hath flown ere love, to expiate
Its sinful stay where he did habitate.
Ah me! if they had left a sepulchre!
But no—the light hath changed not and in it
Of its same colour stir   20
Spirits I see not but phantasm'd feel to flit.

Air legioned such stirreth
So that I seem to draw them with my breath.
Ghouls that devour each joy they do to death.
Strange glimmering griefs and sorrowing silences,   25
Bearing dead flowers unseen whose charnel smell
Great awe to my sense is
Even in the rose-time when all else is well.

In my great loneliness
This haunted desolation's dire distress,   30
I strove with April buds my thoughts to dress,
Therewith to reach to joy through gay attire;
But as I plucked came one of those pale griefs
With mouth of parched desire
And breathed upon the buds and charred the leaves.   35

[*God looked clear at me through her eyes*]

God looked clear at me through her eyes,
And when her fresh and sweet lips spake,
Through dawn-flushed gates of Paradise
Such silvern birds did wing and shake

God's fervent music on my soul,   5
And with their jewelled quivering feet
Did rend apart the quiet stole
That shades from girl-fanned pulsing heat.

Upon a gold branch in my breast
They made their nest, while sweet and warm   10
Hung wav'ring thoughts like roseleaves drest;
My soul the sky to keep from harm.

In the heart's woods mysterious
Where feelings lie remote and far,
They fly with touch imperious,   15
And loose emotion's hidden bar.

And to dark pools of brooding care,
And blinding wastes of loneliness,
They gleam a Paradisal air,
And warm with a divine caress.   20

The Dead Past

Ah! will I meet you ever—you who have gone from me,
You the I that was then and a moment hath changed into you.
So many moments have passed and changed the I into we,
So many many times but alas I remember so few.

I know you are dead, long perished, the boy that babbled and
    played   5
With the toys like the wind with the flowers and the clouds play
    with the moon,
I know you are dead long ago and hid in the grave I made
Of regrets that were soon forgotten, as snow is forgotten by June.

You too are dead, the shining face that laughed and wept without
    thought
Uttered the words of the heart, wept or leapt as was right.   10
O were you taken to heaven by God in a whirlwind caught,
I do not know yours was best, you not conscious of your delight.

O my life's dead Springtime—why will you haunt me like ghosts
You little buds that have died—and blossom in memory,
Will I meet you in some dead land and see your faces in hosts   15
Saying 'The past is the future and you and the future are we.'

[O! in a world of men and women]

O! in a world of men and women
Where all things seemed so strange to me,
And speech the common world called human
For me was a vain mimicry,

I thought—O! am I one in sorrow?   5
Or is the world more quick to hide
Their pain with raiment that they borrow
From pleasure in the house of pride?

O! joy of mine, O! longed for stranger,
How I would greet you if you came!   10
In the world's joys I've been a ranger,
In my world sorrow is their name.

Love To Be

When at that happy pause that holds sweet rest
As a hard burden, that it doth belate
And make him seem a laggard at the gate
Of long-wished night, while day rides down the west;
I, weighted from my toil, and sore distrest   5
In body and soul, the scourge of partial fate,
At such sweet pause, to silence consecrate,
Came thoughts swift-changing fancy had bedrest
In colours of desire. I thought on her
I never yet have seen, my love to be.   10
I conjured up all glorious shapes that were;
And wondered what far clime, by what sad sea
She roaming? And what spirits minister?
What thoughts, and what vague shadowing of me?

'By what far ways shall my heart reach to thine?   15
We, who have never parted—never met,
Nor done to death the joys that shall be yet,
Nor drained the cup of love's delirious wine.
How shall my craving spirit know for mine
Thine, self-same seeking? Will a wild regret   20
For the lost days—the lonely suns that set,
Be for our love a token and a sign?
Will all the weary nights, the widowed days
That sundered long, all point their hands at thee?
Yea! all the stars that have not heard thy praise   25
Low murmur in thy charmèd ear of me?

All pointing to the ending of the ways,
All singing of the love that is to be?'

The Nun

So thy soul's meekness shrinks,
Too loth to show her face—
Why should she shun the world?
It is a holy place.

Concealèd to itself   5
If the flower kept its scent,
Of itself amorous,
Less rich its ornament.

Use—utmost in each kind—
Is beauty, truth in one,   10
While soul rays light to soul
In one God-linkèd sun.

Heart's First Word [I]

To sweeten a swift minute so
With such rare fragrance of sweet speech,
And make the after hours go
In a blank yearning each on each;
To drain the springs till they be dry,   5
And then in anguish thirst for drink,
So but to glimpse her robe thirst I,
And my soul hungers and I sink.

There is no word that we have said
Whereby the lips and heart are fire;   10
No look the linkèd glances read
That held the springs of deep desire.
And yet the sounds her glad lips gave
Are on my soul vibrating still.

Her eyes that swept me as a wave   15
Shine, my soul's worship to fulfil.

Her hair, her eyes, her throat and chin;
Sweet hair, sweet eyes, sweet throat, so sweet,
So fair because the ways of sin
Have never known her perfect feet.   20
By what far ways and marvellous
May I such lovely heaven reach?
What dread dark seas and perilous
Lie 'twixt love's silence and love's speech?

[*So innocent you spread your net*]

So innocent you spread your net,
I knew not I was caught in it,
Till when I vainly tried to rise
I read the reason in your eyes.

Your silken smiles had bound me fast;   5
Your nestling speech had tangled more;
But when I started up at last
I shook the fetters to the floor.

The Garden of Joy

In honey-essenced bliss of sleep's deceit
My sense lay drowned, and my soul's eyes saw clear,
Unstranged to wonder, made familiar
By instant seeing, Eden's garden sweet,
Shedding upon mine eyelids odorous heat   5
Of the light fingered golden atmosphere
Shaken through boughs whose whisperings I could hear.
Beneath, within the covert's cool retreat
Of the spread boughs stood shapes who swayed the boughs,
And bright fruit fell, laughing to leave green house;   10
While gleeful children dabbled with the sun

Caught the strange fruit, then ran with smiles of love
To earth, whose peoples as they ate thereof
Soft sank into the garden, one by one.

They lie within the garden, outside Time.   15
The ripened fulness of their soul's desire
Glad on their tranquil faces. No fanged fire
Of hot insatiate pleasure, no pulsed chime
To summon to tusked orgy of earth's slime,
Flickers the throne of rapture's flushed empire   20
That glows, mild rays of the divine attire
Upon each face, sun of this day-spring clime.

They seem forever wondering—listening
Unto some tale of marvel, music told,
That the flowers weep in jewelled glistening   25
With envy of the joy that they must hold,
While in the dewy mirrors lady Spring
Trims herself by their smiles, their happy mould.

In the Woods

Let me carve my fantasy
Of this web like broken glass
Gleaming through the fretted leaves
In a quaint intricacy
Diamond tipping all the grass.   5

Hearken as the spirit heaves
Through the branches and the leaves
In the shudder of their pulse.
Delicate nature trembles so
To a ruder nature's touch,   10
And of peace that these convulse
They have little who should much.
Life is so.
Let me carve my fantasy
From the fretwork of the leaves.   15

In Kensington Gardens

I saw the face of God today,
I heard the music of His smile;
And yet I was not far away,
And yet in Paradise the while.

I lay upon the sparkling grass,   5
And God's own mouth was kissing me,
And there was nothing that did pass
But blazèd with divinity.

Divine—divine—upon mine eyes,
Upon mine hair, divine—divine,   10
The fervour of the golden skies,
The ardent gaze of God on mine.

Knowledge

Within this glass he looks at he is fair,
Godlike his reach and shining in his eyes
The light that is the sun of Paradise.
Yet midst his golden triumph a despair
Lurks like a serpent hidden in his hair   5
And says 'Proud wisdom I am yet more wise'.
But swift before his look the serpent dies,
Before his glory's grandeur mirrored there.

This to himself, but what to us looks he?
A lank unresting spectre whose grey gaze   10
A moth by night—a ferret thro' the days—
A hunger that devours all it can see
And then feeds on himself but never slays
Insatiate with his own misery.

[*A woman's beauty is a strong tree's roots*]

A woman's beauty is a strong tree's roots.
The tree is space, its branches hidden lutes,
Wherefrom such music spreads into the air
That all it breathes on doth its spirit share,
And all men's souls are drawn beneath and lie   5
Mixed into her as words mix with the sky.
And as some words before they mix are stayed
And old thoughts live new spirits by their aid,
So souls of some men meet the spirit of love
That sentinels   10

A woman's beauty is like kisses shed,
A colour heard, or thoughts that have been said,
It covers, with infinity between.
The memory sees, but 'twixt you and that seen
A million ages lie. It is a wave   15
That in old time swept Gods, and did enslave
As the broad sea imprisons, savage lands,
It is a wind that blows from careful hands
The grains of gathered wheat, and golden grains
To others bears.   20

It is a diver into seas more strange
Than fishes know. No poison makes such change
As her swift subtle alchemy.

In November

Your face was like a day in June
Glad with the raiment of the noon,
And your eyes seemed like thoughts that stir
To dream of warm June nights that were.

The dead leaves dropped off one by one,   5
All hopeless in the withered sun.
Around, the listless atmosphere
Hung grey and quiet and austere.

As we stood talking in the porch
My pulse shook like a wind-kissed torch,   10
Too sweet you seemed for anything
Save dreams whereof the poets sing.

Your voice was like the buds that burst
With latter spring to slake their thirst,
While all your ardent mouth was lit   15
With summer memories exquisite.

[*When I went forth as is my daily wont*]

When I went forth as is my daily wont
Into the streets, into the eddying throng,
Lady—the thought of your sweet face was strong,
The grace of your sweet shape my ways did haunt.
About this spell clangoured the busy chaunt   5
Of traffic, like some hundred-throated song
Of storm set round some moon-flashed isle in wrong.
But soon usurped your robe's undulant flaunt—
Your last words said—your ruby gaoler's loss—
The instant and unanchored gleams across   10
My soul's mirror that holds you there for aye;
The sounds that beat the guard down of sound's gates,
But memory master not, behind who waits,
Your speech—your face—his text by night and day.

The Key of the Gates of Heaven

A word leapt sharp from my tongue,
Could a golden key do more
Than open the golden door
For the rush of the golden song.
She spoke, and the spell of her speech,—   5
The chain of the heart linked song—
Was on me swift and strong,
And Heaven was in my reach.   [BREAK

A word was the key thereof;
And my thought was the hand that turned.   10
And words that throbbed and burned,
Sweet birds from the shine of love,
Flew clear 'tween the rosebud gate
That was parted beneath and above,
And a chain of music wove   15
More strong than the hand of fate.

The Cage

Air knows as you know that I sing in my cage of earth,
And my mouth dry with longing for your winsome mouth of mirth,
That passes ever my prison bars which will not fall apart,
Wearied unweariedly so long with the fretful music of my heart.

If you were a rose, and I, the wandering invisible air   5
To feed your scent and live, glad though you knew me not there,
Or the green of your stem that your proud petals could never meet,
I yet would feel the caresses of your shadow's ruby feet.

O splendour of radiant flesh, O your heavy hair uncurled,
Binding all that my hopes have fashioned to crown me King
   of the world,   10
I sing to life to befriend me; she sends me your mouth of mirth,
And you only laugh as you pass me, and I weep in my cage of earth.

Bacchanal

If life would come to me
As she has never come,
The music of the spring—
The fullness of its prime—
With roses in her hair,   5
With laughter on her lips,

Ah! life!—we'd dance a tune.
Ah! life! we'd live—we'd live.

If life would come to me
With roses in her lap—   10
With wine between her hands,
And a fire upon her lips—
We would burn Time in that fire,
We would drown care in that wine,
And with music and with laughter   15
We would scare black death away.

If life would come to me
As I would have her come,
With sweet breasts for my bed,
And my food her fiery wine.   20
If life would only come!
For we live not till it comes;
And it comes not till we feel
Its fire through all our veins.

[*Now the spirit's song has withered*]

Now the spirit's song has withered
As a song of last year's June
That has made the air its tomb.
Shall we ever find it after
Sighing in some summer tune   5
That is sealèd now in gloom
Safe for light and laughter?

Now the sky blooms full of colour,
Houses glow and windows shine
Glittering with impatient wings.   10
Where they go to may I follow
Since mine eyes have made them mine?
Shall I ever find these things
Hid in hill or hollow?

[*O heart, home of high purposes*]

O heart, home of high purposes,
O hand with craft and skill,
Say, why this meagre dalliance
To do such greatness ill?

Marshal the flame-winged legions, yours,— 5
The thunder and the beauty;
Sweeten these sunsoiled days of ours,
We need your wizard duty.

Our parched lips yearn for music yet.
Find us some gate in air 10
To leave our worldstained lives behind,
And live a life more fair.

The vagrant clouds are alive with light
When the sun shines and sings,
When the wind blows they race in flight 15
So happy in their wings.

Help us, the helpless, breathe thy breath,
Show us new flowers, new ways to live,
Thy glory thaw our lips of death.
To you your feel of power we'll give.

To J. Kramer

In the large manner and luxury
Of a giant who guests
In a little world of mortals
He condescends a space
His ears to incline, 5
But as tho' list'ning were a trouble.
Who knows! but it were a hazard
To break speech on this matter,
To bid conference with a doctor.

Mayhap Cod-liver-oil   10
Thrice in the day taken
Medicinal might be.

Don Juan's Song

The moon is in an ecstasy,
It wanes not nor can grow.
The heavens are in a mist of love,
And deepest knowledge know.
What things in nature seem to move   5
Bear love as I bear love?
And bear my pleasures so?

The moon will fade when morning comes,
The heavens will dream no more.
In our missed meetings are eyes hard?   10
What shadows fleck the door
Averted, when we part? What guard
Scents death in each vain word?
What haggard haunts the shore?

I bear my love as streams that bear   15
The sky still flow or shake.
Though deep within too far on high,
Light blossoms kiss and wake
The waters sooner than the sky.
And if they kiss and die!   20
God made them frail to break.

You and I

You and I have met but for an instant;
And no word the gate-lips let from out them.
But the eyes, voice audible—the soul's lips,
Stirr'd the depths of thought and feeling in me.

I have seen you somewhere, some sweet sometime,   5
Somewhere in a dim-remembered sometime.
Was it in the sleep-spun realm of dreamland?
In sweet woods, a faery flower of fancy?

If our hands touched would it bring us nearer?
As our souls touched, eyes' flame meeting eyes' flame.   10
If the lips spake would it lift the curtain
More than our mute bearing unaffected
Told the spirit's secrets eloquently?

Strange! this vast and universal riddle!
How perplexing? Manifold the wonder.   15
You and I, we meet but for an instant,
Pause or pass, reflections in a mirror.
And I see myself and wonder at it.
See myself in you, a double wonder.
With my thought held in a richer casket,   20
Clothed and girt in shape of regal beauty.
Strange! we pause! New waves of life rush blindly,
Madly on the soul's dumb silent breakers.
And a music strange is new awakened.
Fate the minstrel smites or holds the chord back.   25
Smites—new worlds undreamt of burst upon us.
All our life before was but embryo
Shaping for this birth—this living moment.

As We Look

As they have sung to me,
So shall they sing to you?
One song have they.
Nay, when the old be new,
Nay, when the blind shall see,   5
Then, when the night is day,
Shall this thing be.

For this is truth, and still
Ever throughout be truth
While the world sings.   10
Gladly it sings to youth;
Sadly to age and ill.
To love sweet whisperings
Its songs fulfil.

One song the roses sing;   15
One song the chirping birds.
But whoso hears,
He makes within the words
To his soul murmuring.
High hopes or lowly fears   20
One song shall bring.

One song, one voice, the sky:
The star, the moon, the cloud:
One song the trees.
But some will see a shroud,   25
And some will dim descry
Immortal harmonies
That never die.

Each looks with eyes that are
But the soul's curtain hung   30
Till thought draws clear.
One hears sweet songs, unsung
To some, and dumb the star,
To these while songs are near,
Fair things are far.   35

Psyche's Lament

O! love, my love! once, and not long,
Yet seems it dreams of ancient days,
When nights were passion's lips of song,
And thou his speech of honeyed praise.

'O love, my love', in murmurs low   5
Burnt in my ears. Then I was thine.
O! love, my love! 'twixt weepings now
The empty words are only mine.

O! sweetest love! O! cruel wings,
The darkening shadow of thy flight   10
Is all that dreary daylight brings
Of all that was so sweet at night.
O! sweetest love! once you called sweet,
Through kisses, her forlorn who weeps
That wings, too swift to hear their beat,   15
Of Time, flew with you . . . How he creeps.

O life my life! I have no life
Whilst thou who hast my soul art far.
When night is not, while day has strife,
What life has the unwakened star?   20
O! life, my life, upon my brow
My tears like flowers are gathered up.
The fruit that sorrow did not sow
She turns to poison in her cup.

[*Like some fair subtle poison is the cold white beauty you shed*]

Like some fair subtle poison is the cold white beauty you shed;
Pale flower of the garden I walk in, your scent is an amorous net
To lure my thoughts and pulses, by your useless phantom led
By misty hours and ruins with insatiate longing wet.

To lure my soul with the beauty of some enthralling sin.   5
To starve my body to hunger for the mystic rapture there.
O cruel; flesh and spirit your robe's soft stir sucks in,
And your cold unseeing glances, and the fantasies of your hair.

And in the shining hollow of your dream-enhaunted throat
My mournful thoughts now wander and build desire a nest,   10

But no tender thoughts to crown the fiery dreams that float
Around those sinuous rhythms and dim languors of your breast.

Tess

The free fair life that has never been mine, the glory that might
    have been,
If I were what you seem to be and what I may not be!
I know I walk upon the earth but a dreadful wall between
My spirit and your spirit lies, your joy and my misery.

The angels that lie watching us, the little human play,   5
What deem they of the laughter and the tears that flow apart?
When a word of man is a woman's doom do they turn and wonder
    and say,
'Ah! why has God made love so great that love must burst her heart!'

Aspiration

The roots of a dead universe are shrunken in my brain,
And the tinsel-leafèd branches of the charred trees are strewn;
And the chaff we deem'd for harvest shall be turned to golden grain,
While May no more will mimic March, but June be only June.

Lo! a ghost enleaguer'd city where no ghostly footfall came!   5
And a rose within the mirror with the fragrance of it hid;
And mine ear prest to the mouth of the shadow of a name;
But no ghost or speech or fragrance breathing on my faint eyelid.

I would crash the city's ramparts, touch the ghostly hands without.
Break the mirror, feel the scented warm lit petals of the rose.   10
Would mine ears be stretched for shadows in the fading of the
    doubt?
Other ears shall wait my shadow,—can you see behind the brows?

For I would see with mine own eyes the glory and the gold.
With a strange and fervid vision see the glamour and the dream.

And chant an incantation in a measure new and bold,   15
And enaureole a glory round an unawakened theme.

Raphael

Dear, I have done; it shall be done. I know
I can paint on and on, and still paint on.
Another touch, and yet another touch.
Yet wherefore? 'Tis Art's triumph to know this,
Long ere the soul and brain begins to flag,   5
And dim the first fresh flashes of the soul,
Before achievement, by our own desire
And loathing to desist in what we love,
Is wrought to ruin by much overtoil,
To know the very moment of our gain,   10
And fix the triumph with reluctant pause.
Come from the throne, sweet, kiss me on the cheek;
You have borne bravely, sweet, come, look with me.
Is it not well—think love—the recompense,
This binds the unborn ages at our feet.   15
Thus you shall look, my love, and never change
Throughout all changes. Time's own conqueror,
While worshippers of climes and times unknown
Lingeringly look in wonder—here—at us.

What have we done—in these long hours, my love.   20
Long—long to you—whose patient labour was
To sit, and sit, a statue, movelessly.
Love we have woven a chain more glorious
Than crowns or Popes—to bind the centuries.
You are tired. I should have thought a little,   25
But you said nothing, sweet, and I forgot,
In rapture of my soul's imaginings.
You,—yes, 'twas thus you looked, ah, look again
That hint of smile—it was like wings for heaven,
And gave my spirit play to revel more   30
In dazzling visions. But ah! it mocked my hand.
There,—there—before my eyes and in my brain
Limned perfect—but my fingers traitors were,

Could not translate, and heartsick was the strife.
But it is done—I know not how—perchance   35
Even as I, maddened, drew on hopelessly
An angel taking pity—mayhap for thee—
Guided my hand and drew it easily.

And they will throng—admire with gaping mouth,
The students, 'Look, what ease, what grace divine.   40
What balance and what harmony serene'.
And some, 'Like noonday lakes to torrents wild,
After titanic Mighty Angelo.'
Ah, Angelo, he has no sweetness—true;
But, ah, I would I had his breadth of wing.   45
Jove's Thunders, and the giant craggy heights
Whose points cleave the high heavens, and at whose feet
The topmost clouds have end, afraid to soar.

And I too, shake my brow amongst the stars.
And this I know and feel what I have done   50
Is but the seed plot of a mightier world.
Yea, world on world is forming in my brain.
I have no space to hold it. Time will show
I could draw down the Heavens, I could bend
Yon hoar age-scorning column with my hand   55
I feel such power. But where there's sun, there's shade!
And these thoughts bring their shadow in their train.
Who lives?—See this, it is my hand—my name.
But who looks from the canvas, no—not me.
Some doubt of God—but the world lives who doubts?   60
Even thus our own creations mock at us,
Our own creations outlive our decay.

What do I labour for if all is thus.
I triumph, but my triumph is my scorn.
'Tis true I love my labour, and the days   65
Pass pleasantly,
But what is it I love in it—desire
Accomplished? never have I reached
The halfway of the purpose I have planned.
A hardship conquered?—a poor juggler's feat   70
And his elatement mayhap betters mine.

The adoration of the gaping crowd,
Who praise, with jest, not knowing why they praise,
Then turn, and sing a lewd and smutty song.
Or kneel—bate breath—to my Lord Cardinal.   75
Or is it the approval of the wise?
I take it—sadly knowing what I know,
And feeling that this marvel of their world
Is little triumph to me, it being my world;
Their deeds being circumscribed—proportionate,   80
Within their limits; and mine loftier,
But (God how bounded yet,) to do as thus
Is but my nature—therefore little pride
Their praises give me. Ah, but this gives pride
To know that there is one that does feel pride   85
When they praise me, and cannot hide the glow
Upon her cheeks to hear me spoken of.
Love—this is better—here—to be with you,
My head upon your bosom while your hair
A loosened fire falls all about my face   90
And thro' its tangles—like a prison bar
To shut my soul in—watch the shadows creep,
The long grey shadows creeping furtively.
I would I were a poet—love—this once.
I cannot tell my feelings . . .   95
How effable in this half-light you look,
Love I would dream—the shadows thickly press.
You fade into my fancy—and become
A thought—a smile—a rapture of the brain,
A presence that embraces all things felt.   100
A twilight glamour—faery fantasy.
Your two eyes in the shadow, stars that dream
In quiet waters of the evening, draw
My spirit to them and enfold me there
Love. I would sleep, dear love I would forget.   105
Love I would sleep, you watching, covering me,
Warmed by your love and sheltered 'neath love's wing,
Sweet let the world pass as this day has passed,
What do you murmur—sleeping? then will I.

To Michael Sherbrooke on hearing his recitation of the 'Raven'. Poe

O! keen magnificent pangs, luxurious opulent doom,
The exquisite tortures of death, felt, seen from the fullness of life,
A harrowing soul despair wrought out of a jewelled gloom,
My overcharged heart can endure not this pinnacled orient strife.

O master—take thought of our weakness, be not like God in His
    might,   5
He may forget—He is God, but why should you play with our
    hearts?
Lift them to ecstasy's sunblaze, steep them in tear-dripping night.

Night and Day

ARGUMENT.

NIGHT. The Poet wanders thro' the night and questions of the stars
    but receives no answer. He walks through the crowds of the
    streets, and asks himself whether he is the scapegoat to bear the
    sins of humanity upon himself, and to waste his life to discover
    the secret of God, for all.
DAY. He wakes, and sees the day through his window. He feels   v
    endowed with a larger capacity to feel and enjoy things, and
    knows that by having communed with the stars, his soul has
    exalted itself, and become wiser in intellectual experience. He
    walks through the city, out into the woods, and lies under the
    trees, dreaming through the sky-spaces
He hears Desire sing a song of Immortality,   x
Hope, a song of Love,
And Beauty, a song of the Eternal Rhythm.
Twilight comes down and the poet hearkens to the song of the
    evening star, for Beauty has taught him to hear, Hope to feel,
    and Desire, a conception of attainment.   xv
By thinking of higher things we exalt ourselves to what we think
    about.
Striving after the perfect—God, we attain nearer to perfection
    than before.

NIGHT.

When the night is warm with wings
Invisible, articulate,
Only the wind sings
To our mortal ears of fault.
And the steadfast eyes of fate   5
Gleam from Heaven's brooding vault,
Through dull corporeal bars
We drink in the proud stars.

These, my earth-sundered fantasy
On pillared heights of thought doth see   10
In the dark heaven as golden pendulous birds,
Whose tremulous wings the wind translates to words,
From the thrilled heaven which is their rapturous nest.
Still, though they sleep not, thoughtful to illume,
They are not silent, only our sundering gloom   15
Makes their songs dumb to us—a tragic jest.

Sing to me, for my soul's eyes
Anguish for those ecstasies
And voluptuous mysteries
That must somewhere be,   20
Or we could not know of them.
Sing to me, O sing to me,
Is your light from sun of them,
Or from boughs of golden stem
Trickling over ye,   25
That your nest is hanging on?

Tho' the sun's face be on high,
Yet his fiery feet do lie
Fixed on earth, to give the sky
In our hands a while.   30
So our mortal hearts make bliss,
And we may a little smile.
Wherefore keep ye all your bliss?
What your gain for gain we miss?
Wherefore so beguile   35
With your shining, heard of none?

How can I burst this trammel of my flesh,
That is a continent 'twixt your song and me?
How can I loosen from my soul this mesh
That dulls mine ears and blinds mine eyes to see?   40

When I had clambered over the walls of night,
Lo! still the night lay unperturb'd behind.
Only in Heaven the starry birds of light
Swarmed as arrested in their showery flight.
O! could I bind your song as night can bind.   45

* * *

Sudden the night blazed open at my feet.
Like splintered crystal tangled with gold dust
Blared on my ear and eye the populous street.

Then, like a dark globe sprinkled with gold heat
Wherein dark waters move—dark gleaming seas,   50
So round the lit-faced shadows seemed the street.

They feel the skeleton rattle as they go.
'Let us forget', they cry. 'Soon we shall know,—
Drown in life's carnival fate's whisperings.'

Foul heat of painted faces, ribald breath,   55
Lewd leer, make up the pageant as they flow
In reeking passage to the house of death.

Then said I, what divides love's name from lust?
Behold, what word can name the life for these?
For starven and not hungered, O! what crust?   60

Lean—starven, and they hunger not increase.
Starven of light, barriered 'gainst purity,
A bruten lust of living their life's lease.

A dream-empearlèd ladder to the moon.
A thought enguarded heavenly embassy   65
To treat with God for a perpetual June,

Colours my youth's flower for them, for me.
One flower whose ardent fragrance wastes for all,
Fed with the sobbings of humanity.

The sobbing of the burden of their sins   70
Is all the guerdon strife to ease them wins.
Who seeks heaven's sign, earth's scapegoat must he be?

God gives no June, and Heaven is as a wall.
No symboled answer to my questionings—
Only the weak wind yearns, the stars wink not at all.   75

DAY.

The fiery hoofs of day have trampled the night to dust;
They have broken the censer of darkness and its fumes
    are lost in light.
Like a smoke blown away by the rushing of the gust
When the doors of the sun flung open, morning leaped
    and smote the night.

The banners of the day flame from the east.   80
Its gorgeous hosts assail the heart of dreams.
They brush aside the strange and cowlèd priest
Who ministers to our pillows with moonbeams
And restful pageantry or lethe draught,
Sleep—who by day dwells in invisibleness—   85
Their noising stirs the waking veils of thought.
Ah! I am in the midst of their bright press.

I went to sleep in the night,
In the awed and shadowy night,
Pleading of those birds delight.   90
Where has the morning borne me to?
What has she done with the night?
And those birds flown whereto?

Surely some God hath breathed upon mine eyes
Between awake and waking, or poured strange wine   95
Of some large knowledge—for I am grown wise
And big with new life—eager and divine.   [BREAK

Last night I stripped my soul of all alloy
Of earth that did ensphere and fetter it.
I strove to touch the springs of all the night. 100
My brow felt spray, but hands and eyes were dry.

Last night my soul thought God—my soul felt God.
I prayed the stars this for my body's dole.
Through prayer and thought to purified desires.
Thro' hallowed thought I was made half divine. 105

Shall I dream of shadow
Now I have the light;
Spoil the sunny meadow
To think of night?

Forth into the woods I will fare. 110
I will walk thro' the great clanging city
To seek what all have sought to find.
No face shall pass me
But I will question therein
Some mirrored subtlety, 115
Some wandering gleam that straggled thro'
Nativity, from the forgotten shelter of God's skirts.
In all that Time has harvested,
Whether a seed from Heaven has sprung;
In all God has made mutable and swift 120
Some lustre of his smile to see.
And the dun monstrous buildings be a book
To read the malediction of lucre
That spreads a shade and shelter for a plague.

Noon blazes in the city, tumult whirled. 125

Flame crowned and garmented
With robes that flaunt
The splash of gold he throws
About my feet,
He weaves above my head 130
A golden chaunt,
A song that throbs and glows
Thro' all the noon-day heat.

No Pan-pipe melodies
Of wind and boughs.   135
No tired waves listless wash,
No silence deep
With spirit harmonies
Night only knows:
No tender breaking flush,   140
Dawn's voice of dreams-asleep.

But buildings glorified,
Whose windows shine
And show the heaven, while far
Down the throng'd street   145
Mingles man's song of pride
With the divine
Song of the day's great star
Struck from the noon-day heat.

*   *   *

Shall I turn me to this tavern   150
And so rest me from the sultriness?

*   *   *

Dim-watery-lights, gleaming on gibbering faces,
Faces speechful, barren of soul and sordid.
Huddled and chewing a jest lewd and gabbled insidious,
Laughter, born of its dung, flashes and floods like sunlight, 155
Filling the room with a sense of a soul lethargic and kindly.
Touches my soul with a pathos, a hint of a wide desolation.

*   *   *

Green foliage kisses my heart's sight
Before I yet have left the street,
My heart feels summer-leaping light   160
These summer silent guests to greet.
The grassy plot—with rows of trees,
Like some sweet pallisaded land
From off some land outcast of these,
Whose air you breathe is grinding sand.   165

These are the outskirts of the woods,
The shore of mighty forest seas,
Where Pan plays to the solitudes
His deep primordial melodies.
Where night and day like ships sail by,   170
And no man knoweth this miracle;
Eternal as the eternal sky
That is the earth's dumb oracle.

                    *   *   *

I saw the face of God to-day,
I heard the music of his smile,   175
And yet I was not far away,
And yet in Paradise the while.

I lay upon the sparkling grass,
And God's own mouth was kissing me,
And there was nothing that did pass   180
But blazèd with divinity.

Divine—divine—upon mine eyes,
Upon mine hair—divine—divine,
The fervour of the golden skies,
The ardent gaze of God on mine.   185

(*Wherein the poet heareth the song of Desire.*)

Let me weave my fantasy
Of this web like broken glass
Gleaming thro' the fretted leaves
In a quaint intricacy,
Diamond tipping all the grass.   190

Hearken as the spirit heaves
Thro' the branches and the leaves
In the shudder of their pulse.
Delicate nature trembles so
To a ruder nature's touch,   195
And of peace that these convulse
They have little who should much.
Life is so.

Let me carve my fantasy
Of the fretwork of the leaves.   200

Then the trees bent and shook with laughter,
Each leaf sparkled and danced with glee.
On my heart their sobs came after,
Demons gurgling over me.
And my heart was chilled and shaken,   205
And I said thro' my great fear,
When the throat of tears is slaken
Joy must come for joy will hear.

Then spake I to the tree,
Were ye your own desire   210
What is it ye would be?

Answered the tree to me,
'I am my own desire,
I am what I would be.

'If ye were your desire   215
Would ye lie under me,
And see me as you see?'

I am my own desire
While I lie under you,
And that which I would be   220
Desire will sing to you.

Thro' the web of broken glass
I knew her eyes looked on me.
Soon thro' all the leaves did pass
Her trembling melody.   225
Yea! even the life within the grass
Made green stir
So to hear
Desire's yearned song of immortality.

(*Desire sings.*)

'Mortals—ancient syllables 230
Spoken of God's mouth,—
Do spirits them chronicle
So they be not lost?

'Music, breathed ephemeral—
Fragrant maid and child: 235
Bellow, croak and droning—
Age and cumbrous man.

'Music that the croaking hears:
Croak, to mate the music:
Do angels stand and throw their nets 240
From the banks Eterne?

'Surely the speech of God's mouth
Shall not be for nought!
Music wrought of God's passion
Less than vanished dew? 245

'As the sea through cloud to sea,
Thought through deed to thought,
Each returneth as they were,
So man to God's mouth?'

(*Here endeth the song of Desire.*)

So man to God's mouth, 250
Mouth whose breath we are!
How far—O—how far!
Spring of the soul's drouth?

I heard a whisper once
Of a way to make it near, 255
And still that whisper haunts
Like a wonder round my ear.

Hope whispered to me,—
I could not hear
The meaning to subdue me 260
Of the music most clear.

*   *   *

'Music that the croaking hears,
Croak, to mate the music.'

Was it lorn echo babbling to herself,
That none would mate and none would hear her?   265

'I wander—I wander—O will she wander here?
Where'er my footsteps carry me I know that she is near.
A jewelled lamp within her hand and jewels in her hair,
I lost her in a vision once and seek her everywhere.

'My spirit whispers she is near, I look at you and you.   270
Surely she has not passed me, I sleeping as she flew.
I wander—I wander, and yet she is not here,
Altho' my spirit whispers to me that she is near.'

Verily my heart doth know the voice of Hope.
What doth he in these woods singing this wise?   275

'By what far ways shall my heart reach to thine?
We, who have never parted—never met,
Nor done to death the joys that shall be yet,
Nor drained the cup of love's delirious wine.
How shall my craving spirit know for mine   280
Thine, self-same seeking? Will a wild regret
For the lost days—the lonely suns that set,
Be for our love a token and a sign?
Will all the weary nights, the widowed days
That sundered long, all point their hands at thee?   285
Yea! all the stars that have not heard thy praise
Low murmur in thy charmèd ear of me?
All pointing to the ending of the ways,
All singing of the love that is to be?'

Of love to be, wherefore of love to be?   290
I never have heard the stars though they look wistfully
     at me.
I have cried to them and they showed me Desire.
She brought me a passionate wistful dream of eternity.
I cried to them, and they showed me Hope—a fire.
He brought me a dream of love—he made my heart to feel   295

Vague shadowy longings—whereon loneliness had
   put a seal.
Wherefore? because love is the radiant smile of God,
Because love's land is a heaven only by angels trod.
Where beauty sings and teaches her fair song
Of the Eternal rhythm—Ah! teach me.   300

(*Beauty sings the song of eternal rhythm.*)

'Close thine eyes and under the eyelids that hide,
The glory thine eyes have seen in thy soul shall abide.
The beauty thy soul has heard shall flow into thy soul.
Lordship of many mysteries will be thine being beauty's
   thrall.

'Close thine eyes and under the eyelids that hide   305
A bridge build from Heaven as the earth is—wide,
For the bright and dense shapes that 'twixt earth and
   heaven do pass,
Lutanists of day and even to the pool and to the grass.

'To the cloud and to the mountains, to the wind and to
   the stars,
Silvern-tonguèd din of fountains, golden at the sunset bars. 310

So they sing the songs I taught them, and they lute the
   songs I made
For the praise of Him who wrought them lauders of His
   sun and shade.

How may there be a silence? for the cosmic cycle would
   cease,
I am but the voice of God and these do lute my litanies.'

            *   *   *

One night and one day and what sang Desire?   315
All that God sings betwixt them is not lost.
One night and one day, what did Beauty choir?
If our souls hearken little is the most,
And nothing is which is not living sound,

All flowing with the eternal harmony 320
That with creation's first day was unwound.
One night and one day—what sang Hope to me?
That the next night and day love's song must fill.
He showed me in a mirror, ecstasy,
And a new dawn break over the old hill. 325

Twilight's wide eyes are mystical
With some far off knowledge,
Secret is the mouth of her,
And secret her eyes.

Lo! she braideth her hair 330
Of dim soft purple and thread of satin.
Lo! she flasheth her hand—
Her hand of pearl and silver in shadow.
Slowly she braideth her hair
Over her glimmering eyes, 335
Floating her ambient robes
Over the trees and the skies.
Over the wind-footing grass.
Softly she braideth her hair
With shadow deeper than thought. 340

To make her comely for night?
To make her meet for the night?

Slowly she heaveth her breast,
For the night to lie there and rest?

Hush, her eyes are in trance 345
Swooningly raised to the sky.
What heareth she so to enthral?
Filleth her sight to amaze?

'From the sweet gardens of the sky
Whose roots are pleasures under earth, 350
Whose atmosphere is melody
To hail each deathless minute's birth,
Between frail night and frailer day

I sing what soon the moon will say,
And what the sun has said in mirth.   355

'I sing the centre of all bliss.
The peace like a sweet-smelling tree
That spreads its perfumed holiness
In unperturbed serenity.
Between the darkness and the light,   360
I hang above my message bright
The clamour of mortality.

'Here, from the bowers of Paradise
Whose flowers from deep contentment grew,
To reach his hand out to the wise   365
My casement God's bright eyes look through.
For him whose eyes do look for Him
He leans out thro' the seraphim
And His own bosom draws him to.'

I heard the evening star.   370

To Nature

Beneath the eternal wandering skies
O wilt thou rest awhile by me,
Immortal mother of mystery,
And breathe on my blind eyes!

Or is it that thou standest nigh,   5
And while I know that I am blind
I live, until thou passest by,
To leave me dead behind.

Dust Calleth to Dust

A little dust whispered—a little grey dust,
As it whirled round my knees in the arms of the wind,

'O wind lift me higher, sweet wind, lift me higher
To see thro' his eyes to the vast of his mind'.

Then I soon heard it murmur—'O brother, dear brother   5
How long must you guard that fierce temple of God?
So fixt to the earth and a foe to the wind—
O haste and with me kiss the cloud and the clod.'

My Songs

Deep into the great heart of things
My mood passed, as my life became
One with the vasty whisperings
That breathe the pure ineffable name.

A pulse of all the life that stirs   5
Through still deep shade and wavering light,
The flowing of the wash of years
From out the starry infinite.

And flowing through my soul, the skies
And all the winds and all the trees   10
Mixed with its stream of light, to rise
And flow out in these melodies.

To the Present

Time leveller, chaining fate itself to thee—
Hope frets her eager pettings on thy sand.
Wild waves that strive to overreach command
Of nature, much in sight. Eternity
Is but thyself made shoreless. Toward thy sea   5
The streams-to-be flow from the shadowland
Of rootless flowers no earthly breeze has fanned,
Weaves with the past thy restless apathy.   [BREAK

Thou art the link 'twixt after and before,
The one sole truth; the final ultimate 10
Endeavour of the ages. The loud roar
Of life around me is thy voice to fate
And Time—who looking on thee has grown hoar
While thou art yet—and freedom is so late.

[*Have we sailed and have we wandered*]

Have we sailed and have we wandered
Still beyond, the hills are blue.
Have we spent and have we squandered,
What's before us still is new.

See the foam of unheard waters 5
And the gleam of hidden skies.
Footsteps of Eve's whiter daughters
Tremble to our dreaming eyes.

Soundless waning to the spirit
Still—O still the hills are blue, 10
Ever and yet never near it,
There where our far childhood grew.

[*We are sad with a vague sweet sorrow*]

We are sad with a vague sweet sorrow
Whose touch is a scent of sighs;
A flower that weeps to a flower
The old tale that beauty dies.

Our smiles are full of a longing, 5
For we saw the gold flash of the years.
They passed, and we know where they came from,
The deep—deep well of tears.

Spring

I walk and I wonder
To hear the birds sing.
Without you my lady
How can there be Spring?
I see the pink blossoms   5
That slept for a year;
But who could have woke them
While you were not near?

Birds sing to the blossoms;
Blind, dreaming your pink.   10
These blush to the songsters.
Your music they think.
So well had you taught them
To look and to sing;
Your bloom and your music;   15
The ways of the Spring.

The Poet [I]

The trouble of the universe is on his wonder-travelled eyes.
Ah, vain for him the starry quest, the spirit's wistful sacrifice.
For though the glory of the heavens celestially in glimpses seen
Illumines his rapt gazing, still the senses shut him in.
No fellowship of suffering to meet his tear-bewildered ways.   5
Alone he bears the burden of alienated days.
He is a part of paradise that all the earth has pressed between,
And when he calls unto the stars of paradise with heaven-sweet
   songs
To his divided self he calls and sings the story of earth's wrongs.

Himself he has himself betrayed, and deemed the earth a path of
   heaven,   10
And wandered down its sunless days, and too late knew himself
   bereaven.

For swiftly sin and suffering and earth-born laughter meshed his
    ways,
And caught him in a cage of earth, but heaven can hear his dewy
    lays.

[O'er the celestial pathways the mortal and immortal strays]

O'er the celestial pathways the mortal and immortal strays;
For earth is a swift dream of God, and man one shape within His brain.
And there man meeteth sun and moon, immortal shapes of nights
    and days,
And in God's glad mood he is glad and in God's petulance has pain.

And there he dreams his dreamer's face; forgets, nor knows himself
    a dream,   5
Until some shadow wavers by and leaves him but a trembling shade
To murmur in his impotence that nothing is, but all things seem,
And what they seem like man shall know when man beneath the
    dust is laid.

Peace

Where the dreamy mountains brood
Ever in their ancient mood
Would I go and dream with them
Till I graft me on their stem.

With fierce energy I aspire   5
To be that the Gods desire
As the dreamy mountains are
And no God can break or mar.

Soon the world shall fade and be
One with still eternity   10
As the dreamy hills that lie
Silent to the passing sky.

Twilight [II]

Mist-like its dusky panic creeps in the end to your proud heart:
O you will feel its kisses cold while it rends your limbs apart.
Have you not seen the withering rose and watched the lovely
    moon's decay,
And more than mortal loveliness fade like the fainting stars away?

I have seen lovely thoughts forgot in wind, effacing dreams;   5
And dreams like roses wither leaving perfume not nor scent;
And I have tried to hold in net like silver fish the sweet starbeams,
But all these things are shadowed gleams of things beyond the
    firmament.

The Poet [II]

He takes the glory from the gold
For consecration of the mould
He strains his ears to the clouds' lips
He sings the song they sang to him
And his brow dips   5
In amber that the seraphim
Have held for him and hold.

So shut in are our lives, so still
What we see not of good and ill,
A dead world since ourselves are dead   10
Till he, the master speaks and lo!
The dead worlds shed
Strange winds, new skies and rivers flow
Illumined from the hill.

Creation

As the pregnant womb of night
Thrills with imprisoned light,

Misty, nebulous-born,
Growing deeper into her morn,
So man, with no sudden stride,   5
Bloomed into pride.

In the womb of the All-spirit
The universe lay, the will
Blind, an atom, lay still,
Docile for birth to bear it.   10
The pulse of matter
Obeyed in awe
And strove to flatter
The rhythmic law.
But the will grew; nature feared   15
And cast off the child she reared,
Now her rival, instinct-led,
With her own powers impregnated.

Brain and heart, blood-fervid flowers!
Creation is each act of yours.   20
Your roots are God, the pauseless cause,
But your boughs swing to self-windy laws.
Perception is no dreamy birth
And magnifies transfigured earth.

With each new light, our eyes receive   25
A larger power to perceive.
If we could unveil our eyes,
Become as wise as the All-wise,
No love would be, no mystery.
Love, joy, dwell in infinity.   30
Love begets love; reaching highest
We find a higher still, unseen
From where we stood to reach the first.
Moses must die to live in Christ.
The seed be buried to live to green.   35
Perfection must begin from worst.
Christ perceives a larger reachless love
More full, and grows to reach thereof.
The green plant yearns for its yellow fruit.
Perfection always is a root,   40

And joy, a motion that doth feed
Itself on light of its own speed,
And round its radiant circle runs,
Creating and devouring suns.

Thus human hunger nourisheth   45
The plan terrific,—true design—
Makes music with the bones of death,
And soul knows soul to shine.

What foolish lips first framed 'I sin'?
The virgin spirit grows within   50
To stature its eyes know to fail.
And all its edges weaken and pale
Where the flesh merges and is one;
A chalice of light for stagnation
To drink, but where no dust can come   55
Till the glass shatters and light is dumb.
Soul grows in freedom natural.
When in wild growths eventual
Its light casts shadow on other light,
All cry 'That spirit is not white'.   60
As when God strides through the wrack of skies,
The plunging seas welcome paradise,
They say not 'This dark period
Sheweth our bitter wrong to God',
But revel in a dark delight,   65
And day is sweet and night is bright.
The jewelled green laughs myriadly.
The yearning pits swing and draw down
The rainbow-splintered mountains thrown
By wrestling giants beneath the sea.   70

Now think how high a mountain is.
Joy, could this tall oak's branches kiss
Its shoulder, less its brow, how blest?
If I lie low the skies are drest
With its broidered branches stretched across   75
Into the sky-scorned mountain's loss,
The sky, it gibbers to forever.
Naught is too low to make so high

As hope, if we stand right, and sever
Waste, the essential to descry.   80

An emanation like a voice
Spreads up, the spirits of our joys.
The sky receives it like an ear
Bent o'er the throbbing atmosphere.
Our thoughts like endless waterfalls   85
Are fed—to fill life's palace halls
Until the golden gates do close
On endless gardens of repose.
A sun, long set, again shall rise
Bloom in annihilation's skies   90
Strong—strong—past ruin to endure
More lost than bliss—than life more sure.
This universe shall be to me
Millions of years beneath the sea
Cast from my rock of changelessness   95
The centre of eternity.
And uncreated nothingness
Found what creation laboured for,
The ultimate silence—Ah, no more
A happy fool in paradise   100
But finite—wise as the All-wise.

[*Even now your eyes are mixed in mine*]

Even now your eyes are mixed in mine.
I see you not, but surely, he—
This stricken gaze—has looked on thee.
From him your glances shine.

Even now I felt your hand in mine.   5
This breeze that warms my open palm
Has surely kist yours; such thrilled calm
No lull can disentwine.

The words you spoke just now, how sweet?
These grasses heard and bend to tell.—   10

The green grows pale your speech to spell,
How its green heart must beat?

I breathe you. Here the air enfolds
Your absent presence, as fire cleaves,
Leaving the places warm it leaves.　　　　　15
Such warmth a warm word holds.

Bruised are our words and our full thought
Breaks like dull rain from some rich cloud.
Our pulses leap alive and proud.
Colour, not heat, is caught.　　　　　20

A Question

What if you shut your eyes and look,
Yea, look with all the spirit's eyes,
While mystic unrevealèd skies
Unfold like pages of a book

Wherein new scenes of wonder rare　　　　　5
Are imaged, till the sense deceives
Itself, and what it sees believes—
Even what the soul has pictured there?

A Careless Heart

A little breath can make a prayer,
A little wind can take it
And turn it back again to air:
Then say, why should you make it?

An ardent thought can make a word,　　　　　5
A little ear can hear it,
A careless heart forget it heard:
Then why keep ever near it?

Twilight [III]

A sumptuous splendour of leaves
Murmurously fanning the evening heaven
And I hear
In the soft living grey shadows
In the brooding evanescent atmosphere   5
The voice of impatient night.

The splendour shall vanish in a vaster splendour,
Its own identity shall lose itself
And the golden glory of day
Give birth to the glimmering face of the twilight   10
And she shall grow into a vast enormous pearl maiden
Whose velvet tresses shall envelop the world,—
Night.

[Invisible ancient enemy of mine]

Invisible ancient enemy of mine
My house's foe
To rich my pride with wrongful suffering
Your vengeful gain
Coward and striker in the pit-lined dark   5
Lie to my friends
Feed the world's jealousy and pamper woe.

When I had bowed
I felt your smile, when my large spirit groaned
And hid its fire   10
Because another spirit leaned on it,
I knew you near.

O that the tortured spirit could amass
All the world's pains,
How I would cheat you, leaving none for life,   15

You would recount
All you have piled on me, self-tortured count
Through all eternity.

In Piccadilly

Lamp-lit faces! to you
What is your starry dew?
Gold flowers of the night blue!

Deep in wet pavement's slime,
Mud rooted, is your fierce prime,   5
To bloom in lust's coloured clime.

The sheen of eyes that lust,
Dew, time made your trust,
Lights your passionless dust.

Midsummer Frost

A July ghost, aghast at the strange winter,
Wonders, at burning noon, (all summer-seeming)
How, like a sad thought buried in light words,
Winter, an alien presence, is ambushed here.

See, from the fire-fountained noon, there creep   5
Lazy yellow ardours towards pale evening,
To thread dark and vain fire
Over my unsens'd heart.
Dead heart, no urgent summer can reach.
Hidden as a root from air or a star from day;   10
A frozen pool whereon mirth dances;
Where the shining boys would fish.

My blinded brain pierced is,
And searched by a thought, and pangful

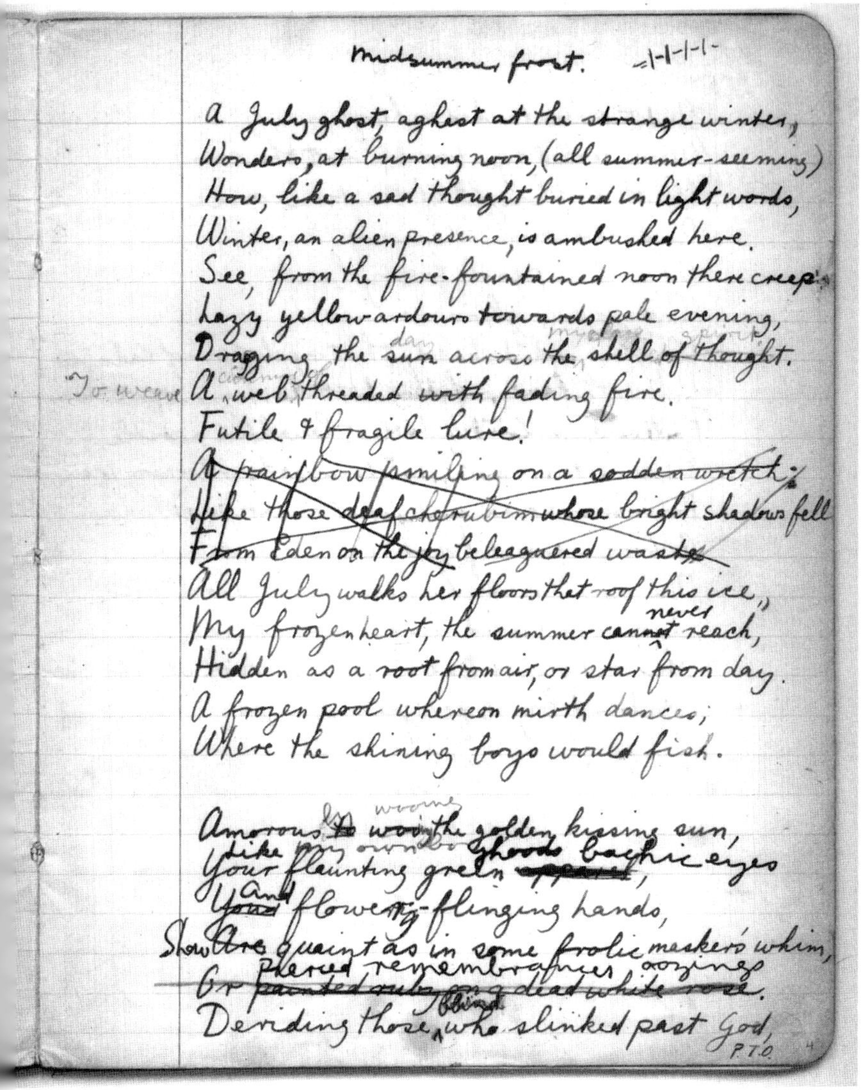

midsummer frost. -|-|-|-|-

A July ghost, aghast at the strange winter,
Wonders, at burning noon, (all summer-seeming)
How, like a sad thought buried in light words,
Winter, an alien presence, is ambushed here.
See, from the fire-fountained noon there creeps
Lazy yellow ardours towards pale evening,
Dragging the sun across the shell of thought.
To weave A web threaded with fading fire.
Futile & fragile lure!
A rainbow smiling on a sodden wretch;
Like those deaf cherubim whose bright shadows fell
From Eden on the joy beleaguered waste
All July walks her floors that roof this ice,
My frozen heart, the summer cannot never reach,
Hidden as a root from air, or star from day.
A frozen pool whereon mirth dances;
Where the shining boys would fish.

Amorous to woo the golden kissing sun,
Your flaunting green bacchic eyes
And flowery-flinging hands,
quaint as in some frolic masker's whim,
Or remembrances dead white rose.
Deriding those who slinked past God,
P.T.O.

FIG. 2 'Midsummer Frost'. Ink draft, begun as a fair copy with ink and pencil alterations.

With bitter ooze of a joyous knowledge   15
Of some starred time outworn.
Like blind eyes that have slinked past God,
And light, their untasked inheritance,
(Sealed eyes that trouble never the Sun)
Yet has feel of a Maytime pierced.   20
He heareth the Maytime dances;
Frees from their airy prison, bright voices,
To loosen them in his dark imagination,
Powered with girl revels rare
And silks and merry colours,   25
And all the unpeopled ghosts that walk in words.
Till wave white hands that ripple lakes of sadness,
Until the sadness vanishes and the stagnant pool remains.

Underneath this summer air can July dream
How, in night-hanging forest of eating maladies,   30
A frozen forest of moon-unquiet madness,
The moon-drunk, haunted, pierced soul dies;
Starved by its Babel folly, lying stark,
Unvexed by July's warm eyes.

Wedded [I]

The knotted moment that untwists
Into the narrow laws of love,
Its ends are rolled round our four wrists
That once could stretch and rove.

See our confinèd fingers stray   5
O'er delicate fibres that recoil,
And blushing hints as cold as clay;
Love is tired after toil.

But hush! two twin moods meet in air;
Two spirits of one gendered thought.   10
Our chained hands loosened everywhere
Kindness like death's have caught.

Song

A silver rose to show
Is your sweet face,
And like the heaven's white brow
Sometime God's battle place
Your blood is quiet now.   5

Your body is a star
Unto my thought.
But stars are not too far
And can be caught,—
Small pools their prisons are.   10

A Mood

You are so light and gay,
So slight, sweet maid;
Your limbs like leaves in play,
Or beams that grasses braid;
O! joys whose jewels pray   5
My breast to be inlaid.
Frail fairy of the streets;
Strong, dainty lure;
For all men's eyes the sweets
Whose lack makes hearts so poor;   10
While your heart loveless beats,
Light, laughing, and impure.

O! fragrant waft of flesh
Float through me so,—
My limbs are in your mesh,   15
My blood forgets to flow.
Ah! lilied meadows fresh,
It knows where it would go.

[*If you are fire and I am fire*]

If you are fire and I am fire,
Who blows the flame apart
So that desire eludes desire
Around one central heart?

A single root and separate bough,   5
And what blind hands between
That make our longing's mutual glow
As if it had not been.

None Have Seen the Lord of the House

Stealth-hushed, the coiled night nesteth
In woods where light has strayed;
She is the shadow of the soul,
A virgin and afraid,
That in the absent Sultan's chamber resteth,   5
Sleepless for fear he call.

Lord of this moon-dim mansion,
None know thy naked light.
O! were the day, of Thee dim shade,
As of the soul is night,   10
O! who would fear when in the bourne's expansion,
With Thy first kiss we fade.

But the sad night shivers,
And palely wastes and dies;
A wraith under day's burning hair,   15
And his humid golden eyes.
He has browsed by immortal meadowed rivers;
O! were she nesting there!

[*What if I wear your beauty as this present*]

What if I wear your beauty as this present
Wears infinite aeons yet is only now.
The spirit opens but to receive
Close hid, nought yet departing—
But the world's gaze lessens love.   5

O softer pearl whose iridescent fountain
Hath been my sky, my sun, my stream of light
From the first dazzling dayspring, the enfolden
Sweet thirst, a mother prattle
To a new babbled birth.   10

I like an insect beautiful wings have gotten
Shed from you, let me hide, O like a vessel
That you have marvel-laden, burdened
With new rich fears of pirates
I droop dark penurious sails.   15

[*Her fabled mouth love hath from fables made*]

Her fabled mouth love hath from fables made.
She tells the same old marvels and sweet stories.
Chaos within her eyes his jewels laid.
Our lips and eyes dig up the antique glories.

The wonder of her heavy-coloured hair   5
Still richly wears the hues of faded Eden;
There, where primeval dream hath made its lair,
Joy subtly smiles, in his arms sorrow hidden.

O! as her eyes grow wide and starlight wanes,
Wanes from our hearts that grow into her splendour,   10
We melt with wronging of love's fabled pains,
Her eyes so kind, her bosom white and tender.

[*A bird trilling its gay heart out*]

A bird trilling its gay heart out
Made my idle heart a cage for it
Just as the sunlight makes a cage
Of the lampless world its song has lit.

I was half happy and half vexed   5
Because the song flew in unasked
Just as the dark might angry be
If sudden light her face unmasked.

I could not shut my spirit's doors
I was so naked and alone   10
I could not hide and it saw that
I would not to myself have shown.

Beauty [I]

An angel's chastity
Unfretted by an earthly angel's lures,
The occult lamp of beauty
Which holds? Is truth? Whose spreaded wing endures?

Say—beauty springs and grows   5
From the flushed night of the nun solitude
And the deep spirit's throes.
Unconscious as in Eden—chaste and nude.

His self-appointed aim
Whose bloodless brows bloom with austere delight,   10
O'er his entombed fame,
Whose ghost, an unseen glory, walks in hidden light.

Her sire and her lover.
He burns the world to gloat on the bright flame,
Her absence doth him cover.   15
Her silence is a voice that calls his name.

From the womb's antechambers
He, list'ning, moves thro' life's wide presence-hall,
Blindly its turret clambers,
Then searches his own soul for the flying bacchanal.   20

Is she an earthly care
Moulding our needs unto her gracious ends,
Making the rough world fair
With softer meanings than its rude speech lends?

Of Any Old Man

Wreck not the ageing heart of quietness
With alien uproar and rude jolly cries,
Which satyr-like to a mild maiden's pride
Ripens not wisdom, but a large recoil.
Give them their withered peace, their trial grave,   5
Their past youth's three-scored shadowy effigy.
Mock them not with your ripened turbulence,
Their frost-mailed petulance with your torrid wrath,
While edging your boisterous thunders shivers one word,
Pap to their senile sneering, drug to truth.   10
The feignèd ramparts of bleak ignorance,
'Experience'—crown of naked majesties,
That tells us naught we know not—but confirms.
O think! you reverend, shadowy austere,
Your Christ's youth was not ended when he died.   15

Dawn

O tender, first cold flush of rose!
O budded dawn, wake dreamily,
Your dim lips as your lids unclose
Murmur your own sad threnody.

O! as the soft and frail lights break   5
Upon your eyelids, and your eyes
Wider and wider grow and wake,
The old pale glory dies.

And then, as sleep lays down to sleep
And all her dreams lie somewhere dead,   10
(While naked day digs goldly deep
For light to lie uncoverèd),
Your own ghost fades with dream-ghosts there,
Our lorn eyes see, mid glimmering lips,
Pass through the haunted dream-moved air,   15
Slowly, their laden ships.

Subjectivity

At my eyes' anchoring levels
The pigmy skies foam over
The flat earth my senses see;
A vapour my lips might stir—
The heat of my breath might wither.   5
Strong eyes unfed, not baffled,
Yon bright and moving vapour
In a moment fades.

The beamy air, the roofless silence,—
The smoke-throated, man-thundered street,   10
Die to an essence, a love spirit.
Whose feet compound are
As my own breath back brought.
All things, that, brooding, are still,
Speak to me, untwist and twine   15
The shifting links of consciousness,
Speak to the all-eyed soul,
And tread its intricate infinities
Immured in two hands' breadth
Behind the mask of man.   20

On Receiving News of the War: Cape Town

Snow is a strange white word.
No ice or frost
Have asked of bud or bird
For Winter's cost.

Yet ice and frost and snow 5
From earth to sky
This Summer land doth know.
No man knows why.

In all men's hearts it is.
Some spirit old 10
Hath turned with malign kiss
Our lives to mould.

Red fangs have torn His face.
God's blood is shed.
He mourns from His lone place 15
His children dead.

O! ancient crimson curse!
Corrode, consume.
Give back this universe
Its pristine bloom. 20

To Wilhelm II

It is cruel Emperor
The stars are too high
For your reach Emperor,
Far out they lie.
It is cruel for you Emperor 5
The sea has a stone,
England—they call it England,
That cannot shine in your crown. [BREAK

Cruel the seas are deep,
Cruel for you Emperor   10
That all men are not in blind sleep,
And free hearts burn, Emperor.
It is cruel when a wronged world turns
And draws the claws of the beast
Cruel, cruel for you Emperor   15
Who would be most is least.

The Female God

We curl into your eyes.
They drink our fires and have never drained.
In the fierce forest of your hair
Our desires beat blindly for their treasure.

In your eyes' subtle pit   5
Far down, glimmer our souls,
And your hair like massive forest trees
Shadows our pulses, overtired and dumb.

Like a candle lost in an electric glare
Our spirits tread your eyes' infinities.   10
In the wrecking waves of your tumultuous locks
Do you not hear the moaning of our pulses?

Queen! Goddess! animal!
In sleep do your dreams battle with our souls?
When your hair is spread like a lover on the pillow,   15
Do not our jealous pulses wake between?

You have dethroned the ancient God.
You have usurped his sabbaths, his common days.
Yea! every moment is delivered to you.
Our Temple! our Eternal! our one God!   20

Our souls have passed into your eyes,
Our days into your hair.

And you, our rose-deaf prison, are very pleased with the
    world.
Your world.

Beauty [II]

Far and near, and now, from never
Thy calm beauty burns for ever,
Through the forests deep and old
Which loose their miser secrets hold
Unto the fountains of the sky,   5
Whose showers of radiant melody
Delight the laughter-burdened ways,
And dress the hours to light the days,
While hand in hand they reel their round;
For the burning bush is found.   10

Joy has blossomed, joy has burst;
And earth's parched lips and dewy thirst
Hath found a shroud of summer mirth,
And Eden covers all the earth
Whose lips love's kisses did anoint,   15
And straight our ashes fell away.
Our lives are now a burning point,
And faded are its walls of clay,
Purged of the flames that loved the wind
To the pure glow that has not sinned.   20

The Dead Heroes

Flame out, you glorious skies,
Welcome our brave,
Kiss their exultant eyes;
Give what they gave.

Flash, mailèd seraphim,   5
Your burning spears;

New days to outflame their dim
Heroic years.

Thrills their baptismal tread
The bright proud air;   10
The embattled plumes outspread
Burn upwards there.

Flame out, flame out, O Song!
Star ring to star,
Strong as our hurt is strong   15
Our children are.

Their blood is England's heart;
By their dead hands
It is, their noble part
That England stands.   20

England—Time gave them thee;
They gave back this
To win Eternity
And claim God's kiss.

[*I have lived in the underworld too long*]

I have lived in the underworld too long
For you O creature of light
To hear without terror the dark spirit's song
And unmoved hear what moves in night.

I am a spirit that yours has found   5
Strange, undelightful, obscure,
Created by some other God, and bound
In terrible darkness impure.

Creature of light and happiness
Deeper the darkness when you   10
With your bright terror eddying the distress
Grazed the dark waves and shivering further flew.

[*Under these skies, that take the hues*]

Under these skies, that take the hues
Of metals locked beneath earth
According as the spirit woos
What changing mood to birth.
Delicate silver gleaming   5
In threads of tender thought,
Gold in a proud dreaming
Our dream ships have brought.
But the skies of lead
When our hearts are dead   10
And the skies relentless
Of an iron petal scentless
That brooding like a shadow
Weighs down the sunless meadow.

[*Break in by subtler nearer ways*]

Break in by subtler nearer ways;
Dulled closeness is too far,
And separate we are
Through joinèd days.

The shine and strange romance of time   5
In absence hides and change.
Shut eyes and hear the strange
Perfect new chime.

On a Lady Singing

She bade us listen to the singing lark
In tones far sweeter than its own.
For fear that she should cease and leave us dark
We built the bird a feignèd throne,—
Shrined in her gracious glory-giving ways   5

From sceptred hands of starred humility.
Praising herself the more in giving praise
To music less than she.

[*As a sword in the sun*]

As a sword in the sun—
A glory calling a glory—
Our eyes seeing it run
Capture its gleam for our story.

Singer, marvellous gleam   5
Dancing in splendid light,
Here you have brought us our dream—
Ah! but its stay is its flight.

A splendour of moving wings
Drifting the infinite.   10
Like a procession of starry kings
Passing us out of the light.

[*Sacred, voluptuous hollows deep*]

Sacred, voluptuous hollows deep
Where the unlifted shadows sleep
Beneath inviolate mouth and chin.
What virginal woven mystery
Guarding some pleadful spiritual sin   5
So hard to traffic with or flee,
Lies in your chaste impurity?

Warm, fleshly chambers of delights,
Whose lamps are we, our days and nights.
Where our thoughts nestle, our lithe limbs   10
Frenzied exult till vision swims
In fierce delicious agonies;
And the crushed life bruised through and through

Ebbs out, trophy no spirit slew,
While molten sweetest pains enmesh   15
The life sucked by entwining flesh.

O rosy radiance incarnate,
O glowing glory of heaven-dreamt flesh,
O seraph-barred transplendent gate
Of paradisal meadows fresh.   20
O read—read what my pale mouth tells.
God! could that mouth be but the air
To kiss your chasteness everywhere
Bound with lust's shrivelling manacles!

As weary water dreams of land   25
While waves roll back and leave wet sand,
Their white tongues fawning on its breast,
But turns it to the thing that prest,
Though my thoughts drown you sweet, and cover,
Your shape in me is my mad lover.   30

Love and Lust

We dream of mortal joy;
Yet all the dreamers die.
We wither with our world
To make room for her sky.

O lust! when you lie ravished,   5
Broken in the dust,
We will call for love in vain,
Finding love was lust.

At Sea-Point

Let the earth crumble away,
The heavens fade like a breath,
The sea go up in a cloud,
And its hills be given to death.

For the roots of the earth are old,   5
And the pillars of heaven are tired.
The hands that the sea enfold
Hath seen a new desired.

All things upon my sense
Are wasted spaces dull   10
Since one shape passed like a song
Let God all things annul.

A lie with its heart hidden
Is that cruel wall of air
That held her there unbidden,   15
Who comes not at my prayer.

Gone, who yet never came.
There is the breathing sea,
And the shining skies are the same,
But they lie—they lie to me.   20

For she stood with the sea below,
Between the sky and the sea,
She flew ere my soul was aware,
But left this thirst in me.

[*I know you golden*]

I know you golden
As summer and pale
As the clinging sweetness
Of marvels frail.

A touch of fire   5
A loitering thrill.
My dancing spirit
Has passed the will

And love and living
And Time and space   10
My naked spirit
Hath seen its face.

The Mirror

It glimmers like a wakeful lake in the dusk-narrowing room.
Like drowning vague branches in its depths floats the gloom,
The night shall shudder at its face by gleams of pallid light
Whose hands build the broader day to break the husk of night.

No shade shall waver there when your shadowless soul
   shall pass,   5
The green shakes not the air when your spirit drinks the
   grass,
So in its plashless water falls, so dumbly lies therein
A fervid rose whose fragrance sweet lies hidden and shut
   within.

Only in these bruised words the glass dim showing my spirit's
   face,
Only a little colour from a fire I could not trace,   10
To glimmer through eternal days like an enchanted rose,
The potent dreamings of whose scent are wizard-locked beneath
   its glows.

The Exile

A northern spray in an all human speech
To this same torrid heart may somewhat reach,
Although its root, its mother tree
Is in the North.
But O! to its cold heart, and fervid eyes,   5
It sojourns in another's paradise,
A loveliness its alien eyes might see
Could its own roots go forth.

O! dried-up waters of deep hungering love!
Far, far, the springs that fed you from above,   10
And brimmed the wells of happiness
With new delight.
Blinding ourselves to rob another's sun

Only its scorching glory have we won,
And left our own homes in bleak wintriness   15
Moaning our sunward flight.

Here, where the craggy mountains edge the skies,
Whose profound spaces stare to our vain eyes;
Where our thoughts hang, and theirs, who yearn
To know our speech.   20
O! what winged airs soothe the sharp mountains' brow?
From peak to peak with messages they go,
Withering our peering thoughts that crowd to learn
Words from that distant beach.

[*A flea whose body shone like bead*]

A flea whose body shone like bead
Gave me delight as I gave heed.

A spider whose legs like stiff thread
Made me think quaintly as I read.

A rat whose droll shape would dart and flit   5
Was like a torch to light my wit.
.

A fool whose narrow forehead hung
A wooden target for my tongue.

A meagre wretch in whose generous scum
Himself was lost—his dirty living tomb.   10

But the flea crawled too near
His blood the smattered wall doth smear.

And the spider being too brave
No doctor now can him save.

And when the rat would rape my cheese   15
He signed the end of his life's lease.

Expression

Call—call—and bruise the air!
Shatter dumb space!
Yea! we will fling this passion everywhere,
Leaving no place

For the superb and grave   5
Magnificent throng,
The pregnant queens of quietness that brave
And edge our song

Of wonder at the light,
(Our life-leased home)   10
Of greeting to our housemates. And in might
Our song shall roam

Life's heart, a blossoming fire
Blown bright by thought,
While gleams and fades the infinite desire, 15
Phantasmed naught.

Can this be caught and caged?
Wings can be clipt
Of eagles, the sun's gaudy measure gauged,
But no sense dipt   20

In the mystery of sense.
The troubled throng
Of words break out like smother'd fire through dense
And smouldering wrong.

[Who loses the door that the wind]

Who loses the door that the wind
Of the after silence swings?
But lost—lost—lost, are the things
We seek, and the seekers blind.
And broken are all our wings.   5

Is a cold kiss blown from the surge
Of the dark tides of the night?
We sleep, and blind is their flight
The dreams of whose kisses urge
The soul to endure its plight.   10

Blown words, whose root is the brain,
Live over your ruined root.
For other mouths is the fruit
And the songs so rich with pain
Of a splendour whose lips were mute.   15

God Made Blind

It were a proud God-guiling, to allure
And flatter, by some cheat of ill, our Fate
To hold back the perfect crookedness, its hate
Devised, and keep it poor,
And ignorant of our joy,—   5
Masqued in a giant wrong of cruel annoy,
That stands as some bleak hut to frost and night,
While hidden in bed is warmth and mad delight.

For all Love's heady valour and loved pain
Towers in our sinews that may not suppress   10
(Shut to God's eye) Love's springing eagerness,
And mind to advance his gain
Of gleeful secrecy
Through dolorous clay, which his eternity
Has pierced, in light that pushes out to meet   15
Eternity without us, heaven's heat.

And then, when Love's power hath increased so
That we must burst or grow to give it room,
And we can no more cheat our God with gloom,
We'll cheat Him with our joy.   20
For say! what can God do
To us, to Love, whom we have grown into?

Love! the poured rays of God's Eternity!
We are grown God—and shall His self-hate be?

[Summer's lips are aglow, afresh]

Summer's lips are aglow, afresh
For our old lips to kiss,
The tingling of the flesh
Makes life aware of this.

Whose eyes are wild with love?   5
Whose hair a blowing flame
I feel around and above
Laughing my dreams to shame?

My dreams like stars gone out
Were blossoms for your day;   10
Red flower of mine I will shout,
I have put my dreams away.

[O be these men and women]

O be these men and women
That pass and cry like blowing flakes,
Seeking the parent cloud,
Seeking the parent sea.
Or like famished flames that fly   5
On a separate root of fire
Far from the nurturing furnace.
Or like scent from the flower
That hovers in doubt afar,
Or the colour of grasses   10
That flies to the spirit and spreads.

Are these things your dreams
That I too can watch?

When I dream my dreams
Do you see them too?　　　　　　15
When the ghosts depart
Can you follow them,
Tho' I see them not.

Nocturne

Day, like a flower of gold, fades on its crimson bed,
For the many-chambered night unbars to shut its sweetness up;
From earth and heaven fast drawn together a heavy stillness is
　　shed,
And our hearts drink the shadowy splendour from a brimming cup.

For the indrawn breath of beauty thrills the holy caves of night,　　5
Shimmering winds of heaven fall gently and mysterious hands
　　caress
Our wan brows with cooling rapture of the delicate starlight
Dropping from the night's blue walls in endless veils of loveliness.

A Girl's Thoughts

Dim apprehension of a trust
Comes over me this quiet hour,
As though the silence were a flower,
And this, its perfume, dark like dust.

My individual self would cling　　　　　5
Through fear, thro' pride, unto its fears;
It strives to shut out what it hears,
The founts of being, murmuring.

O need, whose hauntings terrorize,
Whether my maiden ways would hide,　　10
Or lose, and to that need subside,
Life shrinks, and instinct dreads surprise.

The Blind God

Streaked with immortal blasphemies
Betwixt His twin eternities
Shaper of mortal destinies
Sits in that limbo of dreamless sleep,
Some nothing that hath shadows deep.   5

The world is only a small pool
In the meadows of Eternity
And the wise man and the fool
In its depths like fishes lie,
When an angel drops a rod   10
And he draws you to the sky
Will you bear to meet your God
You have streaked with blasphemy?

[*Walk you in music light or night*]

Walk you in music light or night
Spelled on your brows, plain to men's sight
Is death and darkness written clear.
God only can neither read nor hear.

Ah men ye are so skilled to write   5
This doom so dark in letters bright.
But how can God read human fear
Who cannot dry a human tear.

At Night

Crazed shadow from no golden body
That I can see, embraces me warm;
All is purple and closed
Round by night's arm.

A brilliance wings from dark-lit voices,   5
Wild lost voices of shadows white.
See the long houses lean
To the weird flight.

Star-amorous things that wake at sleep-time—
(Because the sun spreads wide like a tree   10
With no good fruit for them—)
Thrill secrecy.

Pale horses ride before the morning
The secret roots of the sun to tread,
With hoofs shod with venom   15
And ageless dread,

To breathe on burning emerald grasses
And opalescent dews of the day,
And poison at the core
What smiles may stray.   20

April Dawn

Pale light hid in light
Stirs the still day-spring;
Wavers the dull sight
With a spirit's wing.

Dreams, in frail rose mist   5
Lurking to waylay,
Subtle-wise have kist
Winter into May.

Nothing to the sight—
Pool of pulseless air.   10
Spirits are in flight,
And my soul their lair.

Wedded [II]

They leave their love-lorn haunts,
Their sigh-warm floating Eden;
And they are mute at once;
Mortals, by God unheeden;
By their past kisses chidden.   5

But they have kist and known
Clear things we dim by guesses;—
Spirit to spirit grown:—
Heaven, born in hand caresses:—
Love, fall from sheltering tresses.   10

And they are dumb and strange;
Bared trees bowed from each other.
Their last green interchange
What lost dreams shall discover?
Dead, strayed, to love-stranged lover   15

Chagrin

Caught still as Absalom,
Surely the air hangs
From the swayless cloud-boughs,
Like hair of Absalom
Caught and hanging still.   5

From the imagined weight
Of spaces in a sky
Of mute chagrin, my thoughts
Hang like branch-clung hair
To trunks of silence swung,   10
With the choked soul weighing down
Into thick emptiness.
Christ! end this hanging death,
For endlessness hangs therefrom.   [BREAK

Invisibly—branches break   15
From invisible trees—
The cloud-woods where we rush,
Our eyes holding so much,
Which we must ride dim ages round
Ere the hands (we dream) can touch.   20
We ride, we ride, before the morning
The secret roots of the sun to tread,
And suddenly
We are lifted of all we know
And hang from implacable boughs.   25

The Cloister

Our eyes no longer sail the tidal streets,
Nor harbour where the hours like petals float
By sensual treasures glittering thro' thin walls
Of woman's eyes and colour's mystery.

The roots of our eternal souls were fed   5
On the world's dung and now their blossoms gleam.
God gives to glisten in an angel's hair
These He has gardened, for they please His eyes.

[My soul is robbed by your most treacherous eyes] [I]

My soul is robbed by your most treacherous eyes
Treading its intricate infinities.
Stay there rich robbers! what I lose is dross;
Since my life is your dungeon, where is loss?

Ah! as the sun is prisoned in the heaven,   5
Whose walls dissolve, of their own nature bereaven,

So do your looks, as idly, without strife,
Cover all steeps of sense, which no more pasture life,
Which no more feel, but only know you there,
In this blind trance of some white anywhere.   10

Come—come—that glance engendered ecstasy—
That subtle unspaced mutual intimacy
Whereby two spirits of one thought commune
Like separate instruments that play one tune,
And the whole miracle and amazement of   15
The unexpected flowering of love,
Concentrates to an instant that expands
And takes unto itself the strangest of strange lands.

[*A warm thought flickers*]

A warm thought flickers
An idle ray—
Being is one blush at root.

For the hours' ungentle doom
When one forsaking face   5
Hides ever—hides for our sighing
Is a hard bright leaf over clover
And bee-bitten shade.

What moons have hidden
Their month-long shine,   10
What buds uncover
And plead in vain
While one opaque thought wearies
The weary lids of grief?

One thought too heavy   15
For words to bear,
For lips too tired
To curl to them.

[*My soul is robbed by your most treacherous eyes*] *[II]*

My soul is robbed by your most treacherous eyes
Treading its intricate infinities,
Some pale light hidden in light and felt to stir
In listening pulse, an audible wonder,
Delighting me with my immortal loss;   5
While you stay in its place, rich robbers, that is dross.
Wine of the Almighty who got drunk with thee.
(The reason sin—God slumbering then—flew free.)
Alas! if God thus, what will hap to me?
Ah! even now drunken while your sweet light beams,   10
You, far as Heaven, I am drunk on my dreams.
Not yet, that glance engendered ecstasy,
That subtle, unspaced, mutual intimacy,
Whereby two spirits of one thought commune,
Like separate instruments that play one tune.   15
The music of my playing is lost in thine.
Does the sun see when noonday torches shine?
Mine is not yours though you have stolen mine.
Beautiful thieves, I cannot captive ye,
Being so bound even as ye rifle me.   20
My limbs that moved in trembling innocence
You harden to knowledge of experience
Till honour rings upon the ear as crime.

Night

With sleek lascivious velvety caresses
The nestling hair of night strays on my cheeks.
My heart is full of brimless fervid fancies
Ardent to hear the imperious word she speaks.

O purple-hued—O glimmering mouth that trembles!   5
O monstrous dusky shoulders lost above,

Wrapt in bleak robes of smoke from eye, star embers;
You smouldering pyres of flaming aeons of love.

The straining lusts of strenuous amorists
Smoking from crimson altars of their hearts,   10
In burning mists are shed upon my dreaming.

Relax—relax. I have not strength to withstand thee;
My soul will not recoil, so full of thee.
Thy loathesomeness and beauty fill my hunger,
O! splendid, thy lithe fingers gripping me.   15

Naked and glorious, like a shining temple
I fill with adorations, fervent psalm,
Anoint with honey of kisses, while thy bosom
Throbs music to my unprofaning palm.

See! how thy breasts, those two white grapes of passion   20
Look mixed in mine, like globed fruit mixed with leaves.
Lo! where I press, what crimson stains come leaping,
Bright juice of inexhaustible dreams, lust weaves.

Apparition

From her hair's unfelt gold
My days are twined.
As the moon weaves pale daughters
Her hands may never fold.

Her eyes are hidden pools   5
Where my soul lies
Glimmering in their waters
Like faint and troubled skies.

Dream pure, her body's grace,
A streaming light   10
Scatters delicious fire
Upon my limbs and face.

[*Wistfully in pallid splendour*]

Wistfully in pallid splendour
Drifts the lonely infinite,
A wan perfume vague and tender,
Dim with feet of fragile light.

Drifts so lightly thro' the spirit,   5
Breathes the torch of dreams astir
Till what promised lands lie near it
Wavering are betrayed to her.

Ghostly foam of unheard waters,
And the gleam of hidden skies,   10
Footsteps of Eve's whiter daughters
Tremble to our dreaming eyes.

O! sad wraith of joy lips parted,
Hearing not a word they say—
Even my dreams make broken-hearted   15
And their beauty falls away.

Far Away

By what pale light or moon-pale shore
Drifts my soul in lonely flight?
Regions God had floated o'er
Ere He touched the world with light?

Not in Heaven and not in earth   5
Is this water, is this moon;
For there is no starry birth,
And no dawning and no noon.

Far away—O far away,
Mist-born—dewy vapours rise   10
From the dim gates of the day
Far below in earthly skies.

[*Glory of hueless skies*]

Glory of hueless skies
What pallid splendour flies
Like visible music touched
From the lute of our eyes.

The stars are sick and white   5
Old in the morning light,
Like genius in a rabble
The obscure mars their might.

The forest of the world
Lights scattering hands have uphurled,   10
The branches of thought are driven
The vapours of act are uncurled.

Deed against strenuous deed
Dark seed choking the seed
The impulses blind that blacken   15
The ways of life's rough need.

Mountain and man and beast
Live flower and leaf diseased
Riot or revel in quiet
At the broad day's feast.   20

Auguries

Fading fire that does not fade
Only changing its nest,
Sky-blown words of cloudlike breath
Live in another sky.
Days that are scrawled hieroglyphs   5
On thunder-stricken barks,
First our souls have plucked the fruit.
Here are time's granaries.

Has my soul plucked all the fruit?
One waits somewhere for me   10
Holding fresh the fruit I left,
And I hold fruit for one.
What screen hid us gathering
And lied unto our thirst,
While two faces looked singly to the moon?   15
But the moon was secret and chill.

Will my eyes know the fruit I left?
Will her eyes know her own?
This broken stem will surely know
And leap unto its leaf.   20
No blossom bursts before its time
No angel passes by the door
But from old Chaos shoots the bough
While we grow ripe for heaven.

[*I am the blood*]

I am the blood
Streaming the veins of sweetness; sharp and sweet
Beauty has pricked the live veins of my soul
And sucked all being in.

I am the air   5
Prowling the room of beauty, climbing her soft
Walls of surmise, her ceilings that close in.
She breathes me as her breath.

I am the death
Whose monument is beauty and forever   10
Altho I lie unshrouded in life's tomb
She is my cenotaph.

Heart's First Word [II]

And all her soft dark hair,
Breathed for him like a prayer.
And her white lost face,
Was prisoned to some far place.
Love was not denied—   5
Love's ends would hide.
And flower and fruit and tree
Were under its sea.
Yea! its abundance knelt
Where the nerves felt   10
The springs of feeling flow
And made pain grow.
There seemed no root or sky
But a pent infinity
Where apparitions dim   15
Sculptured each whim
In flame and wandering mist
Of kisses to be kist.

As a Besieged City

In the hushed pregnancy
And gleaming of hope,
When a joy's infancy
Fills our star's horoscope,
Flowering like a mist   5
Heaven mixed but light unkist,
The soul is mixed in anguish,
For joy has not yet burst.

Expectant is the fear—
O! why the doubt?   10
Surely our friends are near,

And the strong foe cast out.
Ah! but if we are dead
In their loving fears, and shed
The tears for us in anguish, 15
And they turn from gates not burst.

The One Lost

I mingle with your bones.
You steal in subtle noose
This lighted dust Jehovah loans,
And now I lose.

What will the Lender say 5
When I shall not be found
Safe sheltered at the Judgement Day,
Being in you bound?

He'll hunt throng'd wards of Heaven;
Call to uncoffined earth, 10
'Where is this soul unjudged, not given
Dole for good's dearth?'

And I, lying so safe
Within you, hearing all,
To have cheated God, shall laugh, 15
Freed by your thrall.

[Past days are hieroglyphs]

Past days are hieroglyphs
Scrawled behind the brows
Scarred deep with iron blows
Upon the thundered tree
Of memory. 5

Marvellous mad beliefs
(To believe that you believed!)

Plain and time-unthieved
Scratched and scrawled on the tree
Of memory. 10

Time, good graver of griefs,
Those words sapped with my soul
That I read as of old and whole
What eye in the world shall see
On this covered tree. 15

Torpor

Upon my lips like a cloud
To burst on the peaks of light
Sit cowled impossible things
To tie my hand's young might.
Power! break through their shroud. 5
Pierce them quite thoroughly,
Thoroughly enter me,
Know me for one dead.
Break the shadowy thread,
The cowering spirit's bond 10
Writ by illusions blonde.

Ah! let the morning pale
Throb with a wilder pulse,
No delicate flame shall quail
With terror at your convulse. 15
Thin branches cross the white skies
To lips and spaces of song
Chanting a mood to my eyes,
Ah! sleep can be overlong.

God

In his malodorous brain what slugs and mire
Lanthorned in his oblique eyes, guttering burned!

His body lodged a rat where men nursed souls.
The world flashed grape-green eyes of a foiled cat
To him. On fragments of a skull of power,   5
On shy and maimed, on women wrung awry,
He lay, a bullying hulk, to crush them more.
But when one, fearless, turned and clawed like bronze,
Cringing was easy to blunt these stern paws,
And he would weigh the heavier on those after.   10

Who rests in God's mean flattery now? Your wealth
Is but his cunning to make death more hard.
Your iron sinews take more pain in breaking.
And he has made the market for your beauty
Too poor to buy, although you die to sell.   15

Only that he has never heard of sleep;
And when the cats come out the rats are sly.
Here we are safe till he slinks in at dawn.

But he has gnawed a fibre from strange roots,
And in the morning some pale wonder ceases.   20
Things are not strange and strange things are
      forgetful.
Ah! if the day were arid, somehow lost,
Out of us, but it is as hair of us,
And only in the hush no wind stirs it.
And in the light vague trouble lifts and breathes,   25
And restlessness still shadows the lost ways.
The fingers shut on voices that pass through,
Where blind farewells are taken easily.

Ah! this miasma of a rotting God!

Evening

My roses loiter, their lips to press
Vague emerald winds
Fall'n from sky chasms of sunset stress, . . .
Amongst each petal grope
Displacing hands of vapoured heliotrope.   [BREAK   5

The vague viols of evening
Call all the flower clans
To some abysmal swinging
And tumult of deep trance.

[*I did not pluck at all*]

I did not pluck at all,
And I am sorry now,
The garden is not barred,
But the boughs are heavy with snow,
The flake blossoms thickly fall,   5
And the hid roots sigh, 'how long will our flowers
    be marred?'

Strange as a bird were dumb,
Strange as a hueless leaf.
As one deaf hungers to hear,
Or gazes without belief,   10
The fruit yearned 'fingers come'.
O, shut hands, be empty another year.

Sleep [I]

Godhead's lip hangs
When our pulses have no golden tremors,
And his whips are flicked by mice
And all star-amorous things.

Drops, drops of shivering quiet   5
Filter under my lids.
Now only am I powerful.
What though the cunning gods outwit us here
In daytime and in playtime,
Surely they feel the gyves we lay on them   10

In our sleep.
O! subtle gods lying hidden!
O! gods with your oblique eyes!
Your elbows in the dawn, and wrists
Bright with the afternoon,   15
Do you not shake when a mortal slides
Into your own unvexed peace?
When a moving stillness breaks over your knees,
(An emanation of piled aeons' pressure)
From our bodies flat and straight,   20
And your limbs are locked,
Futilely God's,
And shut your sinister essences.

Lusitania

Chaos! that coincides with this militant purpose.
Chaos! the heart of this earnest malignancy.
Chaos! that helps, chaos that gives to shatter
Mind-wrought, mind-unimagining energies
For topless ill, of dynamite and iron.   5
Soulless logic, inventive enginery.
Now you have got the peace-faring Lusitania,
Germany's gift—all earth they would give thee, Chaos.

Dusk and the Mirror

Where the room seems pondering,
Shadowy hovering,
Pictured walls and dove-dim ceiling,
Edgeless, lost and spectral,
In a quaint half farewell   5
Away the things familiar fall
In some limbo to a spell.
Mutation of slipped moment

When nothing and solid is blent.
O! dusk palpitant! 10
Prank fantastical!
You hide and steal from morning
What you give back from hiding,
You prank before the dawning
And run from her frail chiding, 15
And all my household Gods
When he who worships nods
You tweak and pinch and hide
And dabble under your side
To drop upon the shores 20
Of an old tomorrow
Shut with the same old doors
Of sleep and shame and sorrow.

But naked you have left
One jewel, dripping still 25
From plundering plashless fingers.
Lying in a cleft
Of your surging-bosomed hill
It dreams of dreams bereft
And warm dishevelled singers, 30
Safe from your placeless will.

Or you are like a tree now,
And that is like a lake,
Sinister to thee now
Its glimmer is awake 35
Like vague undrowning boughs
Above the pool
You float your gloom in its low light
Where Narcissian augurs browse,
Dreaming from its cool 40
Apparition a fear;
Behind the wall of hours you hear
The tread of the arch light.

Significance

The cunning moment curves its claws
Round the body of our curious wish
But push a shoulder through its straitened laws
Then are you hooked to wriggle like a fish.

Lean in high middle 'twixt two tapering points,   5
Yet rocks and undulations control
The agile brain the limber joints
The sinews of the soul.

Chaos that coincides, form that refutes all sway,
Shapes to the eye quite other to the touch,   10
All twisted things continue to our clay
Like added limbs and hair dispreaded overmuch.

And after it draws in its claws
The rocks and unquiet sink to a flat ground,
Then follow desert-hours, the vacuous pause   15
Till some mad indignation unleashes the hound.

And those flat hours and dead unseeing things
Cower and crowd and burrow for us to use
Where sundry gapings spurn and preparing wings
And O! our hands would use all ere we lose.   20

Marching—as seen from the left file

My eyes catch ruddy necks
Sturdily pressed back,—
All a red-brick moving glint.
Like flaming pendulums, hands
Swing across the khaki—   5
Mustard-coloured khaki—
To the automatic feet.   [BREAK

We husband the ancient glory
In these bared necks and hands.
Not broke is the forge of Mars;   10
But a subtler brain beats iron
To shoe the hoofs of death,
(Who paws dynamic air now).
Blind fingers loose an iron cloud
To rain immortal darkness   15
On strong eyes.

Sleep [II]

A spray of shivering quiet
Filters under my lid.
Thinnest veils are shaken, are dropt—
Silver is tarnished from whispers hid.
Outside the world, their twilight stone,   5
Our unfamiliar ghosts are known . . .
Though the cunning Gods outwit us,—nay,
We have dear gyves and torpor as they.

The Gods with their oblique eyes,
The subtle Gods lying hid,   10
Elbowed in dawn their twilight wrists
Shake where sudden a mortal slid
Into their own unvexed peace,
And the moving stillness breaks over their knees
Far from our bodies flat and straight   15
That bears like a stone the whole night's weight.

Upon my lips, like a cloud
To burst on the peaks of light,
Sit cowled lost impossible things
To tie my hands at the noon's height.   20
And breath floats like a twilight old
Of some spent words pale shredded gold;
And soft hair laid on a feathered fur
Sinks dim as a thought of a sound astir.

Spring 1916

Slow, rigid, is this masquerade
That passes as through a difficult air;
Heavily—heavily passes.
What has she fed on? Who her table laid
Through the three seasons? What forbidden fare   5
Ruined her as a mortal lass is?

I played with her two years ago,
Who might be now her own sister in stone,
So altered from her May mien,
When round the pink a necklace of warm snow   10
Laughed to her throat where my mouth's touch
        had gone.
How is this, ruined Queen?

Who lured her vivid beauty so
To be that strained chill thing that moves
So ghastly midst her young brood   15
Of pregnant shoots that she for men did grow?
Where are the strong men who made these
        their loves?
Spring! God pity your mood.

[*A worm fed on the heart of Corinth*]

A worm fed on the heart of Corinth,
Babylon and Rome.
Not Paris raped tall Helen,
But this incestuous worm
Who lured her vivid beauty   5
To his amorphous sleep.
England! famous as Helen
Is thy betrothal sung.

To him the shadowless,
More amorous than Solomon.   10

The Troop Ship

Grotesque and queerly huddled
Contortionists to twist
The sleepy soul to a sleep,
We lie all sorts of ways
But cannot sleep.   5
The wet wind is so cold,
And the lurching men so careless,
That, should you drop to a doze,
Wind's fumble or men's feet
Is on your face.   10

In the Trenches

I snatched two poppies
From the parapet's edge,
Two bright red poppies
That winked on the ledge.
Behind my ear   5
I stuck one through,
One blood red poppy
I gave to you.

The sandbags narrowed
And screwed out our jest,   10
And tore the poppy
You had on your breast . . .
Down—a shell—O! Christ.
I am choked . . . safe . . . dust blind—I
See trench floor poppies   15
Strewn. Smashed you lie.

Break of Day in the Trenches

The darkness crumbles away.
It is the same old Druid Time as ever.
Only a live thing leaps my hand,
A queer sardonic rat,
As I pull the parapet's poppy   5
To stick behind my ear.
Droll rat, they would shoot you if they knew
Your cosmopolitan sympathies.
Now you have touched this English hand
You will do the same to a German   10
Soon, no doubt, if it be your pleasure
To cross the sleeping green between.
It seems, odd thing, you grin as you pass
Strong eyes, fine limbs, haughty athletes,
Less chanced than you for life,   15
Bonds to the whims of murder,
Sprawled in the bowels of the earth,
The torn fields of France.
What do you see in our eyes
At the shrieking iron and flame   20
Hurl'd through still heavens?
What quaver—what heart aghast?
Poppies whose roots are in man's veins
Drop, and are ever dropping,
But mine in my ear is safe—   25
Just a little white with the dust.

August 1914

What in our lives is burnt
In the fire of this?
The heart's dear granary?
The much we shall miss?

Three lives hath one life—   5
Iron, honey, gold.

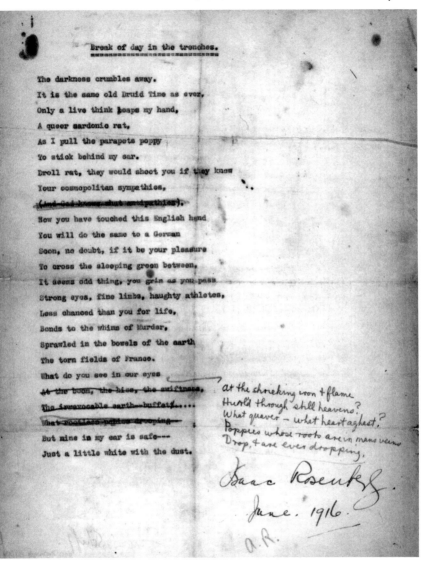

FIG. 3 'Break of Day in the Trenches'. Complete typescript, with pencil alterations.

The gold, the honey gone—
Left is the hard and cold.

Iron are our lives
Molten right through our youth.   10
A burnt space through ripe fields,
A fair mouth's broken tooth.

The Dying Soldier

'Here are houses' he moaned,
'I could reach but my brain swims.'
Then they thundered and flashed
And shook the earth to its rims.

'They are gunpits' he gasped,   5
'Our men are at the guns.
Water... Water... O water
For one of England's dying sons.'

'We cannot give you water,
Were all England in your breath.'   10
'Water!... Water!... O! Water!'
He moaned and swooned to death.

[*Wan, fragile faces of joy!*]

Wan, fragile faces of joy!
Pitiful mouths that strive
To light with smiles the place
We dream we walk alive.

To you I stretch my hands;   5
Hands shut in pitiless trance
In a land of ruin and woe,
The desolate land of France.

Dear faces, startled and shaken
Out of wild dust and sounds,   10
You yearn to me, lure and sadden
My heart with futile bounds.

Pozières

Glory! glory! glory!
British women! in your wombs you plotted
This monstrous girth of glory, this marvellous glory.
Not for mere love-delights Time meant the profound
   hour
When an Englishman was planned.   5
Time shouted it to his extremest outpost.
The illuminated call through the voided years
Was heard, is heard at last,
And will be heard at the last
Reverberated through the Eternities,   10
Earth's immortality and Heaven's.

The Immortals

I killed them but they would not die.
Yea! all the day and all the night
For them I could not rest or sleep,
Nor guard from them nor hide in flight.

Then in my agony I turned   5
And made my hands red in their gore.
In vain—for faster than I slew
They rose more cruel than before.

I killed and killed with slaughter mad;
I killed till all my strength was gone.   10
And still they rose to torture me
For Devils only die in fun.

I used to think the devil hid
In women's smiles and wine's carouse.
I called him Satan, Balzebub.   15
But now I call him, dirty louse.

Louse Hunting

Nudes—stark aglisten
Yelling in lurid glee. Grinning faces of fiends
And raging limbs
Whirl over the floor one fire,
For a shirt verminously busy   5
Yon soldier tore from his throat
With oaths
Godhead might shrink at, but not the lice.
And soon the shirt was aflare
Over the candle he'd lit while we lay.   10
Then we all sprung up and stript
To hunt the vermin brood.
Soon like a demons' pantomime
The place was raging.
See the silhouettes agape,   15
See the gibbering shadows
Mixed with the battled arms on the wall.
See gargantuan hooked fingers
Dug in supreme flesh
To smutch the supreme littleness.   20
See the merry limbs in hot Highland fling
Because some wizard vermin
Charmed from the quiet this revel
When our ears were half lulled
By the dark music   25
Blown from Sleep's trumpet.

From France

The spirit drank the Café lights;
All the hot life that glittered there,

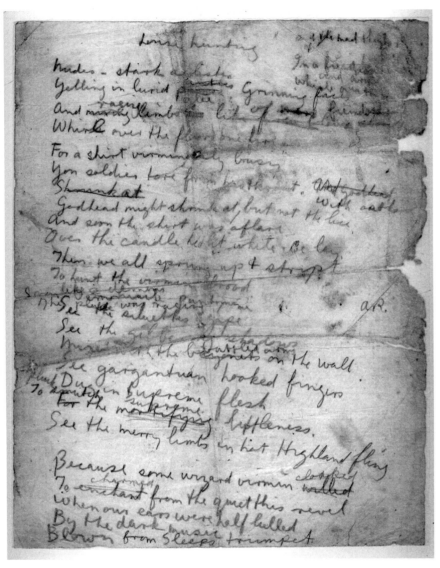

And heard men say to women gay,
'Life is just so in France'.

The spirit dreams of Café lights,   5
And golden faces and soft tones,
And hears men groan to broken men,
'This is not Life in France'.

Heaped stones and a charred signboard shows
With grass between and dead folk under,   10
And some birds sing, while the spirit takes wing.
And this is life in France.

The Destruction of Jerusalem by the Babylonian Hordes

They left their Babylon bare
Of all its tall men,
Of all its proud horses;
They made for Lebanon.

And shadowy sowers went   5
Before their spears to sow
The fruit whose taste is ash
For Judah's soul to know.

They who bowed to the Bull god,
Whose wings roofed Babylon   10
In endless hosts darkened
The bright-heavened Lebanon.

They washed their grime in pools
Where laughing girls forgot
The wiles they used for Solomon.   15
Sweet laughter! remembered not.

Sweet laughter charred in the flames
That clutched the cloud and earth
While Solomon's towers crashed between
The gird of Babylon's mirth.   20

Returning, we hear the larks

Sombre the night is.
And though we have our lives, we know
What sinister threat lurks there.

Dragging these anguished limbs, we only know
This poison-blasted track opens on our camp—   5
On a little safe sleep.

But hark! joy—joy—strange joy.
Lo! heights of night ringing with unseen larks.
Music showering our upturned list'ning faces.

Death could drop from the dark   10
As easily as song—
But song only dropped,
Like a blind man's dreams on the sand
By dangerous tides,
Like a girl's dark hair for she dreams no ruin lies there,   15
Or her kisses where a serpent hides.

Dead Man's Dump

The plunging limbers over the shattered track
Racketed with their rusty freight,
Stuck out like many crowns of thorns,
And the rusty stakes like sceptres old
To stay the flood of brutish men   5
Upon our brothers dear.

The wheels lurched over sprawled dead
But pained them not, though their bones crunched,
Their shut mouths made no moan,
They lie there huddled, friend and foeman,   10
Man born of man, and born of woman,
And shells go crying over them
From night till night and now.

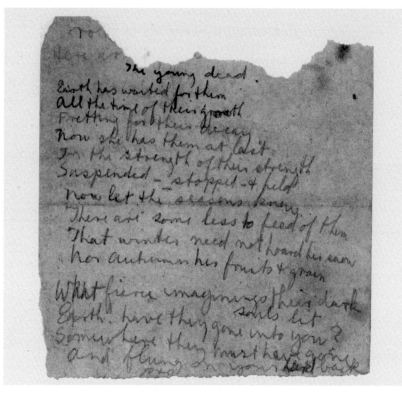

FIG. 5 'The young dead'. An early pencil draft of a poem, most of which was later
incorporated into 'Dead Man's Dump'.

Earth has waited for them
All the time of their growth   15
Fretting for their decay:
Now she has them at last!
In the strength of their strength
Suspended—stopped and held.

What fierce imaginings their dark souls lit   20
Earth! have they gone into you?
Somewhere they must have gone,
And flung on your hard back

Is their soul's sack,
Emptied of God-ancestralled essences.   25
Who hurled them out? Who hurled?

None saw their spirits' shadow shake the grass,
Or stood aside for the half used life to pass
Out of those doomed nostrils and the doomed mouth,
When the swift iron burning bee   30
Drained the wild honey of their youth.

What of us, who flung on the shrieking pyre,
Walk, our usual thoughts untouched,
Our lucky limbs as on ichor fed,
Immortal seeming ever?   35
Perhaps when the flames beat loud on us,
A fear may choke in our veins
And the startled blood may stop.

The air is loud with death,
The dark air spurts with fire   40
The explosions ceaseless are.

Timelessly now, some minutes past,
These dead strode time with vigorous life,
Till the shrapnel called 'an end!'
But not to all. In bleeding pangs   45
Some borne on stretchers dreamed of home,
Dear things, war-blotted from their hearts.

A man's brains splattered on
A stretcher-bearer's face;
His shook shoulders slipped their load,   50
But when they bent to look again
The drowning soul was sunk too deep
For human tenderness.

They left this dead with the older dead,
Stretched at the cross roads.   55

Burnt black by strange decay
Their sinister faces lie
The lid over each eye,

The grass and coloured clay
More motion have than they,   60
Joined to the great sunk silences.

Here is one not long dead;
His dark hearing caught our far wheels,
And the choked soul stretched weak hands
To reach the living word the far wheels said,   65
The blood-dazed intelligence beating for light,
Crying through the suspense of the far torturing
    wheels
Swift for the end to break,
Or the wheels to break,
Cried as the tide of the world broke over his sight.   70

Will they come? Will they ever come?
Even as the mixed hoofs of the mules,
The quivering-bellied mules,
And the rushing wheels all mixed
With his tortured upturned sight,   75
So we crashed round the bend,
We heard his weak scream,
We heard his very last sound,
And our wheels grazed his dead face.

Daughters of War

Space beats the ruddy freedom of their limbs—
Their naked dances with man's spirit naked
By the root side of the tree of life
(The underside of things
And shut from earth's profoundest eyes).   5

I saw in prophetic gleams
These mighty daughters in their dances
Beckon each soul aghast from its crimson corpse
To mix in their glittering dances.
I heard the mighty daughters' giant sighs   10
In sleepless passion for the sons of valour,
And envy of the days of flesh

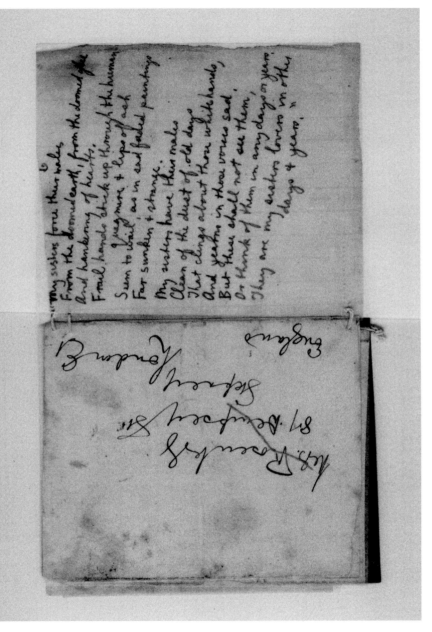

FIG. 6 'Daughters of War', p. 6 (ll. 49–61) of a presentation fair copy given by Rosenberg to Gordon Bottomley in May 1917.

Barring their love with mortal boughs across,—
The mortal boughs—the mortal tree of life,
The old bark burnt with iron wars   15
They blow to a live flame
To char the young green days
And reach the occult soul;—they have no softer lure—
No softer lure than the savage ways of death.
We were satisfied of our Lords the moon and the sun   20
To take our wage of sleep and bread and warmth—
These maidens came—these strong everliving Amazons,
And in an easy might their wrists
Of night's sway and noon's sway the sceptres brake,
Clouding the wild—the soft lustres of our eyes.   25

Clouding the wild lustres, the clinging tender lights;
Driving the darkness into the flame of day,
With the Amazonian wind of them
Over our corroding faces
That must be broken—broken for evermore   30
So the soul can leap out
Into their huge embraces.
Tho' there are human faces
Best sculptures of Deity,
And sinews lusted after   35
By the Archangels tall,
Even these must leap to the love-heat of these maidens
From the flame of terrene days,
Leaving grey ashes to the wind—to the wind.

One (whose great lifted face,   40
Where wisdom's strength and beauty's strength
And the thewed strength of large beasts
Moved and merged, gloomed and lit)
Was speaking, surely, as the earth-men's earth fell away;
Whose new hearing drunk the sound   45
Where pictures lutes and mountains mixed
With the loosed spirit of a thought,
Essenced to language, thus—

'My sisters force their males
From the doomed earth, from the doomed glee   50

And hankering of hearts.
Frail hands gleam up through the human quagmire,
   and lips of ash
Seem to wail, as in sad faded paintings
Far sunken and strange.
My sisters have their males   55
Clean of the dust of old days
That clings about those white hands,
And yearns in those voices sad.
But these shall not see them,
Or think of them in any days or years,   60
They are my sisters' lovers in other days and years.'

The Jew

    Moses, from whose loins I sprung,
    Lit by a lamp in his blood
    Ten immutable rules, a moon
    For mutable lampless men.

    The blonde, the bronze, the ruddy,   5
    With the same heaving blood,
    Keep tide to the moon of Moses,
    Then why do they sneer at me?

Girl to Soldier on Leave

    I love you—Titan lover,
    My own storm-days' Titan.
    Greater than the son of Zeus.
    I know who I would choose.

    Titan—my splendid rebel—   5
    The old Prometheus
    Wanes like a ghost before your power—
    His pangs were joys to yours.

Pallid days arid and wan
Tied your soul fast.　　　　　　　　　10
Babel cities' smoky tops
Pressed upon your growth

Weary gyves. What were you?
But a word in the brain's ways,
Or the sleep of Circe's swine.　　　　15
One gyve holds you yet.—

It held you hiddenly on the Somme
Tied from my heart at home.
O must it loosen now?—I wish
You were bound with the old old gyves.　20

Love! you love me—your eyes
Have looked through death at mine.
You have tempted a grave too much.
I let you—I repine.

Soldier: Twentieth Century

I love you, great new Titan!
Am I not you?
Napoleon and Caesar
Out of you grew.

Out of unthinkable torture,　　　　　5
Eyes kissed by death,
Won back to the world again,
Lost and won in a breath,

Cruel men are made immortal.
Out of your pain born.　　　　　　　10
They have stolen the sun's power
With their feet on your shoulders worn.

Let them shrink from your girth,
That has outgrown the pallid days,

When you slept like Circe's swine,   15
Or a word in the brain's ways.

In War

Fret the nonchalant noon
With your spleen
Or your gay brow,
For the motion of your spirit
Ever moves with these.   5

When day shall be too quiet,
Deaf to you
And your dumb smile,
Untuned air shall lap the stillness
In the old space for your voice—   10

The voice that once could mirror
Remote depths
Of moving being,
Stirred by responsive voices near,
Suddenly stilled for ever.   15

No ghost darkens the places
Dark to One;
But my eyes dream,
And my heart is heavy to think
How it was heavy once.   20

In the old days when death
Stalked the world
For the flower of men,
And the rose of beauty faded
And pined in the great gloom,   25

One day we dug a grave:
We were vexed
With the sun's heat.

We scanned the hooded dead:
At noon we sat and talked   30

How death had kissed their eyes
Three dread noons since,
How human art won
The dark soul to flicker
Till it was lost again: 35

And we whom chance kept whole—
But haggard,
Spent—were charged
To make a place for them who knew
No pain in any place.   40

The good priest came to pray;
Our ears half heard,
And half we thought
Of alien things, irrelevant;
And the heat and thirst were great.   45

The good priest read: 'I heard . . . '
Dimly my brain
Held words and lost . . .
Sudden my blood ran cold . . .
God! God! it could not be.   50

He read my brother's name;
I sank—
I clutched the priest.
They did not tell me it was he
Was killed three days ago.   55

What are the great sceptred dooms
To us, caught
In the wild wave?
We break ourselves on them,
My brother, our hearts and years.   60

The Burning of the Temple

Fierce wraith of Solomon
Where sleepest thou? O see
The fabric which thou won
Earth and ocean to give thee—
O look at the red skies.   5

Or hath the sun plunged down?
What is this molten gold—
These thundering fires blown
Through heaven—where the smoke rolled.
Again the great king dies.   10

His dreams go out in smoke,
His days he let not pass
And sculptured here are broke
Are charred as the burnt grass
Gone as his mouth's last sighs.   15

[*Through these pale cold days*]

Through these pale cold days
What dark faces burn
Out of three thousand years,
And their wild eyes yearn,

While underneath their brows   5
Like waifs their spirits grope
For the pools of Hebron again—
For Lebanon's summer slope.

They leave these blond still days
In dust behind their tread   10
They see with living eyes
How long they have been dead.

FRAGMENTS

I

When the heart wakes and hears

II

Hymn to Life

Born with me die with me
Mother mistress friend

III

L——and M——

Once on a time in a land so fair
That the air you breathed was as wine,
And everything that you looked on there
Made you at once divine,

There lived two maidens, little and sweet,
Whose dear names I may not tell
Because that would call me blab and cheat,
Which would be terrible.

The eldest whom I will just call L,
Was most ladylike and smart,
And of M the youngest,—she had ways that—well,
One had to guard one's heart.

And in this land, as of course you'd guess,
They did not live all alone,

And all the blessings that God could bless
These two could call their own.

A mother, so wise and good and kind,
A father as young as they
In heart, who while he formed their mind,
He did not mind their play.

They were taught music, and painting, and all
Of culture's thousand pothers,
To dance and to ply the bat and ball,
And also feel for others.

But sad to say, most sad it should be,
They were not always good;
Although they looked so fairily,
They oft did what no fairy would.

When they were set to drawing flowers
Then Lilly in pique would say,
'I hate drawing, especially flowers,
Let's throw the flowers away'.

And Maisy, that buxom rosy Miss,
Would set the teacher riddles,
And his brain with 'Can you solve this and this?'
Buzzed as if with a hundred fiddles.

IV

Tom is so reserved and quiet
Before he married was so blatant
  he finds his Prue
Will talk enough for two.

V

'I live for you', says Ted to Jane
And if you died, so I'd die too'.

'I'm sure you would' said working Jane
'You live for me—to live for you.'

VI

Your hand that sings your soul's music
Your soul the plummet of my soul

VII

Nature, indeed, the plot you spin's so stale,
And each man's story is so like another,
I should advise—it's such a boring tale,
Suppress all copies and begin some other.

VIII

I know all men are withered with yearning
O forest flame guarded with swords that are
    burning
O eyes that sea-like our madness entombs
Gold hair whose rich metal enlocks us in terror

IX

Such fond conceits my heart may have

X

Wood and forest, drink
Of the blue delight,
Only of its brink.
But my mind and sight
Drink from brink to brink

XI

Poets have snared thee in sweet word.
Such cage immortal singing bird
Each soul finds you while tread your eyes
Its intricate infinities.
Stirring the veins whose heart is God
To ecstasy with roseate rod
Ah could they only keep you there
To make their prison a palace fair

Bounding infinity in a mood
Whose habit is your roseate hood
To ecstasy—to ecstasy
More sweet than Paradise can be
Where every thought and pulse and vein
Melts into joy—till sense is fain
To cease lest

Poets have snared you in sweet word,
Such cage, immortal singing bird
Each soul finds you while tread your eyes
Its intricate infinities

XII

In dimpled depths of smiling innocence
In dimpled labyrinths of innocence
My sunless sorrow made its rosy grave
In laughing liquid eyes that Time had wardened
Fifteen skiey years,—my sad soul looked
My sad soul looked and all its sadness vanished.

This were we searching all our lives to find

XIII

A mood

Over my glad heart's summer
There floats a breath of spring
The honey of happy laughter

XIV

And the skies ran leaping to me
And in my veins danced
All things praised me

XV

A shimmering rose coloured elegance
Rose and silver and streaked
With a tender blue of a luminous sky

The warm lit fountain quivers in the lake
The chequered green of emerald grass
Shakes and quivers and throbs and twinkles

XVI

I have pressed my teeth in the heart of May
I have dabbled my lips in the honey of June
And the sun shot keen and the grass laughed gay
And the earth was buoyed on the tide of noon
And earth sailed swift
And all was young
And the skies were old and young
And my soul to the tide I flung,
And the bloom of my soul to the tide I fl[   ]

XVII

A gurgling drip perpetual
To make the silence seem more still

XVIII

Whoso is neither deaf nor blind,
Hath oped the gates of sin,
For circumstances form the mind,
And moulds the thought within
By that which is about around
In wills and hearts despite
In fetters fearful we are bound
Dark—dark our moral night.

If then that purity of mind
Essential, for no wrong
Is shattered by a fate unkind
That did not make us strong
If sin is woven with our frame
If nature bids desire
If this must be, why call it shame
Must nature's wants expire?

XIX

What songs do fill the pauses of our day
When action tires and motion begs to stay.
And life can give to life a little heed
Then when life only seems to pause
A life divine from heaven she draws
From labour's earthly trammels freed

XX

The flowers I gather bloom with me
By meditation fed

XXI

The heavens are black

XXII

And walk again my righteous ways
And then thy foes shall vanquished be
And I again shall hear thy praise

XXIII

The vanishing spire

XXIV

Power that impels
Pulse of the void working
My unwilled|willess grappling fingers.
Like a grave star drawing
Our gazes forlorn
To kiss the sister star that is my soul

Must kiss the sister star that is my soul
And unimaginable fires of dawn
The brooding stones and the dissolving hills
The summer's leafy gladness
The winter shrewd
And all thy changing robes, thy myriad forms
Stirless to our

Power that impels
Pulse of the void to our vain grappling fingers
Like a star|grave that draws my gazes forlorn
The poet's dead soul whose flung word lights the world
The struck music that panic whirls the world
The hills decay and pass to blossoms of fire

In this slow dust God kneads his changing forms
Sculptor of exhaustless|infinite dreams we thank our dreamer

Power that impels
Pulse of the void to my willess grappling fingers.
Like a grave star drawing our gazes forlorn
Will kiss the sister star that is my soul
So I a visible star, would penetrate the vast
The unimaginable chasms and abysses
That is thy body—all natures
To reach the fountain star and hides the soul of thee.

XXV

Sensual

Or where absence, silence is,
Of fleshy strings whose strains are Paradise
And paven ecstasies
For the untravelled ardours leashed in eyes.

Youth's fearless wings are spread
O Cynic life! fine mirrors are your walls.
O voice and lip unwed
Hands beckon but my own wild shadow calls.

Is not love loveliness
Truth beauty and all natural harmony
Unstriving happiness
The mystic centre of all unity.

Life mirrors love and truth
Even as our love and truth within be deep
His own self dazzles youth

XXVI

The stars are out of gear the heavens' motion
Slopes wrecked upon the human sinewed housetops
The tyrant manacles of thought have chained the

XXVII

By the Euphrates
forests hung
In my ears a rustle

XXVIII

And all their faces yearn to thee

XXIX

The grasses tremble and quiver

Shake your tiny heads and shower
All the love you bear

Now at the set of day
The host of colours come
In gorgeous disarray

Marvelous hour of peace and memory
Fold me as in a chamber
And my tumultuous youth

XXX

In mingled skies of dark and red

XXXI

Kiss me once more
You have been fair
And cruel and foul.
You have been fair
Kiss me once more.

XXXII

Not all the fruit that hung thereon
The trees whose barks were pictured days,

XXXIII

She kindles fire

Her icy flame is like the moon

She is like the moon
In her icy flame
As a giant turns in sleep

XXXIV

From the|your sunny clime
Dream of earthly time
And the chill mist
Wonder at earth's wreck
And the sorrow strewn deck,
By friend death unkist

Sailing as for joy
Happy girl and boy,
In these waters grim
See their faces pale
The broken sail,
For an idle whim.
God's dream, God's whim
All for a whim
Their parents
To suit God's whim

XXXV

Heart is there hope—or is there sighing|ordeal still
  in thy stars' horoscope

Come, the keen years, the fierce years, laughing cruel
Heap on your trouble

Maiden in my troubled heart
Look not thou
It would trouble you

XXXVI

  The trees suffer the wind
  And the sunbeams leap in their mail
  The shadows slide from leaf to leaf
  And sudden and brief
  Resounds like an avalanche
  The throats of these things frail

XXXVII

  The satyr prompting of his blood

XXXVIII

Where the rock's heart is hidden from the sea
The unwearied sea whose white tongues fawn upon its breast
The rock's heart hidden from the unwearing sea
Whose white tongues fawn upon its dumb cold breast|cheeks
  |wet cheeks
It knows the hunger
O As the rock heart is her heart
And my thoughts fawn and my eyes cover her
O wonderful sea—it is a little rock
Her eyes, deep heavens|that are the hours whose depth reach
  not to me

XXXIX

O cockney who maketh negatives
You negative of negatives.

XL

Shall this be ever thus
All our swiftness, our wrath

I have heard the Gods
In their high conference
As I lay outside the world
Quiet in sleep

Shall all immortal
If the Gods perish

Babylon was built on Babylon
How comes it cities have such faith in stones

Babylon was built on Babylon
And heaven was builded on heaven
And all immortal things
And the ensuing way Apollo watched

The mountains are but clouds

XLI

Ah if your lips might stir
With one moods wind|breath behind
As easily as it alters
To all swift moods but this
But you are afraid to smile
And bewitch yourself to a chain|place
Where tho your moods might alter
One mood would come in vain

Ah if your lips might stir
With one mood's wind|breath behind
To the touch of a certain mood
As easily as it alters
To all swift moods but this!
But you are afraid to smile
And bewitch yourself to a place
Where though your moods might alter
One mood would come in vain.

XLII

There are sweet chains that bind
And gains that are strange loss
Your ruddy freedom falters
And pales at hint of these
You change bewilder and gleam
In a labyrinth of light
But one change calls dark and dumbly
To you and calls in vain.

XLIII

Dyed with a superb light

And the west is stained with superb light

O filled with ephemeral light

XLIV

The moon.

The pigmy skies cover
No mood in my simple eyes
The flat earth foams over
With pallour when I first rise
Thin branches like whips

Whiten the skies
To gibbuous lips

Thin branches threaten like whips
Caught in the spell of the windy moon
They are changed to bells

The leaves are burning emerald lamps
The air is a wall of shining sounds

Girl's song

The pigmy skies cover
The roots of my eyes;
The flat earth foams over
The shores of moonrise.
Thin branches like whips
Writhe in the skies. Whiten the skies
Where anchor star ships
That keep my mad lover.

What is his knowledge
Knowing not this?
I'll send him a message,
My life in a kiss.
Why is he mad?
I hold fire for him, bliss
He has not had
And dare not aspire.

Girl's song

The pigmy skies cover
No mood in my eyes,
The flat earth foams over
My pallour's moonrise.
Thin branches like whips
Whiten the skies
To gibbuous lips
Calling for my mad lover.

What is his knowledge
Knowing not this?
I'll send him a message,
My life in a kiss.
Why is he mad?
I hold fire for him, bliss
He has not had
And dare not aspire,

XLV

All pleasures fly.
O Clinging lights
And wavering glory
Adieu you sigh,
Half told your story
To you we die

XLVI

Voluble like light

XLVII

The apples have wine
Witchcraft is in your voice
Cunning like wine

XLVIII

Wag your heads and wink your eyes
Kick your feet right thro the skies
Naked dive into the water

XLIX

The weight of wonder in this age of ours

L

And every face to watch him raised
Puts on the light of children praised

LI

Each handshake where the souls do not touch
Bread for the hungry soul to [?]
Starved the soul a little more
Words no accent makes alive
A handshake where the souls do not touch,
As words no accent makes alive

The topped clouds

Sweetheart in each handshake
My soul like fawns not yet
That place where my heart must be unpressed|
    untouched on the land's breast
The sea with her white tongues are fawning
Cloud their wealth for my eye
Abraham's was no riches,
You were strange to him as to me
Sarah's rival
You are old to me as to him

Love forged one soul of two atoms soluble

LII

My desires are as the sea
Whose white tongues fawn on the breast
Of sand and turns it again to sea
Back to itself that prest
My desires feed to me

LIII

The silver leaf we call the sky

LIV

Green thoughts are
Ice block on a barrow
Gleaming in July
A little boy with bare feet
And jewels at his nose stands by.

LV

Her ways are like sour gooseberries
Sometimes, when her sweets become|change to so sour
Her legs in rosy satiny folds

LVI

What bird dropt a stone from the sky
Or slipped dead from a cloud

O knarled grotesque
You have a key to unlock my box of fancies
And your feet roam in the dim recess.

LVII

She could not share in my ambitious feast
She could not breast me in my flight of fire
She burnt herself
Poor girl [   ] our natures grow
Coaxed mine grow too fast
How could it rest in thee who only knew
Coax me from my rival ambition
You had a key to unlock my box of fancies
And had no key to lock it up again

LVIII

Over the chasm they rolled together
Chasm that lay in tumult of trance

Blue is the sky and calm the spring weather,
Careless of two who have ended their dance,
Over the two who were lovely once,
What shall we write here. There were once

Flies are down hurrying insects are busy
Blue is the sky and quiet the air—

They only slipped out of despair

Across Sky chasms in|of a sunset stress
Burn swart for sorrowless
Roses in storm adance.
Abysmal as they swing
Thro a tumult of deep trance
They burn for sorrowless roses

Across sky chasms of a sunset stress
My roses loiter their last breath to press
The dawn of the vague evening
Calls them to dance to dance,
Abysmal still they swing
Over tumult of deep trance

LIX

And all imaginary traces bare
In such dear casuistry
That I too in the fond delusion share

LX

In a concentrated thought a sudden noise startles

LXI

Sensual motions of nerves
Vibrate from hushed shy curves

Helpless obscene and cruel
My fires must drain that jewel
Of all its virgin rays
Crunched in one black amaze

My life inert goes out
Dissolved voluptuously

LXII

You can never bury him
He can never die
Like a worm you cut in two
Still doth wriggle by
Though you kill him with your tongue

LXIII

All violet and amethyst
With green flung here and there

LXIV

Her grape green eyes have stained in weird
Lustrous phantasies the urn
Of one mood and ever they burn,
And the heart stands there to learn

They are old carvings so long heard
In oldest struggle of man's brain
One of restlessness
One greed God's jealousy to gain,
Death dim her fair hair in vain

One mood

LXV

O spear girt face too far
Save for the sorcery that makes soft
Those points or turns them inward on herself
I cannot cleave thro that inviolate tract
That virginal

LXVI

Through what forbidden fare
Ruined as a mortal lass is

LXVII

Amber eyes with ever such little red fires
Face as vague and white as a swan in shadow

LXVIII

Learn not such music here
The grave's door
Shall hear that music
The Eternal taciturn.

LXIX

Yea I a soldier, say I have not suffered at all before
If this is suffering

A mother watching her son die, a soldier
With thews used, cursing|despair blasphemies
God's unthinkable imagination
Invents new tortures for nature.
New anguish new despairs, strange thirsts|humiliations|
    indignities
If this were natural

Our thews stretch to the largeness of th[?]
And makes the wrong thin and used, but all my [?]
Trodden under the unearthly hoofs of this a soldier
　　tried in the wars　　　all human suffering
Till the stricken soul wails in anguish, intolerable
Till the wilful soul breaks all [?]
To the largeness of the intolerable wrong to st[?]
And writhes all thin and used, a shuddering pain
No man can say he's suffered till this thing
Which has been hidden from me, a soldier
Whose conceit grew [?] experience

LXX

What wind has bowed the world's face from the light
Not Paris loved Helen so

LXXI

What may be, what hath been, and what is now?
God. God! if thou art pity, look on me;
God! if thou are forgiveness, turn and see
The dark within, the anguish on my brow!
O! wherefore am I stricken in grief thus low?
For no wrong done, or right undone to thee?
For, if that thou hast made me, what must be
Thou hast made too. How canst thou be thy foe
To retribute what thou thyself hast done?
A little pity, or if that be vain,
If tears are dumb since there to hear are none,
If that the years mean lingering hours of pain.
If rest alone through death's gates is but won,

LXXII

Is your life bruised and would you rest
And your bruised life would bear the hurt

The careless world
Sleep there is nothing here
There yet may be some pleasant hours
Perhaps there waits

Unto each destruction

And we have suf[

How have we come to be men

LXXIII

In the dusk of Time|the world

LXXIV

O lady—little am I skilled to sing

LXXV

If all my tears were gathered up like flowers
To gleam a coronet upon my brow

LXXVI

and like the artist he who doth create|who creates
From dying things what never dies.

LXXVII

Wild Undertones

I wash my soul in colours, in a million undertones,
And then my soul shines out—and you read—a poem.

LXXVIII

Unlock our faces of their glow
And tear the fruit and flower of love
Still there were sparkles on the snow
And scent round the torn branch would move
Can you be drenched in love and dry
Without a stain to haunt to linger
The damned disease will never die
Where syphil[is] has placed its corroding finger

LXXIX

But I am thrown with beauty's breath
Climbing my soul, driven in
Like a music wherein is pressed
All the power that withers the mountain
And maketh trees to grow.

LXXX

From the neck of a God your hands are odorous.
Now I am made a God and he without you is none.
Your eyes still wear the looks of Paradise.
I look upon its shining fields and mourn for the outcast
    angels
Who have no Eden now since it shines in your eyes.
     .   .   .   .
My soul is a moulten cup with brimming music of your
    mouth;—
Somewhere is a weeping silence and I feel a happy thief.

LXXXI

Like a voice compressed in a box
Coming out through a tiny crack

LXXXII

Your own sweet leave to love you

You gave me leave to love you
In my own way I will
Your leave you gave in your way

In shy delight of loving
The ways we two had met
Those ways we still must wander
There is one thing to forget

We must forget ourselves sweet
Too much we know|feel the kiss
Forget the bliss of loving,
And strive for God love's bliss
For love's eternal bliss

LXXXIII

Drowsed in beauty
Of her face,
Waking fancies
Two souls embrace
Strive to chase

LXXXIV

He was mad
Brain drenched by luxury of pulsing blood
While to his heart's throat his cold spirit pressed,
And ever rippled waves of golden curls,
Rose hue made of his thoughts a coloured fire,

LXXXV

Love, hide thy face—why in thy land
This garden blooms we understand

A little—not at all—but men
Live not who are not drunk sometime
With fragrance|power of its scents that climb
Their towers of soul and melt and sting
The thoughted throng unburnishing
The spiritual shining

We turn aside from love's holy feast
Is not man [   ] God man the beast
And sex

Rapid the flames and swords, the chains
Flash and are flung, we burn, we writhe
The blood is emptied from our veins
And wine streams through fiercely and blithe
The royal flesh whose panting legions

LXXXVI

The thronging glories ringing round our birth
The angels worshiping th' adoring kings
Enroofs nativity with a marvel of gold
The inspired presence

Surely the songs are heard the worship known|the worship
   and the burden
Of light washes beneath the lidded slumber
Of the shut soul

LXXXVII

Beautiful is the day
And the beloved night
Deep the speech they say
From the fathomless height
For they fade like flowers
And their speech
And their fragrance reaches

Beautiful is the day
Of the beloved night
Between his breast there play
Dark forms waving bright
In stars' vague disarray
The hills have taken flight.
He has unsheathed his mail

Beautiful is the day
Sighs the beloved night
Why do you fly away
When I come with my stars bright
Your gaudy disarray

LXXXVIII

In half delight of shy delight
In a sweetness thrilled with fears
Like grass that trembles as for flight
As a perfume fills the night

In half delight of shy delight
In a sweetness thrilled with fears—
She walks where the night
Has stored her maiden years
He loves me he loves me
O glory for a girl

Her eyes on this rich storied night
Reads love—and strangely hears
Love guests with wintered years

So a rich storied night
Guests with the wintered years
She looks strangely with life's wonder

In half delight of shy delight
In a sweetness thrilled with fears
Her eyes on the rich storied night
Reads love and strangely hears

Love guests with wintered years.

We know the summer plaited hours

O maiden still plaiting
Your men unruffled curls.
For fierce loving and hating
No trap to keep you girls
She walks so delicately grave
And builds a house for her heart's|hope's love
And unbuilds so love is made brave

As lovely as her unroofed fancies
In waters of soft night they love
Of Thro measureless expanses
Of love's far linked|mermaiden dances

LXXXIX

Girl! how quiet you are

LXXXX

Even as a paper burns and curls
And the obliterating mind and heart
Symboled in writing is not quite gone

Sweet years walling up the sky
Five and twenty piled up very high
What blue spaces still are left to wall
Are there any—any at all.

Even as a letter burns and curls
And the mind and heart in the writing blackens
Words that wane as the wind unfurls—
Obliteration never slackens
Fate who wrote it and addressed it here
Life who read it loved it called it dear
Peace who slumbered love who tore it thro

XCI

For one thrilled instant am I you, O skies.
It passes, I am hunted, and the air
Lives with revengeful momentary fires.
O wilderness of heaven, O scroll of fate
Whose profound spaces like some God's blank eyes
Roll in a milky terror, move and move
While our fears make vague shuddering imprints there
And character such chained up forms of sorrow
That a breath can unloose; in its white depths
Dream unnamed gulphs of sudden traps for souls|men
For all men's thoughts go up and form one soul
With unimagined powers|might of evil scheming
Wrought by the texture of man's|selfish desires
Of puny plotting, and inspired dreaming.

Or if a thought like spray by sudden moon
Is lit, that holy amorous instant knows
Transplanted time to make twin time in space
My new born thought touch aeon dusted thoughts
From softly lidded lights, from breaking gleams
Into a rainbow radiance, some pale light springs,
And the dim sun stands midwife to this child

XCII

The monster wind prowls in the writhen trees
The wind dives in the writhen trees
They strain in angered leash
They are strong in their green ease

Soft forward inarticulate
Warm, wayward, drooping, or aburst,
Rushing, it tires, rests|slacks to abate

The wind wakes in the writhen trees

XCIII

Duplicate hours, moods that are valueless

XCIV

Frail hours that love to dance
To hear your princely sun
His golden countenance
Scatters you pale and wan
Scatters your ghostly love
That was the breath of a dream
Scatters light from above
Till day flows like a stream

The stars fade in the sky
Taking our dreams away
Day's banners flame on high
In gaudy disarray
Love that my dream fashioned
Leaving no song has gone

XCV

Sunlight gave new birth to new hues
In Pearl translucency wavered

XCVI

Pale mother night suckling thy brood of stars
My fire too, yearns for thy giant love
But they are calm, and mine is frenzy fire

XCVII

Where we wander shadow shaken
Where we revel in our fear
In a spell no charm can waken

XCVIII

Violet is the maddest color I know
And opal is the color of dreams
But a girl is the color of snow
The violet like noon haze she seems.
And of opal the lights on her brow

The root's hidden secrecy
Laughs out in fruit

XCIX

Dawn like a flushed rose petal flecked with gold
Broke glowingly
Throbbed ardently—Upon my barb I leaped
Filled my heart's sinew
Quickened youth's glow
While the black deserts stretchèd leaguers slept
And loosed his bridle of flame from idling cold
We flew—I said"

The search

Dawn like a flushed rose petal fleck'd with gold
Quickened youth's glow. Upon my barb I leap'd
While the blank desert's stretchèd leaguers slept,
And loosed his bridle of flame from idling cold.

C

Be the hope or the fear,
Be the smile or the tear,
In the strife of a life
On Time's rolling river
That rolls forever.

CI

The brooding stones and the dissolving hills,
The summer's leafy luxury,
The winter shrewd,
And all thy changing robes, thy myriad forms.

CII

The first by such hands
And aged and tired battalions
Stand to and kiss us with their gold
It was not so five hundred years ago
When the terrific plumes of Edward the black
Towered to dark these shuddering w[   ]
And all the band of rabble

PLAYS

Moses

MOSES (An Egyptian Prince)
ABINOAH (An Overseer)
TWO HEBREWS
KOELUE (Abinoah's Daughter)
MESSENGER

SCENE I

Outside a College in Thebes. Egyptian Students pass by.
MOSES *alone in meditation.*

Enter MESSENGER.

MESSENGER (*Handing papyrus*) Pharaoh's desires.
MOSES (*Reads*) To our beloved son, greeting. Add to our thoughts
of you, if possible to add, but a little, and you are more than old
heroes. Not to bemean your genius, who might cry 'Was that all!'
We pile barriers everywhere. We give you idiots for tools, tree   5
stumps for swords, skin sacks for souls. The sixteenth pyramid
remains to be built. We give you the last draft of slaves. Move!
Forget not the edict. PHARAOH.
(*To* MESSENGER) What is the edict?
MESS. The royal paunch of Pharaoh dangled worriedly,   10
Not knowing where the wrong. Viands once giant-like
Came to him thin and thinner. What rats gnawed?
Horror! The swarm of slaves. The satraps swore
Their wives' bones hurt them when they lay abed
That before were soft and plump. The people howled   15
They'd boil the slaves three days to get their fat,
Ending the famine. A haggard council held
Decrees the two hind molars, those two staunchest
Busy labourers in the belly's service, to be drawn
From out each slave's greased mouth, which soon,   20
From incapacity, would lose the habit

Of eating.

MOSES Well should their bones stick out to find the air,
    I'll make a use of them for pleasantness.
    Droll demonstrations of anatomy.   25
MESS. And when you've ended find 'twas one on sharks.

(MOSES *signs* MESSENGER *to go*)

Exit MESSENGER.

MOSES Fine! Fine!
    See in my brain
    What madmen have rushed through,
    And like a tornado   30
    Torn up the tight roots
    Of some dead universe.
    The old clay is broken
    For a power to soak in and knit
    It all into tougher tissues   35
    To hold life,
    Pricking my nerves till the brain might crack,
    It boils to my finger tips,
    Till my hands ache to grip
    The hammer—the lone hammer   40
    That breaks lives into a road
    Through which my genius drives.
    Pharaoh well peruked and oiled,
    And your admirable pyramids,
    And your interminable procession   45
    Of crowned kings,
    You are my little fishing rods
    Wherewith I catch the fish
    To suit my hungry belly.

    I am rough now, and new, and will have no tailor.   50
    Startlingly,
    As a mountain side
    Wakes aware of its other side,
    When from a cave a leopard comes,
    On its heels the same red sand,   55
    Springing with acquainted air,
    Sprang an intelligence
    Coloured as a whim of mine,

Showed to my dull outer eyes
The living eyes underneath,   60
Did I not shrivel up and take the place of air,
Secret as those eyes were,
And those strong eyes call up a giant frame;
And I am that now.

Pharaoh is sleek and deep;   65
And where his love for me is set, under
The deeps, on its floor, or in the shallow ways,
Tho' I have been as a diver, never yet
Could I find . . . I have a way, a touchstone!
A small misdemeanour, touch of rebelliousness;   70
To prick the vein of father, monitor, foe,
Will tell which of these his kingship is.
If I shut my eyes to the edict,
And leave the pincers to rust,
And the slaves' teeth as God made them,   75
Then hide from the summoning tribunal,
Pharaoh will speak, and I'll seize that word to act.
Should the word be a foe's, I can use it well,
As a poison to soak into Egypt's bowels,
A wraith from old Nile will cry   80
'For his mercy they break his back'
And I shall have a great following for this,
The rude touched heart of the mauled sweaty horde,
Their rough tongues fawn at my hands, their red streaked eyes
Glisten with sacrifice. Well! Pharaoh bids me act.   85
Hah! I'm all abristle. Lord! his eyes would go wide
If he knew the road my rampant dreams would race.
I am too much awake now—restless, so restless.
Behind white mists invisibly
My thoughts stood like a mountain.   90
But Power, watching as a man,
Saw no mountain there,
Only the mixing mist and sky,
And the flat earth.
What shoulder pushed through those mists   95
Of gay fantastic pastimes
And startled hills of sleep?
                    (*He looks in the mirror*)

Oh! apparition of me!
Ruddy flesh soon hueless!
Fade and show to my eyes   100
The lasting bare body.
Soul sack fall away
And show what you hold.
Sing! Let me hear you sing.
                    (*A voice sings*)

      Upon my lips, like a cloud   105
      To burst on the peaks of light,
      Sit cowled, impossible things
      To tie my hands at their prime and height.
      Power! break through their shroud,
      Pierce them so thoroughly,   110
      Thoroughly enter me,
      Know me for one dead.
      Break the shadowy thread,
      The cowering spirit's bond
      Writ by illusions blonde.   115

      Ah! let the morning pale
      Throb with a wilder pulse.
      No delicate flame shall quail
      With terror at your convulse.
      Thin branches whip the white skies   120
      To lips and spaces of song
      That chant a mood to my eyes—
      Ah! sleep can be overlong.

MOSES Voices thunder, voices of deeds not done.
    Lo! on the air is scrawled in abysmal light   125
    Old myths never known, and yet already foregone,
    And songs more lost, more secret than desert light.
    Martyrdoms of uncreated things,
    Virgin silences waiting a breaking voice—
    As in a womb they cry, in a cage beat vain wings   130
    Under life, over life,—is their unbeing my choice?

    Dull wine of torpor—the unsoldered spirit lies limp.
    Ah! if she would run into a mould
    Some new idea unwalled
    To human by-ways, an apocalyptic camp   135

Of utterest and ulterior dreaming,
Understood only in its gleaming,
To flash stark naked the whole girth of the world.

I am sick of priests and forms,
This rigid dry-boned refinement.   140
As ladies' perfumes are
Obnoxious to stern natures,
This miasma of a rotting god
Is to me.
Who has made of the forest a park?   145
Who has changed the wolf to a dog?
And put the horse in harness?
And man's mind in a groove?

I heard the one spirit cry in them,
'Break this metamorphosis,   150
Disenchant my lying body,
Only putrefaction is free,
And I, Freedom, am not.
Moses! touch us, thou!'

There shall not be a void or calm   155
But a fury fill the veins of time
Whose limbs had begun to rot.
Who had flattered my stupid torpor
With an easy and mimic energy,
And drained my veins with a paltry marvel   160
More monstrous than battle,
For the soul ached and went out dead in pleasure.

Is not this song still sung in the streets of me?

          A naked African
          Walked in the sun   165
          Singing—singing
          Of his wild love.

          I slew a tiger
          With your young strength
          (My tawny panther)   170
          Rolled round my life.

          Three sheep, your breasts,
          And my head between,

Grazing together
On a smooth slope. 175

Ah! Koelue!
Had you embalmed your beauty, so
It could not backward go,
Or change in any way,
What were the use, if on my eyes 180
The embalming spices were not laid
To keep us fixed,
Two amorous sculptures passioned endlessly?
What were the use, if my sight grew,
And its far branches were cloud-hung, 185
You, small at the roots, like grass,
While the new lips my spirit would kiss
Were not red lips of flesh,
But the huge kiss of power.
Where yesterday soft hair thro' my fingers fell 190
A shaggy mane would entwine,
And no slim form work fire to my thighs.
But human Life's inarticulate mass
Throb the pulse of a thing
Whose mountain flanks awry 195
Beg my mastery—mine!
Ah! I will ride the dizzy beast of the world
My road—my way.

SCENE II

Evening before Thebes.

The Pyramids are being built. Swarms of Hebrews labouring.
Priests and Taskmasters. TWO HEBREWS *are furtively talking.*

KOELUE *passes by singing.*

The vague viols of evening
Call all the flower clans 200
To some abysmal swinging
And tumult of deep trance;
He may hear, flower of my singing,
And come hither winging.

OLD HEB. (*gazing after her in a muffled frenzy*)
    Hateful harlot. Boils cover your small cruel face.   205
    O! fine champion Moses. O! so good to us,
    O! grand begetter on her of a whip and a torturer,
    Her father, born to us, since you kissed her.
    Our champion! O! so good to us.
YOUNG HEB. For shame, our brother's twisted blood-smeared
       gums   210
    Tell, we only, have more room for wreck curtailed,
    For you, having no teeth to draw, it is no mercy
    Perhaps, but they might mangle your gums;
    Or touch a nerve somewhere. He barred it now.
    And that is all his thanks, he, too, in peril.   215
    Be still old man, wait a little.
OLD HEB. Wait!
    All day some slow dark quadruped beats
    To pulp our springiness.
    All day some hoofed animal treads our veins,   220
    Leisurely—leisurely our energies flow out.
    All agonies created from the first day
    Have wandered hungry searching the world for us
    Or they would perish like disused Behemoth.
    Is our Messiah one to unleash these agonies   225
    As Moses does, who gives us an Abinoah?
YOUNG HEB. Yesterday as I lay nigh dead with toil
    Underneath the hurtling crane oiled with our blood,
    Thinking to end all and let the crane crush me,
    He came by and bore me into the shade.   230
    O what a furnace roaring in his blood
    Thawed my congealed sinews and tingled my own
    Raging through me like a strong cordial.
    He spoke! since yesterday
    Am I not larger grown.   235
    I've seen men hugely shapen in soul
    Of such unhuman shaggy male turbulence
    They tower in foam miles from our neck-strained sight.
    And to their shop only heroes come.
    But all were cripples to this speed   240
    Constrained to the stables of flesh.
    I say there is a famine in ripe harvest
    When hungry giants come as guests,

Come knead the hills and ocean into food.
There is none for him.   245
The streaming vigours of his blood erupting
From his halt tongue, is like an anger thrust
Out of a madman's piteous craving for
A monstrous baulked perfection.
OLD HEB. He is a prince, an animal   250
    Not of our kind, who perhaps has heard
    Vague rumours of our world, to his mind
    An unpleasant miasma.
YOUNG HEB. Is not Miriam his sister, Jochabed his mother?
    In the womb he looked round and saw   255
    From furthermost stretches our wrong.
    From the palaces and schools
    Our pain has pierced dead generations
    Back to his blood's thin source
    As we lie chained by Egyptian men   260
    He lay in nets of their women,
    And now rejoice, he has broken their meshes.
    O! his desires are fleets of treasure
    He has squandered in treacherous seas
    Sailing mistrust to find frank ports.   265
    He fears our fear and tampers mildly
    For our assent to let him save us.
    When he walks amid our toil
    With some master mason
    His tense brows critical   270
    Of the loose enginery.
    Hints famed devices flat, his rod
    Scratching new schemes on the sand.
    But read hard the scrawled lines there,
    Limned turrets and darkness, chinks of light,   275
    Half beasts snorting into the light,
    A phantasmagoria, wild escapade,
    To our hearts' clue; just a daring plan
    To the honest mason. What swathed meanings peer
    From his workaday council, washing to and from   280
    Your understanding till you doubt
    That a word was said.
    But a terror wakes and forces your eyes
    Into his covertly . . . to search his searching.

Startled to life starved hopes slink out   285
Cowering, incredulous.
OLD HEB. (*to himself*) His youth is flattered at
Moses' kind speech to him.
                    (*To the* YOUNG HEBREW)
I am broken and grey, have seen much in my time,
And all this gay grotesque of childish man   290
Long passed. Half blind—half deaf, I only grumble
I am not blind or deaf enough for peace.
I have seen splendid young fools cheat themselves
Into a prophet's frenzy; I have seen
So many crazèd shadows puffed away,   295
And conscious cheats with such an ache for fame
They'd make a bonfire of themselves to be
Mouthed in the squares, broad in the public eye.
And whose backs break, whose lives are mauled, after
It all falls flat? His tender airs chill me   300
As thoughts of sleep to a man tip-toed night-long
Roped round his neck, for sleep means death to him.
Oh! he is kind to us!
Your safe teeth chatter when they hear a step.
He left them yours, because his cunning way   305
Would brag the wrong against his humane act
By Pharaoh; so gain more favour than he lost.
YOUNG HEB. Help him not then, and push your safety away.
I for my part will be his backward eye,
His hands when they are shut. Ah! Abinoah!   310
Like a bad smell from the soul of Moses dipt
In the mire of lust, he hangs round him.
And if his slit-like eyes could tear right out
The pleasure Moses on his daughter had,
She'd be as virgin as ere she came nestling   315
Into that fierce unmanageable blood,
Flying from her loathed father. O, that slave
Has hammered from the anvil of her beauty
A steel to break his manacles. Hard for us,
Moses has made him overseer. O, his slits   320
Pry—pry...for what...to sell to Imra...
                 (ABINOAH *is seen approaching*)
Sh! the thin-lipped abomination!
Zig-zagging hashish tours in a fine style.

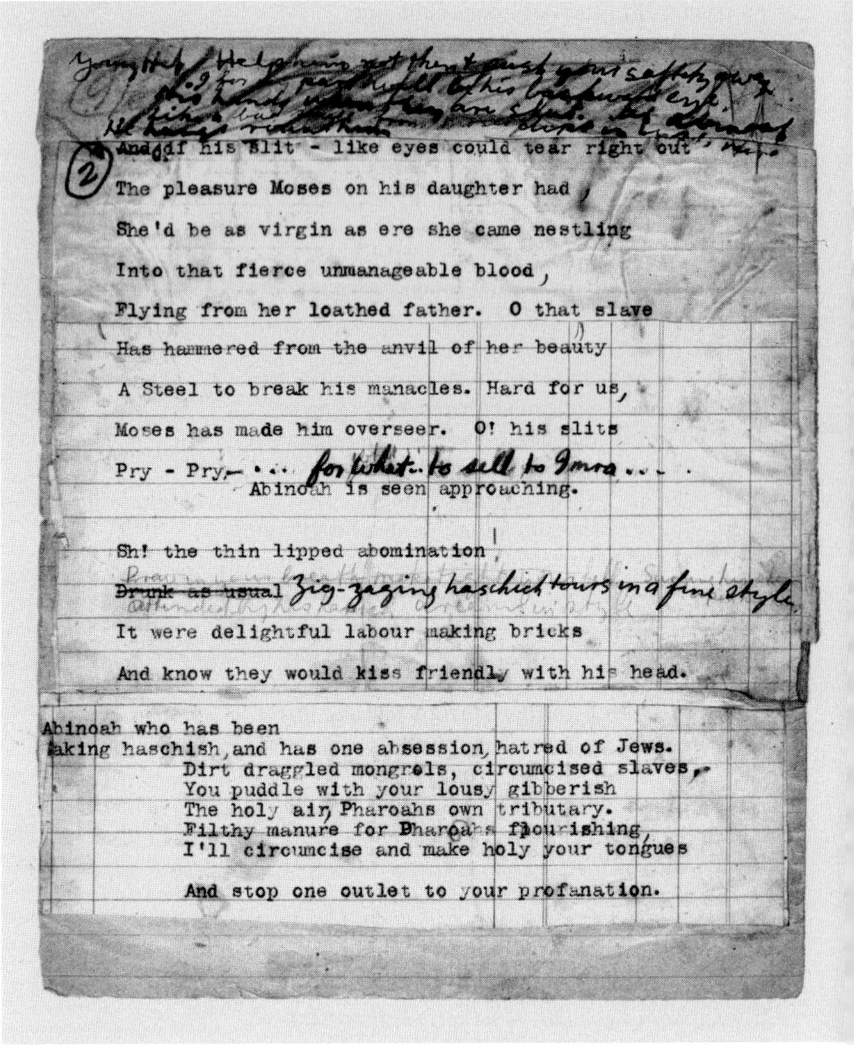

And if his slit - like eyes could tear right out
The pleasure Moses on his daughter had,
She'd be as virgin as ere she came nestling
Into that fierce unmanageable blood,
Flying from her loathed father. O that slave
Has hammered from the anvil of her beauty
A Steel to break his manacles. Hard for us,
Moses has made him overseer. O! his slits
Pry - Pry, ... for what.. to sell to Imra... .
Abinoah is seen approaching.

Sh! the thin lipped abomination,
~~Drunk as usual~~ Zig-zaging haschich tours in a fine style
It were delightful labour making bricks
And know they would kiss friendly with his head.

Abinoah who has been
making haschish, and has one obsession, hatred of Jews.
Dirt draggled mongrels, circumcised slaves,
You puddle with your lousy gibberish
The holy air, Pharoahs own tributary.
Filthy manure for Pharoahs flourishing,
I'll circumcise and make holy your tongues
And stop one outlet to your profanation.

FIG. 7 *Moses*, p. 14 (ll. 308–31) of an incomplete typescript with ink and pencil alterations.

It were delightful labour making bricks
And know they would kiss friendly with his head. 325
ABINOAH (*who has been taking hashish, and has one obsession,*
hatred of Jews)
Dirt-draggled mongrels, circumcised slaves.
You puddle with your lousy gibberish
The holy air, Pharaoh's own tributary,
Filthy manure for Pharaoh's flourishing,
I'll circumcise and make holy your tongues, 330
And stop one outlet to your profanation.
(*To the* OLD HEBREW)
I have never seen one beg so for a blow,
Too soft am I to resist such entreaty.
(*Beats him*)
Your howling holds the earnest energies
You cheat from Pharaoh when you make his bricks. 335
(*An aged* MINSTREL *sings from a distance*)
MINSTREL Taut is the air and tied the trees.
The leaves lie as on a hand.
God's unthinkable imagination
Invents new tortures for nature.

And when the air is soft and the leaves 340
Feel free and push and tremble,
Will they not remember and say
How wonderful to have lived?
(*The* OLD HEBREW *is agitated and murmurs*)
OLD HEB. Messiah, Messiah... that voice...
O, he has beaten my sight out... I see 345
Like a rain about a devouring fire...
(*The* MINSTREL *sings*)
MINSTREL Ye who best God awhile,—O, hear, your wealth
Is but His cunning to make death more hard.
Your iron sinews take more pain in breaking.
And he has made the market for your beauty 350
Too poor to buy although you die to sell.
OLD HEB. I am crazed with whips... I hear a Messiah.
YOUNG HEB. The venerable man will question this.
ABINOAH (*overhearing*) I'll beat you more, and he'll question
The scratchiness of your whining; or may be, 355

Thence may be born deep argument
With reasons from philosophy
That this blow, taking longer, yet was but one,
Or perhaps two; or that you felt this one . . .
Arguing from the difference in your whine   360
Exactly, or not, like the other.
MINSTREL You labour hard to give pain.
ABINOAH (*Still beating*) My pain is . . . not . . . to labour so.
MINSTREL What is this greybeard worth to you now.
All his dried up blood crumbled to dust.   365
　　(*Motions* ABINOAH *to desist, but not in time to prevent the old man*
　　　　fainting into the hands of the YOUNG HEBREW)
ABINOAH Harper, are you envious of the old fool?
Go! hug the rat who stole your last crumbs,
And gnawed the hole in your life which made time wonder
Who it was saved labour for him the next score of years.
We allowed them life for their labour—they haggled.   370
Food they must have—and, god of laughter! even ease;
But mud and lice and Jews are very busy
Breeding plagues in ease.
　　　　(*The* MINSTREL *pulls his beard and robe off*)
Moses!
MOSES You drunken rascal!   375
ABINOAH A drunken rascal! Isis! hear the Prince.
Drunken with duty, and he calls me rascal.
MOSES You may think it your duty to get drunk!
But get yourself bronze claws before
You would be impudent.   380
ABINOAH When a man's drunk he'll kiss a horse or king,
He's so affectionate. Under your words
There is strong wine to make me drunk; you think,
The lines of all your face say, 'Her father, Koelue's father'.
MOSES This is too droll and extraordinary.   385
I dreamt I was a prince, a queer droll dream,
Where a certain slave of mine, a thing, a toad,
Shifting his belly, showed a diamond
Where he had lain. And a blind dumb messenger
Bore syllabled messages soaked right through with glee.   390
I paid the toad—the blind man; afterwards
They spread a stench and snarling. O, droll dream!

I think you merely mean to flatter me
You subtle knave, that, more than prince, I'm *man*,
And worth to listen to your bawdy breath.   395
ABINOAH Yet my breath was worth your mixing with.
MOSES A boy at college flattered so by a girl
Will give her what she asks for.
ABINOAH Osiris! burning Osiris!
Of thee desirable, for thee, her hair . . .   400
       (*He looks inanely at* MOSES, *saying to himself*)
Prince Imra vowed his honey-hives and vineyards.
Isis! to let a Jew have her for nothing.
       (*He sings under his breath*)

    Night by night in a little house
    A man and woman meet.
    They look like each other,   405
    They are sister and brother;
    And night by night at that same hour
    A king calls for his son in vain.

MOSES (*to himself*) So sister Miriam, it is known, then. Slave,
    you die.
(*Aloud*) O, you ambiguous stench.   410
You'll be more interesting as a mummy
I have no doubt.
ABONOAH I'm drunk, yes—drenched with the thought
Of a certain thing. (*Aside*) I'll sleep sounder tonight
Than all the nights I've followed him about.   415
Worrying each slight clue, each monosyllable
To give the word to Imra. The prince is near,
And Moses' eyes shall blink before next hour
To a hundred javelins. I'll tease him till they come.
(*Aloud*) On Koelue's tears I swam to you, in a mist   420
Of her sighs I hung round you,
As in some hallucination I've been walking
A white waste world, we two only in it.
MOSES Doubtless the instinct baulked to bully the girl,
Making large gapings in your hashish dreams,   425
Led you to me, in whom she was thoroughly lost.
Pah! you sicken me.
      (*He is silent awhile then turns away*)

ABINOAH Prince Imra is Pharaoh's choice now, and Koelue's.

(MOSES *turns back menacingly*)

MOSES Silence, you beast!

(*He changes his tone to a winning softness*)

I hate these family quarrels, it is so   430
Like fratricide. I am a rebel, well!
Soft! You are not, and we are knit so close.
It would be shame for a son to be so honoured
And the father still unknown. Come, Koelue's (so *my*) father.
I'll tell my plans. You'll beg to be rebel, then,   435
Look round on the night,
Old as the first, bleak, even her wish is done,
She has never seen (though dreamt perhaps of the sun,)
Yet only dawn divides; could a miracle
Destroy the dawn, night would be mixed with light,   440
No night or light would be, but a new thing.
So with these slaves, who perhaps have dreamt of freedom,
Egypt was in the way, I'll strike it out
With my ways curious and unusual.
I have a trouble in my mind for largeness,   445
Rough-hearted, shaggy, which your grave ardours lack.
Here is the quarry quiet for me to hew,
Here are the springs, primeval elements,
The roots' hid secrecy, old source of race,
Unreasoned reason of the savage instinct.   450
I'd shape one impulse through the contraries
Of vain ambitious men, selfish and callous,
And frail life drifters, reticent, delicate.
Litheness thro' bulk; a nation's harmony.
These are not lame, nor bent awry, but placeless   455
With the rust and stagnant. All that's low I'll charm;
Barbaric love sweeten to tenderness.
Cunning run into wisdom, craft turn to skill.
Their meanness threaded right and sensibly
Change to a prudence, envied and not sneered.   460
Their hugeness be a driving wedge to a thing,
Ineffable and useable, as near
Solidity as human life can be.
So grandly fashion these rude elements
Into some newer nature, a consciousness   465

Like naked light seizing the all-eyed soul,
Oppressing with its gorgeous tyranny
Until they take it thus—or die.

*(While speaking he places his hand on the unsuspecting Egyptian's
head and gently pulls his hair back (caressingly), until his chin is
above his forehead and holds him so till he is suffocated.*

In the darkness ahead is seen the glimmer of javelins and spears.

It is Prince Imra's cohorts come to arrest MOSES).

Moses I

ONE-ACT VERSION (1915)

MOSES *An Egyptian Prince*
ABINOAH *An Overseer*
TWO HEBREWS

Scene before Thebes. A pyramid is being built. Priests and taskmasters.
Hebrews bearing burdens. TWO HEBREWS *are seen whispering.*

IST HEBREW But he, the father of this venture
Against our masters, is their foster child.
His flesh is wild, and we will suffer for it.
2ND HEBREW I have seen men hugely and large proportioned
In spirit, of such noble indignation,   5
Accoutred to no credence of the times;
Lodgings of swift barbaric tenderness,
Wherein the towers of Babel found a top,
Whose ears were prest against Jehovah's mouth,
But all were cripples to this mettled speed   10
Constrained to the stables of proud flesh.
The streaming vigours of his fire-forced blood,
Tempered by high august philosophies,
From his halt tongue is like an anger thrust
Out of a madman's piteous craving for   15
A monstrous baulked perfection.
IST HEB. He is a prince pampered in palaces,
And such division in his splendid sphere
Rolls that from ours; what can he know of ours?
2ND HEB. Nine months he drew the dreaming years to him   20
As dark in antenatal womb he lay
Papped with the life of Abram's prophecy.
We trodden careless under
The riding pomp of heavy handed years,
Have pierced him with our pain a tunneled way   25
Back to the springs of being, his blood's old source.
He has the deep schools drained of their brain ore,
And his desires are fleets of sunbright treasure
Sailing mistrust to find the frank eyed ports.
He fears our fear and tampers for our assent   30

To lift the temperate level of our hopes,
So politic, his tense brows search our toil,
As purposing some loose machinic laws
To perfect, or some builded base to touch,
With prophecy and wisdom, bettering it.   35
Sleek ambush mild! For covert under council
Peer muffled meanings, doubled-tongued words,
Like doubtful sounds scarce heard; terror in you
Forces your eyes into his covertly
To search his searching. Startled into life   40
The dead desires seek for some shape of trust.
2ND HEB. But others watch that shape to read distrust.
Here's Abinoah follows him about.
And if his slit-like eyes could tear right out
The pleasure Moses on his daughter had   45
She'd be as virgin as ere she came nestling
Into that fierce unmanageable blood
Flying from her loathed father. O that slave
Has hammered on the anvil of her beauty
A steel to break his manacles. Hard for us   50
Moses has made him overseer. O his slits
Pry—pry—
             (ABINOAH *is seen approaching*)
Sh! the thin lipped abomination!
It were delightful labour making bricks
And know they would kiss friendly with his head.   55
ABINOAH Dirt draggled mongrels, circumcised slaves!
You puddle with your lousy gibberish
The holy air, Pharaoh's own tributary.
Filthy manure for Pharaoh's flourishing.
I'll circumcise and holy make your tongues,   60
And stop one outlet to your profanation.
I've never seen one beg so for a blow.
Too soft am I to resist entreaty so. (*Beats him*)
Your howling holds the earnest energies
You cheat from Pharaoh when you make his bricks.   65
             (MOSES *is heard from a distance singing*)
MOSES   A naked African
            Walked in the sun

Singing singing
Of his wild love.

'I slew the tiger   70
With your young strength
(My tawny panther)
Rolled round my life.

'Three sheep, your breasts
And my head between   75
Grazing together
On a smooth slope.'

HEBREW Here comes one will ask you a question.
ABINOAH I'll beat you more and he'll question
   The scratchiness of your whining, or maybe,   80
   Thence might be born some learned argument
   Riched with deep reasons from philosophy,
   That this was one or two blows, or your felt
   This like the other.
MOSES You labour hard to give pain.   85
ABINOAH My pain is not to labour so.
MOSES But he is grey and all his dried-up blood
   Is crumbling in your hands to dust.
ABINOAH We buy their labour with a lease of life,
   And they would haggle, want ease.   90
   What do the locusts with their stinking ease?
   The mud, the lice are busy breeding plagues
   In ease.
MOSES You drunken rascal.
ABINOAH A drunken rascal is your father then.   95
   Give back his daughter to the drunken rascal.
MOSES Remember that your rod is in your hands
   But what you are in mine. Because you're dung
   Out of which grew a lovely rose for me.
   Because you're like some blind deaf messenger   100
   That bore a shining message for my ear.
   I put the rod in your hands for that service.
   Now you are impudent and scratch at me.
   What wrong by these, o'er rides obsequiousness
   To sting you to forget—or subtly meanst   105
   This flattery—more than prince I'm man,

And worth to listen to all braggart breath.
ABINOAH You thought my breath worth fouling with your lust,
  I am a man also, a father, prince.
  Or was mere man until you honoured me   110
  And mixed your princely blood and made me
  The father of a prince's concubine.
  I was a father till you stole my daughter.
MOSES A boy at college flattered by a girl
  Will give her what she asks for.   115
ABINOAH No love but hatred of Egypt made you
  Steal love that should be Egypt's. I know
  A story of a bark by rushes placed
  Cunningly to attract where naked girls
  Sang to a barren princess and the Nile   120
  Flowed by, as clean as Egypt's royal blood.
  You hate the Egyptians and would ruin Pharaoh
  As my poor girl. This slave you hate me beat
  Is more my Father than is Pharaoh yours.
  I beat all with that thought.   125
MOSES I'll smudge your life out like a bug's.
ABINOAH Why should I fear? If you were Pharaoh's son,
  You have in mind should make you fear, not me.
  Your frequent hooded whispers amongst these,
  And loose words dropt, and quick looks backward cast;   130
  The strained aspect and dissimulation,
  These are your own accusers.
  Your fearful wrong to me making me mad
  To shadow you, to drain in some strange way
  The smirch you made, the good you drew in you;   135
  I have found you plotting your own dreadful ruin.
MOSES You have marvellous skill to move me.
ABINOAH She was my child.
MOSES Your dog you mean. You beater of girls and old men.
  Why do I vindicate myself to you?   140
  You blind rod in the throned hand of kings.
  Can I give to the blind eyes of your brain
  Clear light? Your pigmy spirit denies
  Stature above it, in its narrow mould
  Pens the infinite, and in its denseness muds   145
  All sunlike actions and original.
  Your private anger would turn to my hurt,

'Neath justices' colour my unusual means.
I would be skilled in arts of government
And shape one impulse thro' the contraries   150
Of vain ambitious men, selfish and callous,
And frail, life-drifting natures, reticent,
Litheness thro' bulk—nation's grand harmony.
Here are the springs—primeval elements;
The roots' hid secrecy, old source of race.   155
Unreasoned reason of the savage instinct.
And can all Thebes deepest teach me more?
So, doctor-like I'd force from these wild herbs
Virtues more potent than we know on earth,
Barbaric love to bring forth tenderness.   160
Cunning, to nurture wisdom, wise desires.
Meanness enlarged to prudence, timely brave.
And hugeness be a driving wedge to truth.
Thus rude elements I would grandly fashion
Into some newer nature, a consciousness   165
Like naked light seizing the all-eyed soul,
Oppressing with its gorgeous tyranny
Until they take it thus—or die.

*Places his hand on the unsuspecting Egyptian's head and gently pulls
his hair back until his chin is above his forehead and holds him so till
he is suffocated.*

The Amulet

LILITH
SAUL
AMAK
NUBIAN

SCENE I

LILITH *sits under the pomegranate trees watching* AMAK *playing with his father's helm and spear. A light smoke is ascending from the chimney of the hut, and through the doorway a naked* NUBIAN *man is seen stirring the embers.* SAUL *sleeps.*

LILITH Amak, you'll break your father's sleep.
Come here and tell me what those spices are
This strange man bakes our cakes with.
It makes the brain wild. Be still, Amak.
I'll give you the strange man your father brought today   5
And he will run with you upon his back.
Come from your father or you'll get no cake;
He's been a long journey.
Bring me the pictured book he brought for you.
What! already cut to pieces.   10
Put away that horn from your father's ear
And stay that horrid noise. Come, Amak.
  (AMAK *runs to his mother with a jade amulet, shouting,*)
AMAK Look mother what I've found.
  (*He runs back again making great shouts*)
LILITH It dances with my blood. When my eyes caught it first
I was like lost, and yearned and yearned and yearned   15
And strained like iron to stay my head from falling
Upon that beggar's breast where this jade stone hung.
Perhaps the spirit of Saul's young love lies here
Strayed far and brought back by this stranger so.
Saul said his discourse was more deep than heaven.   20
For the storm trapped him ere he left the town
Loaded with our week's victuals. The slime clung
And licked and clawed and chewed the clogged dragging wheels
Till they sunk nigh to the axle. Saul sodden and vexed

Like fury smote the mules' mouths, pulling but sweat   25
From his drowned hair and theirs, while the thunder knocked
And all the air yawned water, falling water,
And the light cart was water, like a wrecked raft,
And all seemed like a forest under the ocean.
Sudden the lightning flashed upon a figure   30
Moving as a man moves in the slipping slime
But singing not as a man sings thro the storm,
Which could not drown his sounds. Saul bawled to him,
And the man loomed, naked vast, and gripped the wheels.
Saul fiercely dug from under. He tugged the wheels,   35
The mules foamed, straining, straining,
Sudden they went.
Saul and the man leapt in, Saul miserably sodden
Marvelled at the large cheer in a naked gleaming glistening man.
And soon fell in with that contented mood,   40
That when this hut's light broke on his new mind
He could not credit it. Too soon it seemed
The strange man's talk was witchery.
I pray his baking be as magical.
The cakes should be nigh burnt.   45

(*She calls the* NUBIAN. *He answers from within*)

NUBIAN They are laid by to cool, housewife.
LILITH Bring me a sherbet from the ledge and the fast-dried figs.

(*The* NUBIAN *brings sherbet and figs and a bowl of ice, and lays it
down. She looks curiously at him. He is an immense Nubian with
squat, mule-skinned features. His jet-black curled beard, crisp hair,
glistening nude limbs, appear to her like some heathen idol of ancient
stories. She thinks to herself*)

Out of the lightning
In a dizzying cloven wink
This apparition stood up,   50
Of stricken trunk or beast's spirit,
Stirred by Saul's blasphemies.
So his heart feared aghast.
But lo! he touched the mischance and life ran straight.
Was it the storm-spirit, storm's pilot   55
With all the heaving debris of Noah's sunken days
Dragged on his loins;
Law's spirit wandering to us

Through Nature's anarchy,
Wandering towards us when the Titans yet were young?   60
Perhaps Moses and Buddha he met.
                    (*She speaks aloud*)
The shadow of these pomegranate boughs
Is sweet and restful. Sit and ease your feet.
Eat of these figs.
You have journeyed long?   65
NUBIAN All my life, housewife.
LILITH You have seen men and women,
    Soaked yourself in powers and old glories,
    In broken days and tears and glees,
    And touched cold hands,   70
    Hands shut in pitiless trance where the feast is high.
    I think there is more sorrow in the world
    Than man can bear.
NUBIAN None can exceed their limit, lady.
    You either bear or break.   75
LILITH Can one choose to break? To bear,
    To wearily bear is misery.
    Beauty is this corroding malady.
NUBIAN Beauty is a great paradox.
    Music's secret soul creeping about the senses   80
    To wrestle with man's coarser nature.
    It is hard when beauty loses.
LILITH I think beauty is a bad bargain made of life.
    Men's iron sinews hew them room in the world
    And use deceits to gain them trophies.   85
    O when our beauty fails us did we not use
    Deceits, where were our room in the world?
    Only our room in the world.
    Are not the songs and devices of men
    Moulds they have made after my scarlet mouth   90
    Of cunning words and haughty contours of bronze,
    And viols and gathered air.
    They without song have sung me
    Boldly and shamelessly.
    I am no wanton, no harlot.   95
    I have been pleased and smiled my pleasure.
    I am a wife with a woman's natural ways.
    Yet thro the shadow of these pomegranates

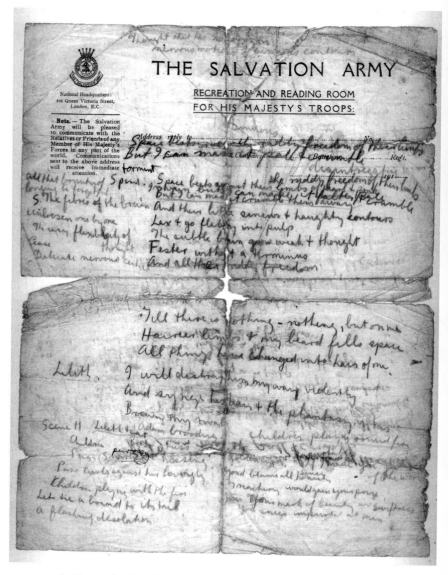

FIG. 8 *The Amulet*. Pencil draft, written on Salvation Army paper supplied to the troops on the Western Front. The state of the manuscript, damaged by mud, water, and wear, gives an idea of the conditions under which Rosenberg often worked.

Filters a poison day by day,
And to a malady turns   100
The blonde, the ample music of my hair.
Inward to eat my heart
My thoughts are worms that suck my softness all away.
I watch the dumb eyeless hours
Drop their tears, their shapeless moaning drop.   105
Unfathomable is my mouth's dream
Do not men say?
So secret are my far eyes
Weaving for iron men profound subtleties.

Sorceress they name me,   110
And my eyes harden, and they say
How may those eyes know love
If God made her without a heart?

Her tears, her moaning,
Her sad profound gaze,   115
The disheveled lustres of her hair
Moon-storm like, they say,
These are her subtleties, men say.
My husband sleeps.
The ghosts of my virgin days do not trouble him.   120
His sleep can be overlong,
For there is that in my embers,
Pride and blushes of fire, the outraged blood,
His sleep makes me remember.

Sleep! hairy hunter, sleep!   125
You are not hungry more
Having fed on my deliciousness.
Your sleep is not adultery to me,
For you were wed to a girl
And I am a woman.   130
My lonely days are not whips to my honour.
        (*She dries her tears with her hair, then fingers the amulet
                        at her throat*)
Yours, friend.
NUBIAN (*eagerly*) My amulet! my amulet! (*He speaks gravely*)
    Small comfort is counsel to broken lives,
    But tolerance is medicinal.   135
    In all our textures are loosed

Pulses straining against strictness
Because an easy issue lies therefrom.
(Could they but slink past the hands holding whips
To hunt them from the human pale 140
Where is the accident to cover; spite fears bias.)
I am justified at my heart's plea;
He is justified also.

For the eyes of vanity are sleepless, are suspicious,
Are mad with imaginings 145
Of secret stabs in words, in looks, in gestures.
Man is a chimera's eremite
That lures him from the good kindness of days
Which only asks his willingness.

There is a crazed shadow from no golden body 150
That poisons at the core
What smiles may stray.
It mixes with all God-ancestralled essences
And twists the brain and heart.
This shadow sits in the texture of Saul's being 155
Mauling your love and beauty with its lies;
I hold a power like light to shrivel it
There, in your throat's hollow that green jade.

(*He snatches at it as she lets if fall. He grows white and troubled,
and walks to where* AMAK *is playing and sees minutely strewn pieces
of paper. He mutters.*)

Lost—lost.
The child has torn the scroll in it 160
And half is away. It cannot be spelt now.
The mould of it is in an ancient world
Unhaunted by illusions. Far and not far.
LILITH God, restore me his love.
Ah! Well! 165
(*She rises*)
I will go now prepare our evening meal
And waken my lost husband, my lover once.
NUBIAN (*musing*) The lightning of the heavens
Lifts an apocalypse.
The dumb night's lips are seared and wide. 170
The world is reeling with sound.

Was I deaf before, mute, tied?
What shakes here from lustral-seeded pomegranates
Not in the great world
More vast and terrible?   175
What is this ecstasy in form,
This lightning
That found the lightning in my blood,
Searing my spirit's lips?
Aghast and naked   180
I am flung in the abyss of days
And the void is filled with rushing sound
From pent eternities.
I am strewn as the cypher is strewn.
A woman—a soft woman!   185
Our girls have hair
Like heights of night ringing with never-seen larks,
Or blindness dim with dreams.
Here is a yellow tiger gay that blinds your night,
Mane—Mane—Mane!   190
Your honey spilt round that small dazzling face
Shakes me to golden tremors.
I have no life at all,
Only thin golden tremors.
Light tender beast!   195
Your fragile gleaming wrists
Have shook the scaled glaciers from under me,
And bored into my craft
That is now with the old dreamy Adam
With other things of dust.   200
LILITH   You lazy hound. See my poor child.

(*He turns to see* LILITH *drop the bowl of cakes and run to* AMAK *who is crying, half stifled under* SAUL*'s huge shield.* SAUL *opens his eyes.*)

The Unicorn

SAUL

LILITH

TEL

ENOCH

UMUSOL (The Unicorn)

*Scene. A track through a woody place. Against the hedge is a half
sunk wagon in a quagmire. The mules stand shivering.* SAUL *sits with
his head between his knees. Thunder and lightning.*

SAUL Ah! miserable! miserable!
  Is it gone . . . oooooh! that wild might of wind
  Still howling in my ears . . . the glittering beast.
  If I look up and see it over me
  I will shrink up . . . I cower, I quail;   5
  I am a shivering grass in a chill wind.
  There is no mortal terror . . . spectres wail.
  Stricken trunks and beasts' spirits wail across to mine
  And whirl me, strew me, pass and repass me:
  Let me look up; break this unnatural fear.   10
  Ah God! Ah God! what black thing towers towards me
  Wailing . . .
      (*A young man on horseback sweeps past, crying in
      a despairing voice, 'Dora, Dora!'*)
  Is there no end? murderers are suffered to die.
  What have I done, these ghosts that seek their loves
  The fearful unicorn has devoured, pass me   15
  As if I was the road to it.
  It has breathed on me, and I must reek of it,
  Twice have I seen the flaring thing.
  My life stormed in the wind of this.
  And always wailing, wails and floats away.   20
  The shouts of women and the wail of men.
  How chilled my spirit is, how clutched with terror.
  Lilith, my Lilith.
  Like my hands in the membranes of my brain
  To pluck your blonde hair out.   25
  I'll run to you. I totter. A wavering wall
  Against me is the air; what pulls me back?

God! in that dizzying flash I saw just now
Phantoms and nomads
And balls of fire pursuing   30
A panting streaming maenad.
What ghosts be these so white and mute?
Stay... Stay... Ah miserable
That crash... thunder... no...
O God it falls on me.   35
My brain gives way; look, look...

    (*The* UNICORN *flashes by, lit by lightning, and a voice calls
'Umusol'.* SAUL *sinks moaning and shivering against a tree.*)
Ooowe... Ooowe... I sink.
A breath will lift me up and scatter me.
My name was wailed and all my tissues
Untwined and fell apart.   40
Sick... Sick... I will lie down and die. How can I die?
Kind lightning, sweetest lightning, cleave me through,
Lift up these shreds of being and mix me with
This wind, this darkness.
I'll strive once more. See how the wheels are sunk   45
Right to the axle... Ah impotent puny me...
Vain! Futile!
Hi hi hi hi! is there no man about.
Who would be wandering in a storm like this?
Hark... was that a human voice?   50
Sh!... when that crash ceases.
Like laughter... like laughter.
Sure that was laughter... just the laughter of ours.
Hi hi hi hi hihi...
My voice fears me.   55
God cover my eyes.

    (*The* UNICORN *rushes by and when he looks up again, his hair
stands up. A naked black giant stands there and signs for* SAUL*'s hand.
Mechanically as in a trance,* SAUL *gives his hand and together they
heave and lift the wheels. The mules suddenly start;* SAUL *is lifted into
the cart and the black drives. The exertion has revived* SAUL *who is
    thinking of the warm humanlike grasp of the hand in his.*)
Why quails my heart? God riding with
A mortal would absorb him.
He touched my hand, here is my hand the same.

Sure I am whirled in some dark phantasy   60
A dizzying cloven wink, the beast, the black,
And I ride now ... ride, ride, the way I know
That rushing terror ... I shudder yet
The haughty contours of a swift white horse
And on its brows a tree, a branching tree,   65
And on its back a golden girl bound fast.
It glittered by
And all the phantoms wailing.
Then sudden, here I ride
His monstrous posture, why his necks turn   70
Were our thews adventures some Amazon's son doubtless
From the dark countries. Can it be
That storm spirit, storm's pilot
With all the heaving debris of Noah's sunken days
Dragged on his loins.   75
What have I lived and agonised today, today.
It seems long centuries since I went to the town
For our weeks victuals, and I saw the beast
And rode into the town a shaken ghost,
Not Saul at all, but something that was Saul   80
And saw folk wailing; and men that could not weep.
And my heart utterance was Lilith,
Whose face seemed cast in faded centuries
While the beast was rushing back towards her
Sweeping past me leaving me with the years.   85
Mere human travail never broke my spirit
Only my throat to impatient blasphemies.
But God's unthinkable imagination
Invents new tortures for nature
Whose wisdom falters here.   90
No used experience can break, make aware
The imminent unknowable.
Sudden destruction
Till the stricken soul wails in anguish
Torn here and there.   95
Man could see and live never believed.
I ride ... I ride ... thunder crowned
In the sheltering of a glist'ning chanting giant,
What flaring chaunt the storm's undertones
Full of wild yearning,   100

And makes me think of Lilith
And that swift beast, it went that way.
My house my blood all lean to its weird flight
But Lilith will be sleeping... ah miss my Lilith.
Swifter my mules swifter   105
Destroy the space... transport me instantly
For my soul yearns and fears.
TEL How his voice fears... If I strove utterance
What fear would be in mine
I saw her... I fled... he brings me back.   110
Umusol... a golden mane shall mingle with your horns
Before the storm shall cease.
SAUL Yonder, my house is yonder.
I feared to see it vanished
On the ground from Lilith.   115
TEL The powered storm means such devastation (I dread to
enter)
Yet my soul hungers so intense.

(SAUL *springs from the cart and hurries into the room where* LILITH *sits
white and terror stricken, wringing her hands.*)

LILITH Pity me. Where is Saul...
Do not touch me.
SAUL Lilith dear, look up, it is me.   120
LILITH Saul, oh Saul, do not go away,
Who is that?

(SAUL *kisses her.*)

SAUL How frightened you are...
See, where I sunk in the mire, the mud,
His was the healing hand.   125
Lilith, your viol
To force this gloom away even while I dry
In the inner chamber.
I am dank and tired.
LILITH Saul do not leave me!   130
I dread to look up and see again
Two balls of fire casement glaring.
SAUL This is some fantasy: play music till I come.

(TEL *crouches in the shadow and she turns to take the viol down*)

LILITH The roots of a torn universe are wrenched,

See the bent trees like nests of derelicts in ocean   135
That beats upon this ark.
TEL   Unearthly accents float amid the howling storm.
Her mouth moves... is it thence...
Secret Mother of my orphan spirit
Who art thou?   140
LILITH   I think he speaks, this howling storm sheets out all so.
I'll play and ease my heavy heart.
TEL   Was that the lightning?
These fragile gleaming wrists untangle me,
Those looks tread out my soul.   145
Somewhere I know those looks, I lost it somewhere.

           (LILITH *draws nearer and sings softly*)

LILITH   Beauty is music's secret soul
Creeping about man's senses.
He cannot hold it or know it ever,
But yearns and yearns to hold it once.   150
Ah! when he yearns not, shall he not wither?
For music then will have no place
In the world's ear, but mix in windless darkness.
TEL   Am I gone blind?
I swim in a white haze.   155
What shakes my life to golden tremors?
I have no life at all... I am a crazed shadow
From a golden body
That melts my iron flesh, I flow from it.
I know the haze, the light   160
I am a shuddering pulse
Hung over the abyss. I shall look up
Even if I fall, fall, fall, fall forever.
I faint, tremble.
LILITH   Still the rain beats and beats.   165

        (TEL *looks up furtively, then prostrates himself*)

TEL   Ah woe, ah woe. (*He sobs*)
LILITH   Has lightning turned his brain?
Is this a maniac? Saul, Saul.
TEL   Hear me, hear me.
Do I speak, or think I speak,   170
I am so faint... Wait!

Let my dazed blood resolve itself to words.
Where have I strayed incomprehensible?
Yet here ... somewhere
An instant flashes a large face of dusk   175
Like heights of night ringing with unseen larks
Or blindness dim with dreams.
I hear a low voice ... a crooning,
Some whisperings and shadows vast,
A crying through the forest—wailing.   180
Behind impassable places
Whose air was never warmed by a woman's lips
Bestial man-shapes ride dark impulses
Through roots in the bleak blood, then hide
In shuddering light from their self loathing.   185
They fade in arid light—
Beings unnatured by their craving, for they know
Obliteration's spectre. They are few.
They wail their souls for continuity,
And bow their heads and knock their breasts before   190
The many mummies whose wail in dust is more
Than these who cry, their brothers who loiter yet.
Great beasts' and small beasts' eyes have place
As eyes of women to their hopeless eyes
That hunt in bleakness for the dread might   195
The incarnate female soul of generation.
The daughters of any clime are not imagined
Even of their occult ears, senses profound
For their corporeal ears and baby senses
Were borne from gentle voices and gentle forms   200
By men misused flying from misuse
Who gave them suck even from their narrow breasts
Only for this, that they should wither,
That they should be as an uttered sound in the wind.
        (*He sees* SAUL's *smouldering eyes in the doorway.*
                It rouses him.)
By now my men have raided the city,   205
I heard a far shrieking.
LILITH This is most piteous, most fearful,
        (I fear him, his hungry eyes
        Burn into me, like these balls of fire.)
TEL There is a tower of skulls,   210

Where birds make nests
And staring beasts stand by with many flocks
And man looks on with hopeless eyes.
LILITH O horrible, I hear Saul rattle those chains in the cellar.
TEL What clanking chains!   215
  When a man's brains crack with longing
  We chain him to some slender beast to breed.
LILITH Tell me, tell me, who took my cousin Dora,
  Oh God, those balls of fire...
  Are you men...? tell me!   220
TEL Marvellous creature.
  Night tender beast.
LILITH Man... man!
TEL Has the storm passed into me?
  What ecstasy, what lightning!   225
  He touched the lightning in my blood.
  Voluptuous
  Crude vast terrible hunger overpowers...
  A gap... a yawning...
  My blood knocks... inarticulate to make you understand,   230
  To shut you in itself
  Uncontrollable.
          (*He stretches his arms out.*)
Small dazzling face I shut you in my soul.

      (*She shrieks.* SAUL *appears, looking about, dazed, holding an
      iron chain, while the door is burst open and* ENOCH *bursts in.
                  He springs on* TEL.)
SAUL Where is my Dora, where?
  Pity, rider of the Unicorn.   235
TEL Yonder!

      (*Through the casement they see riding under the rainbow a black
      naked host on various animals, the* UNICORN *leading. A woman is
      clasped on every one, some are frantic, others white or unconscious,
      some nestle, laughing.* ENOCH *with madness in his eyes leaps through
      the casement and disappears with a splash into the well.* SAUL
      leaps after him shouting 'The Unicorn'. TEL *places the unconscious*
              LILITH *on the unicorn and they all ride away.*)

Tel's Song

Small dazzling face!
I shut you in my soul;
How can I perish now?

But thence a strange decay,
Your fragile gleaming wrists   5
Waver my days and shakes my life
To golden tremours. I have no life at all
Only thin golden tremours
That shudder over the abyss of days
Which hedged my spirit, my spirit your prison walls   10
That shrunk like phantasms with your vivid beauty.

Towering and widening till
The sad moonless place
Throngs with a million torches
And spears and flaming wings.   15

The Tower of Skulls

Mourners

These layers of piled-up skulls,
These layers of gleaming horror—stark horror!
Ah me! Through my thin hands they touch my eyes.

Everywhere, everywhere is a pregnant birth,
And here in death's land is a pregnant birth.   5
Your own crying is less mortal
Than the amazing soul in your body.

Your own crying yon parrot takes up
And from your empty skulls cries it afterwards.

Thou whose dark activities unenchanted   10
Days from gyrating days, suspending them
To thrust them far from sight, from the gyrating days
Which have gone widening on and on and left us here,
Cast derelicts for ever.

When aged flesh looks down on tender brood;   15
For he knows between his thin ribs' walls
The giant universe, the interminable
Panorama—synods, myths and creeds,
He knows his dust is fire and seed.

PROSE

On a Door Knocker

This is essentially an age of romance. We no longer dream but we live the dream. Romance is no more a dim world outside the ordinary world, whose inhabitants are only poets and lovers, but wide, tangible and universal. Poets no longer hold exclusive monopoly of the clouds, but whosoever pleases (except the poet generally) can soar aloft on the wings of an aeroplane beyond the reach and ken of man. No longer is it the poet who brags of the rushing chariot of the whirlwind, for he alone is unable to afford a motor. In fact, the positions are reversed. The philistine has become the romanticist, and the poet the philistine; and he actually presumes to deny the purity of their romanticism on the grounds that achieving the ideal destroys the ideal, and the charm of existence is the illusion of it. Wherever we turn we see the unmistakable atmosphere of romance and strangeness, of a delightful incongruity, that might be a Japanese fantasy. The ragged newsboy bartering news and information to the gentleman in the high hat. The gentleman in the high hat benevolently making a picture of himself for us to enjoy the spectacle; and see, this charming young lady decked out as a draper's front window, as if this were some merry carnival. In this age of romance we are bent so profoundly on romancing ourselves that we have little time to notice the romances of others. We read novels, true; but they are Hardy, Zola, Turgenif;° dreadfully realistic, so as to get more zest from the romance of life, by contrast with this ugly realism. Few ever dream of considering—say—the romance of a door knocker. Its romantic pre-existence—its long subterraneous sojourn in purgatorial mines; its awakening to light, and the kingdom of man; the gradual stages of its development, make of it an object supremely romantic. We will take the knocker as it is, and study it in its aspect and relation to modern conditions; it must be worth while, having had such romantic development. We will see how the manners and customs, the tendencies of the age are reflected in the knocker.

A door knocker is the symbol of an unfinished civilization and an aloof and unassertive aristocracy. Its imperiousness is unquestioning, its meek acquiescence to convention a record of the sham of custom. It is the signpost of politeness and the negative to precipitate familiarity. It is a proof of the decay of religion, for it shows our want of faith in man, and consequently of the God in man. What forces are set in motion by it? In our family alone (there are no servants) its summons is generally the signal whereby the entire faculties of the junior members are exerted in tremendous efforts to ignore and despise its imperiousness. Ah! what a type then of power desolate! of man beating at the doors of knowledge and clamouring vainly at the gates of the unseen. And in repose, what a sense of infinite patience and a world of energy lying dormant—useless, like genius when the circumstances to bring it into light are wanting. It is kissed by the sun and rain, by day and by night, and endures the frost and thunder with supreme immovable dignity.

The comparative insignificance of the knocker lies in the fact of its functions being so startlingly obtrusive that the cause itself is obscured; an important contrast to the chimney-pot in this. The chimney-pot glares at you—fixes you. It is the last stage, the final result of a series of causes that only minister to its service; whereas the knocker is the beginning—the cause of a certain result. It is the touchstone of character. How timidly the timid use it! How impetuously the impetuous! How gently the gentle-hearted! Before the knocker all self-consciousness is abandoned and the natural and spontaneous is brought into play. It is a type of prostitution, for it is sold to all men; of helplessness, for it lies where all can wreak their will in it; of power, for it sets great forces in motion; of aristocracy, for it is lordly and imperious; of democracy, for it makes no distinction between low and high; of wealth, for, like gold, it is the means of opening doors at its magic touch. It is the link of fraternity whereby so many of divergent aims and minds touch hands. Sometimes knockers are peculiarly identified with the families of the houses to which they are attached, and the fate and fortune of the knocker is the fate and fortune of the family. In one family I know, whose reverses and ill-fortune were something miraculous, the knocker invariably found its way behind the door, and the only disposition it ever showed to knock when it was in its place was to fall and knock the head off of a millionaire relation, who had just discovered them, and they were obliged to pay for his funeral. In another, the knocker was the cause of suicide. A friend of mine of aesthetic tastes, visiting his affianced, took prejudice to the knocker, because of its exceedingly ugly shape, and so fastidious was he that he would not knock; but finding the door open, and being of that passionate precipitate nature that despises convention, rushed in, and conceive his horror when he beheld his beloved in the embrace of a man (it happened to be her long lost brother just returned), and, infuriated, he dashed out and went straight to the river (not even stopping to pick up his hat) and there ended his sorrows . . . .

A knocker is so enchantingly romantic and real; so human in its pathetic helplessness; so divine in its terrible significance of power, that we might sum up in it the epitome of humanity. Man, with his vast power over destiny, yet controlled by destiny. Man, with death in his hands yet in the hands of death. Power that is powerless. Sleeping mechanism that is ready to leap and crash at a touch.

Thus far we have seen the knocker as a symbol of general tendencies and vitalities of the present, and an important factor in the lives and destinies of individuals. Let us see in it a prophetic far-reaching symbol of the religion of the future. The only serious drawback is its variety of type; but this of course, would depend on the aesthetic leanings and fashions of the future generation. When we consider that the symbol of the Christian religion was erstwhile a sign of degrad-ation, a gallows; how idealism has converted this type of human degradation into a symbol of divine beatific sanctity, does it need a great wrench of credulity to believe a door knocker, which has so tremendous a significance, and is so much more infinitely romantic in form, when culture has finally reached its ultimate emancipation from barbarism, to take its place and stand for the new religion, Christianity with its limitations, its self-sacrifice, its strange mendicant idealisation of poverty, its crown and banner of austere primitive barbarism, the cross;—be a thing that has been; and a religion, generous, large in its conception of humanity, refined yet homely, usurp the vacated throne; the door knocker, its sceptre, when the doors of this new religion have opened to our knocking.

On Noses

It has often struck me as a fact of paramount significance in life that noise, projectivity and ostentation, though always in themselves signs of uselessness and the superficial, are generally the echoes and heralds of the great, the useful and substantial. If we take religion as an instance, or a great cause, like dandyism or woman suffrage, is not the spouting, the shouting, the foppishness but the effervescence, the first dribblings of a solid and profound idea, of an earnest soul-enthralling basis? Nature has constructed each of us, rightly or wrongly, as an individual demonstration of this principle. The apparent important feature, the centre, the arresting portion of the face, the part that stands before all others in singleness of leadership, ostentatious and projecting, is the nose. Wherever it leads the face, the entire body must follow after it. There is no protesting, no argufying, we must endure. The eyes may close in chagrin, mortification, the mouth may howl in disgust, the ears twitch in agony, but still we must endure. Yet what is this apparent leadership? It is only a station it has appropriated to secure a position, a prominence which otherwise it had not got, and it only heralds the will, the larger, the grander beauty of the face. Be that as it may, in itself the nose has dominated. [Its] shape and quality too has exercised remarkable influence on the fate of not only individuals but world movements, conquests, death and life. We owe all our heritage of sin and shame, [we] have evidence in the bible, even at the creation that [it was] the extraordinary length of Eve's nose which lost us the world. Columbus discovered a world for that very same reason, Polonius lost his life [

Rudolph

Poor Rudolph! He was an artist and a dreamer—that is, one whose delight in the beauty of life was an effective obstacle to the achievement of the joy of living; whose desire to refine and elevate mankind seemed to breed in mankind a reciprocal desire to elevate him to a higher and still higher—garret. Though a nearer view of heaven and though a poet, he would have preferred° a less lofty dwelling place to preserve, what he facetiously termed, his ancestor's remains, from the chill November weather—but so it was. In this garret, in the dim waning light, God could see day by day the titanic wrestlings of genius against the exigencies of circumstances, the throbbings of a sensitive organism, touched to emotion at the subtlest changes on the face of nature; the keen delight simply in endeavour, the worship and awe of genius before the altar of genius. But day after day of unrequited endeavour, of struggle and privation, brought depression, and in the heaviness of his spirit the futility of existence was made manifest to him. Often inspiration was dead within, and all his aspirations and ideals seemed to mock at his hollow yearning. In his social and spiritual isolation, in his utter desolation, he felt as if he was God's castaway, out of harmony with the universe, a blot upon the scheme of humanity. Life appeared so chaotic, so haphazard, so apathetic—O! it was miserable. He—a spark struck from God's anvil, he—who could clasp the Heavens with his spirit—to whom beauty had revealed herself in all her radiance—and to what end? What purpose was there is such wasted striving—and supposing success did come would it be sufficient recompense for the wasted life and youth, the starved years—the hopelessness of the barren Now?

In one of these moods he strayed to the National Gallery. It was Students' Day, and he wandered round without being able to concentrate himself on his old loves and longings, till at length he sat down on a seat brooding and revolving 'the fragments of the broken years . . . '. He was awakened from his reverie by hearing a feminine voice saying 'O!' please, don't rise, oblige me.' He looked up and saw a lady at an easel gazing intently at him and painting.

'I am painting the interior and you just happen to fit in well. I won't be many minutes,' she called out to him.

'O! certainly,' murmured Rudolph, 'as long as you like.' She was a pleasant faced lady of about thirty-five, rosy and buoyant, and he wondered what her work would be like. He thought what a strange thing Art was, life was. Around were the masters, to whom Art was life, and life meant Art. Here were the dilettanti to whom Art was a necessity as an alternative to the boredom of doing nothing; an important item in the ingredients that go to make up culture.

She was soon finished and asked Rudolph to see it, which he accordingly did, and was, and expressed himself, greatly struck by the result.

'Dutch in idea and influence and yet exceedingly modern,' he told her.

She assented, and then in a tone of defiant confession 'Do you know I think Van Eyck° the greatest Artist that ever lived. I adore him because he makes the commonplace so delightfully precious.'

'I think a picture should be something more,' protested Rudolph. 'Van Eyck is interesting to me just as a pool reflecting the clouds is interesting, or a landscape seen through a mirror. But it is only a faithful transcript of what we see. My ideal of a picture is to paint what we cannot see. To create, to imagine. To make tangible and real a figment of the brain. To transport the spectator into other worlds where beauty is the only reality. Rossetti is my ideal.'

She smiled, amused at his enthusiasm.

'But why go out of the world for beauty when we can find beauty in it?'

'I admit an artist with imagination might make a most exquisite picture out of what may seem most uncompromising in nature. But it is his imagination, his refinement of sentiment that only uses the object itself as a basis to give expression to his vision. Why then were we given the creative faculty? What, if not this, is the meaning of God?'

The lady laughed. 'I have a nephew who used to think like you, until he saw Degas, and now he raves over the beauty of ugliness. He said to me, "We are all idealists when we are young. We begin in the clouds and as we are slipping away from existence we come nearer to existence in thought and feeling. We are born with wings but we find our feet are safest." Perhaps you have heard of him, Leonard Harris, the poet.'

'Leonard Harris! he could never have said that,' incredulously exclaimed Rudolph, and added: 'Though the expression sounds his. Surely Heaven hasn't got too bright for him.'

'Anyway that's how he talks now. Do you know him?' she asked.

'No, but I should very much like to', he replied eagerly.

"Well, I shall talk to him about you. Are you an artist?' she questioned. 'You certainly have the artistic spirit.'

'I am unfortunately.'

'Why unfortunately? It is a golden gift.'

'A golden gift; but I could not exchange it for a pair of shoe laces if I wanted to. Unless one has the golden means the gift is only one of misery.'

'You are young to be a pessimist.'

'I am not old enough to be an optimist. When I will have experienced occasion for optimism I will be one.'

She looked concerned. 'Dear, dear, you are young to talk like that. I think that if one has the golden means, and everything made smooth for him, one does not try so much; that is why the geniuses are always those who have had great difficulties to contend against.'

He smiled bitterly. 'When one has to think of responsibilities, when one has to think strenuously how to manage to subsist, so much thought, so much energy is necessarily taken from creative work. It might widen experience and develop a precocious mental maturity of thought and worldliness, it might even make one's work more poignant and intense, but I am sure the final result is loss, technical incompleteness, morbidness and the evidence of tumult and conflict.'

'Well, it may be so,' she admitted half doubtingly. 'But you must see my nephew on those matters. I will talk to him and leave you his address in case you'd care to write to him.'

'I'd write this moment. I too am a poet.'

'How nice. Yes! Well, send your poems. I myself am not very poetical in my tastes. In any case you'll hear from me, as I cannot let a sinner so young go on sinning,' she said smilingly as she bade him goodbye.

'Then I shall owe my good fortune to my wickedness. The way of the world, Madam.'

Some time after this Rudolph received a letter from Leonard Harris, to whom he had sent his poems, inviting him to dine with him the following evening. Rudolph immediately wrote back accepting the invitation, and in the elation caused by the turn fortune seemed to be taking with him, rushed off to communicate the wonderful intelligence to a friend.

'And you've accepted the invitation?' his friend asked sceptically.

Rudolph looked at him. 'Why—I never waited to finish reading the letter before I answered.'

His friend shook his head pityingly. 'You Simple Simon. Do you know what a wealthy supper is? Evening dresses, immaculate shirt fronts, diamond pins, and sparkling patent boots. If you don't look as if you'd just stepped out of a fashion plate, you're a pariah, you'll be trampled on, pulverised. And probably the whole family will be there. You haven't even got an ordinary dress. Why, I'd sooner think of dropping through a chimney-pot than going.'

Rudolph rubbed his cheek, perplexed; this view of the case had never presented itself to him.

'Then what shall I do?' he questioned disconsolately. 'Can't you suggest something in my dire extremity? Go I must, even if it's in this', pointing to his transparent alpaca, which had the appearance of a turkish carpet for he had used it as a palette once or twice by mistake.

'Good God! If you can pretend that you mistook the invitation for one to a fancy-dress ball it might work. But I'll tell you what. My landlady, who, as you know, is very sweet on me, possesses a husband, who possesses an evening dress, which God knows what he uses for, unless it's to hide a hole in the wall which they want no one to see; for I've lived there two years and that suit has never shifted. It's in a state of remarkable preservation except for some green paint spots on the shoulder little Madge dropped on [it] when the house was being repaired; but that wouldn't notice in the evening. She'll lend it me if I say it's for myself.'

'Dave, you've saved me. Thou art indeed a friend in need. But you must have a swell landlord.'

'He seems to have some mysterious connections with 'igh society, from what I can make out from his missis. I rarely see him.'

Next day Dave brought the prize round. He had succeeded in borrowing it without much difficulty, but with a caution from the landlady to be careful, as it was a particular favourite of her ole man's, being the one in which he had captivated and conquered his Mary Ann, it being so precious that he would not wear it but look at it only to remind him of their honey days.

The suit was laid out, and Rudolph proceeded to make his entrance into the uniform of a gentleman, into which he completely disappeared. When gradually his limbs one by one emerged from its recesses, and he had managed to extricate his head from the vacuity, he desired to know Dave's unbiased impression as to its decorative qualities. After careful examination from all points of view, Dave delivered judgment to the effect that he thought its decorative qualities immense, but that one was inclined to lose sight of the object it was intended to decorate.

'Do you really think it is slightly too big?' queried Rudolph anxiously; 'I feel somehow I am lost in it. But don't you think it will make me look bigger?'

'It might, if one could see you, but I think we can do it with pins. I expect it'll look a little creasy but it won't notice at night.'

'And these green spots, are they noticeable?'

'O! they won't notice at night.'

'And now, the shirt front. Didn't she have one?'

'Well, he couldn't keep the shirt front for two years. Possibly he might if he had foreseen this emergency. I don't know what to suggest unless we buy one. We may get one at the pawnbroker's shop. You might even exchange your alpaca for one; these stains won't notice in this light.'

Thus arrayed in swallow-tail and shirt front, enveloped by his friend's overcoat, with his portfolio under his arm, and the inevitable sombrero on his head, the transformed Rudolph set out on his way to Harris. This was just the opportunity he desired; now he would assert himself. For one night the evening dress was his, for one night would he revel in the privileges it meant. He felt transformed, transfigured; and in his sense of power he mentally pictured society as a beautiful lady, deferential and smiling, showering flowers and delights... These thoughts were counteracted by a sudden inrush of natural shyness; of embarrassment; and he suddenly felt bewildered and mute in the presence of this beautiful creature. While he listened to her mellifluous voice, masculine voices seemed to respond in rich tones, and elegant forms of perfect ease made him appear to shrink—shrink but unable to escape. 'St John's Wood', he heard the conductor call, and he rushed out just in time. He soon found the house and rang. The servant after inquiring his name asked him to follow and announced him. A young man came out, shook hands and pulled him in. After the preliminaries of introduction and the inevitable weather discussion, Rudolph undid his portfolio and arranged his drawings round the room, then stood by to explain and elucidate where elucidation was necessary, which was not seldom; for he painted on the principle that the art of painting was the art of leaving out, and the pleasure in beholding a picture was the pleasure of finding out. Where he had not left out the whole picture, sometimes it was successful. After he had inculcated Harris with a sense of the sacred supremacy of his principles and proved his principles without justifying his pictures, and bewildered and mystified him into acceptance of his creed with a suspicion of its results, Harris found breath to ejaculate, 'I should say you take more trouble in defending your pictures than in painting them'.

'Yes!' flashed Rudolph. 'A religion may be the conception of a moment but it takes ages to spread. Propaganda is a necessary evil.'

At supper, Mrs Harris asked Rudolph whether his father had literary or artistic propensities. Rudolph smiled, 'The only deviation into artistic endeavour I have ever seen my father make was when he, in a frenzy of inspiration, turned and decorated my left eye most beautifully in blue and black (which decorative effect, unfortunately, I was not in a condition to appreciate, not being able to see it), and he accompanied that extraordinary feat with a fervour of exuberant flowery language. The most complete combination of poetry and painting I have ever experienced. But otherwise our genealogical tree has not many blossoms of genius. I am the first to scandalise the family with a difference. They consider it perfectly immoral to talk and think unlike them—and—well what can I do—they show their sense of superiority by being ashamed of me!'

'Perfectly atrocious,' broke in young Harris. 'But as I am rather interested in heredity I am curious to know whether you acquired your taste for art and literature after or before your father's (private or public) exhibition of his skill.'

'Oh! domestic exhibition. I had always practised it to some extent. I wanted to do a sketch of Romeo and Juliet. I got my father to pose for Romeo, and the servant girl for Juliet. When it was finished my mother came across it and of course thought I had sketched my father kissing the servant girl as I had seen it. Well, I have told you the consequences. It was a practical demonstration of his abhorrence for realism—and preference for decoration. I have altered my style since.'

'A sure proof,' gravely asserted Harris, smothering laughter, 'that the genius of the child is sprung from seed in the parent.'

Rudolph assented. 'But my father also had mature qualifications which have descended to me. I have inherited from him a remarkable genius for taciturnity and an amazing facility for forgetting things. Just now I am exercising the latter to exorcise the former.'

The plates clattered with the laughter: under its cover Miss Lily said sweetly to Rudolph, 'Len says you also write'.

'I am afraid I must plead guilty.'

He almost flushed, while young Harris said, 'You should see his verses, mother, he writes beautifully.'

'Which do you prefer, writing or drawing?' enquired Mrs. Harris.

'Drawing when I must write, writing when I must draw,' replied Rudolph becoming flippant.

'Then you never enjoy either, as you must do what you don't want to do: I condole with you!' sympathised Harris with mock pathos on his face.

'No need!' retorted Rudolph. 'I enjoy my disappointment and laugh at myself.'

From this glimpse of Rudolph we might surmise he was one of those superficial wits who are like bottles of soda-water just being opened, and never open their mouths but to fizzle like a chinese cracker. This apparent superficiality was the natural consequence of a super-self-consciousness, a desire not to frustrate expectation, and a lack of sustaining inspiration to keep up with desire. Constructively and inherently he was serious, because he was an enthusiast;—and because he was an enthusiast the comic in his nature would run riot once begun. Wit is the flash of the knit brows of a refined intellect, capped by the smile of achievement. Superficiality is the easy snatch at wit when the knit brows refuse to work, and in him the comic always strove to snatch: sometimes happy, sometimes not.

Brought up as he had been: socially isolated, but living in spiritual communion with the great minds of all ages, he had developed a morbid introspection in all that related to himself, and a persistent frivolousness in relations with others; a dark book for his bedside and a gaudy one for the street. The development of temperament had bred a disassociation from the general run of the people he came in contact with, that almost rendered him inarticulate when circumstances placed him amongst those of more affinity to himself, from disuse of the ordinary faculties and facilities of conversation. Naturally these circumstances would be such where his vanity suggested he had a reputation to sustain, and he would be perpetually on the strain to say something clever. He was totally lacking in the logic of what might be called common sense, but had a whimsical sort of logic of his own which was amusing till it became too clever, and then—patience was a crime.°

Now although Rudolph was in the conversational mood, and felt that in the small talk of the table he was acquitting himself well, he was not wholly at his ease. Some of the pins of his evening dress had come out and he had a feeling of general discomfort, and that they were all looking at him and eyeing his suit particularly. He was beginning to curse inwardly the artificialities of convention, the forms that bound each man to be a mechanical demonstration of its monotony, extremely aggravated at not having made more sure of the arrangement of his temporary disguise. When they adjourned for coffee he was afraid to rise lest he would disappear and only an evening dress be seen walking about. He held his chair in front of him as he manoeuvred gingerly along.

'And how do you find people take your poetry?' Harris was saying to him. Rudolph sat down. 'My poetry? well I find that the poet is to the mass so respected that they consider his creations too sacred even to look at. It would be profanation to open a book of poems. The beggar who carried a menagerie in his rags and the poet are the most respected characters we have. Veneration is carried so far that contact with them is unthought of.'

'I have not been so fortunate as you in that respect,' replied Harris. 'Since I published my poems I have been practically suffocated by the pressure of contact. I am in the throes of a ———'

He was interrupted by a crash behind. He turned; the butler had dropped the tray with the coffee and was glaring at Rudolph, and his mouth was open in astonishment.

'What is it?' exclaimed Rudolph amazed. 'Surely there is no need to be terrified at so trivial an accident.'

'There is,' broke in Harris. 'It would be an accident if he did not drop it. You are always dropping things, Henry, and—'

'Er—er—I beg pardon, sir,' stammered Henry, and turning to Rudolph, 'I... I... I... you... I don't know how to explain myself—' and he pointed to the suit. 'You are wearing my clothes,' he gasped out.

'Wha... what do you mean?' almost whispered Rudolph, oppressed by vague misgivings.

They all stood by, dumbfounded at the strange scene.

The butler pointed to the spots.

'You see these spots, five of 'em, heart shaped. Those very spots were done by my little niece Madge two years ago. That was the very suit I wore when

[Missing Page]

the crestfallen Rudolph as by degrees he made himself visible. 'My extraordinary choice... my situation rendered... my point of observation was somewhat confusing. I did not notice the ladies.'

They were all laughing uproariously while Rudolph, having recovered his self-possession, explained the situation.

'You see, Henry,' put in Harris, 'Mr. Rudolph was under the impression that he was going to a fancy-dress ball, and he borrowed the suit on account of the spots from your lodger.'

Rudolph interposed. 'I'm sorry, Henry, that your wife has suffered on my account, and I hope you feel more comfortable in your property than I do. And I can't help thinking that if you had paid more attention to your property, and not allowed those spots to find their way on, there would have been no necessity for this disturbance. Besides, your latest additions in coffee stains, although they may be very creditable to your decorative capabilities, do not show a just sense of the relative values of time and place. It positively destroys the harmony. However, Henry, I forgive you.'

It was two hours past midnight when he got out into the street and he experienced a wonderful feeling of rejuvenation. The air was tingling and pure, and he walked under the limpid heaven as under a vague, vast tree. The golden lamplights hung in narrowing perspective and shimmered and scintillated on the iridescent bluish pavement. He walked along, the shadowy trees of the park appearing to creep beside him. Some outcasts of the night slept on benches, some looked wistfully: the miserable blasted fruit of this tree of heaven.

Praises rang in his ear, fragments of wit, flashes of lyric, and night played vibrations on the chord of emotion. His mind was in a whirl. His past—what a horrible waste of God's faculties—unused. If he had only been taken up and moulded; but life had been cruel to him. Now she showed signs of remorse and atonement. He was young, upon the threshold of life. Life would hold the doors for the golden stairs. Chamber after chamber of the house of delight would be thrown open to him and he would wander in the gardens of pleasure holding the hand of love. The fountains of song would make perpetual music and they would glide down the rivers of twilight in an ecstasy of repose. Glimpses of undulating robes, shimmer of pearl gleam dresses, creamy arms and gleaming shoulders—Ah! life! was it not time?

And now the dawn broke quietly and rich upon his dream. The vast blue flower of heaven over the dark rim of quaint angular buildings changed dreamily into broken gold and green and rose. The pearly waves of shimmering twilight seemed rising like a tide to meet the dawn into the light which stole inch by inch the kingdom that was night's.

Uncle's Impressions in the Woods at Night

The moon shed its clear effulgent beam upon a scene of sylvan beauty wrapped in its garments of night.

I smiled with glee as a gentle breeze came softly whirring round me, fanning me with its light and delicate touch, and dispelling the heat of a summer's night. The trees, my companions for years, invested with new life this beautiful still night, intermingled a soothing, incessant rustling of their leaves with the slight noises which arose now and then from an awakened insect.

The trees around me stood in ghostly array, huge blotches of shadow in the night shades, but here and there inexpressibly lovely and fairylike, when a beam outlined and touched with a silvery light, a leaf, a twig, or a notch of the gnarled bark.

No daylight could make these trees look lovelier, thought I.

The golden light of the sun with its bold, artistic touch, transforming dull greens into golden magnificence, flooding with its arrogant beneficence a peaceful vale, could not compete, thought I, with the gentler splendour of his sister Moon.

The Lady of the Moon showed me a study of silver and black. Thus the night as the daytime has a peculiar atmosphere of its own. Here, everything was still: a prolonged silence, an unearthly stillness, stole over the woods. The silence was broken by an impudent insect, the watchman of the night, who, curious to know why all was so still, called to its sleeping companions. A little babel arose, yet sweet and appropriate to the woods. It pleased me to think that I was not alone in noting the wonders of Nature by night. Again silence fell, to be interrupted as before by the insect life which dwelt at my feet. They were innumerable, but having respect for my age, they did not often drop in upon my meditations. I like the little things though, and when they ask me to tell them events I have seen in bygone ages, they listen entranced till I cease.

Thus my thoughts ran on in the same groove as they had run on years before, and still, I looked at the Lady touching up a little pool with her wand. The inky blackness of the pool would have disguised its presence but those light touches accentuated the undulations of each ripple, revealing its presence as She revealed each tree. Thus my friends were not merged into the shadows, but with becoming dignity stood out individually and displayed their noble proportions. I ceased thinking and with the rest of the world around me slept.

The Slade and its Relations to the Universe

'The Slade,° what is the Slade?' nine-tenths of our readers will cry. Is it a building or a threshing machine? Well, in Gower St[reet]° there is a noble edifice dedicated to the science of learning and to the manu-facture of the intellect of the future generation. It is known as [the] University. [The Slade] is merely an art school. In Gower Street, concealed in a corner of that noble edifice the University, the Slade reposes in promiscuous obscurity.

You pass through the gate and take the small path to the left. You pass a building which you take no notice of, and then pause before a stately imposing [one], and on proceeding to enter you are intercepted by a buttoned authority and you find you have mistaken the porter's lodge for the Slade. You retrace your footsteps and hesitate before the insignificant building we passed before. Then you catch glimpses of girls in painting overalls through the glass doors, and are oppressed by an uncomfortable feeling of being watched by numberless eyes from rows and rows of windows and you pluck up courage and look, and you know then that it is the Slade.

What is the Slade? You don't know yet. Well, I can't find it in my heart to blame you. I know what the Slade is. I have been a student there, and so I ought to know. The first day I came I thought I had wandered into a Seminary, and I spent the whole day in trying to find my way out without being seen, but I only succeeded in getting myself grabbed by a student—a male luckily—the first I had seen, who told me the model was taken ill and they generally had new students [to take their place]. Afterward I ran across some stray waifs of youthful males on descending to the lower regions [where] the atmosphere distinctly became more masculine.

The Slade and Modern Culture

If we consider the Slade as it stands related to modern culture we will find one fundamental principle exemplified—one guiding law, one fact that is of paramount interest in our endeavour.

We find that the law of change only proves the futility of change, that it is a circle revolving round the rock of fixity. From Greek Art in ever widening circumference Art revolved round Egypt, Renaissance, decadence, romantics and continues revolving.

The Slade marks an era in the history of Art. Constable, French Impressionists, had given flashes to the world of an attempt to wrest her secret from her; of the endeavour to show to the world the beauty that lies around us if our souls will only see; with more or less adequate power and concentration of vision. Whistler,° exquisite, dainty and superficial, dandified through the slushy sentimentalism that had saturated English art, and taught art not to despise the moods of nature; that a pigsty in twilight was a poem, and even a church could be hallowed—by a fog.

But these, though they were forces, were not as one might say an organized force; they were flashes; the final culmination, the concentration of the blaze is the Slade.

This is the paradox of the Slade.

To be ourselves, we must not forget others—but forget ourselves. We must not look at nature with the self-conscious, conventional|mannered eye of a stylist, whose vision is limited by his own personal outlook but assimilate the multifarious & widened vision of masters to widen our outlook to the natural, to attain to a completeness of vision which simply means a total sinking of all conscious personality, a complete absorption & forgetfulness in nature, to bring out one's personality.

The Pre-Raphaelite Exhibition: Notes for an Article

Whether it is intentional on the Director's part or unconscious, the present exhibition of the P[re-]R[aphaelite] B[rotherhood] on view at [the Tate Gallery] running side by side with A[lfred] Stevens° is a perfect antithesis and brings into projectivity the significance of the PRB. Here we have two great activities—both reactions against a school of sickly[   ] that was existent, both an indignant protest against the art around, and both a revival, a return to a principle of a form of art apparently forgotten and obsolete, and yet both utterly different. The PRB, temperamentally disgusted with the affectations, the low sentiment, the want of spiritual fervour and sincerity which was guiding Art, saw all this in the early Italians, and taking nature as material and guide, formed themselves on the principles of[   ] They were fascinated by the almost childishness, the naiveness, the genius of their outlook on nature, and the esoteric feeling, the purity [and] earnestness, and strove to see these qualities in nature, and interpret nature on these principles.

A. Stevens, also disgusted[   ] not from the P[RB] point of view, took another standpoint. He felt the lack of largeness, dignity and style in art, and he turned to the greatest stylist of all, M[ichel] Angelo,° not as a guide and index whereby to see the dignity of nature but[   ]

The soul's hunger.

His ideal simplicity was the simplicity of a giant, the large languor of grandly moulded limbs, and titanic vast sweep of contour in design. Purity of design to him meant harmonious and sinuous arrangement, to compel nature into a preconception of balance. Thus the soul's hunger for perfection sought and found in two temperaments a realisation.

The P[RB] had the acquiescence of a body perhaps because the path was more natural; Alfred Stevens with his sense of monumental, academic design was alone.

What strong and sympathetic lovers of nature these were. How nature is enhanced and how lovingly and earnestly each exquisite

blade of grass, each petal assumes a beauty, a fragrance, an import-
ance, and [is] yet subsidiary to the entire effect. Often the sentiment is
trivial and mean, as in many of Millais'° and Hughes',° but enough is
compensated by the treatment, the evident delight in earnest endeav-
our. A quaintness of effect, a Gothic [

Rossetti and his rich luxurious medievalism, his romantic sensu-
ous revelry in colour, the poetic charm and glowing wealth of his
designs.

In 1850 three young Academy students were furiously discussing
art round the tea-table at the house of the youngest. One,° who was
evidently the domineering spirit, and to whom the others were some-
what deferential considering the tense state they were in, spoke in a
rich loud voice of Keats° and the glowing colour of Botticelli° and the
passion of soul in art, of the correct soulnessness of Raphael—'O, if he
hadn't lived' then art had continued uninterrupted—of the crying
need of a return to the men before Raphael.

Before they parted for the night they had planned to work a subject
on the principle of earnestness and fundamental literalness and exact-
ness to subject and nature. The subject chosen was from Keats,
Lorenzo and Isabel.° Millais' drawing is here. It is incredible for his
age, and disregarding age it is amazing. For psychological accuracy,
consistency and continuity of thought, for variety of minute accessor-
ies and yet subordinated to the main interest, and for charm of
executive quality, it is remarkable.

The cream of the collection is Rossetti's pen-and-ink drawings for
Tennyson,° etc. The wealth of design, the poetic exuberance of the
idea, and the extraordinary dramatic and fervid execution of them,
make them unique in art.

The most astonishing for technical achievement is Millais' 'Mari-
ana at the Moated Grange'.° It is Dutch in idea, in minuteness of
detail and exquisiteness of finish, but it possesses a richness, a dar-
ingness, an arrangement of colour that Dutch art never attained to.

] with the sumptuous exotic ardours of Rossetti's women around,
and the trivial passions of the others. The colour is so quiet and
reticent, and yet so beautiful, and the arrangement is in perfect accord
with the scheme.

The charm|essence of Pre is its earnestness and its reverence.

It does not aim|It lacks the epic quality of the grand style [ ] it
possesses the lyrical exquisiteness|the jewel-like perfection of [ ]

Ingenuity of imagination is the prime requisite in their design.
They recognised the limitations of the grand style of design and

widened the possibilities of natural design. They imagined nature, they designed nature. They were so accurate in design that the design is not felt; and yet though it defies criticism from the naturalistic side we are projected into an absolutely new atmosphere that is real in its unreality.

When I say the naturalistic I mean it in its absolute sense, in the sense that Velasquez painted and Rembrandt,° in the sense the post-impressionists paint. Each of these saw nature in their own way and interpreted it so. All are as truthful to nature and all as unlike each other, in so much as the artist was bent more or less on a particular effect in nature which appealed more to his temperament. Velasquez aimed for realising light as affected by atmosphere. Rembrandt saw nature as one effective chiaroscuro which brought into relief the character and psychology. The post-impr[essionists]° paint nature according to the sensation a perception produced upon them, and the PR combine all these qualities. If we desire to see them we can[

Simeon Solomon° is to me the finest in the room. It is so spiritual in feeling, so perfect in design, the gracious reticence of its colour.

In looking at Simeon Solomon's work we are brought face to face with a psychological contradiction that is not uncommon in the history of art; the antagonism of the relation of art to conduct. In natures like Simeon Solomon's, who know life only through their art, beyond their art their faculties for the controlling and management of their life are undeveloped; they have poured their souls out with creation and possess none for actuality.

The Pre-Raphaelites and Imagination in Paint

We are apt to confuse imagination with literature, with the psychological interest of a picture, as a quality apart from its technical qualities. Literature, I think, is permissible if it can increase|enhances the interest of a picture, but it only increases the difficulties of imagination. A picture must be a perfect consistency of thought and execution of colour and design and conception; the more dramatic or psychological a picture is the more intense must be the imagination of colour and design to harmonise with the idea. The psychology is helpless without the other elements; the p[sychology] itself is only part of the imagination and perhaps the smallest.

Whatever the subject, nature is always our resort, a basis for creation. To feel and interpret nature, to project yourself beyond nature through nature and yet convince of the veracity of the sensation is imagination.

Romance at the Baillie Galleries: The Works of J. H. Amschewitz and the late H. Ospovat °

If one were to walk into the Baillie Galleries, Bruton Street, without knowing the names of the artists, the children of whose brain we are dealing with here, one would not suspect for a moment the Jewish parentage of this remarkable progeny.

Whether this is something to be deplored or not is beside the question here, as it is the inevitable result of ages of assimilation and its blame (if a defect) is to be placed on the causes that made us a race, and unmade us as a nation. Yet though these causes have deprived us of any exclusive atmosphere such as our literature possesses, they have given that which nothing else could have given. The travail and sorrow of centuries have given life a more poignant and intense interpretation, while the strength of the desire of ages has fashioned an ideal which colours all our expression of existence. We find this exemplified in the work before us. Where nature has inspired, the hold on life is strong, but there is an added vitality, the life of ideas and, as all great and sincerely imaginative work must be, the result is more real. Life that is felt and expressed from the immediate fires of conception must naturally be more convincing than what is merely observed and described from without. First is the portrait of a young poet, ° gazing as if out of 'dream dimmed' eyes, holding the pen in his hand, apparently waiting for an inspiration. This he doubtless does as a protest against the legendary unpractical habits of poets. With such prudence and foresight, so long-headed a precaution as the pen implies, no poet surely could incur the stigma of impracticability. It is well studied, except for the mannered and unpleasant way the forms of the shadows repeat themselves, which makes it appear as though style were aimed at rather than exact interpretation. The portrait of Michael Sherbrooke is a most vivid and vivacious rendering of this frank good-humoured modern Roscius. ° Those who know the original know what a living likeness it is of a mood of a man whose moods are so many. The ease and fluency of the handling, so consistent with the buoyancy of the expression, is characteristic of the spontaneous unlaboured technique, which Mr. Amschewitz knows as well how not to abuse. Then there is the portrait of the painter's mother, a sympathetic and most gracious piece of painting. The scheme is one of gold and black, rich, yet reserved, beautiful in delicate treatment of the lace drapery, besides being a most human piece of subtle portraiture. The series of illustrations to 'Everyman' show, perhaps more than any isolated treasure, the remarkable fertility of Mr. Amschewitz's versatile and extraordinary powers. Here he combines a vehement yet orderly dramatic intuition with (to the artist) the larger issues of decorative fitness and harmony. One perhaps might have preferred the text to be illustrated in a purer and more fervid religious spirit. The passion of sense is here more than the passion of soul. But that is merely personal preference. The wealth and opulent colour of some, the restrained delicacy of others, notably No. 10 for this, the breadth, spaciousness and dignity in the conception of one or two, No. 13 particularly, make the series an extraordinary achievement. Then we come to the landscapes. Some, unaffected fantasies, where nature is used simply as a basis for creation, others, faithful transcripts of recognisable localities, but seen through a richly glowing temperament. They all have the authority and air of experience, autobiographical records of moods, lovely and glad, tinged with the merest grace of melancholy—moods sunny and joyous, brooding and pensive, retiring and shy, or sombre with presentiment of storm and tragedy. There is no space except just to mention as another phase of this artist's talent the powerful black and white study, 'The hungry', for its intensity, the yearning tragedy that is its motive.

The works of H. Ospovat shown here are entirely comprised of pen-and-ink illustrations to Matthew Arnold, Browning, and some Shakespeare sonnets. They are very forcible and beautiful interpretations, and show a keenness of insight, and sympathetic appreciation of the poets, wonderful in their way. His influences are apparent, and it seems to me that though he possessed in a great measure the poetic feeling and refinement of the Pre-Raphaelite school of illustrators, he lacked the tenderness and charm of their execution, their patient and honest endeavour for exactness. Sometimes his work recalls Fred Walker,° sometimes Rossetti, but neither at their best. When he is personal, as in the 'Last ride together', 'The wandering Jew', he shows a strength sweetened by refinement that is very rare.

Joy

And when we had seen Time die, and passed through the porches of silence, we came to a land where joy spread its boughs, and we knew that the dreams we had dreamed before Time were but the shadows of the tree of joy mirrored in the waters of life. For the roots of joy lie beyond the valleys and hills of life, and the branches thereof blossom where weeping earth mists come not near, and only the sounds of the laughing of ripples, the running of happy streams, and the rapturous singing of birds is heard. Where delight lies coolly shadowed, overburdened by the weariness of joy, lulled by the songs of joy. Joy—joy the birds sing, joy—the rivers, joy—the happy leaves, for the fear of Time haunts not, and the hands of fate are afar.

Emerson

The great poets of the earth have been manly intellects with a kind of coarseness engrained. At the most delicate and rare there is a sense of solidity and bulk, close knit, that is like some unthinkably powerful chemical contained in some dewlike drop. We question a poet like Shelley because we feel this lack of robustness where we do not question Keats or Donne or Blake. We ask in a poet a vigorous intellect, a searching varied power that is itself, and an independent nature.

We know our poem by its being the only poem. The world is too full of echoes and we seize on the real voice. Does it happen that the real voice is sometimes not heard or is mistaken for an echo? It not infrequently happens that the real voice, sickened by echoes and shy of its own sound, withdraws and only calls to ears it is its delight to call to. The Masters must needs have the whole earth for their bough to sing on or they burst their throats, but there are voices humbler in their demands, but nowise less imperious in their result. The ebullition of the heart that seeks in novel but exact metaphor to express itself, the strong but delicate apocalyptical imagination that startles and suggests, the inward sanity that controls and directs—the mainspring of true poetry—is Emerson's. Does he possess in any eminent degree, does he possess at all, that manly intellect, that solidity and bulk, which is the certificate of legitimacy for a great poet?

We have here no tradition—no tricks of the trade. Spontaneity, inspiration, abysmal in its light, is the outer look these poems have to the eye. The words ebulliate and sparkle as fresh as a fountain. But we are always near a brink of some impalpable idea, some indefinable rumour of endlessness, some faint savour of primordial being that creeps through occult crevices and is caught back again. We know nothing better than Shakespeare's lyrics that have this suggestiveness in perfection:

> Full fathom five thy father lies;
> Of his bones are coral made:
> Those are pearls that were his eyes:
> Nothing of him that doth fade,
> But doth suffer a sea-change
> Into something rich and strange.
> Sea-nymphs hourly ring his knell...

Or from the sonnets:

> Not mine own fears, nor the prophetic soul
> Of the wide world dreaming on things to come...

*   *   *

This man paved the way for Whitman. His freedom, his daring, his inspiration, in Whitman's hands became a roodway right through humanity.

Art

We all, more or less, feel a work of art, and I should like in this paper to find a sort of philosophic connection between one's thoughts and work created by mind. I also want to say a word on modern aims; and no doubt all here have heard of the fermented state of culture now in Europe. The multiplexity and elaborately interwoven texture of modern life,—the whole monstrous fabric of modernity—is rapidly increasing in complexity; and art, which is a sort of summing up and intensification of the spirit of the age, increases its aims accordingly. A great genius is, at once, the product and the creator of his age. It is in him that a marked stage of evolution is fulfilled. His ideas are absorbed and permeate, even when the natures who feel them are not large enough to contain them. These ideas weaken as they become absorbed into the indrawing and everwidening complexities of life, and no longer have their original force, and a new stimulus is necessary. So we have these new movements and their energetic repudiation of preceding movements. To make my point clear I shall be obliged to run roughly through the evolution of art, before I can speak of its present state.

We all have impressions from nature. Our consciousness of these impressions is life. To express and give shape to such impressions on our consciousness, by artificial means, is art. Man's natural necessities, his instinct to communicate his desires and feelings, found shape in corresponding signs and sounds; symbols which, at first crude, gradually developed and refined. Special emotions found expression in the nearest and most sufficient ways. Singing and dancing for joy, for awe and worship, the reverential mien and solemn incantation. Victories, festivities, marriage, love, all these were occasions for art. Shouting became singing; more and more rhythmical and orderly. From the expression of private joy and sorrow, it told tales of others' joys and woes. It became art. Hunters whose eyes were keen and hands were skilful, gloating over the image of the power they chased, strove to record it, cutting sharply with their rude hunting knives on the stone of their rough cave dwelling. Architecture developed, then sculpture as a natural result.

We begin with high culture at the Egyptians. A land of high profound, austere philosophy—their art expressed their priestly natures. Art went hand in hand with their religion, grave and austere. With a profound knowledge of form and perfect craftsmanship, all their energies were directed to express deity, an abstraction of simple, solemn profundity, the omnipresent sprit. Their art was angular and severe.

The Greeks followed. More idealistic, they cultivated a more effeminate conception of beauty, an idea of grace, of rounded forms, suavity. Body's strength and body's beauty was the ideal of this lovely land, and this pagan philosophy has produced art, lovely indeed, but of no intensity, no real hold on man's spirit.

We are moved by a work of art. Is an artistic emotion similar to an ordinary emotion got from actual life? Is fear, horror, pride, called into play? Yet we are moved, aesthetically. What moves us? Just as figures stand for quantities, so we have subtle but intelligible symbols to correspond to the most delicate and imperceptible shade of emotion; and it is by bringing these varied symbols into a coherent unity that a work of art is constructed. To detach a part from nature, and give it the completeness of the whole, by applying to that part of the principle of rhythmic law that is instinctive in our consciousness, and harmonises us to the exterior nature. A law of repetition and contrast, continuity in variety. It is this principle that our consciousness responds to. Art becomes, by this, a living thing, another nature, a communicable creation. To convey to all, in living language, some floating instant in time, that, mixing with the artist's thought and being, has become a durable essence, a separate entity, a portion of eternity. Art widens the scope of living by increasing the bounds of thought. New moods and hitherto unfelt particles of feeling are perpetually created by these new revelations, this interfusion of man's spirit, eager to beget and crown existence with every finer possibility. Thus art is an intensification and simplification of life, which is fragmentary and has no order and no coherent relationship to us, until it has passed through the crucible of Art. Science explains nature physically by atoms, philosophy explains life morally, but art interprets and intensifies life, representing a portion through the laws of unity that govern the whole.

How do we know a vital composition? We know it by its newness and by its rightness. Do you know Blake's° drawing of 'The Song of the Morning Star?' Do you know why it was not conceived before Blake? Yet it is as natural and magnificent a conception as the sun, as familiar and holy when we are with it as the name of God in our hearts, and as mysterious and holy and as new. Perhaps it is irreverent to analyse, but as we are endeavouring to discover a principle in art, we must see how the most inspired art (and no art is perfect without appearing inspired) conforms to this principle. It is a vital composition because its content is an infinite idea expressed coherently in a definite texture. The spaces harmonise in unexpected ways, the forms are expressive and consistent, the gestures are rhythmical, but surprise us, as though one's own private thought, too secret even to reveal to ourselves, were suddenly shown to us from outside. It is limitless idea, responsive to the emotion but ungraspable by the intellect. A poem contains in itself all it would convey, which is infinity. This is brought about through movement, the rapid succession of images and thoughts, as in nature itself. Painting is stationary, it only begins a process of thought, it suggests. But you think outside the painting, not in it. Now this brings us to a point I wish to insist on. In appreciating a picture, it is the general tendency to confuse literary ideas with painting ideas. An idea in painting is only one because it cannot be put into words, just as an idea in music can only receive form through the medium of sound. Each art has its own special ideas and special qualities to express them, though they all have a common basis, the expression of emotional truth. Incident, in a picture, can give some sort of human interest, it might even be that which has inspired the artist to his rhythmical arrangement, but the emotional truth under-lying is brought about by insistence on the plastic unity, the beauty and harmony purely of shapes and forms.

If one takes nature as a standpoint, to a cold judgement, how whimsical and odd it is to see limbs suspended in motion, expressions wrought to the utmost limits of intensity, and remaining so. But pictures depend on gestures and expressions. True—but the gesture must be part of some unfathomable, preponderating idea, hovering on the borderland of revelation. We are struck by no particular gesture, but some rhythmical and unexpected quality that helps in some tentative way our approach to this idea. Art has never received purer or higher utterance than the Italian primitives° gave it. No formal, cold, lifeless arrangement, but some elaborately organised pattern, instinct with some vital conception, rich with variety of texture; simple in result. Every space brimful of meaning, touched with adumbrations of some subtly felt idea. Clear and definite in form, their whole outlook was expressiveness. Nature had no other sign-ificance to them save as a means to symbolise some more intimate nature. Sometimes their passion for something deeper and occult, something never seen by eye or thought of man, led them a little out of the way, to bring back fantastic blossoms and things strange and curious, but which men might like or be angered by as with a child's or a woman's whim. But always their vision of beauty was pure and entire, and their failures rose from their eagerness to obtain a more intimate and profounder sense of her. It was this wishfulness to know, this passionate hunger to reach into the inmost heart of things, by men of such depth, and profundity, this deep imaginative understanding of natural things that drove them burningly to give the clearest utterance to their conclusions of destiny. Art gradually took on different aims. The School founded by Giotto,° which might be called the naturalistic school, nature being their immediate inspiration, gave place to a more scholarly group of painters, whose idea of life was largely woven up with Greek culture and learning, Botticelli and Mantegna being the chief.

We come now to Leonardo Da Vinci,° a mind of unhuman vastness, of the deepest poetry, and extraordinary logic and invention. Too fertile in his ideas to ever go through with one completely, he has yet left us some single achievements which stand supreme in Art. He might be said to have invented chiaroscuro,° for he was enamoured of the mystery of shadow. He was enamoured of all mysteries, and strove to fathom most, and in art made many revelations of form. His drawings, particularly of woman's heads, for perfect loveliness and pure realisation of form have never been surpassed—few indeed have ever come near them. In the primitives the paintings are in a light bright key, the shadows are light and pearl, and the lights delicate rose, their patterns of colour are definite, and subordinated to the linear effect. But Leonardo, eager to express mystery, the elusiveness of natural aspects, particularly the smiling of women, sought in shadow a symbol of this. You might call his pictures colour monochromes.

Then we have Michael Angelo, whose solitary spirit sought in huge titanic limbs and volcanic energy of motion, to express the grandeur of his conceptions of nature. Sculpturesque, architectural, within these arbitrary bonds he unloosed his vast writhing universe, and poured his lonely cries into the void.

With the primitives true decoration passed. Art became more and more concerned with the aspect of things. Plastic unity was achieved, not as in the primitives, by linear design, by expressive spaces and clearly defined planes, but by tonal relationship of shapes of dark and light. Sloven in their form, the work of the Venetians° is soft and inexpressive. Their colour is artificial and has neither the refinement, truth, nor variety of the primitives. Their designs are almost always commonplace, picturesque, and grandiose. Always sensuous, clever and pleasant. Seldom noble and profound—never intense.

With Velasquez we reach the beginning of a new epoch in painting, the objective attitude. Truth to him was not a reaction of the concrete on his sensitiveness in such a way as to become new and unlike—and yet the same. His truth was more the practical truth of the mirror, and yet so clear was his understanding that, even as the sun is drawn into the dark roots of the earth, so his soul too was drawn beneath the surface and gave birth to new combinations.

I will say nothing of Rembrandt, who of all artists came nearest to realising the highest of all, the union of the abstract and concrete, the purest interpretation of the concrete, and the clearest translation of the abstract.

In Ingres° we have the first draughtsman since the old men. Not the picturesque—but the profound ideal of form. Degas° followed, and this ideal of form learned from Ingres he used to express in his powerful way, certain phases of modernism. He is perhaps the chief power of modern times. Monet, Pissarro—and the other French Impressionists,° made an attempt to reconquer the active vital spirit, to connect the inner with the outer by means of a more spontaneous and intelligent understanding of the actual.

We come now to what is known as the Post Impressionist movement. This was an attempt by men of the deepest culture, and reverence for art, to see nature as a child might see it. However profound their ideas, however mixed with the multiplexity of modern life, their presentation of that idea must be a sort of detachment from all they know—it must be purely that one thing. We know that children see colours bright and unmixed. A drawing by a child of an animal running would express speed by lines that could mean nothing else. It is when we begin to think, and thought begins to modify all our perceptions of an object, that we can no longer see a thing as a thing without associated ideas. The presentation of an object then would be sentiment. It was in Chinese Art these men found similar aims, but joined to a perfect sense of craft, and in Rembrandt. Art to them was inspiration not mere craft and secondhand enthusiasm, and this they strove to destroy. With a feverish impatience of the bonds of technique, in a vehement spontaneity, they poured on canvas their direct visions. Their attempt always for vital rhythms, more vehement and startling connections, their colour is perhaps too lyrical for the fiercer qualities of their design. In Cézanne, rose and green and pearl, in definite patterns of colour, make beautiful harmonies. To feel continuity in variety, both in colour and in form, to feel freshness and intimacy—life and genuine communion of man's spirit with the universal spirit, was the aim of these men.

But a new being has arisen. Hitherto all art has been an attempt to reconcile the present with the age of artists, the standard has always been the highest achieved. The forms have always remained the same though the content has changed. But the Futurist,° the last spark struck from this seething modernism, this mechanical age of speed and convulsive machinery, must create a new form to completely express this entirely new and changed humanity. The old forms to him are useless, they served for the outworn creed that made the beauty of woman, or some quietist searching for ideal beauty its object, always taking some commonly recognised symbol to express this. This quietist detachment from life to watch from outside is not for the Futurist. Violence and perpetual struggle—this is life.

Dynamic force, the constantaneous rush of electricity, the swift fierce power of steam, the endless contortions and deadly logic of machinery; and this can only be expressed by lines that are violent and struggle, that are mechanical and purely abstract. Theirs is an ideal of strength and scorn; the tiger must battle with the tiger. The world must be cleansed of the useless old and weak, for the splendour of battle must rage between the strong and the strong. Theirs is the terrible beauty of destruction and the furious energy in destroying. They would burn up the past, they would destroy all standards. They have wearied of this unfair competition of the dead with the living. To express these new ideals they have invented forms, abstract and mechanical, remote from and unassociated with natural objects, and by the rhythmic arrangement of these forms, to convey sensation. This presupposes a sympathetic intuition—an understanding of the symbols in the spectator.

We can only see ingenuity. The forms are not new, but dead and mechanical. There is no subtlety nor infinity. The only sensation I have ever got from a Futurist picture is that of a house falling—and however unlike the pictures were, that has always been the sensation. We can never strip ourselves completely from associated ideas, and art, being in its form at least, descriptive, the cubes and abrupt angles call to mind falling bricks. It is too purely abstract and devoid of any human basis to ever become intelligible to anybody outside the creator's self. The symbols they use are symbols of symbols. But they had introduced urgency—energy into art and striven to connect it more with life.

Art is now, as it were, a volcano. Eruptions are continual, and immense cities of culture at its foot are shaken and shivered. The roots of a dead universe are torn up by hands, feverish and consuming with an exuberant vitality—and amid dynamic threatenings we watch the hastening of the corroding doom.

But we believe that the Gioconda° will endure, and Albrecht Dürer° will never be forgotten, and that the reign of Blake is yet to begin.

I have said nothing of Art in England. We have never had a tradition. Gainsborough° in a small charming way, Blake in his magnificent great way, Alfred Stevens in his noble reminiscent way, and Rossetti in a romantic way, with Turner and Constable°, are perhaps all the English artists who count at all, and of all these, only Blake can be ranked amongst the highest order. But lately Art has sprung into flower. In Augustus John,° we have a power—perhaps the first English artist with a genuine conception of the ideals of Art.

About 30 years ago the Slade School was started. Before the Slade, with the exception of Alfred Stevens and Legros,° both of whom learnt abroad and were unrecognised here, no drawings worthy of the name had been done by an English artist. Blake was not a good draughtsman, but he had a noble idea of form. It was a great pity he had Flaxman° for a teacher instead of Dürer. I here mean drawing as we understand it in the classic sense. Blake knew the end but grasped at it too quickly; he recognised a result and conceived too simple a cause. What else could he do? The unbroken tradition that runs right from Egypt through Da Vinci, Dürer to John, passed by him; there were none to hand it on to him. Drawing is a science, the final result of a slow growth, and continual criticism of ages, and no man however divine can be expected to invent it. I hold Blake to be the highest artist England has ever had, as high above the next highest as it to the lowest. No artist that ever lived possessed in so high a degree that inspired quality, that unimpaired divinity that shines from all things mortal when looked [at] through the eye of imagination. Each touch is interpenetrated with sense, with life that breathes from the reachless and obscure heights and depths, deep, profound, and all embracing. And this in spite of a bad and mannered way of drawing, which sometimes obtrudes and obscures our pure appreciation. I will not enter into the claims of Leighton, Watts,° Millais as draughtsmen. In England they have been forgotten long ago and nobody dreams of disturbing their memories. While these men were still alive and England mute and wondering at their powers, real drawings were being done by students at the Slade. John burst upon London with amazing drawings, some that could be hung side by side with Da Vinci without suffering. At last we were able to boast of a draughtsman, such as Italy once had, and France now possessed. A man who could apprehend a fact, its significance, and translate into terms of expressive line the visual substance of things. You look at a drawing. Can I read it? Is it clear, concise, definite? It cannot be too harsh for me. The lines must cut into my consciousness, the waves of life must be disturbed, sharp, and unhesitating. It is nature's consent, her agreement that what we can wrest from her we keep. Truth, structural veracity, clearness of thought and utterance, the intelligent understanding of what is essential. I should like to make the distinction between the picturesque and the profound, the swagger and the stately. Rubens, Vandyke, Watteau° are considered good but not serious enough. They are the 'knuts' of the Renaissance. These glib and aristocratic hunger marchers, who were too clever to sweat, are as shallow as they are fertile. Compare an etching of Rembrandt with Vandyke, a drawing by Ingres or Degas with Rubens or Watteau. It is the difference of the Temple to the Playhouse, of the Prophet to the balladmonger. It is the difference between the accessory and the essential, the accidental and the inevitable. The difference between the pretty plausible and the fierce straightforward.

The French Impressionists were the reaction from the traditional and lifeless. Art somehow had lost touch with nature and lay simpering, cosy and snug, propped up by sweet anecdote and delicious armchair sentiment. It was the day of Dickens' slime and slush.° Then Baudelaire published 'The Flowers of Evil', Swinburne his ballads, and Meredith 'Modern Love',° while at the same time Degas, Manet,° Pissarro, Puvis de Chavannes° tried to get at the core of nature with paint. In their anxiety to get at truth, the Impressionists like Puvis and Degas overlooked one great point, which was, the form by which truth is to be conveyed must be concise and arbitrary, to isolate and impress its significance. Post Impressionism is that criticism of Impressionism. Vitality is expressed by patterns of clear form.

In England Impressionism manifested itself in Wilson Steer, Professor Brown, Sargent, Walter Sickert, Henry Tonks.° To my mind the personality of Sickert is the most interesting of this school. It is very forbidding and sombre and stands alone in its ruthless philosophy. Steer is more lyrical and gay, and has recaptured the golden splendour of Turner. Clausen° serves as a good populariser of other men while Sargent pains one by his smartness. Then we have a group of artists whose ideal is mixed up with Dutch Art, with Vermeer and Van Hooch, William Rothenstein, Orpen and Walter Russell.° Rothenstein's picture of 'The Doll's House' is very beautiful and haunting.

But the young men have been taught by John that a sharp contour means more than the blending of tone into tone. Nature can be a lure and a snare and be used as an end and not as a means to an end. The concise pregnant quality of poetry rather than prose.

Henry Lamb° is shy, a tremulous and ever-shaken life in shadow. Compared to Lamb, John is the broad ocean with the sun on it, and Lamb the sea with the moon. Innes° paints landscapes very much like the Chinese and Mantegna. They have the vague beauty of perfumes and luxuriant reverie. Mark Gertler° has a deep understanding of nature and sometimes achieves to that intensity we call imagination. John Currie° has painted lovely things without being very convincing

PLATE 1. Self Portrait, 1914. Oil on panel. National Portrait Gallery, London.

PLATE 2. Caxton and Edward IV. 1901. Pen, ink and watercolour on paper. Mrs Gerda Horvitch.

PLATE 3. Head of Barrister. 1910. Red chalk on paper. Joseph Cohen Collection of World War I Literature, Rare Books and Special Collections, University of South Carolina.

PLATE 4. Hark, Hark, the Lark. 1912. Charcoal and monochrome wash on paper.
Joseph Cohen Collection of World War I Literature, Rare Books and Special Collections,
University of South Carolina.

PLATE 5. Portrait of the Artist's Father, 1912. Oil on canvas. Stern Pissarro Gallery, London.

PLATE 6. Study of nude. Charcoal on grey paper. British Museum.

PLATE 7. First Meeting of Adam and Eve, 1915. Charcoal on paper. Tullie House Museum & Art Gallery.

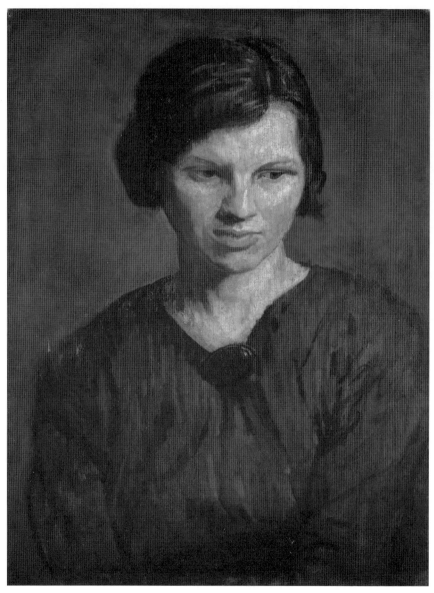

PLATE 8. Portrait of Sonia Rodker. *c*.1915. Oil on canvas. Joan Rodker.

as a draughtsman. David Bomberg° has crude power of a too calcu-
lated violence—and is mechanical, but undoubtedly interesting.
Roberts,° who is yet a boy, is a remarkable draughtsman in a stodgy
academic way, clear, logical, and fervent. But the finest of all is Stanley
Spencer.° He is too independent for contemporary influence and goes
back to Giotto and Blake as his masters. He strikes even a deeper note
than John, and his pictures have that sense of everlastingness, of no
beginning and no end, that we get in all masterpieces.

Thoughts on Art

We are not affected by Art in the same way as life.° The spiritual
consciousness is stirred to aesthetic emotion.

Colour being more imitative, is responded to by the senses. Form
has a greater interest for the mind. Here nature becomes an abstrac-
tion, an essence. Mere representation is unreal, is fragmentary. The
bone taken from Adam remains a bone.

To create is to apply pulsating rhythmical principles to the part, a
unity, another nature is created.

The renaissance was the revival of learning. Civilization has been
tamed by the commercial spirit, a logic without imagination, mechanical,
scientific, practical. Impetuous ideals, Art has become too self-conscious.

The sky stagnates, life become inert, arid, a perishing tomb for
itself. Dust are the stars, dust the sun, the whole world dust. Obscured
and effaced, the life force fails and like a pricked balloon subsides. Out
of this nothingness, out of this dust, art is born and philosophies.

Life stales and dulls, the mind demands noble excitement, half appre-
hended surprises, delicate or harsh, the gleams that haunt the eternal
desire, the beautiful. It is a vain belief that Art and life go hand in
hand. Art is as it were another planet, which does indeed reflect the
rays of life, but is nevertheless a distinct and separate planet.

Passivity and detachment is a need, even as a mirror to reflect truly
must be calm and undimmed. The vivifying organism that is the pulse
of a work of art does not come from the ardour of the limbs, or the
impulse to mix with men, and do what men do (an external life) but
from the imaginative understanding, a necessary consequence of hav-
ing something genuine to express. We all experience all emotions
possible to be experienced. Similar sentiments may dwell in dissimilar

conditions, and qualities that appear to be unapprehensible because their activities are possible only in certain conditions have their corresponding elements in apparently [   ] though the connection would be difficult to trace.

Vitality is a necessary consequence° of having something genuine to express.

An artist who depends on his art° for his living must be an advertiser.

Art to be great° must be unforgettable. Leaving the picture or poem, the impression remains, the quintessence, epitome. Suggestiveness, mystery, vagueness, something underlying what is actually put down, a hauntingness of [

Thoughts on Beauty

The ultimate end of all the arts should be beauty.° Poetry and music achieve that end through the intellect and the ear; painting and sculpture through the eye. The former possess advantages which the latter do not; and the latter, *vice versa*. Painting is stationary while poetry is motion. Through the intellect the emotion is enchained; feeling made articulate transmits its exact state to the reader. Each word adapts itself to the phase of emotion, (I include sensation of the soul) and carries one along from degree to degree. Painting can only give the moment, the visual aspect, and only suggest the spiritual consciousness; not even a mood, but the phase of a mood. By imagination in paint we do not encroach on the domain of the writer; we give what the writer cannot give, with all his advantages, the visible aspect of things, which the writer can only suggest, and give that aspect a poetic interest; and by that a more intensely human interest: for here the body and the soul are one, and beauty the crown thereof.

Thoughts on Words and Writing

We have hints, suggestions°—as if we have just woken up in time to note the passing; there are moments in thought where thought almost knows—words are not delicate or intimate enough; that instant we have died—our souls truly abstracted|etherealised—that instant we have truly lived.

We all build the tower of Babel to reach to God and he has stricken us [with] confusion of speech who understand each other.

Is not each soul solitary, condemned in its separate prison? Yet when all the prisoners assemble in the courtyard, we suspect each other and talk guardedly and opposite, fearing to be betrayed.

If I could die and leave no trace, ah, that thought of mine must live, incomplete and imperfect, maimed. Could I destroy all I have ever thought and done.

You the world, will sneer: 'Young fool—mad ... ' But my quiet undisturbed serenity rebukes your despairs and vexations and the joys that pass. I go to meet Moses who assuredly was a suicide, and the young Christ who invited death, I who have striven to preach the gospel of beauty—

How small a thing is art. A little pain; disappointment, and any man feels a depth—a boundlessness of emotion, inarticulate thoughts no poet has ever succeeded in imaging.

Death does not conquer me, I conquer death, I am the master.

An age that believes in Blake and tolerates Tennyson,° that has forgotten Pope° and worships Shelley, to whom Keats is simply sensuous and Shakespeare not subtle or intense enough—this is our age of poetry. Rossetti I think is the keynote of the demand, and in the 'Monochord' and 'The Song of the Bower'—in the first all poignancy—a richness and variety, a purity of imagination—a truth, far beyond wit, or thought. There are poets who delight in the morbid, for whom life always is arrayed in crape; whose very vigour and energy find its outlet in a perverse and insistent plucking at the wings of death. The poet is so not because he is weak but because he is perverse. His life is a paradox—he does not live, if what other men do is life. This poet will make a song out of sorrow and find in a tear a jewel of perpetual delight. Love is his theme, life is the background, and the beauty of woman stands to him as the manifestation of the beauty of spiritual nature and all outer aspects of the workings of nature.

'Crossing the Bar'° has this consistency, this perfect oneness of tone. A sense of unutterable life in quiet, a depth of yearning, the fading greyness of the whole piece ...

Hidden in air, in nature, are unexplored powers° which the earlier masters had no hint of. We are immeasurably in advance of them in range and scope of subject.

The spirit of enquiry wrestled with superstition. Luther° brought to bear upon the moral world what Darwin° has upon the physical world. Marlowe° foreshadows Nietzsche.° Tamburlaine, the towering colossus|creation, symbolises the subjection of matter to will—the huge blind forces of nature shrink terrorised before this indomitable energy of purpose, clay for some colossal plastic shaping.

We of this age stand in the same relation to things as then, but with a sharpened curiosity. Religious freedom, freedom of thought, has prepared the way for heights of daring and speculation. Social freedom is still as far off as ever, but we dare dream of it.

the last vivid word° one uses in conversation clings to him, becomes the main part of his vocabulary for a week till the next word

Speech|Language is the mask° Politeness is a mask which betrays the speaker

Miscellaneous Thoughts

Lack of depth,° of profundity, makes our age an age of sceptics.

We never excuse the absolute want of spirit° and dignity of character, or a proper sense of what is due to oneself, in society and the common intercourse of life. This vice constitutes what we properly call *meanness*; when a man can submit to the basest slavery, in order to gain his ends; fawn upon those who abuse him, and degrade himself by intimacies and familiarities with undeserving inferiors. A certain degree of generous pride or self-value is so requisite that the absence of it in the mind displeases.

Very few people say what they mean,° though they may say what they think. Few can shape their feelings into words, and in the hurry of conversation say the first words that come. Few people's actions are expressions even of their nature—we are different with different persons.

Poor people are born in troubles° & spend all their lives trying to get
out of them. Rich, born free, try all [ ] to get into them.

Youth is still childhood.°
    When we cast off every cloudy vesture and our thoughts are clear
and mature; when every act is a conscious thought, every thought an
attempt to arrest feelings; our feelings strong and overwhelming, our
sensitiveness awakened by insignificant things in life
    When the skies race tumultuously with our blood and the earth
shines and laughs, when our blood hangs suspended at the rustling of
a dress. Our vanity loves to subdue—battle, aggressive. How we
despise those older and duller. We want life, newness, excitement.

Sometimes in listening to a man° [ ] obscene feelings came over him
he felt inert dissolved a loss of mastery over his will [ ] threatened
with madness
    Sensual
    Like one set of nerves continually being twisted wrenched
    What could be ignoble or depraved?
    What idle name honour Self esteem
    We can do no wrong. Sin does not exist.
    A weird silence

Conversation on trial of car° on Blackfriars Bridge.
Jim. 'I wonder why they opened the bridge and closed it again for.'
John. 'Ask Joe.'
Joe. 'O they wanted to see that it was firm enough to bear the car.
    How far is it across?'
Jim. 'Four miles, I should say.'
Joe. 'Four miles when you come from Pelles. It's all zigzag then.'

'How are you getting on with the picture?'°
'I think I'll call it finished.'
'Why not call it done?
'It suggests dramatic possibilities. Swindled by a sharper.'

If there must be a quarrel,° let's quarrel in a letter and get over it.
What shall we quarrel about? I can't quarrel with anything you've
said, so I'll quarrel with what you have not said.

I'll quarrel for your writing being so nice it leaves me no room to
hope for nicer.

I suppose I haven't qu[arrelled] with Rowarth because he never
hears what I say he is so tall. Mrs ?Din I might have q[uarrelled]
with but she won't qu[arrel] with me.

LSW°

I beg to state that 2/7° has been unjustly stopped from my weekly
money, the reason being that I travelled from Fr[imley]. to W[aterloo]
without paying my fare.

I beg to state that when travel. fr[om].   on Sat on pass I was
robbed and His Majesty's uniform insulted by the Railway Co.

I was robbed and His Majesty's uniform in my person was insulted
by the R. Co.

Whether the robber was intentional|purposeful and deliberate or
accidental I cannot say. There was no two questions about the insult

<Because I do not see that my being in khaki was any reason>

<Khaki may stand for public service but>

<We stand used by the public but not abused>

LETTERS

Wherever possible, the text has been taken from the originals of the letters. However, some have now disappeared, and with these the text has been taken from *1937*. With some letters, all that appears to have survived are the edited extracts used by Laurence Binyon in his Introductory Memoir to *1922*. These are taken from *1922*, and given as 'Extract from letter to', and the name of the recipient.

It has been impossible to date many of the letters; the order in which these are given suggests a possible, not a certain, sequence. In letters dated by IR, or where there is a postmark, this date is given without brackets. Those undated by him but for which a likely date, or range of dates, can be given, are placed in square brackets. Where the date given is conjectural, it is preceded by a question mark.

Spelling mistakes have been tacitly corrected, and punctuation has occasionally been introduced for the sake of clarity. Ampersands have been given as 'and', and apostrophes have been introduced into words such as 'I'll'. Because of shortage of paper, many of IR's letters are not broken into paragraphs; I have introduced paragraph breaks where these seem obvious.

On a few occasions I have reintroduced an excised, or censored, sentence. These are enclosed thus < >.

In a number of letters, IR wrote out a poem that he wished his correspondent to see. To avoid duplication, the text is not repeated here, and the title of the poem is placed in square brackets. However, where IR quotes only a few lines, or an incomplete draft which is not in the Poems section, and this relates directly to the text of the letter, it is given in the letter.

Extract from letter to Winifreda Seaton°

Before March 1911

It is horrible to think that all these hours, when my days are full of vigour and my hands and soul craving for self-expression, I am bound, chained to this fiendish mangling-machine,° without hope and almost desire of deliverance, and the days of youth go by [...] I have tried to make some sort of self-adjustment to circumstances by saying, 'It is all *experience*'; but, good God! it is *all* experience, and nothing else [...] I really would like to take up painting seriously; I think I might do something at that; but poetry—I despair of ever writing excellent poetry. I can't look at things in the simple, large way that great poets do. My mind is so cramped and dulled and fevered, there is no consistency of purpose, no oneness of aim; the very fibres are torn apart, and application deadened by the fiendish persistence of the coil of circumstance.

Extract from letter to Winifreda Seaton

[Jan. 1911]

Congratulate me! I've cleared out of the——shop°, I hope for good and all. I'm free—free to do anything, hang myself or anything except work [...] I'm very optimistic, now that I don't know what to do, and everything seems topsy-turvy.

Extract from letter to Winifreda Seaton

[Jan. or Feb. 1911]

I am out of work. I doubt if I feel the better for it, much as the work was distasteful, though I expect it's the hankering thought of the consequences, pecuniary, etc., that bothers me [...] All one's thoughts seem to revolve round to one point—death. It is horrible, especially at night, 'in the silence of the midnight'; it seems to clutch at your thought—you can't breathe. Oh, I think, work, work, any work, only to stop one thinking.

Extract from letter to Winifreda Seaton

No date.

One conceives one's lot (I suppose it's the same with all people, no matter what their condition) to be terribly tragic. You are the victim of a horrible conspiracy; everything is unfair. The gods have either forgotten you or made you a sort of scapegoat to bear all the punishment. I believe, however hard one's lot is, one ought to try and accommodate oneself to the conditions; and except in a case of purely physical pain, I think it can be done. Why not make the very utmost of our lives? [. . .] I'm a practical economist in this respect. I endeavour to waste nothing [. . .] Waste words! Not to talk is to waste words [. . .] To most people life is a musical instrument on which they are unable to play: but in the musician's hands it becomes a living thing [. . .]

The artist can see beauty everywhere, anywhere [. . .]

Extract from letter to Winifreda Seaton

No date.

You mustn't forget the circumstances I have been brought up in, the little education I have had. Nobody ever told me what to read, or ever put poetry in my way. I don't think I knew what real poetry was till I read Keats a couple of years ago. True, I galloped through Byron° when I was about fourteen, but I fancy I read him more for the story than for the poetry. I used to try to imitate him. Anyway, if I didn't quite take to Donne° at first, you understand why. Poetical appreciation is only newly bursting on me. I always enjoyed Shelley and Keats. The 'Hyperion' ravished me [. . .]

Whenever I read anything in a great man's life that pulls him down to me, my heart always pleads for him, and my mind pictures extenuating circumstances.

Extract from letter to Winifreda Seaton

No date.

Have you ever picked up a book that looks like a Bible on the outside, but is full of poetry or comic within? My Hood° is like that, and, I am afraid, so am I. Whenever I feel inclined to laugh, my visage assumes the longitude and gravity of a church spire.

Extract from letter to Winifreda Seaton

No date.

Do I like music, and what music I like best? I know nothing
whatever about music. Once I heard Schubert's 'Unfinished Sym-
phony' at the band; and—well, I was in heaven. It was a blur of
sounds—sweet, fading and blending. It seemed to draw the sky
down, the whole spirit out of me; it was articulate feeling. The
inexpressible in poetry, in painting, was there expressed. But I have
not heard much, and the sensation that gave me I never had again. I
should like very much to be one of the initiated.

Extract from letter to Winifreda Seaton

No date.

Some more confidences. I've discovered I'm a very bad talker: I find
it difficult to make myself intelligible at times; I can't remember the
exact word I want, and I think I leave the impression of being a
rambling idiot.

Extract from letter to Winifreda Seaton

No date.

Thanks so much for the Donne. I had just been reading Ben Jonson
again, and from his poem to Donne° he must have thought him a
giant. I have read some of the Donne; I have certainly never come
across anything so choke-full of profound meaningful ideas. It would
have been very difficult for him to express something commonplace, if
he had to.

Extract from letter to Winifreda Seaton

[After visiting the Japanese–British Exhibition which opened at
Shepherd's Bush on 27 July 1910.]

The thoroughness is astounding. No slipshod, tricky slickness, trusting to chance effects, but a subtle suggestiveness, and accident that is the consequence of intention.

Extract from a letter to ?Winifreda Seaton

[Oct. 1910]

Whitechapel Gallery.° The paintings are in the upper gallery. Some wonderful Re[y]nolds and Hogarths. There is Hogarth's Peg Woffington° the sweetest the most charming, most exquisite portrait of a woman I've ever seen. A Rossetti drawing—fine and a lot of good things. It's open Sunday as well. You could easily manage to go in the afternoon.

I read the Ivan Turgeneff. Panshin is very good—and the aunt does live. It is very sad; I almost think books like that are immoral; in this sense that one leaves them with a discouraging sense of the futility of life; a sort of numbing effect. I like to read something joyous— buoyant, a clarion call to life, an inspirer to endeavour, something that tells one life is worth living, and not death only is worth having. You can keep 'The man of feeling' if you want it, I've got it again somewhere at home, I think.

I've got a letter from Dr Eder.° Of course his criticism does not refer to the latest things I showed you; but I know he's right. Here it is, word for word

Dear Mr Rosenberg

Do you want your verse back now. I have been keeping them to show to a friend—but he is not back yet in England. Much I like very much. You are young, and your verse shows that much. My own counsel would be not to think of publishing yet awhile (I never thought of publish). You have the artist's feeling for expression and for words. I should say you have not yet developed your own technique. That is not meant as a fault—for the contrary. But there is a fault. And that is, you have so far not given utterance to your own personality and it is all too reminiscent. I think you want courage to strike out into a line of your own. I should not write thus to anyone whom I did not respect for what he had done. We have all done a little versifying in our green days and hence these counsels.

Eder.

I am sending these poems in type so you can read easier but I'll let you have copies if you like.

Yours sincerely
I. Rosenberg

Extract from letter to Winifreda Seaton

No date.

I forgot to ask you to return my poetry, as I mean to work on some. I agree the emotions are not worth expressing, but I thought the things had some force, and an idea or so I rather liked. Of course, I know poetry is a far finer thing than that, but I don't think the failure was due to the subject—I had nothing to say about it, that's all. Crashaw,° I think, is sometimes very sexual in his religious poems, but it is always new and beautiful. I believe we are apt to fix a standard (of subject) in poetry. We acknowledge the poetry in subjects not generally taken as material, but I think we all (at least I do) prefer the poetical subject—'Kubla Khan', 'The Mistress of Vision', 'Dream-Tryst'; Poe, Verlaine.° Here feeling is separated from intellect; our senses are not interfered with by what we know of facts; we know infinity through melody.

To Winifreda Seaton

[Jan. 1911]

159 Oxford St | Mile End E

Dear Miss Seaton

I'm sure I don't know what to say, or how to say it; my brains, as Sterne says,° are as dry as a squeezed orange; but I've got your letter to answer; and my conscience wouldn't let me sleep if I didn't do that. Not that I don't enjoy writing to you, (writing to and hearing from you is a real treat) but even enjoyment is a laggard at times with the end in view, and must be spurred by conscience. 'Gee up' says conscience, cracking his whip. 'Where?' cries enjoyment with dancing heart but empty head. 'To Mademoiselle Seaton, or course, you noodle.' 'But how? I don't know the road; besides my feet are heavy though my heart is light'. 'That matters not', says conscience, 'Up, and look for it; be sharp about it too', and here, giving a cut with the whip, enjoyment comes galloping delighted but astounded at the wide prospect of white fields of blank paper; and here I am groping for what to say, and beating about the bush for ideas that won't come. Now, you know the state of mind I'm in, or rather the mindless state I'm in, you'll know how to take what I say. In your last letter you deprecated your powers as critic. I most emphatically disagree with your verdict, and absolutely deny your right to judge yourself. Before a less prejudiced court you are found guilty of that most heinous crime of modesty. You are convicted (the jury are all agreed) of having vilely slandered your critical abilities; of having perjured yourself by forswearing and denying the 'gifts the gods gave you'. But I'm not going to flatter or say anything, (though I could hardly flatter); I'm sure if anyone's got anything in one it will out, in spite of everything, though it may take time. I wish you had a little more faith in yourself.

Here is an answer to what you say about too much has been written on books. It is by Rossetti. I suppose you've read it. It is called 'the choice'.

'Think thou and act: tomorrow thou shalt die.
Outstretched in the sun's warmth upon the shore
Thou say'st "Man's measured path is all gone o'er:
Man clomb until he touched the truth; and I,
Even I am he whom it was destined for".
How should this be? Art thou then so much more
Than they who sowed, that thou should'st reap thereby?

Nay come up hither. From this wave-washed mound
Unto the furthest flood-brim look with me:
Then reach on with thy thought till it be drowned.
Miles and miles distant though the last line be
And though thy soul sail leagues and leagues beyond,
Still leagues beyond those leagues there is more sea.'

Isn't it magnificent. What space, what suggestion of immensity.

I suppose Flint's poems° gave me pleasure because of their newness to me. They don't seem to be ambitious, they seem to me just experiments in versification except some, which are more natural; and I think those are the ones I like best. I like the first lot, 'The hearts hunger', for the energy intensity and simplicity with which it expresses that strange longing for an indefinite ideal; the haunting desire for that which is beyond the reach of hands. I like the one called 'Exultation', very much. The image in the last stanza; of the—

'birds, unrooted flowers of space,
    Shaking to heaven in a silver chime of bells',

I think is fine.

   I don't think the measure he generally uses allows the poems to stamp itself on the mind. I've got a particularly bad memory, I seldom remember the words of any poem I read; but the tone of the poem, the leading idea, nearly always fix their impression. I didn't find that with these poems; but Dr Eder told me he was very young, about 22; and I expect he'll do something yet.

   Last Sunday, I got up early, and feeling very energetic, I locked myself in till about two o'clock and worked on a painting to 'La Belle dame Sans Merci',° 'I set her on my pacing steed', you know the rest, I should like you to see it. I didn't quite get what I wanted, but—so—so. It was the first bit of painting I've done for months.

   Here is a sonnet I wrote to Mr Amschewitz; he hasn't seen it yet.

['To J. H. Amschewitz']

   Well, enjoyment must come to a full stop here, breathless. Conscience growls out a sort of inarticulate monosyllable of—is it satisfaction or disgust?—but I construe the former, and—well, that is all, while enjoyment can just manage to gasp out
I am

Yours sincerely
I Rosenberg

   Does this sound as if I'm glad to come to a stop. No!—I mean the enjoyment stops with the letter, and I'm sorry I can't think of any more—no doubt—luckily for you.

To Israel Zangwill°

[Summer 1911]

                               159 Oxford Street, | Mile End, E.
I hope I am not taking too great a presumption by intruding in this matter on your valuable time. If the poems do not merit any part of the time you may do me the honour to bestow on them, then the presumption is the more unpardonable; but though I myself am diffident about them, one has, I suppose, whether one has reason or not, a sort of half-faith; and it is this half-faith—misplaced or not—that has led me to this course. If you think them worth criticism, (which is more

than I expect,) on that depends whether this half-faith is to be made an entire one or none at all. I don't know whether it's justifiable, and I do not mention it to abate one jot of your candour, but only in extenuation of my presumption, to remind you that this is not the first time I have wearied you with my specimens of desperate attempts to murder and mutilate King's English beyond all shape of recognition; for about five years ago, when I had just been apprenticed to Carl Hentschel's as a Photo Etcher, I had the hardihood to send you some verses which you were kind enough to think were 'promising', and told me I would hear from you again. Of course, it isn't likely you will remember the occasion, amid your multifarious duties of your valuable life but to me it was an event; and I only mention it to show that I have some sort of right to bother you with these; it being in a way your own kind criticism of the poem five years ago that encouraged me to continue in these.

Yours humbly,
Isaac Rosenberg

To Winifreda Seaton

[Autumn 1911]

159 Oxford St | Mile End E.

Dear Miss Seaton

I saw Miss Cook and she told me what has fired me to write this letter—that you think I don't want to do the drawing I promised of you. Or at least she hinted so. I thought it was plain that the conditions were awkward—no convenient place to do it—but Mr Amshewitz has kindly promised to lend his studio for the purpose Sat—as he will not be in. If you cared to come there, I should be delighted to do the drawing.

I don't suppose you have aged much since I saw you although it seems ages ago; because I don't seem to be in sympathy with old heads, I am seldom successful. You must be prepared to sit about 2 hours as I draw slowly—of course resting when you like. I wrote you a letter some time ago which perhaps you never received. I have a habit of forgetting to address my letters which often has disastrous results. When I heard about you then you were ill and had been away to the country. I hope you are allright now and don't work too hard.

I am studying at the Slade, the finest school for drawing in England. I do nothing but draw—draw—You've heard of Professor Tonks— he's one of the teachers. A most remarkable man. He talks wonderfully. So voluble and ready—crammed with ideas—most illuminating and suggestive—and witty. I am still keen on writing. I sent some poems to the English Review.° I heard nothing for several months and then I got them back—with a letter from Austin Harrison° saying he kept them so long because he liked two of them (I sent 3) very much, and he asked me to send more. I have done so this week—I have not heard yet. I have been writing some prose, I will bring with me.

Hope you will come

Yours sincerely

I Rosenberg

To Laurence Binyon

[1912]

159 Oxford St | Mile End E.

Dear Sir,

I must thank you very much for your encouraging reply to my poetical efforts.° Rambles in the wake of the muse generally end in ditchwater—and I expected a good sousing for my boldness in way-laying so staunch an upholder of the Muse's honour. As you are so kind enough to ask about myself I am sending a sort of autobiography I wrote about a year ago which I hope you will excuse not being in type. You will see from that, that my circumstances have not been very favourable for artistic production, but generally I am optimistic, I suppose because I am young and do not yet properly realize the difficulties.

I am now attending the Slade, being sent there by some wealthy Jews who are kindly interested in me, and of course I spend most of my time drawing. I find writing interferes with drawing a good deal and is far more exhausting. Amongst modern artists Rossetti appeals very much to me and also his poems. I think his 'Beata Beatrix'° has as much of the divine in it as any Lippi Lippi°—more I should say, because in it Rossetti has deified a human passion and not as the Italians did, humanized deity. I do not know much of early Italian art, but I consider that form of art—*Art*. For emotional fervour and lyrical

ecstasy, expression through passionate colour and definite design;—
because instead of confining themselves to rules of Architectural line,
they took the infinitude of nature to build their design from;—because
instead of appearing an affectation of beauty—a moment frozen into
canvas—they have the grace and quality—the spontaneity of unself-
conscious and childlike nature,—infinity of suggestion,—that is as
much part and voice of the artist's soul as the song to the bird.

I know little of modern poets as they are difficult to get hold of—
but Francis Thompson° a little. I think he is tremendous. In fact that
is the sort of poetry that appeals most to me,—richly coloured without
losing that mysteriousness, the hauntingness which to me is the subtle
music—the soul to which the colour is flesh and raiment.

I have not yet done anything in painting or drawing which I would
care to show—but when I have got anything done I wonder whether
you would have time to see them if I brought or sent them. Of course
I would like to do imaginative work but I have hardly attempted
anything—practising portraiture mostly as I feel that is the most
paying—and one must live.

I sincerely hope I have not bored you.

Yours sincerely
Isaac Rosenberg

To Laurence Binyon

[1912]

159 Oxford St | Mile End E.

Dear Mr Binyon

I enclose the things you promised to look at,—They are all small so
even if they are worthless they will not take up much of your time.
I don't know whether I have quite followed your advice about being
more concrete—I'm afraid my mind isn't formed that way—I believe,
though, my expression is more simple. My muse is a very conven-
tional muse, far-away and dreamy, she does not seek her beauty in
common life.

I trust it is not impertinent to bother you about private affairs but
I wonder if you could give me introductions to Editors or people who
might consider my things. I have sent a few times but without
success—I thought they might be considered more attentively if

I had an introduction. I believe I could write Art articles,°—if you fall in with this idea, I could send you one I am writing, and you could judge.

I would be so obliged, but if you think all this is too previous I shan't trouble any more about it.

Yours sincerely
Isaac Rosenberg

To Ruth Löwy

[March 1912]

159 Oxford St | Mile End E.

Dear Miss Löwy

I feel very elated at Mr Picciotto° liking my poems, as I was very anxious to know. Nothing is rarer than good poetry—and nothing more discouraging than the writing of poetry. One might write for pleasure but I doubt if there is no stronger motive whether one would be incited to ambitious work. Circumstances and other considerations have prevented me from applying myself assiduously, and also diffidence—so you can imagine what a rare pleasure it is to me when people appreciate my efforts. As to the prose I sent him, it was an early thing I did some years ago—I had no other by me when I sent. You did not say whether the poem I sent you° would do for the publication. Since I sent it I found in my copy the typist had been trying to improve on parts, which, when I noticed, sent me into ecstasies°— and also, the two or three verses about the parents and brother should be left out. I expect though, there's plenty of time and I may hit off something better.

So your commission bothers you. That's a calamity indeed. All I can suggest is that you should bother it, and bother it, until you bother it into shape.

I have been doing practically nothing—except leading a lordly life—not getting up till tea time and then cursing myself for letting the daylight go. It's getting terribly on my conscience. I shan't torture you with my adventures in the land of Nod, or accounts of the wonderful dream castles I have built and unbuilt by myriads,—also not quite so substantial architecturally as those of Mr Joseph's building.

The other night I met Michael Sherbrooke,° the actor I told you of. He took me home with him and almost made me delirious with delight at some of his marvellous recitations. His power is almost incredible— I have never seen anything like it and could hardly conceive anything so. He gave the Raven. The melancholy insistence—the perpetual recurring note of despair—the gradual tightening to the climax— which is almost unbearable—and then the unutterable broken pathos of the last verse—has so tremendous a grip on you—and so supreme is the acting—one almost faints. I wish you heard it—I should like you to.

If Mr Picciotto would like to see me I should not like to go unprepared—I mean, would it be inquisitive on my part to ask you for information—you needn't give me all his autobiography, his genealogy etc, I might know more than he knows, then, about himself—and that would be unfair,—but I have a dread of meeting people who know I write, as they expect me to talk and I am a horrible bad talker. I am in absolute agonies in company and it needs a sympathetic listener like yourself to put me at ease,—

I have been tempted into a letter and I need very little tempting—so you must excuse this egotism—if a letter isn't that it's nothing.

The Pre-Raphaelite show at the Tate° closes very shortly—when you get back I wish you could come with me—and exchange impressions. We would both learn. I think the Rossetti drawings would be a revelation to you.

Yours sincerely
I Rosenberg

To Alice M. Wright

No date.

Dear Miss Wright,°

I am so sorry about not being able to fix up to come round. Monday evening I joined some classes, and Sunday I am having a friend at my place—could we leave it to the Sunday after. Trust you find the school agrees with you again. Remember me to your sister.

Yours sincerely
I Rosenberg

To Alice M. Wright

Postmarked 15 July 1912

32 Carlingford Rd | Hampstead.

Dear Miss Wright

I am so glad you and your sister like my poems—and I should so like to be able to agree with you about their merits. I would have sent them to you long ago but I always had an idea of going up to the Birkbeck° which somehow never came off. I should be delighted to be able to come round some evening—in the day my times are rather muddled and don't think it would be safe to make an appointment—

I am just going to paint a fairly big picture for the school competition 'Joy'.° If you could find time ever to come and see how it was getting on and give suggestions I should be so pleased.

Yours sincerely
Isaac Rosenberg.

To Laurence Binyon

[Between mid-July and Nov. 1912]

32 Carlingford Road | Hampstead.

Dear Mr Binyon

I have not been able to return your poem° sooner as I have been very busy—I hope you have not been uneasy about it. Thank you so much for the pleasure it has given me. I like some of it tremendously. The opening two stanzas especially appeal to me—and the 2nd stanza in the second part about the moon as earth's mirror, and all the end part from 'Peace is it peace'. I like the whole poem but these especially appeal to me for the rapture they rise into. I like the restraint of it as a whole and the metre. Forgive these jerky observations but I felt I had to say something even if I could not say what I felt.

Yours sincerely
Isaac Rosenberg.

Fragment of a letter to Ruth Löwy

[July or Aug. 1912]

I hope you have a good time when you are away—live in the garden of Joy so that when you get back you will know what sort of expression to wear when I put you in my 'garden of Joy'. If you find you can spare a line when you are away I should be so glad to hear.

Yours sincerely
Isaac Rosenberg

To Alice M. Wright

Postmarked 6 Aug. 1912

32 Carlingford Rd | Hampstead.

Dear Miss Wright

Thank you for the post card. I don't think I shall be able to come either Wed or Thur—as Wed I have to see the dentist and Thur I believe I am getting a model in my studio—If no one turns up here I may come as I like the idea very much. I have been frantically busy— I have the working fever this week. I have started my picture again, having taken a violent dislike to my first design—it is absolutely another thing now, though the literary idea is the same. My colour conception is a wonderful scheme of rose silver and gold—just now it is all pink yellow and blue—but I have great hopes in it.

My appointment with the dentist is not till 12, so I may be able to come at 10 and leave early.

Yours sincerely
Isaac Rosenberg.

To Alice M. Wright

Postmarked 10 Aug. 1912

32 Carlingford Rd | Hampstead.
Friday

Dear Miss Wright

I have not seen the pearl by day but it looks gorgeous by night—it is just the iridescence—that shimmering quality I want to make the whole

scheme of my picture—and that will help me tremendously—Thank
you so much—I had Miss Grimshaw this afternoon and we both worked
hard—She is a very good sitter—though her figure was much too
scraggy for my purpose—I practically finished the drapery, and the
upper part I will do from some more titanic model if I can get the type—

I forgot when you were here to ask you to put your names in the
Shelley you gave me—I think a present is no present without the—
I mean a book is no present without it has the names of the giver—
I would appreciate it very much. I owe some of the most wonderful
sensations I have ever experienced to that book—the speech by
Beatrice about death°—I think it is quite the most intense passage in
the whole of literature—the literature I know.

Yours sincerely
Isaac Rosenberg.

To Ruth Löwy

[Aug. 1912] Thursday.

32 Carlingford Road | Hampstead

Dear Miss Löwy,

Thanks for letter—I did not think your holiday was going to be
over so soon, but as long as you have rested and been happy the time
has done its duty. The weather here is terrible, I suppose the sun has
gone somewhere for his holidays and has forgotten to leave a substi-
tute to attend to his business,—my God—the elements are having a
lark—The wind plays shuttlecock with the trees—and all the work
I've been doing is chasing my hat through the streets—writing doleful
ditties—and wondering when the deuce the rain is going to stop. I
have seriously thought—knowing the wickedness of the times—(with
suffragettes throwing hatchets at Kings—and poets compelling people
to read their poems,) that God has sent another deluge—and have
been looking about for a carpenter to build me an ark.

I started my picture all again and have been working day and night at
it since Friday and feel very tired. It is a gorgeous scheme of rose pearl
and gold—a dream picture. My landlady asked me if it was a dream—a
splendid proof of the dream like quality it has. Everything now depends
on the models—(if I can afford any) and the types I get for them.
Fine types are so rare and when you see them circumstances make it
impossible to use them. There was a girl with just the head I wanted

came to our place the other day—but her father said he didn't like the idea of her sitting—I don't know what the man imagined I was going to do. But I think I know someone who may do—and then there are two more—one, you promised to sit for—though it seems wrong of me to ask you to waste your time so—but I don't think it'll take long—and perhaps I may be of use to you for small things in yours. But I can't get anyone for my chief head Joy—I think I will leave it until I come across someone. You must buck up if you want to do anything—there is about 7 weeks I think and as soon as you get back—I should get in the big canvas and go ahead—you'll find when you transfer your sketch down and get models that it will come. I feel mine though it looks vague now—improves with each touch—though I haven't use[d] models yet.

I hope Lena is enjoying herself.

Could you come round Monday and get over the sitting—or if you liked I could come round to you and do it though that would be a bit awkward as I may want to paint direct on the picture. If you haven't ordered your canvas you could do so on the way.

Yours sincerely,
I. Rosenberg

You will continue your holiday in going on with your picture.

To Alice M. Wright

Postmarked 5 Sept. 1912

32 Carlingford Rd | Hampstead.

Dear Miss Wright

I have been very busy on my picture and have not been able to come round. Besides, I thought I may not find you in unless I made an appointment which is rather difficult for me just now as I never know when I am to be busy or not. It is very good of you to interest yourself so—in a few weeks perhaps you will come round and see my picture—I have no more copies of my poems° here—but I fancy my printer has some and I will see this week—if I get any I shall send them. Boss and Dickson came to see me a short while back and liked my picture. Ought I to have shown up their bad taste so?

Yours sincerely
I. Rosenberg

Regards to your sister

To Alice M. Wright

Postmarked 16 Sept. 1912

159 Oxford St | Mile End E

Dear Miss Wright

I was far from expecting the pleasure that awaited me when I got home last night in your letter and your sister's poems. I read them while having supper, and, I can assure you, I have seldom enjoyed a supper more, a proof that the ordinary material facts of life can be made more pleasurable with the assistance of some intellectual garnish. They seem to me very beautiful, though I cannot quite agree with the pessimistic tone of the mirror poem. When Milton writes on his blindness,° how dignified he is! how grand, how healthy! What begins in a mere physical moan, concludes in a great triumphant spiritual expression, of more than resignation, of conquest. But I think the concluding idea very beautiful. I like the sonnets very much, an uncommon artistic expression of the artist's common lament. But this pettifogging, mercantile, money-loving age is deaf, deaf as their dead idol gold, and dead as that to all higher ennobling influences.

After seeing these, the poems, I wonder how I could ever have shown mine; still you must understand I showed mine not so much out of vanity, as, on the contrary, out of a consciousness of their poverty, to have their defects pointed out.

I should be much obliged for a criticism.

Yours
I Rosenberg

To Alice M. Wright

?26 Sept. 1912°

32 Carlingford Rd | Hampstead.

Dear Miss Wright

I cannot come round either Wed or Thur—but Friday if you do not write to the contrary—I can come—about 5. My picture is undergoing a transforming process, it is as it were—in the frying pan—not quite raw—nor yet quite done—I think in another week I shall be quite decided on the arrangement—then I hope it will be plain sailing. I managed to find another copy of my poems which I enclose.

Yours sincerely
Isaac Rosenberg

To Alice M. Wright

[Autumn 1912]

32 Carlingford Rd | Hampstead

Dear Miss Wright

I am sorry not to have turned up Sat as I promised. Sat. is a very awkward day for me and the other days I am at the Slade or the N[ational]. G[allery].

Yours sincerely
I Rosenberg

Here is a poem I wrote.°

To Mrs Herbert Cohen

[Late Sept. or Oct. 1912]

32 Carlingford Rd | Hampstead.

Dear Mrs Cohen

I am sorry if there was any confusion about paying the Slade fees.° I still have the cheque and was waiting for the other 5 shillings so as to pay it all. I thought I could pay it out of this week's money but I have had extra expenses—mending boots and other little necessities, which made it awkward. I must thank you for returning my letter as it gives me a chance of doing that which you said ought to be done—of throwing it in the fire. I am very sorry that you noticed it as of course I did not, or I shouldn't have sent it. I said what I had to say, and had done with it, it must have been quite an accident its smudging. I don't think any other letters of mine are in that state. No stranger could receive such a letter of mine as I never write to strangers.

I sent a letter before I received this asking you to see the picture. I am not at the Slade—Tuesdays Thursdays—the picture has to go in by next Monday. I suppose you will let me know.

Yours sincerely
I Rosenberg

To Mrs Herbert Cohen

[Oct. 1912]

32 Carlingford Rd | Hampstead.

Dear Mrs Cohen,

I am very sorry I have disappointed you. If you tell me what was expected of me I shall at least have the satisfaction of knowing by how much I have erred. You were disappointed in my picture for its unfinished state—I have no wish to defend myself—or I might ask what you mean by finish:—and you are convinced I could have done better. I thank you for the compliment but I do not think it deserved—I did my best.

You did ask me whether I had been working hard, and I was so taken back at the question that I couldn't think what to say. If you did not think the work done sufficient evidence, what had I to say? I have no idea what you expected to see. I cannot conceive who gave you the idea that I had such big notions of myself, are you sure the people you enquired of know me, and meant me. You say people I have lately come in contact with. I have hardly seen anyone during the holidays—and I certainly have not been ashamed of my opinions, not about myself, but others—when I have; and if one does say anything in an excited unguarded moment—perhaps an expression of what one would like to be—it is distorted and interpreted as conceit—when in honesty it should be overlooked. I am not very inquisitive naturally, but I think it concerns me to know what you mean by poses and mannerisms—and whose advice do I not take who are in a position to give—and what more healthy style of work do you wish me to adopt?

I feel very grateful for your interest in me—going to the Slade has shown possibilities—has taught me to see more accurately—but one especial thing it has shown me—Art is not a plaything, it is blood and tears, it must grow up with one; and I believe I have begun too late.

I suppose I go on as I am till Xmas. Till then I will look about. I should like all the money advanced on me considered as a loan—but which you must not expect back for some years as it takes some time settling down in art.

Yours sincerely
I Rosenberg

The Slade pictures will be on view shortly, I will let you know more if you care to see them.

To Ruth Löwy

[Oct. 1912]

32 Carlingford Road | Hampstead

Dear Miss Löwy

Thank you for sending the cards. If you see Mr Kohan will you thank him for me—I am always eager to hear Newbolt°—I enjoyed his lecture on Milton very much.

I don't think the professor was at all fair to Bomberg.° He may have been perfectly right from his point of view, but not to enter into Bomberg's at all I don't think was just.

I have had a bit of a scuffle with Mrs Cohen lately. She was very disappointed at my picture and said she was sure I could have done better. I thanked her for the compliment and assured her it was quite undeserved—I did my best. She said that unless I get into a more healthy style of work she won't help me—and many other things that showed great invention. I told her she could do what she liked—God knows what she means by a more healthy style of work—Do you feel ill when you see my work?° I know some people feel faint looking at a Michel Angelo.—How are you getting on?

Yours sincerely
I. Rosenberg

To Alice M. Wright

[Oct. or Nov. 1912]

32 Carlingford Rd | Hampstead

Dear Miss Wright

I forgot to mention in my last letter the result of the criticism. The 'Nativity' took the prize° as was expected. Mine got well praised— The Pro°—said it showed a hopeful future—had great charm etc but I wanted more study. I am sending a drawing and perhaps a painting to the New English° as the Pro—advised me to. I am moving from here Monday so shall be busy Sunday but I shall try and be round at four. I have written other poems which I shall bring round. Trust you don't find the weather too cold.

Yours sincerely
Isaac Rosenberg

To Alice M. Wright

[Late Nov. or Dec. 1912]

159 Oxford St | Mile End E

Dear Miss Wright

I have been very unsettled since I saw you so I could not write as I promised. I moved to Hampstead Rd° and only slept there a night when I found I had to move again—on account of the train noises going on all night. I could not find another room so have gone back to my people. I have not been able to find prose things but if your friend will come to a decision I shall hunt up for them.

My drawing was accepted and bought, but not my painting. MacEvoy° told me it was liked very much, and hung half a dozen times but ...

Yours sincerely
I Rosenberg

To Mrs Herbert Cohen

[Dec. 1912]

159 Oxford St | Mile End E

Dear Mrs Cohen

I saw Mr Lesser today and he is going to put my case before the committee° next meeting.—that is, Friday a week. I told him that my reasons for applying were, firstly my reduced allowance, and that we couldn't agree, which made my position very awkward. I told him I was very vague as to what you expected me to do, or in which way you wished me to show my appreciation of what you had done,—and that I was accused of all sorts of things, and that I was put into a state of mind which made working very difficult.

Perhaps I was wrong in not consulting you, and I suppose if I tell you there was no time to consult you, you will think I am trying to make myself out right. The fact of the matter was, I looked about for a room and couldn't find any. When I went home Sunday as usual, and mentioned my difficulty of sleeping, my mother made me sleep at home that night, which decided me to stay till I found a place. You can call me rude, ungentlemanly ungrateful &c—but you know it is only my honesty in not concealing what it think that leaves me open to this. You know I am not in a position to gain anything—I mean I can only be the loser by being so. Naturally I am concerned at being thought all this by people I respect, but as I, being ignorant of the existence of the qualities that go to make the opposite, can't be expected to agree with them, I certainly don't feel conscience stricken.

Quarrelling° is an unnecessary waste of energy, and the reason I broke with Mr Sherbrooke was to prevent quarrelling.

It was only when Mr Sherbrooke's goodness became unendurable that I broke with him. When I was at Hampstead I worked all day and walked about in the rain all the evening until I was wet through and tired out—that was the only amusement I got.

The isolation there so preyed on my spirits that I don't think I'd be far wrong if I attributed the unfinished state of my picture to the mental and physical looseness so caused.

I shall return the £2 you lent me for printing out of the £4 I shall get for my drawing.°

Yours sincerely
Isaac Rosenberg

To Alice M. Wright

?1912

Slade School of Art | University College, London. |
Gower Street, W.C.

Dear Miss Wright

You must forgive me for not having written before, but things are still very unsettled and all sorts of annoyances happened to interfere. I could not come on Sunday as Sundays I am especially busy. I enclose another poem.°

Yours sincerely,
Isaac Rosenberg

To Alice M. Wright

?1912

159 Oxford St

Dear Miss Wright

I saw Miss Cook at the N[ational].G[allery]. and she told me Mr Quick had seen my poems and wished to see my drawings. I have not got a room yet so it's difficult to arrange about seeing them—in fact I've hardly got anything to show. I am very bothered—I think I've been saying that in all my letters to you—but I really am in a very serious situation. I have thrown over my patrons they were so unbearable, and as I can't do commercial work, and I have no other kind of work to show, it puts me in a fix. I only mention these private troubles to excuse my backwardness in answering your letter—

I trust you and your sister enjoy the holidays.

I have written other poems since I sent the last one° as I can't find the others just now.

Yours sincerely
Isaac Rosenberg

To Alice M. Wright

Postmarked 27 Dec. 1912

159 Oxford St | Mile End E

Dear Miss Wright

Thank you for your letter. My affairs have cleared up a little, I have managed to get fixed up for some time at least satisfactorily. I shall not be able to turn up Sat, as I have work to do, but I think Thursday I could. By then I think I shall be living in Fitzroy St,° I have come across a place there, but haven't quite made up my mind.

I haven't got the poems I promised but will try and remember on the other side.°

Yours sincerely,
Isaac Rosenberg

To Ernest Lesser

[Late Dec. 1912]

1 St Georges Sq | Chalk Farm

Dear Mr Lesser

I enclose another receipt dated last Monday when I received it. I saw Dr Davis but couldn't do anything as he has nothing to do with eyes— but he gave me a card for the Ophthalmic Hospital which I haven't been able to use yet because of the Xmas holidays. I shall go some day next week. Thanks for the information about my being a British Subject. I am getting along with my things for this competition.°

Yours sincerely
Isaac Rosenberg

To Edward Marsh

[Late 1912 or early 1913]

1, St George's Square | Regent's Park, N.W.

Dear Mr Marsh

Thanks for your criticisms which of course I agree with. If a poem doesn't sound real it has missed its end,—but I think you can understand one's fondness for an idea or a line prompting one to show poems that one knows are otherwise poor.

I have seen Bobbie—he has not been able to get his drawings yet, being busy at the workshop, but he expects to get them this week.

Yours sincerely
Isaac Rosenberg

To Ernest Lesser

[Spring 1913]

87 Dempsey St | Stepney E

Dear Mr Lesser

I have failed in the Prix Da Rome competition, but when I get the things back, I can do a little more to them and send them to Exhibitions.° Since I did those things I have been unwell, and been coughing very badly for about two months. Last week I saw a doctor and though at first he thought it was serious and said I had a very bad chest, the next time he said it wasn't so bad but I needed to go away for a couple of weeks and be out in the open. I have been sleeping here while unwell. Do you think the Society° would let me have some money to go away so that I would be fairly comfortable and I could go somewhere on the South Coast.°

The 'Prix Da Rome' things, successful and not, are on show at the Imperial Institute, South Kensington, from 10 till 4, all this week. No Slade people got it, though Prof Tonks thought they should have done so.° He was disgusted with the decision. I trust you will let me know soon.

Yours sincerely
Isaac Rosenberg

To Winifreda Seaton

Between Oct. 1913 and Jan. 1914

1 St Georges [Square]

Dear Miss Seaton

Excuse me writing in pencil as my pen has gone wrong and I want to write just now. I have not been reading Donne much as I am drawing a lot, and when I'm not drawing my mind is generally occupied that way. A great deal of Donne seems a sort of mental gymnastics, the strain is very obvious, but he is certainly wonderful, 'The ecstasy' is very fine, but F. Thompson's 'Dream tryst'° to me is much finer. There is a small book of contemporary Belgian poetry° like the German you lent me (which by the way I don't feel inclined to open) some Materlinck's seem marvellous to me, and Verhaern in the 'Sovran Rhythm' knocks Donne into a cocked hat. I mean for genuine poetry, where the words lose their interest as words and only a living and beautiful idea remains. It is a grand conception,—Eve meeting Adam. Materlinck has a superb little thing 'Orison'—a most trembling fragile moan of astonishing beauty.

The Blakes at the Tate° show that England has turned out one man second to none who has ever lived. The drawings are finer than his poems, much clearer, though I can't help thinking it was unfortunate that he did not live when a better tradition of drawing ruled. His conventional manner of expressing those astounding conceptions is the fault of his time, not his.

Yours sincerely,
Isaac Rosenberg

[To Rosenberg's mother]

Postcard, postmarked 24 Feb. 1914

195 Wimbourne Rd | Winton Bournemouth |
c/o Cohen

I forgot to put the address yesterday. I'm not lucky with the weather but the air is very good,—I don't cough much. The town here is like a big sanatorium. I'll send a card of the invalids' garden. Pine Woods a few minutes from here. I'm going there now.

Isaac

Extract from letter to Winifreda Seaton

[Between autumn 1913 and spring 1914]

I can't say I have ever experienced the power of one spirit over another, except in books, of course, at least in any intense way that you mean. Unless you mean the interest one awakes in us, and we long to know more, and none other. I suppose we are all influenced by everybody we come in contact with, in a subconscious way, if not direct, and everything that happens to us is experience; but only the few know it. Most people can only see and hear the noisy sunsets, mountains and waterfalls; but the delicate greys and hues, the star in the puddle, the quiet sailing cloud, is nothing to them. Of course, I only mean this metaphorically, as distinguishing between obvious experiences and the almost imperceptible.

I still have no work to do. I think, if nothing turns up here, I will go to Africa.° I could not endure to live upon my people; and up till now I have been giving them from what I had managed to save up when I was at work. It is nearly run out now, and if I am to do nothing, I would rather do it somewhere else. Besides, I feel so cramped up here, I can do no drawing, reading, or anything [...]

Create our own experience! We can, but we don't. Very often it's only the trouble of a word, and who knows what we miss through not having spoken? It's the man with impudence who has more experience than anybody. He not only varies his own, but makes other people's his own.

To Ernest Lesser

?Spring 1914

87 Dempsey St | Stepney E

Dear Mr Lesser

Do you think the E[ducation] A[id] S[ociety]° would make me a grant of 12 or 15 pounds to go to S Africa.

The doctor has told me my chest is weak and that I must live in the country and take care of myself. I cannot live here in the country just now, and it is now that it is so essential. I have a relation in Cape Town° who could put me up until I sold things some way or other, and I believe I could get heaps of good subject matter.

The kaffirs would sit for practically nothing. In a year I'd have a lot of interesting stuff, to send to England. I am sending several things to Whitechapel show.° The fare to S Africa is £12. Could you let me know at once as I am convinced of the importance of not stopping here.

Yours sincerely,
Isaac Rosenberg

Extract from letter to Winifreda Seaton

[Spring 1914]

So I've decided on Africa, the climate being very good, and I believe plenty to do [...] I won't be quite lost in Africa [...] I dislike London for the selfishness it instils into one, which is a reason of the peculiar feeling of isolation I believe most people have in London. I hardly know anybody whom I would regret leaving (except, of course, the natural ties of sentiment with one's own people); but whether it is that my nature distrusts people, or is intolerant, or whether my pride or my backwardness cools people, I have always been alone. Forgive this little excursion into the forbidden lands of egotism.

To Edward Marsh

[May 1914]

87 Dempsey Street | Stepney E.

Dear Mr Marsh

I should feel very pleased and proud to have my drawing printed in your book.° I know someone who might be a subscriber and would like to know what the subscription is,—and I suppose a copy would be sent on.

I am about to sail for Africa as I have been told my chest is not strong and I must live away from towns. If I get the chance I may work on a farm for a year or two as I am young enough to afford it. I might also this way get ideas for real things. One is so cramped up here and one must either do cubism° or what I propose to do to avoid the rut &c. I could not resist mentioning this having this occasion to write to you. I hope you will let me know the subscription for my friend.

Yours sincerely
Isaac Rosenberg

To Edward Marsh

Postmarked 15 May 1914

87 Dempsey St | Stepney E

Dear Marsh

I have been to the Emigration Office and find there are no other restrictions beside those you wrote me. They would want some sort of guarantee that my sister could keep me, but that depends on what the other side (in Africa) take for guarantee. I shouldn't think I need fear anything that way, as I'm sure my sister could put me up for some months during which I could turn out enough work to make some sort of stir. I have no tuberculosis as far as I know, but a weak chest.

It is very very kind of you to go to all that bother—I hope it doesn't interfere with anything you have to do.

I am enclosing the lines I lately wrote,° and those I showed you. I think the more recent read more musically. At present they have no connection with the first but that is the only way I can write, in scraps, and then join them together—I have the *one idea* in mind.

Yours sincerely
Isaac Rosenberg

To Edward Marsh

[May 1914]

87 Dempsey St | Stepney E

Dear Marsh

I shall not be going for about 2 weeks, when I expect to be quite ready. I should be delighted to see your pictures before I go,—I have heard you have a fine collection. I can spare any evening you like and will bring one or two drawings. I'm also having some things at the Whitechapel, but they're very incomplete—I suppose you'll see them there. The address I should like you to send the prospectus is

Mrs Löwy°
11 Ladbroke Terrace
Holland Park W.

Yours sincerely
Isaac Rosenberg

To Edward Marsh

[May 1914]

87 Dempsey St | Stepney E

Dear Marsh

Thank you very much—I am very eager to see your pictures. I will be at the restaurant° Fri, with some silly drawings.

Yours sincerely
Isaac Rosenberg

To Edward Marsh

[May 1914]

87 Dempsey St | Stepney E

Dear Marsh

Thanks very very much for the book.° I know so little of these men, and from that little I know how much I miss by not knowing more. I think the Queen's Song of Flecker,° delicious; And 'The end of the world' by Bottomley,° very fine imagination and original. That is all I have had time to read yet. What strikes me about these men are they are very much alive, and have personal vision—and what is so essential, can express themselves very simply. But writing about a poem is like singing about a song—or rather, as Donne says, fetching water to the sea, and in my case, very dirty water. You can talk about life, but you can only talk round literature; you will be talking about life, I think.

Yours sincerely
Isaac Rosenberg

To Edward Marsh

[May or June 1914]

87 Dempsey St | Stepney E

Dear Marsh

This is my rest while packing. My things have to be on board by Wed—and I only knew today—so you can imagine the rush I'm in.

Your criticism gave me great pleasure; not so much the criticism, as to feel that you took those few lines up so thoroughly, and tried to get into them. You don't know how encouraging that is. People talk about independence and all that—but one always works with some sort of doubt, that is, if one believes in the inspired 'suntreaders'. I believe that all poets who are personal—see things genuinely, have their place. One needn't be a Shakespeare and yet be quite as interesting. I have moods when Rossetti satisfies me more than Shakespeare—and I am sure I have enjoyed some things of Francis Thompson more than the best of Shakespeare. Yet I never meant to go as high as these— I know I've come across things by people of far inferior vision, that were as important in their results, to me.

I am not going to refute your criticisms; in literature I have no judgment—at least for style. If in reading a thought has expressed itself to me, in beautiful words; my ignorance of grammar &c, makes me accept that. I should think you are right mostly; and I may yet work away your chief objections. You are quite right in the way you read my poem,° but I thought I could use the 'July ghost' to mean the Summer, and also an ambassador of the summer, without interfering with the sense. The shell of thought is man; you realise a shell has an opening. Across this opening, the ardours—the sense of heat forms a web—this signifies a sense of summer—the web again becomes another metaphor—a July ghost.—But of course I mean it for summer right through. I think your suggestion of taking out 'woven' is very good. I enclose another thing which is part of this. I told you my idea—The whole thing is to be called the poet, and begins with the way external nature affects him, and goes on to human nature.

In packing my things I found a little painting of a boy that I don't think looks at all bad. I could show it to you if you cared to see it—

Yours sincerely
Isaac Rosenberg

Postcard to Rosenberg's mother

June 1914

Jamestown, St Helena

Just got here; haven't looked round yet. Seems fine. Napoleon buried here.

Isaac

To Edward Marsh

[Early June 1914]

c/o Mrs Horvitch | Hill House |
43 De Villiers St | Cape Town.

Dear Marsh

Thank you very much for your letter to your friend.° I hope he will be in C[ape] T[own] and that I'll be able to see him. I'm eagerly waiting for Sat. The above will be my address, but I'll write when I get there and know what sort of outlook it is.

Yours sincerely
Isaac Rosenberg

To Edward Marsh

Letter card, postmarked 20 or 30 June 1914

43 De Villiers St | C[ape] T[own]

Dear Marsh

I've had a fearfully busy week—seeing people and preparing for work. I want to write a long letter I have lots to write about,—wait till next week. Stanley° has given me a small job—painting two babies. I'm just off to do them.

The place is gorgeous—just for an artist.

Yours sincerely
Isaac Rosenberg

To Edward Marsh

Postmarked Cape Town 24 July 1914

43 Devilliers St | Cape Town

Dear Marsh

I should like you to do me a favour if it's not putting you to too much bother. I am in an infernal city by the sea. This city has men in it—and these men have souls in them—or at least have the passages to souls.

Though they are millions of years behind time they have yet reached the stage of evolution that knows ears and eyes. But these passages are dreadfully clogged up; gold dust, diamond dust, stocks and shares, and heaven knows what other flinty muck. Well I've made up my mind to clear through all this rubbish. But I want your help. Now I'm going to give a series of lectures on modern art° (I'm sending you the first, which I gave in great style. I was asked whether the Futurist[s]° exhibited at the Royal Academy.) But I want to make the lectures interesting and intelligible by reproductions or slides. Now I wonder whether you have reproductions which you could lend me till I returned or was finished with them. I want to talk about John, Cézanne° Vangogh, Innes, the early Picasso (not the cubist one) Spencer, Gertler, Lamb, Puvis De Chavannes, Degas. A book of reproductions of the P[ost] Impressionist[s] would do and I could get them transferred on slides. I hope this would not put you to any great trouble but if you could manage to do it you don't know how you would help me.

Stanley gave me a little job to paint two babies, which helped me to pay my way for a bit. I expect to get pupils and kick up a row with my lectures. But nobody seems to have money here, and not an ounce of interest in Art. The climate's fine, but the Sun is a very changeable creature and I can't come to any sort of understanding with this golden beast. He pretends to keep quiet for half an hour and just as I think, now I've got it, the damned thing has frisked about.

There's a lot of splendid stuff to paint. We are walled in by the sharp upright mountain and the bay. Across the bay the piled up mountains of Africa look lovely and dangerous. It makes one think of savagery and earthquakes—the elemental lawlessness. You are lucky to be in comfortable London and its armchair culture.

I've painted a kaffir, and am pottering about. I expect if I get pupils to get a room and shall be able to work better. Do write to me—think of me, a creature of the most exquisite civilization, planted in this barbarous land. Write me of Spencer Lamb Currie and the pack of them. I mean to write to Gertler myself, but so far I've not been able to get away from my own people here, to write. They don't understand the artist's seclusion to concentrate, and I'm always interrupted. Write me of poetry and do send me that little thing of Binyon's in your album.

Yours sincerely
Isaac Rosenberg

I'll send my lecture next week as they may be printing it in a local paper.°

To Edward Marsh

Postmarked 8 Aug. 1914

'Hill House' | 43 Devilliers St | Cape Town

Dear Marsh

I enclose the lecture. By the time it reaches you I expect the world will be in convulsions and you'll be in the thick of it. I know my poor innocent essay stands no chance by the side of the bristling legions of war scented documents on your desk; but know that I despise war and hate war, and hope that the Kaiser William will have his bottom smacked—a naughty aggressive schoolboy who will have *all* the plum pudding. Are we going to have Tennyson's 'Battle in the Air',° and the nations deluging the nations with blood from the air? Now is the time to go on an exploring expedition to the North Pole;° to come back and find settled order again.

Yours sincerely
Isaac Rosenberg

To Edward Marsh

[Oct. or Nov. 1914]

'Hill House' | 43 de Villiers St | Cape Town

Dear Marsh

You are very kind to think of me. I see though from the papers your friend is not coming out but is going to hotter places than this.° It's a fearful nuisance, this war. I think the safest place is at the front,—we'll starve or die of suspense, anywhere else.

I feel very much better in health; I keep a good deal in the open and walk a lot. We have had very damp weather and wonderful storms and winds; houses blown over,—the very mountains shaken. We are expecting the fine weather, which I mean to see right through and then come back. I've been trying to get pupils to teach, but this war has killed all that. I painted a very interesting girl, which I'm rather pleased with. It's very quiet and modest and no fireworks. I may send it to the New English if I don't bring it back myself in time. Also a self portrait, very gay and cocky, which I think will go down very well. I'm waiting for better weather to paint the kaffirs against characteristic landscapes. Also I've written poems, of which I'm sending the small ones. By the time you get this things will only have just begun I'm afraid; Europe will have just stepped into its bath of blood. I will be waiting with beautiful drying towels of painted canvas, and precious ointments to smear and heal the soul; and lovely music and poems. But I really hope to have a nice lot of pictures and poems by the time all is settled again; and Europe is repenting of her savageries.

I know Duncan Grant's dance,° and if the one you have is better, it must be very fine indeed. I've just written to Cokeham;° I hadn't his address so sent it to Cokeham on Thames. I hope he got it. His brother is very lucky. I also just wrote to Gertler. I really get no privacy here and can't write or even think. But this coming away has changed me marvellously, and makes me more confident and mature. Here's a chance to exercise any bloodthirsty and critical propensities.

['The Female God']

This is the last thing° I've written but I've got more, which I may enclose in this letter. What's become of Currie?

Yours sincerely
Isaac Rosenberg

To his family

[Late 1914]

Dear Mother—Father—and everybody.

I have not read your letters this week as I've been staying out at a pretty suburb with a very pretty name Rondebosch, and with very nice people. It was through my lecture and poems being printed. I went one day to see the lady who is the editor of the paper it was printed in, and there I met a Miss Molteno—who told me how delighted she was with my poems. She asked me to come to Rondebosch where she lives; and there she took me to see some beautiful places, and then asked me whether I'd like to be her guest there for a week or two. She is a sister of the speaker to the House of Parliament here. Her father was famous out here—Sir John Molteno,° and she has crowds of relations. Anyway I'm here at Rondebosch having a happy time, you will be glad to hear—I'm anxious to know how you all are and will run down to town about the letters tomorrow, today being Sunday. I'm living like a toff here. Early in the morning coffee is brought to me in bed. My shoes (my only pair) are polished so brightly that the world is pleasantly deceived as to the tragedy that polish covers. I don't know whether there are snakes or wild animals in my room but in the morning when I get up and look at the soles of my shoes, every morning I see another hole. I shan't make your mouths water by describing my wonderful breakfasts—the unimaginable lunches—delicious teas, and colossal dinners. You would say all fibs. I won't tell of the wonderful flowers that look into my window and the magnificent park that surrounds my room. Of the mountain climbing right to the sheerest top until the town and the sea and fields were like little picture postcards lying on the pavement to one looking from the top of the Monument. In a few months I hope to be back in England—I should like to get there for the warm weather—about March or so.

Isaac

To Miss Molteno

[March 1915]

87 Dempsey St | Stepney | London E.

Dear Miss Molteno

I've been a whole day in London and feel very happy, in spite of not being able to see London because of a very thick fog. My voyage was pretty vile and I'm very glad it's over. The moment I got on board I was waylaid and seized and taken charge of by one of those busy servants of death who are known in life as colds and coughs. He stuck pretty tight to me and worried and annoyed me all through the voyage, but he wearied of me at last, or got frightened by the searchlight at Dover, for he left me there. I had no other company on board.

I have not seen anybody yet, as my baggage with my pictures has not arrived and the letters and addresses are all there. By next week I hope to have nice long accounts to give you.

I trust you enjoyed your holiday and are well. Remember me to Miss Greene and say as soon as I get hold of good new poems I'll send them over.

Yours sincerely
Isaac Rosenberg

Extract from letter to Winifreda Seaton

[Spring 1915]

I saw Olive Schreiner last night. She's an extraordinary woman—full of life. I had a little picture for her from a dear friend of hers° in Africa I stayed with while I was there. She was so pleased with my pictures of Kaffirs. Who is your best living English poet? I've found somebody miles and miles above everybody—a young man, Lascelles Abercrombie°—a mighty poet and brother to Browning.

To Edward Marsh

[Spring 1915]

87 Dempsey St | Stepney E

Dear Marsh

Thank you for the cheque. I love poetry—but just now the finest poem ever written would not move me as the writing on that cheque. I saw Olive Shreiner last night. She's an extraordinary woman. Full of go and makes every word live. I think I gave her real pleasure with my kaffir pictures and if I'd done more I'd have given her one.

If you do not find time to read my poems, and I sent them because I think them worth reading, for God's Sake! don't say they're obscure. The idea in the poem I like best° I should think is very clear. That we can cheat our malignant fate who has devised a perfect evil for us, by pretending to have as much misery as we can bear, so that it withholds its greater evil, while under that guise of misery there is secret joy. Love—this joy—burns and grows within us trying to push out to that. Eternity without us which is God's heart. Joy-love, grows in time too vast to be hidden from God under the guise of gloom. Then we find another way of cheating God. Now through the very joy itself. For by this time we have grown into love, which is the rays of that Eternity of which God is the sun. We have become God Himself. Can God hate and do wrong to Himself?

I think myself the poem is very clear, but if by some foul accident it isn't, I wonder if you see that idea in it.

I'll bring the picture Wed. I want to get the hands and feet a bit more explained.

Yours sincerely
Isaac Rosenberg

To Winifreda Seaton

?Spring 1915

87 Dempsey St | Stepney E

Dear Miss Seaton

Could you let me have the 'Georgian book'° back, unless you have not finished with it. I want to show somebody some poems there. I do not know whether I lent you Abercrombie's 'Olympians' in *New Numbers*,° will you tell me? The book you lent me of G. Bottomley made me buy the second 'Chambers of Imagery'.° The fine things in this are simpler and more harmoniously complete than the first book. I like Bottomley more than any modern poet I have yet come across. I will lend you this book.

I have been writing better than usual, (I think) lately, but the things are slight—they all have the same atmosphere and I may be able to work them into one, if I can hit on an episode to connect them. When they're all together I'll show you them. Trust you're doing well.

Yours sincerely
Isaac Rosenberg

To Edward Marsh

?Spring 1915

87 Dempsey St | Stepney E

Dear Marsh

I hope you won't think it too forward of me to try and keep myself in your mind by writing to you, as you promised to buy something of me. I don't know which of mine you liked best but I could bring them all again when you have more time.

Yours sincerely
Isaac Rosenberg

How's this for a joke?

> You cleave to my bones,
> Prop and hold in a noose

One of the lives God loans.
Sinew of my sinews!

What will the Lord say
When I shall nowhere be found
At the judgement day,
My life within you being wound?

To Winifreda Seaton

?Spring 1915

87 Dempsey St | Stepney E

Dear Miss Seaton

Thanks for copying those things for me. I do wish though you had copied that 'Marriage of convenience' it is more interesting to me than these. I am sending you a thing I copied out years ago from one of our greatest poets and I think one of his best. It is very unlike his usual style, and it is not by F. Thompson. I am showing you this because I think it's a discovery of mine. I don't like L. Douglas' sonnets° very much. Rossetti never published anything that wasn't good, but he must have written a good deal very much like those sonnets and burnt them. I like that line 'And thy great oak of life a rotten tree'. I will be able to give you your Goethe° back when I see you. It's the most interesting autobiography I've ever read. It is as much like an autobiography of Shakespeare as one could be. He is the most comprehensive of writers since Shakespeare.

I met somebody yesterday who is a great friend of G Bottomley. He also thinks he is the best modern poet. He tells me B lives in Yorkshire has only one lung and writes in great pain. He is a large giant of a fellow but mustn't exert himself much. He will lend me some of his plays. I have never come across your London poem° before. Why do you ask me who wrote it? 'Truth should have no man's name.'

Yours sincerely
Isaac Rosenberg

Do write me exactly what you think of my play.°

To Edward Marsh

[Spring 1915]

87 Dempsey St | Stepney E

Dear Marsh

I've done a lovely picture I'd like you to see. It's a girl who sat for Da Vinci, and hasn't changed a hair since, in a deep blue gown against a dull crimson ground. If you have time to see it I'd also like Gertler to be there if he can. I don't know whether you've shown my things to Abercrombie yet—if you haven't I'd like you to show these also I enclose,—one of them you have is corrected here.

Yours sincerely
Isaac Rosenberg

To Edward Marsh

[Spring 1915]

87 Dempsey St | Stepney E

Dear Marsh

I will bring the picture tomorrow. I think you will like to see it, though if I had a little longer on it it would have been very fine indeed but the model cleared off before I could absolutely finish. I've also been working hard at my poems. I'm glad you haven't shown A[bercrombie]. my things. I've made that poem quite clear now I think. I've a scheme for a little book called 'Youth',° in three parts.

1. Faith and fear.
2. The cynic's lamp.
3. Sunfire.

In the first the idealistic youth believes and aspires towards purity. The poems are. Aspiration. Song of Immortality (which by the way, is absolutely Abercrombie's idea in the Hymn to Love, and it's one of my first poems). Noon in the city. None know the Lord of the House. A girl's thoughts. Wedded. Midsummer frost.

In the second. The cynic's lamp,—the youth has become hardened by bitter experience and has no more vague aspirations, he is just sense. The poems are Love and lust. In Piccadilly. A mood. The cynic's path. Tess.

In the third. Change and sunfire. The spiritualizing takes place. He has no more illusions, but life itself becomes transfigured through Imagination, that is, real intimacy.—love.

The poems are. April dawn. If I am fire. Break in by nearer ways. God made blind etc. Do you like the scheme?

Yours sincerely
Isaac Rosenberg

To Sydney Schiff

[Late March or early April 1915]

87 Dempsey St | Stepney E

Dear Mr Shiff,°

I am always glad to show people my work and if you ever feel inclined to come down and see it, let me know a little beforehand and it will be alright. Buying pictures of me is the last thing in the world I expect people to do, in the best of times, so you needn't worry about that.

I believe I was introduced to you as a poet, and as poems are not quite so bulky and weighty, at least outwardly, as pictures, I am sending some.

Yours sincerely
Isaac Rosenberg

On second thoughts I will l wait till I've printed some in a few weeks.

To Alice Meynell°

87 Dempsey Street.

Dear Madam,

Mrs Siordet once showed you some poems of mine and drawings I did at the Slade. You liked the drawings very much and said the poems wanted more work. I think there are too few poems to ask you

to forgive the intrusion on your time, and only hope you will not think
there are too many that require forgiveness.

Yours sincerely
Isaac Rosenberg

To Edward Marsh

[April or May 1915]

87 Dempsey St | Stepney E

Dear Marsh
Don't you think this is a nice little thing now

> The one lost
> I mingle with your bones.
> You steal in subtle noose
> This starry trust He loans,
> And in your life I lose.
>
> What will the Lender say
> When I shall not be found,
> Sought at the Judgement Day,
> Lost—in your being bound?

I've given my things to the printer—he's doing 16 pages for £2.10.
I know for certain I can get rid of ten. My notion in getting them
printed is that I believe some of them are worth reading, and that like
money kept from circulating, they would be useless to myself and
others, kept to myself. I lose nothing by printing and may even make a
little money. If you like you can have my three life drawings for the
money if you think they're worth it. You don't know how happy you
have made me by giving me this chance to print.°

Yours sincerely
Isaac Rosenberg

To Sydney Schiff

[April or May 1915]

87 Dempsey Street | Stepney E

Dear Mr Shiff,
Thank you for your letter and for what you say. I have already sent
my poems to the printer and you will have a copy in about 2 weeks.

But I am sending poems I wrote before I was 20 and I leave you to pick out anything good in them.

Yours sincerely
Isaac Rosenberg

   It is the only copy I have
   I shall want it back

To Edward Marsh

[1915]

                                          87 Dempsey St | Stepney E

Dear Marsh
   I'm doing a nice little thing for Meredith's 'Lark ascending'°
     (Their faces raised
     (Puts on the light of children praised.
Everybody is in a sort of delirious ecstasy, and all, feeling in the same way, express the same feelings in different ways, according to their natures. I think you'll like it. I'll bring others, in case you don't. I can't refrain from sending my last poems which I think are much better and clearer than my others.

Yours sincerely
Isaac Rosenberg

To Edward Marsh

[April 1915]

                                          87 Dempsey St | Stepney E

Dear Marsh
   I left a parcel of pictures for you to see, at the porter's lodge. Friday. I remember now I did not put your address on as I could not think of the number, so I am rather worried to know whether you got them. There may be somebody else of your name there. If you have, I suppose you have been too busy to see them—my fear that you might be was the reason I never wrote to you first to bother you for replies. I want to cart those things round London to try and sell as

I am very low and I took them round to you first thinking you might like something there. Do drop me a line to say you have them—I don't want them to get lost.

Yours sincerely
Isaac Rosenberg

To Edward Marsh

[Late April 1915]

87 Dempsey St | Stepney E

My dear Marsh
 I am so sorry°—what else can I say?
 But he himself has said 'What is more safe than death?' For us is the hurt who feel about English literature, and for you who knew him and feel his irreparable loss.

Yours sincerely
Isaac Rosenberg

Extract from letter to Winifreda Seaton

[April or May 1915]

 Do you know Emerson's poems?° I think they are wonderful. 'Each and All' I think is deep and beautiful. There is always a kind of beaminess, like a dancing of light in light, in his poems. I do think, though, that he depends too much on inspiration; and though they always have a solid texture of thought, they sometimes seem thin in colour or sensuousness.

To Edward Marsh

[Late April or May 1915]

87 Dempsey St | Stepney E

My dear Marsh
 I am very sorry to have had to disturb you at such a time with pictures.° But when one's only choice is between horrible things you

choose the least horrible. First I think of enlisting and trying to get my head blown off, then of getting some manual labour to do—anything—but it seems I'm not fit for anything. Then I took these things to you. You would forgive me if you knew how wretched I was. I am sorry I can give you no more comfort in your own trial but I am going through it too.

Thank you for your cheque it will do for paints and I will try and do something you'll like.

Yours sincerely
Isaac Rosenberg

To Edward Marsh

[Late April or May 1915]

87 Dempsey St | Stepney E.

My dear Marsh,

Forgive my weak and selfish letter. I should not have disturbed you at all but one gets so bewildered in this terrible struggle. Thank you for showing my things to Abercrombie and thinking of that now. He has not written yet. I can come if you like Tuesday or any day. I will come Tue if you do not write.

Yours sincerely
Isaac Rosenberg

Incomplete letter to Miss Molteno

[Late April or May 1915]

87 Dempsey St | Stepney | London E

Dear Miss Molteno

I am so glad you are happy in Garden's Bay and am very glad to hear this from yourself for Olive Schreiner had already told me. Your letter makes very vivid to me that strange time in my life (though everything in life is strange to me) when my mind was so full of dark thoughts and terrors and I seemed to myself to be an accidental flame God's heat had lit and He unknowing of it; a flame blown away from the furnace of its birth.

What I want to say is when I felt so isolated and lost you came and took some of the isolation away and your letter brings back very vividly the only time of all that time I wish to remember. I dislike saying such things as I believe people ought to understand; but I am beginning to change my notions about these matters, for I find that by keeping silent, people not only [do] not understand, they misunderstand, and I would dread to be thought unfeeling as much as I would to be thought overfeeling or sentimental.

I have seen Mrs Murray and Mrs Moltino. I do not know whether Mrs Murray has set out yet for S.A. (she told me she was soon going,). I left the books and picture with her. I should have liked to have got more books but when I found that the money I asked for had already covered the frames for [?] picture and Mrs M. with the books, I did not like asking for more.

You will like Meredith's selection. One of the poets in the 'Georgian Poets' has just died at Lemnos. Rupert Brooke who has so wonderful a poem on death° in that book will never write more. He was only 27 and was beginning to do great things. Everybody is upset. Flecker, whose poem on the nativity° Miss Green read so beautifully on New Year's Day is also dead, also the same age.

Olive Schreiner has just written to me asking whether I wanted to sell and the price for a kaffir picture—and I expect to see her shortly.

I have painted some things I am sending to an exhibition where I may sell, but I find it horrible difficult to even do anything and am trying to get a post as a teacher, which, if I should get, my mind would be more settled and I could work. If you heard of a post as teacher in Johannesburg or anywhere in Africa I would go, in fact I'm rather [

To Sydney Schiff

4 June 1915

87 Dempsey St | Stepney E

Dear Mr Shiff

Here are some poems I've had printed. I am selling them at half crown a book. I am also enclosing a sketch for a play, which may interest you; but I want this back as I have no spare copies.

Hope you enjoyed your holiday. We just missed being blown to pieces by a bomb the other night, a factory near by was burnt to pieces and some people killed.°

Yours sincerely
Isaac Rosenberg

You will notice I've torn out a page in the book.° The poems were very trivial and I've improved the book by taking them out.

To Sydney Schiff

8 June 1915

87 Dempsey Street | Stepney E

Dear Mr Schiff,

Thank you for your P[ostal].O[rder]. I am sending you another copy and one to Mr Clutton Brock° as you asked me. I am very glad you have taken the trouble to read my things and have found something you like in them—most people find them difficult and won't be bothered to read into them. What people call technique is a very real thing, it corresponds to construction and command of form in painting. Rossetti was a supreme master of it in poetry and had no command of form whatever in painting. My technique in poetry is very clumsy I know.

I wonder whether Mr Clutton Brock could get me some Art writing to do for any journals he is connected with. I shall mention it in writing to him.

I am thinking of enlisting if they will have me, though it is against all my principles of justice—though I would be doing the most criminal thing a man can do—I am so sure my mother would not stand the shock that I don't know what to do.

Yours sincerely
Isaac Rosenberg

To Sydney Schiff

[Mid-July 1915]

87 Dempsey Street | Stepney E

Dear Mr Shiff

I heard from Mr Clutton Brock and he says he likes my things. If I have the letter I will send it to you. He writes he is overworked but was kind enough to go thro them (I should think with care) and mentions those he likes most. I do not know whether you are still away, but when you are in town and you care to see my pictures you can let me know.

Gertler has a remarkable painting at N[ew].E[nglish].° which puts him easily next to John amongst our painters. John has a very fine head of B. Shaw,° vivid and alive and serious. Gertler's appears clever beside the high seriousness of his.

Yours sincerely
Isaac Rosenberg

To Sydney Schiff

[Mid-July 1915]

87 Dempsey Street | Stepney E

Dear Mr Shiff

Do you mind sending the enclosed to Mr Clutton Brock. I did not answer his letter as I mislaid it and your card has made me think of it. I believe they are getting up a show of Gaudier's work°—at least they are talking of it but nothing is settled as far as I know. I do not know his work but I met him once. He gave one a good impression. It is awful bad luck.

Yours sincerely,
Isaac Rosenberg

Draft of part of a letter to Ezra Pound

[Late summer or autumn 1915]

87 Dempsey St | Stepney E

Dear Mr Pound

Thank you very much for sending my things to America.° As to your suggestion about the army I think the world has been terribly damaged by certain poets (in fact any poet) being sacrificed in this stupid business. There is certainly a strong temptation to join when you are making no money.

To Sydney Schiff

[Early-mid Sept. 1915]

87 Dempsey Street | Stepney E

Dear Mr Shiff

I sent you two drawings I hope you will like, though I had meant to do a composition but have not been able to in my present state of mind. I have decided not to think of painting at least until I have achieved some kind of (no matter how small) independence, by doing what is called an honest trade—I am going to learn something and in a few months I may start earning a little. Painting was once an honest trade, now a painter is either a gentleman, or must subsist on patronage—anyway I won't let painting interfere with my peace of mind—If later on I haven't forgotten it I may yet do something. Forgive this private cry but even the enormity of what is going on all through Europe always seems less to an individual than his own struggle.

Yours sincerely
Isaac Rosenberg

The drawings will follow

To Sydney Schiff

[Early Oct. 1915]

87 Dempsey Street | Stepney E.

Dear Mr Shiff

In my last letter I wrote you I was learning 'an honest trade'. I don't know whether I told you what it was but what I meant was that I was learning to do work that I would not be put to all sorts of shifts and diplomatics to dispose of. It is very mechanical work though my skill in drawing is of great use in it. It is process work—preparing blocks for the press—but it is very unhealthy having to be bending over strong acids all day—and though my chest is weak I shall have to forget all that. But I have yet to learn it and when I have learnt it it may take some time before I find work. I am attending an evening school° where this work is taught and it may take some months to learn as the hours at the school are so few. I also have to pay this evening school, it is not very much but it is more than I can afford. You have shown that you are interested in me so I thought you would not mind lending me the 10 shillings to pay as it is so very little and I could so easily return it as soon as I get work. I hope you will not think this impudence, but all my friends seem to have disappeared. I hope very soon and by this means that I shall need none.

I am sending some small poems I have managed to write in my awful state of mind, or rather as a relief from it.

Yours sincerely
Isaac Rosenberg

To Sydney Schiff

[Oct. 1915]

87 Dempsey St | Stepney E

Dear Mr Shiff

Thank you for the cheque which is as much to me now as all the money in America would be to the Allies. When I am settled I hope you will allow me to return it either in drawings or money. I expect to know enough for my purpose in 2 months, and I will let you know how I get on. As to what you say about my being luckier than other victims I can only say that one's individual situation is more real and important to oneself than the devastation of fates and empires especially when they do not vitally affect oneself. I can only give my personal and if you like selfish point of view that I feeling myself in the prime and vigour of my powers (whatever they may be) have no more free will than a tree; seeing with helpless clear eyes the utter destruction of the railways and avenues of approaches to outer communication cut off. Being by the nature of my upbringing, all my energies having been directed to one channel of activity, crippled from other activities and made helpless even to live. It is true I have not been killed or crippled, been a loser in the stocks, or had to forswear my fatherland, but I have not quite gone free and have a right to say something.

Forgive all this bluster but—salts for constipation—moral of course.

Yours sincerely
Isaac Rosenberg

I have not seen or heard of Bomberg for ages but he was pretty bad 5 months ago.

To Sydney Schiff

[Oct. 1915]

87 Dempsey Street | Stepney E

Dear Mr Shiff

I shall send you a drawing either this week or next for your cheque, which I hope you will like—I should like to write much more but I don't feel I can now. I will try and write a letter when I send the drawing.

I have changed my mind again about joining the army. I feel about it that more men means more war,—besides the immorality of joining with no patriotic convictions.

Thank you very much for your cheque.

Yours sincerely
Isaac Rosenberg

To Edward Marsh

[End Oct. or early Nov. 1915]

Reply to° Priv I Rosenberg |
Company 12th Suffolk | *Bat.* Bantaam | *Regt.* Suffolks |
Stationed at New Offices.
Recruiting Depot Bury St Edmunds

Dear Marsh

I have just joined the Bantaams° and am down here amongst a horrible rabble—Falstaff's scarecrows° were nothing to these. Three out of every 4 have been scavengers the fourth is a ticket of leave. But that is nothing—though while I'm waiting for my kit I'm roughing it a bit having come down without even a towel. I dry myself with my pocket handkerchief. I don't know whether I will be shifted as soon as I get my rigout—I thought you might like to hear this. I meant to send you some poems I wrote which are better than my usual things but I have left them at home where I am rather afraid to go for a while—I left without saying anything. Abercrombie did not write to me, I hope it is not because he disliked my things. If that is not the reason I should like to send him my new things. Can you tell me anything of Gertler.°

Yours sincerely
Isaac Rosenberg

To Sydney Schiff

[Early Nov. 1915]

Priv I Rosenberg | Bat. Bantam, Regt. 12th Suffolk |
New Depot, Bury St. Edmunds

Dear Mr Shiff

I could not get the work I thought I might so I have joined this Bantam Battalion (as I was too short for any other) which seems to be the most rascally affair in the world. I have to eat out of a basin together with some horribly smelling scavenger who spit[s] and sneezes into it etc. It is most revolting, at least up to now—I don't mind the hard sleeping the stiff marches etc but this is unbearable. Besides my being a Jew makes it bad amongst these wretches. I am looking forward to having a bad time altogether. I am sending some old things to the New English and if they get in you may see them there. I may be stationed here some time or be drafted off somewhere else; if you write I will be glad to hear.

Yours sincerely
I. Rosenberg

To Sydney Schiff

[Early Nov. 1915]

Military Hospital | Depot, |
12th Suffolk Bantams | Bury St Edmunds

Dear Mr Shiff

Don't be frightened at the heading. In running before the Colonel I slipped on some mud and gravel and cut my both hands rather badly. But I shall be right enough in a few days. I shall find out the name of the Colonel before I send this letter. Of course if some kind of sense of difference could be established between myself and the others, not that

my sensitiveness should not be played upon but only that unnecessary
trouble shouldn't be started. I don't object to severe duties or menial
and filthy work as it hardens one. As I won't get paid till I am in khaki
which business takes some time it seems (I've been here over a week
and have had to do all the duties of new recruits in my civvies and have
come quite unprepared expecting to get them the day I joined) natur-
ally your present is very handy. It will do for some shaves and suppers
etc. I hope to be well and get the khaki in a few days. I don't know yet
whether I am staying here or will be sent down to Aldershot. I will
write more when I know. I wanted to join the R[oyal] A[rmy] M[edical]
C[orps] as the idea of killing upsets me a bit, but I was too small. The
only regiment my build allowed was the Bantams.

Yours sincerely
I Rosenberg

To Sydney Schiff

[Pre-12 Nov. 1915]

Priv I Rosenberg |
12th Suffolk Bantams Military Hospital |
Depot | Bury St Edmunds |
Tuesday night

Dear Mr Shiff
    I am still in the hospital and expect to be for at least two days more,
so though I have your present° for which many thanks, I am unable to
make any use of it, but it won't be long before I will be unable to make
any more use of it, as it will be used. Just now I don't quite know
where I can keep books. I have with me Donne's poems and Browne's
'Religion De Medici'° and must carry both in my pocket. I have drawn
some of the chaps in the hospital and I can see heaps of subject matter
all over. If you could send any small books or news that might interest
me I think I could find a place for them. A small box of watercolours
would be handy. I cannot get one in this town. I can only get Sundays
off so have no chance of finding out as the evenings are pitch black and
no shops are visible. Cigarettes or any small eatable luxuries also help
to make things pleasanter. Any sketches I may do I will send though
I don't think I'll be in the frame of mind for doing decent work for
some time. The only thing (and it is very serious to me) that troubles

me is my mother is so upset about me. It was this thought that stopped me from joining long ago.

I hope you are happy with your work. Any kind of work if one [can] only be doing something is what one wants now. I feel very grateful at your appreciation of my position, it keeps the clockwork going. To me this is not a result but one motion of the intricate series of activities that all combine to make a result. One might succumb, be destroyed— but one might also (and the chances are even greater for it) be renewed, made larger, healthier. It is not very easy for me to write here as you can imagine and you must not expect any proper continuity or even coherence. But I thought you might like to hear how I am placed exactly and write as I can. If I could get a very small watercolour box with a decent sketch block pencil paper about 12 × 10 I might do something Sundays. The landscape is quite good. Hospital incidents are good but I may not be here more than two days. If you could send anything at once I'd get it here. They'd give it me if I had left. With cigarettes I could make myself more liked, and eatables I'd like myself. Cakes chocolates etc. I hope you don't mind this but though they would do this for me at home I don't like my mother to feel I haven't everything I want.

Yours sincerely
I Rosenberg

To Sydney Schiff

[Post-12 Nov. 1915]

12th Suffolk Bantams | Military Hospital |
Depot | Bury St Edmunds

Dear Mr Shiff

Many thanks for the paints and sketch book which I received yesterday and are just the things I wanted. I sketched an invalid in the blue uniform° but I must give it to him—I got a deal of pleasure in painting after so long a rest. I expect I'll be out of the hospital Tuesday my hands seem to be so slow to heal. We are pretty near starved in this damned hospital and there is no one to complain to. There are no books to read and one must not stir from the room. I'm impatient to get out. This militarism is terrorism to be sure. Again many thanks for the paints.

Yours sincerely
I Rosenberg

To Edward Marsh

[27 Nov. 1915]

12th Suffolk Bantams | Military Hospital |
Depot | Bury St Edmunds | Sat night

My dear Marsh

I have only just got your letter. They kept it back or it got mislaid—
anyway it only reached me today. First not to alarm you by this
heading I must tell you that while running before the colonel I started
rather excitedly and tripped myself coming down pretty heavily in the
wet grit and am in the hospital with both my hands cut. I've been here
since last Sat and expect to be out by about the beginning of the week.
It is a nondescript kind of life in the hospital and I'm very anxious to
get out and be doing some rough kind of work. Mr Shiff sent me some
water-colours and I amuse myself with drawing the other invalids. Of
course I must give them what I do but I can see heaps of material for
pictures here. The landscape too seems decent though I haven't seen
anything but from the Barracks as this accident happened pretty near
at the start.

I hope you were not annoyed at that fib of mine but I never dreamt
they would trouble to find out at home. I have managed to persuade
my mother that I am for home service only though of course I have
signed on for general service. I left without saying anything because
I was afraid it would kill my mother or I would be too weak and not go.
She seems to have got over it though and as soon as I can get leave I'll
see her and I hope it will be well.

It is very hard to write here so you must not expect interesting
letters; there is always behind or through my object some pressing
sense of foreign matter, immediate and not personal which hinders
and disjoints what would otherwise have coherence and perhaps
weight. I have left all my poems including a short drama° with a
friend and I will write to him for them when I shall send them either
direct to Abercrombie or to you first. I believe in myself more as a poet
than a painter. I think I get more depth into my writing. I have only
taken Donne with me and don't feel for poetry much in this wretched
place. There is not a book or paper here. We are not allowed to stir
from the gate, have little to eat, and are not allowed to buy any if we
have money—and are utterly wretched (I mean the hospital). If you
could send me some novel or chocolates, you would make me very

happy. I think I will be here (in the hospital) till Tuesday night as it is Sunday tomorrow, and if the doctor says Monday I can leave the hospital, it means Tuesday night. You will get this Mon and I will have a whole day left me to eat a box of chocolates in; it is only a short winter's day.

Yours sincerely
Isaac Rosenberg

To Edward Marsh

[Dec. 1915]

Pte I Rosenberg | No 22648 | Platoon No 3 |
12th Suffolks. Hut No 2 | Depot. | Bury St Edmunds

My dear Marsh
    I have devoured your chocolates with the help of some comrades and am now out of the hospital. I have been kept very busy and I find that the actual duties though they are difficult at first and require all one's sticking power are not in themselves unpleasant, it is the brutal militaristic bullying meanness of the way they're served out to us. You're always being threatened with 'clink'.
    I am sending you my little play and some poems. The play I mean to work at when I get a chance. I also enclose a photograph of one of my S African drawings. When you have read the poems will you send them to Abercrombie that is if you think he won't be annoyed.

Yours sincerely
I Rosenberg
    Who is the author of Erebus.° I have a marvellous poem by him.

To Edward Marsh

[Early Dec. 1915]

22648 | C Company Bantams Bat. |
12th Suffolk Regt. | Bury St. Edmunds

My dear Marsh
    I received a letter today (sent over a week ago) from Abercrombie and I feel very flushed about it. He says no one who tries to write poetry would help envying some of my writing. Since I wrote you I have had more mishaps. My feet now are the trouble. Do you know what privates' military boots are? You are given a whole armoury's

shop to wear—but by God—in a few hours my heels were all blistered
and I've been marching and drilling in most horrible pain. I drew
three weeks pay and had some money sent me from home and bought
a pair of boots 3 or four sizes too large for me my feet had swelled so.
Besides this trouble I have a little impudent schoolboy pup for an
officer and he has me marked—he has taken a dislike to me I don't
know why.

I sent pictures to the New English° but I think they have got me
mixed up somehow with Bomberg as they wrote me my things were
accepted addressing me Isaac Bomberg.

Could you send me a pound to buy boots with and to get to London
[for] Xmas if my devil of an officer will give me leave as I must get
another pair when my feet are better. You can have the pick of any
drawing I do after this if I get clear, for it. Has Winston Churchill's
change° made any change to you? I suppose you find a lot to do in
these times.

Yours sincerely
Isaac Rosenberg

To Sydney Schiff

[Early Dec. 1915]

22648 | Company C, Bat. Bantam, |
Regt. 12th Suffolks, | Bury St Edmunds

Dear Mr Shiff

I have a spare moment and am using it to write to you. I feel very
bucked this week and as you are interested in my poems I think it will
please you too. A letter reached me from Lascelles Abercrombie who
I think is our best living poet—this is what he says. 'A good many of
your poems strike me as experimental and not quite certain of
themselves. But on the other hand I always find a vivid and original
impulse; and what I like most in your songs is your ability to make
the concealed poetic power in words come flashing out. Some of
your phrases are remarkable; no one who writes poetry would help
envying some of them.' You must excuse these blots. I'm
writing from pandemonium and with a rotten pen. I felt A. would
sympathise with my work. I haven't been able to draw—we get no
private time.

The money you sent me I was forced to buy boots with as the military boots rubbed all the skin off my feet and I've been marching in terrible agony. The kind of life does not bother me much. I sleep soundly on boards in the cold; the drills I find fairly interesting, but up till now these accidents have bothered me and I am still suffering with them. My hands are not better and my feet are hell. We have pups for officers—at least one—who seems to dislike me—and you know his position gives him power to make me feel it without me being able to resist. When my feet and hands are better I will slip into the work but as I am it is awkward. The doctor here too, Major Devoral, is a ridiculous bullying brute and I have marked him for special treatment when I come to write about the army. The commanding officer is Major Ogalvie and his adjutant Captain Thornhill. If you happen to know them, all I would want is leave for a weekend to see my mother. I have asked and was told if I got it now I should have none Xmas so I have put it off. I think we go to Shoreham next week.

Yours sincerely
Isaac Rosenberg

I believe I have some pictures in the N[ew].E[nglish]. but I fancy they are catalogued as Bomberg's but I'm not sure.

To Sydney Schiff

[Early Dec. 1915]

22648 | C Company | 12th Suffolk Bantams |
Bury St Edmunds

Dear Mr Schiff

You are very good to send me that note. Money is very handy and we get too little of it here. Half of what I get goes to my mother. When I spoke to you of leave I don't think I mentioned that I did not tell my mother I had joined and disappeared without saying anything. It nearly killed my mother I heard and ever since she has been very anxious to see me. I send you here a photo° which I think is pretty alive.

What you say about your nephews I dare say is just, but I have been used to this sort of thing and know the kind of people I am with well. I should have been told to soften my boots and I would not have had this damned bother. I now find everybody softens their boots first and anybody would be crippled by wearing them as I have done. I shall let you know when I am in London.

Yours sincerely
Isaac Rosenberg

To Edward Marsh

[Early Dec. 1915]

22648 | C Company Bantam Bat. |
12th Suffolk Regt. | Bury St. Edmunds

My dear Marsh

I suppose my troubles are really laughable but they do irritate at the moment. Doing coal fatigues and cookhouse work with a torn hand and marching ten miles with a clean hole about an inch round in your heel and bullies swearing at you is not very natural. I think when my hands and feet get better I'll enjoy it. Nobody thinks of helping you— I mean those who could. Not till I have been made a thorough cripple an officer said it was absurd to think of wearing those boots and told me to soak it thoroughly in oil to soften it. Thank you for your note, we get little enough you know, and I allow half of that to my mother (I rather fancy she is going to be swindled in this rat trap affair) so it will do to get to London with.

You must now be the busiest man in England° and I am sure would hardly have time to read my things, besides you won't like the formlessness of the play. If you like you can send them to Abercrombie and read them when you have more time. I don't think I told you what he said, 'A good many of your poems strike me as experimental and not quite certain of themselves. But on the other hand I always find a vivid and original impulse; and what I like most in your songs is your ability to make the concealed poetic power in words come flashing out. Some of your phrases are remarkable; no one who tries to write poetry would help envying some of them'. I have asked him to sit for me—a poet to paint a poet. All this must seem to you like a blur on the window, or hearing sounds without listening while you are thinking. One blur more and I'll leave you a clean window—I think we're shifting to Shoreham in a week.

Yours sincerely
Isaac Rosenberg

Extract from letter to Winifreda Seaton

[Mid-Dec. 1915]

[Bury St Edmunds]

Thanks for your letter and your books which they sent me from home. It is impossible to read as we are, and I don't expect to get proper leisure for reading till this rotten affair is over. My feet are pretty nigh better, and my hands, and I am put down for a Lance-Corporal. The advantage is, though you have a more responsible position, you are less likely to be interfered with by the men, and you become an authority. I expect to be home for four days shortly. I don't know whether I told you Lascelles Abercrombie sent me a fine letter about my work, which made me very bucked. There is nobody living whose praise could have pleased me so much. I have some pictures at the N[ew].E[nglish].A[rt].C[lub]., one of which is likely to be sold.

To Edward Marsh

[Mid-Dec. 1915]

22648 | C Company | 12th Suffolk Bantams |
Bury St Edmunds

My dear Marsh

I am going home on leave Friday and shall have four days in town. I don't know whether you have had time to send my things to L[ascelles].A[bercrombie]. but if not, could you send them to me at 87 Dempsey St so that I might correct them and send them on myself. I am getting on so well that I have been offered a stripe, but I declined. What is Gertler doing? I feel a bit tired to write, and I expect you are to read a long letter. We are being drilled pretty stiffly.

Yours sincerely
Isaac Rosenberg

87 Dempsey St
Stepney E.

To Sydney Schiff

[Mid-Dec. 1915]

87 Dempsey St | Stepney | London E
Thurs.

Dear Mr Schiff

I shall be home for 4 days from tomorrow, Fri, as you asked me to let you know. I must be looking smart, for I was offered a stripe which I declined. I have some more pictures at home if you care to see, though I, since I have joined have hardly given poetry or painting a thought. I feel as if I were casting my coat, I mean, like a snake or butterfly. Here is another one of myself, not much like a poet—I'm afraid.

Yours sincerely
Isaac Rosenberg

To Edward Marsh

[Late Dec. 1915]

22648 | C Company | 12th Suffolk Bantams |
Bury St Edmunds

My dear Marsh

I have sent on the poems to L[ascelles].A[bercrombie]. I sent this one as well which I like.

['Marching—as seen from the left file']

But it is something else I want to write about. I never joined the army from patriotic reasons. Nothing can justify war. I suppose we must all fight to get the trouble over. Anyhow before the war I helped at home when I could and I did other things which helped to keep things going. I thought if I'd join there would be the separation allowance for my mother. At Whitehall it was fixed up that 16/6 would be given including the 3/6 a week deducted from my 7/-. It's now between 2 and 3 months since I joined; my 3/6 is deducted right enough, but my mother hasn't received a farthing. The paymaster at barracks of course is no use in this matter. I wonder if you know how these things are managed and what I might do.

Yours sincerely
Isaac Rosenberg

To Sydney Schiff

[Late Dec. 1915]

22648 | C Company | 12th Suffolk Bantams |
Bury St Edmunds

Dear Mr Schiff

Thanks for your letter. I will try and write to Bomberg. If you wish to buy my thing you can have it for 5 guineas. I am anxious to sell as my mother has received no separation allowance yet and half of my money is deducted which should go to her and it is most difficult to get satisfactory reasons. I have written to Marsh to see whether he would know what to do in the matter.

Yours sincerely
Isaac Rosenberg

To Edward Marsh

[Late Dec. 1915]

22648 | C Company | 12th Suffolk Bantams |
Bury St Edmunds

My dear Marsh

I think this is a decent photo of me and if anything were to happen that would be as far as I got. They talk of sending us out in Spring.

Yours sincerely
Isaac Rosenberg

To Edward Marsh

Postmarked 5 Jan. 1916

22648 | 12th South Lancashires° | A Coy. Alma Barracks, |
Blackdown Camp | Farnborough

My dear Marsh

I have been transferred to this reg and am here near Aldershot. Thanks for writing to W[ar].O[ffice]. I believe my people are getting

FIG. 9 Isaac Rosenberg in uniform [1915].

my 6d a day deducted from my 1s, but not the allowance. We get very little food you know and sometimes none, so if one has only 6d (and often for unaccountable reasons it is not even that) you can imagine what it is like. If I had got into a recent reg that might not have mattered, but amongst the most unspeakably filthy wretches, it is pretty suicidal. I am afraid, though, I'm not in a very happy mood— I have a bad cold through sleeping on a damp floor and have been coal fatiguing all day (a most inhuman job). You must be very busy.—It is a great pity this conscription business,° besides the hope it will give to the enemy to have brought England to that step.

I am sorry [you] didn't like that poem;° I thought I had hit on som[eth]ing there.

Yours sincerely
Isaac Rosenberg

I have heard it is not difficult to get a commission. Do you know anything about it?

To Edward Marsh

Postmarked 29 Jan. 1916

24520 | A Coy | 12th South Lancs | Alma Bks |
Blackdown Camp | Farnborough | Hants.

My dear Marsh

I don't remember whether I told you I'd got transferred to this lot and am now near Aldershot. We are having pretty rigorous training down here and the talk is we are going out the middle of next month. Except for the starvation rations and headachy moments I get it's not so bad down here. I have just been inoculated and asked for 48 hours' leave (we get 48 hrs excused duties) and could not get it. I was told it was a privilege one could insist on, but of course I could not go home without a pass. I sent my poems to Abercrombie about a month ago and have not heard. I hope they won't get lost as I have no copies and I think they're the best things I've done. I added some lines to the Marching poem which you will think vague but I like them.

Yours sincerely
Isaac Rosenberg

To Sydney Schiff

[Early 1916]

24520 | A Coy | 12th South Lancs | Alma Bks |
Blackdown Camp | Farnborough Hants.

Dear Mr Shiff

Thank you for your letter and present, (particularly as I've been unlucky this week and lost 5/- through the post). The latter will be turned into food, which means fitness, and that means proper work. My troubles at the beginning were mostly caused by insufficient food; one felt inert, and unable to do the difficult work wanted; until I got my people to send food from home. The authorities are quite aware of the state of things, but as the authorities have not got to eat of our food, their energy in the matter is not too obvious. I am known as a poet and artist, as our second in command is a Jewish officer who knows of me from his people. I have other copies of those poems I sent you so you needn't return them.

Mr Clutton Brock's address I've lost, though of course, I would be very glad of his interest. I will keep you informed of my whereabouts should we shift, and send you anything I think worth reading, though we get really no time to write or think.

Yours sincerely
Isaac Rosenberg

To Lascelles Abercrombie

11 March 1916

24520 | A Coy, 12th South Lancs |
Alma Bks, Blackdown Camp | Farnborough

Dear Sir

Your letter was sent to me from home and it gave me a lot of pleasure. I really wonder whether my things are worth the trouble you have taken in analysing them, but if you think they are, and from your letter, you do, of course I should feel encouraged. I send you here my two latest poems,° which I have managed to write, though in the utmost distress of mind, or perhaps because of it. Believe me the army is the most detestable invention on this earth and nobody but a private in the army knows what it is to be a slave.

I wonder whether your muse has been sniffing gunpowder.

Thank you for your good wishes

Yours sincerely
Isaac Rosenberg

To Sydney Schiff

[March 1916]

24520 | A Coy, 12th South Lancs | Alma Bks |
Blackdown Camp | Farnborough | Hants

Dear Mr Shiff

I have been in this reg about 2 months now and have been kept going all the time. Except that the food is unspeakable, and perhaps luckily, scanty, the rest is pretty tolerable. I have food sent up from home and that keeps me alive, but as for the others, there is talk of mutiny every day. One reg close by did break out and some men got bayoneted. I don't know when we are going out but the talk is very shortly. I have written two small poems since I joined and I think they are my strongest work. I sent them to one or two papers as they are war poems and topical but as I expected, they were sent back. I am afraid my public is still in the womb. Naturally this only has the effect of making me very conceited and to think these poems better than anybody else's. Let me know what you think of them as I have no one to show them to here.

Yours sincerely
Isaac Rosenberg

Extract from letter to Winifreda Seaton

[Spring 1916]

Blackdown Camp | Farnborough

Thanks very much for the bread and biscuits, which I enjoyed very much. I am in another regiment now, as the old one was smashed up on account of most of the men being unfit.° We that were left have been transferred here. The food is much better, but the conditions are most unsettling. Every other person is a thief, and in the end you become one yourself, when you see all your most essential belongings go, which you must replace somehow. I also got into trouble here the first day. It's not worth while detailing what happened and exposing how ridiculous, idiotic, and meaningless the Army is, and its dreadful bullyisms, and what puny minds control it. I am trying to get our Passover off, which falls Easter. If I do I'll let you know. The bother is that we will be on our ball-firing then, and also this before-mentioned affair may mess it up. This ball-firing implies we will be ready for the front. I have been working on 'Moses'—in my mind, I mean—and it was through my absent-mindedness while full of that that I forgot certain orders, and am now undergoing a rotten and unjust punishment. I'm working a curious plot into it, and of course, as I can't work here, I jot little scraps down and will piece it together the first chance I get.

To Edward Marsh

[Mid-May 1916]

22311 | A Coy | 11th (S) Batt K.O.R.L.° |
Alma Bks | Blackdown Camp | Farnborough.

Dear Marsh

I have not heard from you and did not expect to, as you must be full up with work. I've also had very little inclination to write to anybody though I've been very eager to hear from all. We are pretty certain to be off the beginning of June and are having our last leave this week. I've got quite used to the thing by now though naturally I hate the restraints. The food in this Reg is much better than the other. I am having a small pamphlet printed of a play and some small poems,° all written since I joined; and I want you to make allowances for the play as I had to write it in a very scrappy manner and even got into trouble thro it. It made me a bit absent minded and you know what that means in the army. I expect it will be ready in 2 weeks.

If you are answering this immediately write to

87 Dempsey St
Stepney E

as I think I'm having my 6 days furlough from Friday.

To Edward Marsh

Postcard, postmarked 19 May 1916

I will be at Raymond B[uildings]° Mon morning: Have got 6 days. I'll bring some proofs of my play which will amuse you. The printer is superb.° He's made quite an original thing of it, and given me a million hints for new things. The plot is droll. There is a famine in Egypt caused by the superabundance of slaves who eat up all the food meant for the masters. To prevent this, all the back molars of the slaves are drawn, so they eat less. The plot works round this.

I. Rosenberg

To Sydney Schiff

[Last week of May 1916]

22311 A Coy | 11th Batt. | K.O.R.L. Regt. |
Blackdown Camp

Dear Mr Schiff

I have not written to you for some time because there was nothing much new to write about. We are going overseas at last, some day this week—I fancy Thursday, but whether it's France or the Coloured Countries° I couldn't say. I will write to you from wherever I am. I have had another pamphlet printed of poems as I felt that would be the safest way of keeping my best work if anything should happen. I have not seen the book myself but I believe it is finished by now and I will ask my people to send on a copy to you. When you have seen that, if you would like a bound copy or some for friends, I am selling some to make up the cost of printing—which is not yet paid for. You could write to Miss A. Rosenberg, 87 Dempsey St. Stepney E. but say nothing of my being away as it would pain my mother. A friend sent me a nice letter from Trevelyan the poet (brother of the socialist M.P.)° in which he mentions me and my poems as being 'startlingly fine'. He has not seen my new things yet. For the rest I am in splendid condition and feel ready for the rotten job I'm about.

Yours sincerely
Isaac Rosenberg

To Israel Zangwill

[Late May 1916]

22311 | A. Coy, 11th (S) Batt., K.O.R.L., |
Alma Bks. | Blackdown Camp.

Dear Sir,

I hope you will excuse this liberty I take in sending my poems to you. I believe you will be interested in 'Moses'.° I have not worked him out as a character quite in the way I wished, because I had to hurry to get it finished before I went out. I was not able to correct proofs either. We are going overseas this week. If you are pleased with my book and think friends will like it they are for sale at 1s. each or in cloth, 4/6d. This is only to pay the printer. I thought it necessary to get them printed to prevent them getting lost.

Yours sincerely,
Isaac Rosenberg

If books wanted send here for them:
Miss A. Rosenberg,
87 Dempsey Street,
Stepney,
London E.

To R. C. Trevelyan

[Last week of May 1916]

22311 | A Coy | 11th (S) Batt. K.O.R.L. Regt., |
Blackdown Camp

Dear Sir,

My friend Rodker told me you liked my poems and wanted a copy. I am enclosing one for you and one for Mr Bottomley (who is the most real poet living in England). They will also send you from home copies (one for Bottomley) of some new poems which I've written since I joined. You will excuse the printer's errors as I was not able to correct them. We are leaving for overseas this week (Thursday) but if you write soon I expect I'll get the letter; or write to my people for me, Miss A. Rosenberg. 87 Dempsey St. Stepney. London. E. but don't say anything of my being away as my people are Tolstoyans and object to my being in khaki. My reason for 'castrating' my book before I sent it was simply that the poems were commonplace and you would not have said: 'You do it like a navvy' but, 'You do it like a bank clerk'. You have made me very pleased by liking my work and telling me B[ottomley] liked them.

If my people send you a copy bound in cloth you won't mind paying for it, I'm sure as I have not paid the printer yet. 3/6 will do.

Yours sincerely
Isaac Rosenberg

To Edward Marsh

[27 May 1916]

Dear Marsh,

It was a pity I came late that morning but it could not be helped and I was so anxious to rush my printer through with my poems before I left England. Anyway we're off at last, either tomorrow or Mon. (it's Sat now and we've handed in all our surplus kit and are quite ready). I'll write them at home to send you a copy of my poems, one called 'Spring 1916', I particularly like, and I think you will. But some poems will be in cloth and I am charging for those to make up the cost of printing. If you want any will you write me when I let you know where I am. They are 4/6 each. The king inspected us Thursday. I believe it's the first Bantam Brigade been inspected. He must have waited for us to stand up a good while. At a distance we look like soldiers sitting down, you know, legs so short.

Yours sincerely
Isaac Rosenberg

To Lascelles Abercrombie

[Early June 1916]

Dear Mr Abercrombie

I am sending you copy of new poems. I hope you'll like them. We're off tonight overseas. As soon as we land anywhere I'll let you know as I'd like very much to hear they please you.

Yours sincerely,
Isaac Rosenberg

Some of these books are for sale to make up cost of printing if friends of yours should want any. Send Miss A. Rosenberg 87 Dempsey St Stepney E.

Don't mention my being abroad.

On 2 June 1916 Rosenberg sailed for France

To R. C. Trevelyan

Postmarked 15 June 1916

22311 Pte I Rosenberg |
A. Coy 11th (S) Batt. K.O.R.L. |
British Expeditionary Force
[Number of his division deleted by censor]

Dear Mr Trevelyan

My sister sent me on your letter, which has made me feel very conceited and elated. It is strange why people should be so timid and afraid to praise on their own, and yet so bold to criticise. I know my faults are legion; a good many must be put down to the rotten conditions I wrote it in—the whole thing was written in barracks, and I suppose you know what an ordinary soldier's life is like. Moses symbolises the fierce desire for virility and original action in contrast to slavery of the most abject kind. I was very sorry to hear about Bottomley being bad. I hope by the time this reaches you that will be a thing to joke about. If I get through this affair without any broken bones etc, I have a lot to say and one or two shilling shockers, that'll make some people jump. Here's a sketch of our passage over.

['The Troop Ship']

If you see Mrs Rodker please ask her to write to me about R. as I believe R is in prison.°

The above address will or should find me.

Yours sincerely
Isaac Rosenberg

We are in the trenches now and it's raining horribly.

Extract from letter to Winifreda Seaton

[June 1916]

We made straight for the trenches, but we've had vile weather, and I've been wet through for four days and nights. I lost all my socks and things before I left England, and hadn't the chance to make it up again, so I've been in trouble, particularly with bad heels; you can't have the slightest conception of what such an apparently trivial thing means. We've had shells bursting two yards off, bullets whizzing all over the show, but all you are aware of is the agony of your heels [...]

I had a letter from R. C. Trevelyan, the poet [...] He writes: 'It is a long time since I have read anything that has impressed me so much as your 'Moses' and some of your short poems [...]' He confesses parts are difficult, and he is not sure whether it's my fault or his.

To Edward Marsh

[June 1916]

22311 | 11th (S) Batt. | 40th division |
K.O.R.L. Regt. | B.E.F. France

My dear Marsh

You know we mustn't say very much now we're over the water but as soon as I get a chance I'll try and give you some idea of what's happening to me. Up to now nothing very important has happened, nothing more terrible than uncomfortable regrets at not having learned this infernal lingo when I had the chance. I had a letter from a friend who knows Trevelyan. This letter was from Trevelyan to my friend about my poems—not my recent things. G. Bottomley happened to be staying with him at the time and they both thought some of my things 'startlingly fine'. My new things are miles ahead of those. Write me if you can and if anything occurs to you useful in the trenches that I'm not likely to get here could you send me.

Yours sincerely
Isaac Rosenberg

Here's sketch of passage over.
['The Troop Ship']

I came across your second Georgian book° lately. Why didn't you say anything to me about it. I'm mad to read a play by Bottomley. Is Binyon in London or in France?°

To R. C. Trevelyan

[June or July 1916]

> 22311. A Coy. 11th Batt. | K.O.R.L. Rgt. |
> 3 Platoon British Expeditionary Force | France

Dear Mr Trevelyan

My sister sent me your letter° on, which I answered; but as certain other letters I sent off at the same time went astray I surmise that one was lost as well, so I am writing again. The other side of this sheet is a very crude sketch of how I look here in this dugout. I'll write out at the end of this letter a little poem of the troop ship where I try to describe in words the contortions we get into to try and wriggle ourselves into a little sleep. Of course if you're lucky and get a decent dugout you sleep quite easily—when you get the chance, otherwise you must sleep standing up, or sitting down, which latter is my case now. I must say that it has made me very happy to know you like my work so much; very few people do, or, at least, say so; and I believe I am a poet.

Here in the trenches where we are playing this extraordinary gamble, your letter made me feel refreshed and fine. I hope Bottomley is quite better by now—he is a man whose work (I have only read 'Chambers of Imagery') has made me feel more rare and delicately excited feelings, than any poetry I have ever read. The little poem 'Nimrod' the image in the first stanza° to me is one of the most astonishing in all literature. Another thing that seems to me too astonishing for comment, is Abercrombie's Hymn to Love.

I hope we may some day be able to talk these things over.

['The Troop Ship']

Yours sincerely
Isaac Rosenberg

To Gordon Bottomley

Postmarked 12 July 1916

> 22311 Pte I. Rosenberg. |
> c/o 40th Divisional Coy. Salvage Officer, |
> B.E.F. France.

Dear Mr Bottomley

If you really mean what you say in your letter,° there is no need to tell you how proud I am. I had to read your letter many times before

FIG. 10 Drawing letter to R. C. Trevelyan [June or July 1916].

I could convince myself you were not 'pulling my leg'. People are
always telling me my work is promising—incomprehensible—but
promising, and all that sort of thing, and my meekness subsides before
the patronizing knowingness. The first thing I saw of yours was last
year in the Georgian Book, 'The end of the world'. I must have
worried all London about it; certainly everybody I knew. I had never
seen anything like it. After that I got hold of 'Chambers of Imagery'.

Mr Marsh told me of your plays but I joined the Army and have never been able to get at them. It is a great thing to me to be able to tell you now in this way what marvellous pleasure your work has given me, and what pride that my work pleases you. I had ideas for a play called 'Adam and Lilith' before I came to France, but I must wait now.

Here is a sketch

['The Troop Ship']

I had heard about your weakness with pain, and I beg of you not to trouble yourself to answer if it exhausts you, though a word from you gives me pride and pleasure.

Yours sincerely
Isaac Rosenberg

Enclosed with this letter was a draft of the first two verses on 'In War', written in pencil on a bit of the back of an envelope, and a draft of 'Break of Day in the Trenches' entitled 'In the Trenches'.

To Sonia Cohen

[July 1916]

22311 A Coy. 3. Platoon |
11th. Batt. K.O.R.L. | B.E.F.

Dear Sonia°

I have been anxious to hear from you about Rodker. I wrote to Trevelyan (he thinks me a big knut in poetry) and asked him for news but I fancy my letter got lost. Write me any news—anything. I seem to have been in France, ages. I wish Rodker were with me, the infernal lingo is a tragedy with me, and he'd help me out. If I was taciturn in England I am 10 times so here; our struggle to express ourselves is a fearful joke. However our wants are simple, our cash is scarce, and our time is precious, so French would perhaps be superfluous. I'd hardly believe French manners are so different to ours, but I leave all this for conversation. Here's a little poem a bit commonplace I'm afraid.

['In the Trenches']

Yours sincerely
Isaac Rosenberg

To Edward Marsh

Postmarked 30 July 1916

22311 A Coy | 11th Bttn. K.O.R.L. |
3 Platoon. | B.E.F.

My dear Marsh

I sent you a letter and a copy of my book when I reached here, but am doubtful whether you got it, as several letters I sent off at the time, I know got mislaid. I am aware how fearfully busy you must be, but if poetry at this time is no use it certainly won't be at any other. Miss Asquith° seems to think this too, and I half believe it is at your suggestion. R.C. Trevelyan is a friend of yours I believe. He wrote me a most flattering letter about my 'Moses'. He said no new thing has

[FIG. 11]

impressed him so much for a long time. Bottomley admires my work too, and that has pleased me more than if I were known all over the world. We made straight for the trenches and have spent a wet time and dry one there. I'll write you out a dramatic thing of the trenches sometime and shan't say anything here. I sketched myself in a dug out but lost it. Here's it rough.

If you have anything to say about my poem do write me as soon as you get time. I am busy too but I write. Of course the work I'm busy at doesn't matter as much as yours—I mean it's not so responsible but do write.

Here's a sketch very slight I've done here.

Yours sincerely
Isaac Rosenberg

To Mrs Herbert Cohen

?Summer 1916

22311 A Coy 3 platoon | 11th K.O.R.L. B.E.F.

Dear Mrs Cohen

We are on a long march and I'm writing this on the chance of getting it off; so you should know I received your papers and also your letter. The notice in the Times of your book° is true—especially about your handling of metre. It is an interesting number. The Poetry Review° you sent is good—the articles are too breathless, and want more packing, I think. The poems by the soldier are vigorous but, I feel a bit commonplace. I did not like Rupert Brooke's begloried sonnets for the same reason. What I mean is second hand phrases 'lambent fires' etc takes from its reality and strength. It should be approached in a colder way, more abstract, with less of the million feelings everybody feels; or all these should be concentrated in one distinguished emotion. Walt Whitman° in 'Beat, drums, beat', has said the noblest thing on war.

I am glad Yeats° liked your play: His criticism is an honour. He is the established great man and it is a high thing to receive praise from him. Don't talk of Noyes°—he only cloys. I always think of some twopenny bazaar when I read him.

I am thinking of a Jewish play with Judas Macabeas for hero.° I can put a lot in I've learnt out here. I hope I get the chance to go on with it. I've freshly written this thing—red from the anvil.

['August 1914']

I have a good one in the anvil now but it wants knocking into shape. Thanks very much for the papers.

Yours sincerely
Isaac Rosenberg

To Gordon Bottomley

Postmarked 23 July 1916

22311 Pte I Rosenberg |
c/o 40th Divisional Coy Salvage Officer. |
B.E.F.<France> [deleted by censor]

Dear Mr Bottomley,
   Your letter came today with Mr. Trevelyan's, like two friends to take me for a picnic. Or rather, like friends come to release the convict from his chains with his innocence in their hands, as one sees in the twopenny picture palace. You might say, friends come to take you to church or the priest to the prisoner. Simple *Poetry* that is where an interesting complexity of thought is kept in tone and right value to the dominating idea so that it is understandable and still ungraspable I know, is beyond my reach just now, except perhaps in bits. I am always afraid of being empty. When I get more leisure in more settled times I will work on a larger scale and give myself more room then I may be less frustrated in my efforts to be clear, and satisfy myself too. I think what you say about getting beauty by phrasing of passages rather than the placing of individual words, very fine and very true.
   The poem 'In the Trenches',° I altered a little and have asked my sister to send on to you. I left a line out 'A shell's haphazard fury' after 'Irrevocable earth buffet'. I don't think I made my meaning quite clear that it is a shell bursting which has only covered my [*sic*] and the poppy I plucked at beginning of poem still in my ear, with dust. It is one of a sequence of dramatic war poems I want to write. 'Marching' 'The Troopship', 'Fret the nonchalant moon' and 'In the Trenches' are written. I have plenty of amusing and serious material. Last night we had a funny hunt for fleas.° All stripped by candlelight, some Scots dancing over the candle burning the fleas, and the funniest, drollest and dirtiest songs and conversation ever imagined. Burns 'Jolly Beggars' is nothing to it. I have heaps of material. I feel all your advice and am very grateful for it. If you knew how much I have destroyed because I felt it would be completely unintelligible to most, you would anyway—praise my prudence.

I have not read 'King Lear's Wife'° and have never seen the second Georgian book. Since I've joined the only book I carried with me and read was your 'Chambers of Imagery' with the Nimrod poem.° I lost it when I came to France.

For the last week or two I've been on a quieter but more interesting job than trenches. I've got to rummage behind the lines among shattered houses and ruins for salvage. We come across all kinds of grim and funny odds and ends. More material for poem. I don't know how long this job will last but it's fairly safe, anyway, except for stray shells which don't count. I do trust you are not worried by ill health and are happy.

Yours sincerely
Isaac Rosenberg

To R. C. Trevelyan

[Late July 1916]

Pte I Rosenberg
[address deleted by censor]

Dear Mr Trevelyan

Your letter came with a second one of Bottomley's. His first was all praise and his second all criticism; but his criticism was higher praise than any praise I had been given before. His letter was full of fine writing and useful tips and I feel very grateful for it, and to you for first showing my things to him. I had been meaning to write to him for some time, in fact, when I first read him, but I always thought to myself,—wait till you have something worthy to show him! It was only coming out to France and the risk of being knocked over made me print the poems hurriedly.

I have never read B's plays though Mr Marsh told me of them, but the war interfered and I have read no literature for the last year, till I got yours and B's letters. I have asked my sister to send you a poem Bottomley liked—'Break of day in the trenches'. Perhaps the end is not quite clear and wants working on. I have an idea for a book of war poems. I have already written a few small things but have plans for few longish dramatic poems. Abercrombie's 'Hymn to Love'° is I think, the great thing of modern times, and far above anything else of his I know.

Bottomley is more profound and a purer artist—but the Hymn to love wants some licking. Thank you for showing my work about. I am naturally anxious for discerning people to read my things.

Yours sincerely
Isaac Rosenberg
    I have not heard from J[ohn].R[odker]. and am glad he is not in trouble.

To Sydney Schiff

[Late July 1916]

Pte I Rosenberg 22311 |
C/o 40th Divisional Coy Salvage Officer |
B.E.F. France

Dear Mr Shiff
    I was most glad to get your card today together with the papers. It is a hard job to get any decent literature out here and it has never occurred to any of my friends to send any to me; (though they have sent me things more urgent and necessary, such as chocolates etc). Still, up to now I have had no leisure at all not a moment for books, but by some curious way, some queer change in my military programme has taken place, and now I do get time to read—but there is nothing to read. I am sending you this portrait of the militant poet a bit changed ay! Also my sister will send you a trench poem of mine.° I think I'll also enclose copy of G. Bottomley's letter to me. I wonder whether you have any of his plays to send me.° He was my great god of poetry the moment I read 'The End of the World' in 'Georgian book', and I immediately bought a small book of his and that was the only book I had with me since I joined till I came to France where I lost it somehow.
    I am distressed about your state of mind, but refrain from philoso-phizing. I know Cornwall but not Devonshire. I've found Cornwall in Spring gorgeous and I've done a good deal of sketching there. I do not know Trevor Blackmore's work° though I know his name and his opinion of my work would interest me greatly. It is fine of you to show my work about so, as it may do me a deal of good after the war if I get established some way. My plan is to teach drawing at a school a few days in the week, which leaves plenty of leisure to write as I am convinced I am more deep and true as a poet than painter. I am glad Bomberg has done something definite at last,° I do hope nothing will

happen to him out here, more than ever. Who has he married? What division is he in. I might run across him.

The above address is fairly permanent as far as I know. If you write I am pretty sure to get it, and I am bucked up when I hear from friends.

Yours sincerely
Isaac Rosenberg

To Edward Marsh

4 Aug. [1916]

My dear Marsh

I have only just received your letter, which has been lying about for the last week before it was given to me. By now you must have read a letter I wrote on behalf of a friend, and sent to Whitehall to reach you during the day, as it was so pressing. I trust you have been able to do something; as it is rough luck on the poor fellow. I was most glad to get your letter and criticism. You know the conditions I have always worked under, and particularly with this last lot of poems. You know how earnestly one must wait on ideas, (you cannot coax real ones to you) and let as it were, a skin grow naturally round and through them. If you are not free, you can only, when the ideas come hot, seize them with the skin in tatters raw, crude, in some parts beautiful in others monstrous. Why print it then? Because these rare parts must not be lost. I work more and more as I write into more depth and lucidity, I am sure. I have a fine idea for a most gorgeous play, Adam and Lilith. If I could get a few months after the war to work and absorb myself completely into the thing, I'd write a great thing.

I am enclosing a poem I wrote in the trenches,° which is surely as simple as ordinary talk. You might object to the second line as vague, but that was the best way I could express the sense of dawn.

Since I wrote last I have been given a job behind the lines and very rarely go into the trenches. My address is c/o 40th Divisional Coy Officer, B.E.F. Pte I Rosenberg 22311. It is more healthy but not absolutely safe from shells as we get those noisy visitors a good many times a day even here.

Yours sincerely
Isaac Rosenberg

To Sydney Schiff

[Early Aug. 1916]
Dear Mr Schiff

Thank you for your letter which gave me great pleasure. With your letter was a post card sent a week or so before the letter but which only reached me now. Trevor Blakemore's letter° was a good one and I enjoyed the manner of it. What he says is good, also but though I agree with most part of it about over involved simplification etc. I think we would be at loggerheads in our ideas of technique. I mean to make my next play a model of lucidity. I have never read 'King Lear's Wife'. (Is that the book you're sending me, because Marsh, who brought the book out, gave me the first Georgian B; however, either would delight me.) 'The End of the World' in the first Georgian Book stands by itself in the language. I do not think there is any modern poet with the subtlety and energy of mind and art that Bottomley has. John Drink-water,° I could never read, he seems so dull to me and Rupert Brooke has written one fine poem with depth, 'Town and country'. I don't like his other work much, they remind me too much of flag days. I am so glad you are in a happy place and the weather is all you wish it to be. Gertler once told me you had written a novel and I look forward to seeing it when I get back, and the new one.° Prose is so diffuse and has not the advantages of poetry. The novels I like best are those terrific conceptions of Balzac, and one I read of Stendhal's. Hardy I think is a better poet than novelist.° There is so much unessential writing one puts in a novel and yet which must be there, at the same time, that makes me regard novel writing as a mistaken art.

I will write the moment I receive the book. Did I acknowledge your papers?

Yours sincerely
I Rosenberg

To Sydney Schiff

[Early Aug. 1916]

Dear Mr Schiff

Your Georgian B. has arrived at last; many many thanks. I pounced on King Lear's Wife, and though it was not more than I expected, it was not less. The only fault I can find is in the diction. It has the aspect of talking to children, in some places. Goneril is marvellously drawn. Lear is a bit shadowy perhaps, but altogether as a poetic drama, it is of the very highest kind. The conception of Lear making love to the servant besides the bedside of his dying wife is unsurpassable.

In one way I do not think the play equal to some things in 'Chambers of Imagery'; at least I never got that startling pleasure from the play as I did from those. Rupert Brooke's poem on Clouds is marvellous; his style offends me; it is gaudy and reminiscent. The second half of the second line, and the whole of the 4th line are so uninteresting. Forgetting these it is a really wonderful thing. I also received your packet of papers which I've had no time yet to look into. I trust you've heard well of your nephews. I wonder how Bomberg behaves. I *must* write to him.

Is the novel growing? I am a bad midwife to ideas just lately and only bring out abortions.

Yours sincerely
I Rosenberg

To Gordon Bottomley

Postmarked 8 Aug. 1916

Dear Mr Bottomley,

Since writing to you the new Georgian book arrived. 'King Lear's Wife' is a fine criticism of the Elizabethan manner of writing. You don't waste a word and it is equal throughout. The conception of Lear making love beside the dying Queen's bedside is terrific. The tone of cruelty throughout the play; the marvellous portraiture of Goneril; the vividness of it all gave me a pleasure I have not experienced since I read our great masters.

You must forgive me, if you can, my sister's pestering letter about printing and selling my work. She told me what you said and the whole affair has vexed me very much. I simply asked her to send a clear copy of my poem to you, as I scrawl abominably, and I suppose she has some sort of notion that one can't be a poet unless his things are printed in daily papers. I am very sorry indeed that you have been bothered in this silly way.

I hope when I come back to England I will be allowed to make a drawing of you; as a rule the poets are unlucky in their painters; but I am eager to draw the poets I like.

Yours sincerely
Isaac Rosenberg

To Edward Marsh

Postmarked 17 Aug. 1916

My dear Marsh

You didn't get my letter because it was never sent; however time has put it all to rights again and there's no need to bother you about it. Thank you for showing my thing to Rothenstein.° I value his praise very much.

G. Bottomley sent me 'King Lear's Wife'. I do think it magnificent as a play and some stunning poetry in it too. There are few men living who could whack that as a play.

We are kept pretty busy now, and the climate here is really un-healthy; the doctors themselves can't stand it. We had an exciting time today, and though this is behind the firing line and right out of the trenches there were quite a good many sent to heaven and the hospital. I carried one myself in a handcart to the hospital, (which often is the antechamber to heaven.) <When I get back to the garden of Eden, a sniff at the tree of knowledge will be enough for me.>°

Binyon wrote me a letter about Moses with the paternal rod half raised in one hand <for my hindquarters> and some sweets and chocolates in the other. But it was a letter I feel grateful for and very good criticism. He says my poetry comes out in clotted gushes and spasms. He has been to France and is back in England now.

Write me if you get time as you know a letter (especially Strakers Stationery°) is a bit—a very tiny bit like London.

Yours
I Rosenberg

To Gordon Bottomley

Postmarked 19 Aug. 1916

Dear Mr Bottomley

I wish I were in London now and had plenty of time to put my thoughts about your book in shape. I have not had time to read it again since I last wrote to you, but I am very glad you did send it as it is, and am very very grateful and honoured. A friend sent me the Georgian book a few weeks ago, but it is so awkward out here to have books in cloth that I must send it back again. In fact at any time I prefer cheap bound books I can spoil by reading anywhere. I often find bibles in dead men's clothes and I tear the parts out I want and carry them about with me. I am pretty fagged just now, having just got back from a wild goose chase up the trenches after some stuff. Yesterday we had a lively time carrying chaps to the hospital in a handcart; it's a toss up whether you're going to be the carried or the carrier. I wish you would try your hand at that Flea hunt. I don't think I'll write anything till we've settled down again. It is a thing Goya would go mad on.

I forgot to say I had not read Wells' Biblical play,° except the bits in Swinburne's essay on him. A friend sent me Swinburne out here and Whitman. I could not help comparing Faustine with a thing I read of yours about those small Tangera Greek figures in Chambers of Imagery.° Yours gives the idea in a much more perfect manner. Swinburne writes too much for the ladies. I shan't try your eyes and your patience with more than this.

Yours sincerely
Isaac Rosenberg

To Sydney Schiff

[Aug. 1916]

Dear Mr Shiff

Many thanks for your letter and the papers. I'll wait till I get back to England to learn French as I can't concentrate on it here. The French poets I think have given a nasty turn to English thought. It is all Café Royal poetry now.° The Germans are far finer though they are fine through Baudelaire. Heine, our own Heine,° we must say nothing of. I admire him more for always being a Jew at heart than anything else. Personally I am very fond of our Celtic Rabelais.° Of Butler° I know very little, but Shaw in spite of his topsy turvy manner seems to me to be very necessary. Anyhow his plays are the only plays I can stand at the theatre. I mean of course of the plays that are played on the stage. He has no subtlety, no delicate irony, none of the rarer qualities. But his broad satire is good.

Yours sincerely,
I. Rosenberg

To Edward Marsh

[Aug. 1916]

22311 A Coy 3 Platoon |
11th K.O.R.L. | B.E.F

My Dear Marsh

I know the terrible length of my new address will make an excellent excuse for not replying; I hope however, it will not frighten you. I am back again in the trenches. I have a notion the Artist [R]ifles° have been somewhere about because I fancy I recognized a Fitzroy Street flea,° but I couldn't swear to it. I have been forbidden to send poems home, as the censor won't be bothered with going through such rubbish, or I would have sent you one I wrote about our armies,° which I am rather bucked about. I have asked the 'Nation'° to print it, if they do, you will see it there. The 'Georgian book' was sent out to me here. Brooke's poem on 'Clouds' is magnificent. Gordon Bottomley has been writing me warm letters. He is a great man and I feel most pained about his condition. Do you know anything about artists out here to disguise things, landscape sheds etc. Col S[olomon] J Solomon° is their Chief I believe and I know him a bit. I wonder if I'd be any good at it. Who would I have to approach about it. Do write.

Yours sincerely
Isaac Rosenberg

To Sydney Schiff

[Mid–late Aug. 1916]
Dear Mr Schiff
    As soon as I had sent my letter off to you I wrote this little thing.° I believe Mr Massingham will like it better than the other you showed him, though I of course prefer the other. I am not sending it to any other paper.
    How is the novel progressing?

Yours sincerely
Isaac Rosenberg

To Gordon Bottomley

Postmarked 29 Aug. 1916

['Pozières']

Dear Mr Bottomley
    Our armies deserve something better than I can hymn them; still here is my little mite. I wrote it immediately I had sent my last letter off to you, and now I have just got your new and kind letter I take this chance of letting you see it, and thanking you at the same time for your letter. By now you will have received my letter acknowledging your book, which I would rather have as it is, than the awkward Georgian form. If we had a theatre as you suggest I believe we would get the great age of poetry back again. I thought Yeats had started something of the kind—the theatre I mean, not the great age.
    I have read Abercrombie's comedy.° He writes like Hercules rolling down Hampstead Hill. I doubt whether the slang always suits the

grandeur and vehemence of his writing. But I always enjoy (especially out here) his work; and the wit in this play is strong and robust. It is a rare and enchanting work.

We are still salving France and our peregrinations find us in the trenches about twice a week; we hope it won't be long before we'll be salving the German Trenches. My address is still

    C/o 40th divisional Coy Officer B.E.F.

    Pte I Rosenberg 22311

Please don't trouble to write unless it amuses you to, although the arrival of a letter from you is a real deep pleasure. If I get the chance I will draw a sketch of anything I think might interest you. I leave the Flea hunt for home coming if that event ever comes about. I have a little drawing at home I should like you to accept and when next I write home I will ask them to send it to you if it can be found. It is a drawing of Adam and Eve° when first they see each other and rush in frenzy to meet. If it can not be found I will find it on my return as I am sure you would like it.

Yours sincerely
Isaac Rosenberg

To John Rodker

[Aug. or Sept. 1916]

Dear Rodker

    What on earth is happening to you and why are you so secret about things. Your letter made me quite wild to know what was up. However perhaps you've got to be quiet. I've had some lovely letters from G Bottomley. It is rough luck on him that he's so poor in health. That must be the reason he doesn't produce very much. I had a box of Turkish from Miss Pulley° and if you see her you can tell her that the war has been worth while since it's been the cause of this enormous pleasure to me—Of course a poet must put it on a bit thick. Turn over for a patriotic gush jingo spasm.

['Pozières']

    I am sending this to Sonia as you gave no address.

Rosenberg

To Sydney Schiff

[Aug. or Sept. 1916]

22311 A Coy 3 Platoon |
11th K.O.R.L. B.E.F. | 3 Platoon

Dear Mr Shiff

   I sent the poem to Mr Massingham. Nation. It makes things so complicated when there is no reply, as one can't show it elsewhere. I am back in the Trenches now and my address is altered as you notice.

FIG. 12 'Isaac Rosenberg   his outer semblance?   22311 Pt I Rosenberg 11th K.O.R.L. B.E.F.   I have gone back to the trenches & send you this souvenir. Above is my new address.   The line above the helmet is the Germans front line 100 yards away.'

Thank you for Lawrence° offer but cloth books are so bulky and impossible out here. I have sent home the Georgian book. I know his poems a little and admire his power, but not his outlook. I suppose he is the necessary spokesman for people that way inclined. It is a pity you are chucking your novel, but of course, you would know best. I read an excellent poem in the Westminster Gazette,° it got the prize there; it begins 'Me and Bill and Ginger'. Do you know who wrote it? It's by someone at the front.

I am sorry I can't date my letters as you ask but I never know the date and one can't choose your own time as to sending letters. I generally write when I see the postman coming to collect, if I get the chance.

Yours sincerely
Isaac Rosenberg

To Sydney Schiff

[late Aug. or Sept. 1916]

22311 | A Coy 3 Platoon |
11th K.O.R.L. B.E.F.

Dear Mr Schiff

Thanks very much for papers. I liked the article on the Somme Cinemas.° Of course Chesterton on Zangwill° was nearer home; but C seems sly and certainly anti Jewish.

We are having rotten wet weather in the trenches, mucky and souzing and cold. I don't think I've been dry yet, these last 3 days.

Bottomley is a permanent invalid and lives quietly in the North of England. I don't think he's ever troubled much about his work though they have made more headway in Yankeeland than here. I think him in many ways our best poet. He has an extraordinary dramatic power and quite new. There is a lovely delicacy about his work as if shaken about strength, as powerful as any of those sledge hammer bawlers which many people will accept alone for strength. His enfeebled condition is a great loss to literature as it lessens his output.

Yours sincerely
Isaac Rosenberg

I forgot to mention the rejected masterpiece.° Its adventures must have been various and many, to judge by the interminable length of time it took to reach me again; it must have been handled by angels too, for the printless pressure of their fingers on the paper could be felt but not seen. Gordon Bottomley thought the lines from 2 to 5 first rate poetry, but thought the whole things seemed like a long interjection. Well, I had meant to go on with it.

To Gordon Bottomley

Postmarked 17 Sept. 1916

22311 A Coy 3 Platoon |
11th. K.O.R.L. B.E.F.

Dear Mr Bottomley,

I have not had the chance till now of thanking you for your beautiful thought of me in your letter and book. It has been wet and mucky in the trenches for some time and the cold weather helping, we are teased by the elements as well as by the German fireworks. I don't think I've been dry yet these last few days. I have been able in heavy lidded spasms to dip half asleep into Joseph.° It is magnificent; the barbarous blazonry of Marlowe too much perhaps. I came across Swinburne's notice in an old 'Fortnightly'.° There is fine freshness and vehemence in the writing of Joseph and I am looking forward to reading it properly. I did mean to write Poziers as a hymn with ample proportions, but got stuck somehow.

It gave me fine pleasure that you liked my drawing. I have not written home about the Adam and Eve drawing as I don't remember where it is, but I want you to have it when I get back, if I am lucky. I must draw the 'Flea hunt' if I don't write it, but so far I've not been able to do anything interesting. I forgot about your fine louse song,° which naturally the world would read with visions of Keatings° floating in its mind.

I am most eager to read your early book but it would [be] far from safe to send it here, besides the little time there is for reading.

Yours sincerely
Isaac Rosenberg

Extract from letter to Harriet Monroe

[Summer or autumn 1916]

   Could you let me know whether a poem of mine 'Marching' has been printed by you,° as I understood from J. Rodker, it was accepted. I have no means of knowing, or seeing your magazine out here, I have lost touch with Rodker [. . .] I am enclosing a poem or two written in the trenches [. . .]

To Edward Marsh

Postmarked 10 Oct. 1916

                              22311 A Coy 3 platoon | 11th K.O.R.L. B.E.F.

My dear Marsh

   You complain in your letter that there is little to write about; my complaint is rather the other way, I have too much to write about, but for obvious reasons my much must be reduced to less than your little. My exaggerated way of feeling things when I begin to write about them might not have quite healthy consequences. I was most glad to hear about Bottomley. He has been writing me warm letters and I was greatly pained to find so fine a nature possessing so frail a hold on health and I am always most anxious about him and to hear anything of him.

   My Lilith° has eloped with that devil procrastination, or rather, labours of a most colossal and uncongenial shape have usurped her place and driven her blonde and growing beauty away. I have written something that still wants knocking into shape. I feel too tired to copy if out, but later on I will, if you care to see it. I came across that poem on clouds by poor Rupert Brooke. It is magnificent indeed, and as near to sublimity as any modern poem.

   The poem I like best of modern times is Abercrombie's Hymn to Love. It is more weighty in thought, alive in passion and of a more intense imagination than any I know. I was amused to hear of your gardening experiment. I suppose one must get interested in things different to our usual interests and get our thoughts shaken up a bit nowadays or it would be Hell going on. Do write when you can.

Yours sincerely
Isaac Rosenberg

To Laurence Binyon

[Autumn 1916]

22311 A Coy 3 platoon |
11th Batt K.O.R.L. B.E.F.

Dear Mr Binyon

It is far—very far to the British Museum from here—(situated as I am, Siberia is no further—and certainly not colder—) but not too far for that tiny mite of myself—my letter, to reach there. Winter has found its way into the trenches at last, but I will spare you, and leave to your imagination, the transports of delight with which we welcomed its coming. Winter is not the least of the horrors of war.

I am determined that this war, with all its powers for devastation, shall not master my poetry—that is if I am lucky enough to come through all right. I will not leave a corner of my consciousness covered up, but saturate myself with the strange and extraordinary new conditions of this life and it will all refine itself into poetry later on.

I have thoughts of a play round our Jewish hero Judas Maccabeus. I have much real material here, and also there is some parallel in the savagery of the invaders then to this war.

I am not decided whether truth of period is a good quality or a negative one. Flaubert's 'Salambo'° proves perhaps that it is good. It decides the tone of the work though it makes it hard to give the human side and make it more living. However it is impossible now to work and difficult even to think of poetry one is so cramped intellectually.

The period is about Christ's time and I think I could bring about a meeting between Christ and Judas, in fact Christ could be brought up or spend part of his boyhood with Mathias the high priest and father of Judas.

I am enclosing a poem I think will please you, it being simpler than my usual.

I saw some time ago in the papers a book of yours had appeared.° Your time in France has borne fruit which I hope to taste when I go home on leave if that time ever comes.

If I get the chance I'll write a sequence of poems of trench life which I mean to be a startler. You know all that goes on so I won't worry you with my experiences now, but they the poems will be psychological and individual, and I hope interesting. I hope you will write when you can though I suppose your time is filled up.

Yours sincerely
I Rosenberg

To Rosenberg's father

[Autumn 1916]

22311 A Coy 3 Platoon |
11th K.O.R.L. B.E.F.

Dear Father

I am glad you are satisfied with my Yom Tov° energy. I had a letter from Minnie° which I've answered. I suppose you will be home for the winter now.° I am short of stationery so can't write much, but everything is contained in I'm fit. Will write home as soon as I get stationery.

Isaac

To Gordon Bottomley

Postmarked 12 Nov. 1916

3 Platoon | 22311 A Coy 11th K.O.R.L. | B.E.F.

Dear Mr Bottomley,

I have a few minutes now, for a wonder, to do what I like with, and I'm going to worry you in them with my staggering calligraphy. I asked my people at home to forward my 'Adam and Eve' some months ago. Whether they have done so I have not heard. I heard from Mr Marsh that he had heard from you and I was mightily pleased to hear anything about you. Of course, being the Prime Minister's secretary he is far too busy to write much. We are getting well into November now and have already had it bitter cold in the trenches and warm again and wet. We are now on a long march and have done a good deal towards flattening the roads of France. I wrote a little thing yesterday which still needs working on.

['The destruction of Jerusalem by the Babylonian hordes']

I have also written or rather sketched a thing I fancy will be strong but I'll reserve that for another letter. I do hope you can fight the winter well. I hate the cold.

I have not been able yet to read the 'Joseph' thing. Our time is absolutely filled up and there is little room for Pegasus to ride in or to watch him riding. But I see now why you asked me when you read 'Moses'. There is certainly a semblance of aim, if I may say so. I mean the matter and the subject are not so unalike and yet unusual. I hope you are writing and that I may some day have the delight of seeing it.

Yours sincerely
Isaac Rosenberg.

To R. C. Trevelyan

Postmarked 20 Nov. 1916

22311 A Coy 3 Platoon | 11th K.O.R.L. B.E.F.

Dear Mr Trevelyan

I had just written to Mr Bottomley when your letter reached me last week. Perhaps you were still with him when my letter arrived (if it did arrive) and read the little poem I sent. Just as a reminder that poetry is still alive in my brain. We are pretty busy and writing letters is most awkward, but after some rough days in the trenches, here before the comfortable glare of the camp fire I cannot help using these few odd minutes to answer your letter. It was a treat to get something about something from home. I cannot now enter into your arguments tho that kind of fighting is more in my line than trench fighting—

I am writing this chiefly to let you know I am still safe, and to thank you for your letter. I am most eager to see Bottomley's new work and the rest in your annual.° I read Moore's Sicilian Idyll° in the first Georgian book and it is great. That is all I know of Moore. Judith° and the Hymn to Love made me think Abercrombie the first poet in the world.

If there is any chance of getting home I'll certainly let you know— though things are so vague and in the air we never know what's going to happen for two minutes together.

Yours sincerely
Isaac Rosenberg

To Laurence Binyon

Postmarked 5 Dec. 1916

22311 3 platoon A Coy | 11th K.O.R.L. B.E.F.

Dear Mr Binyon

I have thought about the poem and your suggestions but it's impossible for me to work on it here. If you care to you could send it to a paper—I might get something for it, which would come in handy when I go home on leave—if I do.

We are in a rougher shop than before and the weather is about as bad as it can be but my Pegasus though it may kick at times will not stampede or lose or leave me. I felt your letter very much but we are young and it's excitement for us. I have also learnt a good deal about human nature though perhaps not very flattering to it.

I wonder if you like this new poem. It has my usual fault of intricacy I know but I think the idea is clear. Mr Gibson's new book 'Battle'° was sent me. Most of the poems are really fine and absolutely express the thing. 'Between the Lines' is most vivid and exact. I was never very fond of Gibson's work, it struck me as cultured vigour—but I was delighted with this book.

Yours sincerely

Isaac Rosenberg

Enclosed with this letter was a pencil holograph of 'Daughters of War'.

To Gordon Bottomley

5 Dec. 1916

Pages 1–3 only

Dear Mr Bottomley

I know what it costs you to write a letter, especially now this cruel weather has set in. Mr Trevelyan gave me good and cheering news of you, and also all the literary adventures at 'The Sheiling'.° Since I last wrote to you I have been feeling pretty crotchety—and my memory has become very weak and confused. I fancy the winter has bowled me over, but I suppose we must go lingering on.

What you say of my poem might lend colour to Marsh's belief that you are too indulgent to me, but give me half a chance, and you will see it'll be the other way about. I am enclosing the poem I spoke about. ° I think it has nine parts of my old fault to one of my new merit; but I fancy you will like the idea.

I am grieved at the misunderstanding about Wells. I forget quite what I said; but I know it was one of the rarest pieces of pleasure I have had out here, when you sent me his book.

I also received Gibson's 'Battle', and in one way I think it is the best thing the war has turned out. Personally, I think the only value in any war is the literature it results in.

> 'Where are all your warring kings a tale
> By some stammering schoolboy told'.

[Two lines deleted by censor and illegible. They are signed 'R S Oglethorpe'.]°

To Laurence Binyon

[Autumn 1916]

Dear Mr Binyon

Please don't bother about the poem if you still mean to try and get it printed. 'Poetry' of America are printing it so it might cause complications if it were printed again.

I am feeling a bit knocked up but I hope I'll get over it.

When will this plague be over—everybody and everything seems to be tumbling to pieces.

Yours sincerely
Isaac Rosenberg

To Edward Marsh

[Dec. 1916]

My dear Marsh

If I get two letters from one friend I get none from another. Well—I have not been out here six months for nothing—I have learnt to be a

Stoic and say nothing. We hear very little of what's going on in England, but I did get a rumour of great changes in the government° which may affect you. I wish I were in England just for a while, particularly now that I feel run down and weakened. I am also wishful to meet Gordon Bottomley some day. I hear Abercrombie is over-working himself and doing himself no good; a condition of being I can claim to rival him in.

Gibson's 'Battle' was sent to me and delighted me. It is as good as Degas. In a way it seems a contradiction that a thinker should take a low plane as he does there instead of the most complex and sensitive personality of a poet in such a situation. Most who have written as poets have been very unreal and it is for this reason their naturalness I think Gibson's so fine. The Homer for this war has yet to be found— Whitman got very near to the mark 50 years ago with 'Drum Taps'. I don't know what these Government changes will mean to you but do write if you can and let me know.

Yours sincerely
Isaac Rosenberg

To Gordon Bottomley

Postmarked 5 Jan. 1917

Dear Mr Bottomley

Your letter came to me from home on New Year's day, and it was the best pleasure the new year brought. I feel better than when I last wrote to you, I fancy it was a touch of the flu I had, but that is all over now, though I am not altogether well; and when I get the chance of a rest I will use it well. My poem came when I was brooding over Judas Macabeus, and it is all that did come of it. If I get back all right Judas will come too, and all I have learnt out here will be crammed into it. I've also thought about the louse hunt but so far I've had no chance of working on it properly. It could be worked into Judas and make an entire scene. Where we are now gives us very little chance for this, and also, I've been transferred to a labour batt. My new address now is

Pte I.R. 22311. 7 Platoon F. Coy.
40th Division Works Batt. B.E.F.

It is a sort of navvy Batt to repair the roads. When I went bad we were just going into the trenches and I was shifted into this. Naturally we are in less danger than before, but we are practically always under fire of some sort.

Thank you for asking about books. I shan't say I don't get the time to read; but when we've done our day's work, and get into the tent, (we are in tents just now) it is dark and lights are not easy to get out here. In fact it is desolation everywhere, in diabolical state. Don't trouble to send the book, though there is nothing I'd like more. If we are ever shifted to more convenient quarters I'll remind you of your promise you may be sure.

I cannot remember whose translations I've read; but what I've read have been very few of the Greeks; I have read some of the great dramas, but have always felt (except in Shelley's) the translator use his English in a foreign unnatural and empty way. Not like the Bible translators.

I wonder if Aeschylus as a private in the army was bothered as I am by lice. I am very grateful for your good wishes and your wife's.

Yours sincerely
Isaac Rosenberg

To Edward Marsh

Postmarked 18 Jan. 1917

My dear Marsh

My sister wrote me she would be writing to you.° She'd got the idea of my being in vile health from your letter addressed to Dempsey St, and naturally they at home exaggerated things in their minds. Perhaps though it is not so exaggerated. That my health is undermined I feel sure of; but I have only lately been medically examined, and absolute fitness was the verdict. My being transferred may be the consequence of my reporting sick, or not; I don't know for certain. But though this work does not entail half the hardships of the trenches, the winter and the conditions naturally tells on me, having once suffered from weak lungs, as you know. I have been in the trenches most of the 8 months I've been here, and the continual damp and exposure is whispering to my old friend consumption, and he may hear the words they say in time. I have nothing outwardly to show, yet, but I feel it inwardly. I don't know what you could do in a case like this; perhaps I could be made use of as a draughtsman at home; or something else in my own line, or perhaps on munitions. My new address is

Pte I R 22311
7 Platoon F. Coy
40th Division
Works Battalion
B.E.F.

I wrote a poem some while ago which Bottomley liked so,° and I want you to see it, but I'm writing in most awkward conditions and can't copy it now. 'Poetry' of Chicago printed a couple of my things and are paying me. I should think you find the Colonial Office° interesting particularly after the war.

I hope however it leaves you leisure for literature; for me it's the great thing.

Yours sincerely
Isaac Rosenberg

To Edward Marsh

Postmarked 8 Feb. 1917

My dear Marsh

I was told the other day by the Captain that he had heard from you about me. He had me examined, but it appears I'm quite fit. What I feel like just now—I wish I were Tristram Shandy for a few minutes so as to describe this 'cadaverous bale of goods consigned to Pluto'. This winter is a teaser for me; and being so long without a proper rest I feel as if I need one to recuperate and be put to rights again. However I suppose we'll stick it, if we don't, there are still some good poets left who might write me a decent epitaph.

I've sketched an amusing little thing called 'the louse hunt', and am trying to write one as well. I get very little chance to do anything of this sort, but what I have done I'll try and send you. Daumier or Goya° are far in perspective.

How do [you] find the Colonial Office after the Treasury?

Yours sincerely
Isaac Rosenberg
Pte I. R. 22311
7 Platoon F. Coy 40th Division

Works Batt. B.E.F.
I'll send on the poem G.B. liked so much, next time I write.

To Gordon Bottomley

Postmarked 19 [Feb. 1917]

Dear Mr Bottomley

Your letters always give me a strange and large pleasure and I shall never think I have written poetry in vain; since it has brought your friendliness in my way. Now, feeling as I am, castaway and used up, you don't know what a letter like yours is to me. Ever since Nov, when we first started on our long marches, I have felt weak; but it seems to be some inscrutable mysterious quality of weakness that defies all doctors. I have been examined most thoroughly several times by our doctor and there seems to be nothing at all wrong with my lungs. I believe I have strained my abdomen in some way and I shall know of it later on.

We have had desperate weather, but the poor fellows in the trenches where there are no dugouts are the chaps to pity.

I am sending a very slight sketch of a louse hunt. It may be a bit vague as I could not work it out here. But if you can keep it till I get back I can work on it then.

I do believe I could make a fine thing of Judas. Judas as a character is more magnanimous than Moses, and I believe I could make it very intense and write a lot from material out here.

Thanks very much for your joining in with me to rout the pest out; but I have tried all kinds of stuff; if you can think of any preparation you believe effective I'd be most grateful for it.

Yours sincerely
Isaac Rosenberg

To Ruth Löwy

[Feb. or March 1917]

22311 A Coy 3 Platoon | 11th K.O.R.L. B.E.F.

Dear Miss Löwy,

I did not send K[ing] L[ear's] W[ife] as I hadn't the chance and am most glad you had already read and liked it. We have been on the march almost all the time since I last wrote to you and it has been impossible to do anything one wanted to do. King Lear's Wife is remarkable. The conception of the king's love making at the bedside of his dying wife is marvellous. I chiefly admire the simple beauty of the writing and the characterization of Goneril—hard and beautiful. If you can, do get his 'Chambers of Imagery'. I like some things there perhaps better than the play. He wrote me when he read my 'Moses' that the 'Ah Kolue' speech,° and two or three other speeches was the 'very top of poetry'.

He is a permanent invalid and it gives him hell to write much. He has written me most warm letters out here and I feel really happy when I hear his work is enjoyed.

I spent my wild little pick a back days in Bristol; was born there, too. I have some vague far away memories of the name of Polack in connection I fancy with Hebrew classes and prize giving. It pleases me much that my poems are liked in my natal place—a fate so opposite to the usual—but probably that it because they are unaware of it being my natal place.

G.B. has urged me to write Jewish Plays.° I am quite sure if I do I will be boycotted and excommunicated, that is, assuming my work is understood. My 'Moses' is a hard pill to swallow and should I get the chance of working on it and amplifying it as I wish—it will be harder still. Mrs Cohen sent me her book. It is interesting but my idea of poetry is something deeper than that. She sent me papers too and I notice there Gilbert Cannan has written a novel called 'Mendel'.° I fancy as far as I can make out, Gertler is the hero. Gertler is or was on very friendly terms with Cannan, and lived with him a long time. Cannan is very clever and is ranked very high as a satirical novelist, a kind of Piccadilly Voltaire. I must stop now as we've no more lights.

Yours sincerely
Isaac Rosenberg

To Gordon Bottomley

Postmarked 8 April 1917

Dear Mr Bottomley,

I do wish I could see Mr Trevelyan's Annual.° In his last letter to me he spoke of your things and made me most eager to see them. But the bulkiness of the book, of course, makes it out of the question, my seeing it out here; besides the bad chance I have of reading it properly. Sturge Moore is a poet I like very much though I only know his 'Sycillian Idyll' in G.B.° I want to see Mr Trevelyan's Play° very much, too, as I have seen very little of his work. We all want this rotten business over, that keeps us away from all these good things; and the lively happenings of late sound very promising.°

All through this winter I have felt most crotchety; all kinds of small things kept interfering with my fitness. My hands would get chilblains or bad boots would make my feet sore; and this aggravating a general rundownness, I have not felt too happy. I have gone less warmly clad during the winter than through the summer; because of the increased liveliness on my clothes. I've been stung to what we call 'dumping' a great part of my clothing, as I thought it wisest to go cold than lousy. It may have been this that caused all the crotchetiness.

However, we've been in no danger, that is from shellfire for a good long while; though so very close to most terrible fighting. But, as far as houses or sign of ordinary human living is concerned, we might as well be in the Sahara desert. I think I could give some bloodcurdling touches if I wished to tell all I see; of dead buried men blown out of their graves, and more, but I will spare you all this.

I thought you would like the flea hunt, and your way of commenting on it is infinitely more superior to my sketch.

I do hope when all this is over I shall be able to see you and perhaps get a drawing done of you.

Yours sincerely
Isaac Rosenberg

To Edward Marsh

Postmarked 25 April 1917

My dear Marsh

My sister wrote me you have been getting more of my 'Moses'. It is hardy of you, indeed, to spread it about; and I certainly would be distressed if I were the cause of a war in England; seeing what warfare means here. But it greatly pleases me, none the less, that this child of my brain, should be seen and perhaps his beauties be discovered. His creator is in sadder plight; the harsh and unlovely times have made his mistress, the flighty Muse, abscond and elope with luckier rivals, but surely I shall hunt her and chase her somewhere into the summer and sweeter times. Anyway this is a strong hope. Lately I have not been very happy, being in torture with my feet again. The coldness of the weather and the weight of my boots have put my feet in a rotten state. My address is different now

> Pte IR 22311
> 7 Platoon
> 120th Brigade Works Coy
> B.E.F.

There is more excitement now, but though I enjoy this, my feet cause me great suffering and my strength is hardly equal to what is required.

I hear pretty often from G Bottomley and his letters are like a handshake: and passages are splendid pieces of writing. Have you seen Trevelyan's 'Annual' which G.B. writes me of.

Do write me when you can.

Yours sincerely
Isaac Rosenberg

To Edward Marsh

Postmarked 8 May 1917

My dear Marsh

We are camping in the woods now and are living great. My feet are almost healed now and my list of complaints has dwindled down to almost invisibility. I've written some lines suggested by going out wiring,° or rather carrying wire up the line on limbers and running over dead bodies lying about. I don't think what I've written is very good but I think the substance is, and when I work on it I'll make it fine.

Bottomley told me he had some very old poems in The Annual but of course it's too bulky to send out here. Your extract from his 'Atlantis' is real Bottomleyian. The young Oxford poets you showed my things to I've never come across yet, and I'll soon begin to think myself a poet if my things get admired so.

I'm writing to my sister to send you the lines as she will type several copies.

Yours sincerely

I R

I trust the colonial office agrees with you.

To Edward Marsh

Postmarked 27 May 1917

My dear Marsh

I liked your criticism of 'Dead man's dump'. Mr Binyon has often sermonized lengthily over my working on two different principles in the same thing and I know how it spoils the unity of a poem. But if I couldn't before, I can now, I am sure, plead the absolute necessity of fixing an idea before it is lost, because of the situation it's conceived in. Regular rhythms I do not like much, but of course it depends on where the stress and accent are laid. I think there is nothing finer than the vigorous opening of Lycidas° for music; yet it is regular. Now I think if Andrew Marvell had broken up his rhythms more he would have been considered a terrific poet. As it is I like his poem urging his mistress to love because they have not a thousand years to love in and he can't afford to wait. (I forget the name of the poem)° well I like it more than Lycidas.

I have written a much finer poem° which I've asked my sister to send you. Don't think from this I've time to write. This last poem is only about 70 lines and I started it about October. It is only when we get a bit of rest and the others might be gambling or squabbling I add a line or two, and continue this way.

The weather is gorgeous now and we are bivouacked in the fields. The other night I awoke to find myself floating about with the water half over me. I took my shirt off and curled myself up on a little mound that the water hadn't touched and slept stark naked that night. But that was not all of the fun. The chap next to me was suddenly taken with diarrhoea and kept on lifting the sheet of the bivouac, and as I lay at the end the rain came beating on my nakedness all night. Next morning, I noticed the poor chap's discoloured pants hanging on a bough near by, and I thought after all I had the best of it.

I fancy you will like my last poem, I am sure it is at least as good as my Kolue speech, and there is more of it.

Yours sincerely

Isaac Rosenberg

To Edward Marsh

?Postmarked 29 May 1917°

My dear Marsh

    I hope you have not yet got my poem 'The Amulet' I've asked my sister to send you. If you get it please don't read it because it's the merest sketch and the best is yet to come. If I am able to carry on with it I'll send you it in a more presentable fashion. I believe I have a good idea at bottom. It's a kind of 'Rape of the Sabine Women', idea. Some strange race of wanderers have settled in some wild place and are perishing out for lack of women. The prince of these explores some country near where the women are most fair. But the natives will not hear of foreign marriages and he plots another rape of the Sabines, but he is trapped in the act. Finis. But I fancy poetry is not much bothering you or anybody just now. I've heard of the air raids and I always feel most anxious about my people. Yet out here, though often a troublesome consolation, poetry is a great one to me. G. Bottomley sent me some knock-outs. 'Atlantis' is one of the grand poems in our language; and came to me as the news of a great victory might come. I am still with the R[oyal].E[ngineer]s and go up the line every night, unloading barbed wire etc. In the afternoon we load the stuff. So I have the morning to sleep in, unless I happen to be doing some punishment for my forgetfulness; and then I must do that in the morning. Though furloughs are going about in our Div, it may be a good while before my turn comes.

Yours sincerely

Isaac Rosenberg

To Gordon Bottomley

Postmarked 31 May 1917

My dear Mr Bottomley

    Your last letter was a real precious letter—it touched me in the way a beautiful sad relic might, say a Greek fragment. Because I am always pained to think how dependant your ease of body and mind is upon the weather; and to hear anything distressful happening to you; and then your wonderful poem. We have learnt out here to be a bit callous and have worn the edge off our teeth with much grinding, but the 'spring of tears' remains. 'Sinai' is fine and though I'd like to think my Moses is as fine as you say, I wish I could have got some of that simple greatness Sinai has. It is the first *poem* I have seen since I left England.

> 'They watched me mount the mist
> with steps like threats'

Only the very greatest poets, Job, or Marlowe, could have conceived an image like that. I've had some Poems sent me lately in the Poetry Review but I think the writers should be hung, or the Editor rather. They may be good soldiers but they're poor poets. I came across some poems once in England by 'The author of Erebus'.° There was no name and some of the poems were after my own heart. Do you know who he is.

I am now with the Royal Engineers and we go wiring up the line at night. We took a village and the R.E.s did all the wiring and some digging in front of it. I wrote a poem about some dead Germans lying in a sunken road where we dumped our wire. I have asked my sister to send it on to you, though I think it commonplace; also 'Daughters of war' which I've improved. I've made it into a little book for you,° as I like the poem. We go out at night and sleep in the day in these woods, behind the line. It is that I've had a little more time in the day to myself and am with a small loading party by ourselves that I've been able to write these two things lately. Don't worry about the insect powder. Just when they begin to get unbearable we generally get a change, and I don't think anything else is much use. My address is

　Pte IR. 22311
　7 Platoon. 11th K.O.R.L.
　C/o 229 Field Coy Royal Engineers
　B.E.F.

I suppose I must wait for home to see the Annual and your things.

Yours sincerely
Isaac Rosenberg

To Rosenberg's mother

7 June [1917]

Dear Mother

I have not had a letter since well over a week and hope things are all right at home. My new address is

    Pte I Rosenberg 22311
    11th K.O.R.L.
    c/o 229 Field Coy.
    Royal Engineers,
    B.E.F.

I will send a poem if I can't manage it in this letter, in the next, I want typed and sent back to me not to be shown to anyone, as I want to work on it before it is seen. The weather is still marvellous though last night it lightninged a good deal, it was good to see.

Send me a pencil or chalk pencil. What is Dave doing and Elkon?° I hope Peretz's boys° are good and no trouble. If they are good things should be lively.

Love to all

Isaac

To Gordon Bottomley

Postmarked 23 June 1917

My dear Mr Bottomley

My sister wrote me of your note and it made me very glad to feel you thought in that way about my poem; because I liked it myself above anything I have yet done. I know my letters are not what they should be; but I must take any chance I get of writing for fear another chance does not come, so I write hastily and leave out most I should write about. I wished to say last time a lot about your poem, but I could think of nothing that would properly express my great pleasure in it; and I can think of nothing now. If anything I think it is too brief—although it is so rare and compressed and full of hinted matter. I wish I could get back and read your plays; and if my luck still continues, I shall. Leaves have commenced with us but it may be a good while before I get mine. We are more busy now than when I last wrote but I can generally manage to knock something up if my brain means to, and I am sketching out a little play. My great fear is that I may lose what I've written; which can happen here so easily. I send home any bit I write for safety, but that can easily get lost in transmission. However I live in an immense trust that things will turn out well.

I do hope this weather suits your health and that you are not caused much trouble. Just now I have toothache but otherwise I was never so well.

Do not write because you think you ought to answer; but write when you have nothing else to do and you wish to kill time; it is no trouble for me to write these empty letters, when I have a minute to spare, just to let you know life and poetry are as fresh as ever in me.

Yours sincerely
Isaac Rosenberg

Enclosed with this letter were MS lines 23–6 of 'Dead Man's Dump', and two TSS of 'Daughters of War'.

To Gordon Bottomley

Postmarked 9 July 1917

My dear Mr Bottomley

I really do not want you to write if there is any difficulty at all in writing; as I will always believe even when no letter arrives, in your friendliness to me. Though there is little gives me more pleasure than a letter from you yet that pleasure would be marred if I thought it was at the expense of your ease. But your last letter shows you to be in good condition and happy, and I am greatly pleased at this. Above all your tremendous 'Atlantis' and the others. 'Atlantis' is in Rossetti's way of putting it, 'a stunner'. I think it is as fine as anything you have done, and it fairly knocked me over. It is a marvellously symbolic poem of human life; or rather the dark destiny of man—it is a sad beautiful poem.

The other poems I have not yet read, but I will follow on with letters and shall send the bits of—or rather the bit of a play I've written. Just now it is interfered with by a punishment I am undergoing for the offence of being endowed with a poor memory, which continually causes me trouble and often punishment. I forgot to wear my gas helmet one day; in fact I've often forgotten it, but I was noticed one day, and seven days' pack drill is the consequence, which I do between the hours of going up the line and sleep. My memory, always weak, has become worse since I've been out here.

Your poem beginning 'Within your Roman House'° is a gorgeous little affair, with a most curious music, and 'Homunculus In Penumbra' is strange in your old extraordinary way—The naturalness of your imagination will always be a kind of whip to me, and if I ever do anything high, it will be because of your lesson.

It is real friendship of you to take that workable interest in my poetry and trouble to look after my things. I shall send you stuff when I get the chance though just now—my torturer has this moment come for me.

Yours sincerely
Isaac Rosenberg

To Gordon Bottomley

Postmarked 11 July 1917

My dear Mr Bottomley

I wrote you a day or so ago but my letter was interrupted, so I follow on with this; I want you to know what deep and real pleasure your poems gave me and I owe you much for this; because a rare pleasure like this is something indeed to me, here. I read the 'sermon on the mount' for the first time lately, and got this rare pleasure. It is indeed heroic and great philosophy. I wrote you of your 'Atlantis' which is one of the great poems in our language: Homunculus, is perhaps as marvellous too, certainly no poet has ever conceived a more difficult idea and worked it out more real, more piercingly.

The other poems I enjoyed in their different ways. 'All Souls'° is lovely; though it seems fantastic (if I may say so) to the reality of 'Homunculus'; perhaps fantastic is not the word; fanciful, perhaps. 'Avenglass' is a delightful picture poem: They all gave me that enjoyment that only solid true poetry can give.

I don't suppose my poems will ever be *poetry* right and proper until I shall be able to settle down and whip myself into more clear expression. As it is, my not being able to get poetry out of my head and heart causes me sufficient trouble out here. Not that it interferes with the actual practical work; but with forms and things I continually forget; and authority looks at from a different angle and perspective. This even may (or may not) interfere with my chances of an early leave (the earliest was late enough), but will never break the ardour of my poetry.

I have not read the 'Chronicles of Jeremiah' and thank you for putting me on it. We Jews are all taught Hebrew in our childhood but I was a young rebel and would not be taught, unluckily now. I read Hebrew like a parrot without knowing the meaning. I meant to go on with Moses because I have made ambition to be the dominant point in his character which I've considered is very unfriendly to my ancestor. I did mean to contrast him with a Christ like man, which I may yet do. However I've written a little scribble about him; and my sketch for a play is really too crude and undeveloped, and I am not sure whether I will send it. But I am expecting it any time in its typed form from home, and by that time, if army rigour has not shattered all my dreams of Parnassian peregrinations, I may have thought of improvements. Perhaps you know my little poem 'Wedded', well it is a commentary on that. But the woman is not subtle enough and the man is hardly yet suggested, and the third character is a sort of castrated neuter gender; so I hardly think I will be doing good return for the marvellous 'Atlantis' and the rest.

So Abercrombie is a shell inspector;° that sounds more exciting than school inspector; yet Matthew Arnold° had an exciting enough time, I should think. I swear he (L.A) is laying up stores for great plays gathered from his shell factories, and it gives me great happiness to think of you two together and to learn you are well.

Yours sincerely
Isaac Rosenberg

Enclosed with this letter was a fair copy of 'The Jew'.

To Sydney Schiff

[?July 1917]

22311 Pte I Rosenberg | 11th K.O.R.L. Regt. |
Attached 229 Field Coy, R.Es. | B.E.F. France

Dear Mr Schiff

I was most glad to hear from you. I have just received your letter and its useful enclosure for which many thanks. I say I was most glad—but that is not quite true—your letter is too bitter. I did not get your letters in France and I often wondered about you, but things are

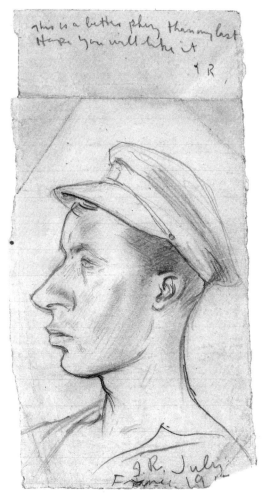

FIG. 13 'This is a better phiz than my last   Hope you like it   I.R. July 19[17]. France.'

so tumultuous and disturbing that unless one has everything handy, like an addressed envelope a pencil and a moment to spare one cannot write letters. One's envelopes get stuck and useless with the damp and you cannot replace them. I managed to jot down some ideas for poems now and then but I won't send them to you because they are actual transcripts of the battlefield and you won't like that, anyway just now. I do hope you have exaggerated your feelings and are not so low in spirits as your letter makes out. We manage to keep cheerful out here in the face of most horrible things but then, we are kept busy, and have no time to brood. I hope your wife is well. My sister and my mother wish you well.

Yours sincerely
Isaac Rosenberg

I am sending you a good photo of myself in a day or two.

To Edward Marsh

Postmarked 30 July 1917

My dear Marsh,

I'm glad you've got your old job again and are Winston Churchill's private sec. once more, though it will be a pity if it will interfere with your literary projects. I thought that would happen when I heard he'd become Minister of Munitions. I can imagine how busy you will be kept and if you still mean to go on with your memoir° and G[eorgian]. P[oetry]., you perhaps can imagine me, though of course my work pretty much leaves my brain alone especially as I have a decent job now and am not as rushed and worked as I was in the trenches. I will be glad to be included in the Georgian Book, and hope your other work won't interfere with it. I've asked my sister (she recognises your helplessness about me, but I hope you were not too annoyed at her persistence; although I was; when I heard of it) not to send the Amulet because I've changed the idea completely and I think if I can work it out on the new lines it will be most clear and most extraordinary. It's called 'The Unicorn' now. I am stuck in the most difficult part; I have to feel a set of unusual emotions which I simply can't feel yet. However if I keep on thinking about it it may come.

We may not begin a letter with our address but work it in the text, I generally forget about it as I go on writing.

    Pte I.R. 22311
    11th K.O.R.L.
    Attached 229 Field Coy R.Es.
    B.E.F.

I think with you that poetry should be definite thought and clear expression, however subtle; I don't think there should be any vagueness at all; but a sense of something hidden and felt to be there; Now when my things fail to be clear I am sure it is because of the luckless choice of a word or the failure to introduce a word that would flash my idea plain as it is to my own mind. I believe my Amazon poem to be my best poem. If there is any difficulty it must be in words here and there the changing or elimination of which may make the poem clear. It has taken me about a year to write; for I have changed and rechanged it and thought hard over that poem and striven to get that sense of inexorableness the human (or inhuman) side of this war has. It even penetrates behind human life for the 'Amazon' who speaks in the second half of the poem is imagined to be without her lover yet, while all her sisters have theirs, the released spirits of the slain earth men; her lover yet remains to be released. I hope however, to be home on leave, and talk it over, some time this side of the year. In my next letter I will try and send an idea of 'The Unicorn'.

If you are too busy don't bother about answering,

Yours sincerely
Isaac Rosenberg

To Edward Marsh

[Late July or Aug. 1917]

My dear Marsh,

Is the poem clearer now. I felt the opening was the weak part and have struggled hard with it.

I am sure once you get hold of it you will find it my best poem and most complete, most epic. I haven't had the chance to work on 'The Unicorn' but will send you the central idea soon.

G. Bottomley wrote me Mr Abercrombie is a shell inspector now at Liverpool, but is living in Arabia between whiles, but says nothing of Parnassus. I shall have to find another daughter of war who elopes with his soul and the background will be a munition factory. Doubtless my usual obscurity will be serviceable this time, and save me from the wrath of a jealous wife.

Pte I R, 22311. 11th K.O.R.L.
attached 229 Field Coy. R.Es. B.E.F.

I hope your job keeps you fit.

Yours sincerely
Isaac Rosenberg

To Gordon Bottomley

Postmarked 3 Aug. 1917

My dear Mr Bottomley
    Do you think this a better opening for my 'Daughters of War'.

> Space knows the ruddy freedom of their limbs.
> Their naked dances with mans spirit naked:
> Here, by the root side of the tree of life
> (Side shut from earths profoundest eyes)
> Their shining dances beckon our dumb faces
>
> This   {Before the pierced voice has ceased in the tree tops,}
> Or   {Before the <?faded> expiring voice has ceased in the
>   boughs.}
> The old bark burnt with iron wars &c

I think it makes the poem clearer for I hate to think my idea is lost, as it must be if the expression is uncertain.

Now Mr Marsh wants to print my 'Kolue' speech in Moses for the Georgian Book, but I am certain my most epic poem, so far, is the Daughters poem, but it is too obscure, he thinks. I believe if one gets hold of the opening it should be easy enough to follow. Where do you think the poem is obscure?

I don't think I'll get my play complete for it in time; though it'll hardly take much space, it's so slight. If I could get home on leave I'd work at it and get it done no doubt, but leaves are so chancy. It's called 'The Unicorn' now, it's about a decaying race who have never seen a woman; animals take the place of women, but they yearn for continuity. The chief's Unicorn breaks away and he goes in chase. The unicorn is found by boys outside a city and brought in and breaks away again. Saul who has seen the unicorn on his way to the city for the week's victuals, gives chase in his cart. A storm comes on, the mules break down, and by the lightning he sees the unicorn race by. A naked black like an apparition rises up and easily lifts the wheels from the rut and together the[y] ride to Saul's hut. There Lilith is in great consternation having seen the unicorn and knowing the legend of this race of men. The emotions of the black (the chief) are the really difficult part of my story. Afterwards a host of blacks like centaurs on horses and buffaloes come rushing up, the unicorn in front. On every horse is clasped a woman. Lilith faints Saul stabs himself, the chief places Lilith on the Unicorn, and they all race away.

I hope you're keeping that pleasantness of condition your last letter showed.

Yours sincerely
Isaac Rosenberg

I'll send bits of the play when I get it into some shape.

To Rosenberg's father

[Aug. 1917]
Dear Father

Ray° wrote me card of the air raid, also you letter. Your miracle amused me very much and the story of the honey delighted me. I hope to be home before the new year but leaves are going very slowly in our division. So it's no used building on it. Mrs Herbert Cohen sent me a little book compiled by the Chief Rabbi of Jewish interest.° There are good bits from the Talmud and from some old writers. A very little bit by Heine, nothing by Disraeli and a lot by Mr Hertz and a few more rash people; I admire their daring, if not their judgement. Mrs Cohen has paid all the expenses and a fuller anthology is coming out shortly; I hope some restraint and caution will be used this time. I think you will find Heine's poems among my books, there is a beautiful poem called 'Princess Sabbath' among them, where the Jew who is a dog all the week, Sabbath night when the candles are lit, is transformed into a gorgeous prince to meet his bride the Sabbath.

I mention this because there is a feeble imitation of this in the anthology. If I am lucky and get home this side of the year you might keep Dave's breeches for me.

Love to all
Isaac

To Gordon Bottomley

Postmarked 19 Aug. 1917

Dear Mr Bottomley°

   Please do not trouble to answer my letters as I am sure it is difficult to write when you are not well. I cannot say how much I feel your taking to my writings, and how I hate to think of you in pain. Does not the open air relieve you, and walking? I will continue to write even if I know my letters helped to make a nice cup of tea, and was the very basis of the fire.

   I am now fearfully rushed but find energy enough to scribble this in the minute I plunder from my work. I believe I can see the obscurities in the 'Daughters', but hardly hope to clear them up in France. The first part, the picture of the Daughters dancing and calling to the spirits of the slain before their last cries have ceased among the boughs of the tree of life, I must still work on. In that part obscure the description of the voice of the daughter I have not made clear I see; I have tried to suggest the wonderful sound of her voice, spiritual and voluptuous at the same time. The end is an attempt to imagine the severance of all human relationship and the fading away of human love. Later on I will try and work on it because I think it a pity if the ideas are to be lost for want of work. My Unicorn play is stopped because of my increased toil, and I forget how much or little I told you of it. I want to do it in one Act although I think I have a subject here that could make a gigantic play. I have not the time to write out the sketch of it as far as it's gone, though I'd like to know your criticism of it very much. The most difficult part I shrink from; I think even Shakespeare might. The first time Tel, the chief of the decaying race sees a woman, (who is Lilith, Saul's wife), and he is called upon to talk. Saul and Lilith are ordinary folk into whose ordinary lives the Unicorn bursts. It is to be a play of terror—terror of hidden things and the fear of the supernatural. But I see no hope of doing the play while out here. I have a way when I write to try and put myself in the situation and I make gestures and grimaces.

   We are fearfully busy now and it has been an effort to write this letter but your letters always give me great delight, and I must let you know.

Yours sincerely
Isaac Rosenberg

To Sydney Schiff

[Between 16 and 19 Sept. 1917]

87 Dempsey St | Stepney E

Dear Mr Schiff

I am home on leave for 10 days. I called at your place but as you are away, I write this. I trust you're fit and having a good time also Mrs Schiff. I'll write a longer letter shortly.

Yours sincerely
Isaac Rosenberg

To Gordon Bottomley

Dated by GB: On leave 21 Sept. 1917

87 Dempsey St | Stepney London. E.

Dear Mr Bottomley

The greatest thing of my leave after seeing my mother was your letter which has just arrived. I am sure you are happy, now, anyway, or you could not have written that letter. I wish I could have seen you but now I must go on and hope that things will turn out well and some happy day will give me the chance of meeting you. I waited to write till this because I wanted you to see my idea of the 'Unicorn' my sister has been typing for you. I am afraid I can do no writing or reading; I feel so restless here and unanchored. We have lived in such an elemental way so long things here don't look quite right to me somehow; or it may be the consciousness of my so limited time here for freedom, so little time to do so many things—bewilders me. This 'Unicorn' as will be obvious is just a basis, its final form will be very different, I hope. But the story is sketched out. Tell me if it appears trashy; I have no feeling at all about it just now, and I am anxious to have yours—if its suggestions are clear to you, of course. My queer situation makes me send it in a state like that as you will understand. One never knows whether one gets the chance again of writing. It happens my young brother is on leave as well now, and brother in law, and all my people are pretty lively and won't let me isolate myself to write.

FIG. 14 Isaac Rosenberg in uniform, 1917.

FIG. 15 Isaac Rosenberg with his brother Elkon, September 1917.

FIG. 16 Isaac Rosenberg with his brother Elkon, September 1917. Inscribed to Gordon Bottomley.

Mr Trevelyan sent me his Comedy.° I think it very very fine for
what it is meant—I had very great pleasure from it. A little more of
that kind of thing might bring people to their senses. I am taking it
back to France with me.

I am sending a Photograph of myself happy in Blighty. I wish you
could send me one of yours. If I can find the 'Adam and Eve' picture I
told you of I'll sent that before I go back.

Yours sincerely
Isaac Rosenberg

My mother and my sister tell me to thank you for the pleasure your
letters to me give them. They thank you for your friendliness—I
thank you for something more.

To Gordon Bottomley

Dated by GB: 1.15 pm 25 Sept. 1917

87 Dempsey St Stepney E | London

Dear Mr Bottomley

I think you will be amused at these things enclosed. I send three
because each is different. The chap with me is my very young brother
and I am in civvies again. The suit and the hat is the family suit and
hat, and fits us all, though my younger brother is growing out of it
now. Your letter about my 'Unicorn' is much better than my 'unicorn'
itself. You have taken a lot of trouble to go over it and it makes me
believe in it. You have got my idea of it exactly as I have, and your
scheme of amplification I had in mind as well, but you have put down
so excellently and concise, and more coherently realised. You know
how impossible it is to work it out, placed as I am—if I had been an
officer I might have managed it, but we Tommies are too full up. I
have other copies of those poems I sent so don't trouble to return
them.

We have been to one theatre and we nearly got turned out for giving
expressing to our feelings about it; we have been to no more. I see
friends and go from one place to another and feel fearfully restless. I
cannot read. But this is a great change; one can also get properly clean
again, and begin afresh. My 'Adam and Eve' I cannot find anywhere,

but if I come across it before I go I will send it. I hope very much you're getting the very best out of your holiday

Isaac Rosenberg

   I go back Thursday

To R. C. Trevelyan

[26 Sept. 1917] not in IR's hand

Dear Mr Trevelyan

   I rec your play and Annual. Thank you very much. The play is gorgeous, one of the chiefest pleasures of my leave days; and for this I thank you indeed. The ideas are exactly what we all think out there—and the court martial of the Kaiser and kings etc might have been copied from one of ours. The fun and the seriousness is splendidly managed together and I only wish the thing had the power of its purpose—I suppose it will be in the end through such literature that we will get satisfaction in the end—just as the French Revolution was the culmination of Revolutionary literature. I have not had the chance of looking at the Annual yet but will do so before I go back.

Yours sincerely
Isaac Rosenberg

To Gordon Bottomley

28 Sept. 1917

                87 Dempsey St | Stepney E

Dear Mr Bottomley

   After missing about three days' trains I'm off again to France now. I hope you have not sent that photo you promised out to France because I hear we've shifted up to Belgium and your letter may miscarry. If you are sending, send it to my people and they will forward it. Have left instructions to send drawing.

IR

To Gordon Bottomley

Postmarked 13 Oct. 1917

> 22311 Pte I Rosenberg |
> 11th K.O.R.L. Attached 229 Field Coy R.E. |
> Ward B.6. | 51 General Hospital B.E.F. France

Dear Mr Bottomley

When I returned from my holiday I was taken sick° and sent down the line. So I can write to you more leisurely than before. When I was in England I felt too restless to write or read; but I went round and made some purchase and one, or two rather, was your Chambers of Imagery. I brought the first series back with me, and reread it. If ever there was a book that tantalised; if ever there was a pleasure that annoyed one—it's your book. Like enjoying some fascinating phenomena through glasses; suddenly the glasses are broken and you can see no more. There are far too few poems in the book. Every one is astonishing; but the book is too brief. Of course I know, your work is spread about in other books, but I had not your other books near me at the time.

The little poem 'Tangera' I once enjoyed so much, I read again with just the same pleasure. 'Sailors' is a bit difficult—the last verse is very, very fine, and the opening pictures of the poem are gorgeous. When I returned I found your letter of Sept 13th waiting for me. It is a beautiful letter and I am very glad it was not lost. I am most glad in that I have been mistaken about your pains. I was told you were in continual suffering—and it is as good to me as the war being over to hear otherwise, from yourself.

I don't know whether you sent that photo you promised—whether it will yet reach me, or has got lost, but I am looking forward to seeing it very much. If ever I get the chance I will remind you of your promise to sit for me—if I still have the skill and power to draw.

I wrote a small poem I'll enclose.° I may now be able to think about my unicorn although so many things happening puts all ideas out of one's head.

Yours sincerely
I Rosenberg

To Gordon Bottomley

Incomplete postmark for Oct. 1917.

22311 Pte I Rosenberg |
11th K.O.R.L. attd 229 Field Coy R.E. |
Lines B.6. 51 General Hospital | B.E.F. France

Dear Mr Bottomley

Though I am denying myself enormous pleasure I feel sure, I want to stop you from sending your book out to me—it will only get lost and if I knew I could buy it again afterwards, of course I should not be so troubled about it. It is a pleasure to be saved up for me and I thank you very very much for this. I believe I am a great tax on your time and invention with my correspondence; however while you do not say so, and give such wonderful exchange for my rubbish, I will go on. I was sorry at the news of your last letter indeed, and don't know what to say—so much sadness is happening in these terrible times that one is either bewildered or becomes insensible. I brought your 'Chambers of Imagery' out with me when I first came out but it vanished as well as Emerson's poems. If you really like the 'Adam and Eve' I am well satisfied with it; I have another at home called the family of Adam which you must see some time. Now your photo—I do wish I had the chance to paint you. I think I'd do a memorable work—you hardly look an invalid from the photo—I hope all that is an exploded myth. So that is Edward Thomas. I used to read his criticisms and thought them very sound and intelligent; but I know very little else of his work. I have been thinking of my Unicorn and your suggestions.°

I want to open with the tower of skulls of the decaying men. An ancient hermaphrodite is about to die and tells the secret of their birth. Tel the chief the rider of the unicorn plans the raid. I have been reading Shakespeare here, the comedies, and can see how hampered he was by a public, though no doubt that also impelled him to work out clearly a large idea. But I fancy Browning—say in Pippa Passes° had in mind certain weaknesses and giving way to the public of Shakespeare and worked out a more interesting form, though no one can touch Shakespeare for masterly handling, and illuminating grasp of character and motives.

Now I should like to write my play in prose a good deal and where it becomes vehement, poetry. As I write it, if I can think of anything,

I will get it typed; but it will hardly be fair to you if I let you see it, till it is more welded together and riper for a verdict.

I am lucky, true, to be here in this poor weather, but it may not be long before I'm out—I cannot say though.

Yours sincerely
Isaac Rosenberg

To R. C. Trevelyan

18 Oct. [1917]

22311 Pte I Rosenberg |
11th K.O.R.L. attd 229 Field Coy R.E. | Lines B.6 51 General
Hospital | B.E.F. France

Dear Mr Trevelyan

My sister sent your letter on to me here. I liked your letter and very much your little boy's verses.

'And the wind blows so violent' takes me most; I hope he will always go direct to nature like that and not get too mixed up with artifice when he has more to say about nature. I brought your play back with me but I'm afraid it's lost now. I lent it to a friend in the Batt[allion] but that day I fell sick and was sent down here to hospital. My sister is sending on Lucretius° and I have time now to read so I will write you how it strikes me. Your play was all I read at home—I read it in bed—the rest of my time I spend very restlessly—going from one place to another and seeing and talking to as many people as I could. G. Bottomley sent me nearly all the poems in the annual before so I knew them. 'Atlantis' is an immense poem—and as good as anything else he has done.

I saw friends of J[ohn].R[odker]. while on leave, and I don't know whether he's having a worse time than us; I hardly think so—Anyway, we're all waiting.

Yours sincerely
Isaac Rosenberg

To Gordon Bottomley

Postmarked 22 Oct. 1917

22311 Pt I Rosenberg |
11th K.O.R.L. attd 229 Field Coy R.E. |
Lines B.6. General Hospital B.E.F. France

Dear Mr Bottomley

I enclose a poem I've just written°—it's sad enough I know—but one can hardly write a war poem and be anything else. It happened to one of our chaps, poor fellow—and I've tried to write it. My sister wrote me you had rec[eived] our unlucky and ancient Adam and Eve; I hope it is not too badly damaged. It was suggested to me by a poem of Verharen° I read in English, where Adam and Eve rush together. I heard from Mr Trevelyan who tells me he is near you. I found a vol of F Thompson's poems here and some of his poems are as good as anything in our language. But I don't like him as I did the first time I read him—he's much too fond of stars. But the Fallen Yew, A Judgment in Heaven, The hymn to the Setting Sun°—and a few more—are equal to any poems written. I do hope for that time to come when I shall be free to read and write in my own time; there will be the worries again of earning a livelihood; painting is a very unsatisfactory business; but I can teach—though after the life I have lived in the army I don't think it would matter much to me what I did. I will write again soon.

Yours sincerely
Isaac Rosenberg

Extract from letter to Winifreda Seaton

[Between Oct. and Dec. 1917]

From hospital

I was very glad to have your letter and know there is no longer a mix-up about letters and suchlike. Always the best thing to do is to answer at once, that is the likeliest way of catching one, for we shift about so quickly; how long I will stay here I cannot say: it may be a while or just a bit. I have some Shakespeare: the Comedies and also 'Macbeth'. Now I see your argument and cannot deny my treatment of your criticisms, but have you ever asked yourself why I always am rude to your criticisms? Now, I intended to show you ——'s letters° and why I value his criticisms. I think anybody can pick holes and find unsound parts in any work of art; anyone can say Christ's creed is a slave's creed, the Mosaic is a vindictive, savage creed, and so on. It is the unique and superior, the illuminating qualities one wants to find— discover the direction of the impulse. Whatever anybody thinks of a poet he will always know himself: he knows that the most marvellously expressed idea is still nothing; and it is stupid to think that praise can do him harm. I know sometimes one cannot exactly define one's feelings nor explain reasons for liking and disliking; but there is then the right of a suspicion that the thing has not been properly understood or one is prejudiced. It is much my fault if I am not understood, I know; but I also feel a kind of injustice if my idea is not grasped and is ignored, and only petty cavilling at form, which I had known all along was so, is continually knocked into me. I feel quite sure that form is only a question of time. I am afraid I am more rude than ever, but I have exaggerated here the difference between your criticisms and——'s. Ideas of poetry can be very different too. Tennyson thought Burns' love-songs important, but the 'Cottar's S[aturday].N[ight].' poor. Wordsworth thought the opposite.°

Extract from letter to Winifreda Seaton

[Between Oct. and Dec. 1917]

Many thanks for book and chocolate. Both are being devoured with equal pleasure. I can't get quite the delight in Whitman as from one poem of his I know—'Captain, my Captain'. I admire the vigour and independence of his mind, but his diction is so diffused. Emerson and not Whitman is America's poet. You will persist in refusing to see my side of our little debate on criticism. Everybody has agreed with you about the faults, and the reason is obvious; the faults are so glaring that nobody can fail to see them. But how many have seen the beauties? And it is here more than the other that the true critic shows himself. And I absolutely disagree that it is blindness or carelessness; it is the brain succumbing to the herculean attempt to enrich the world of ideas.

To R. C. Trevelyan

[Late Oct. or early Nov. 1917]

22311 Pte I Rosenberg 11th K.O.R.L.
Att 229 Field Coy R.E. |
Lines B.6. 51 General Hospital B.E.F. France

Dear Mr Trevelyan

Your Lucretius arrived in all its beauty of type and cover. It is a noble poem and I wish it were printed in a more compressed form so that one could have it in the pocket and read it more. It does not sound like a translation the words seem so natural to the thought. Hamlet's enquiring nature so mixed with theology, superstition, penetration, may be more human and general—But Lucretius as a mood, definite, is fine, proud philosophy. I can say no more than I got deep pleasure from it and thank you very much. I'm reading some Shakespeare— Sturge Moore, G Bottomley, H. G. Wells°—Sturge Moore delights me—they are only small things I mean as number of words go,—but he is after my own heart. You know what I think of G.B. And that old hawker of immortality how glad one feels, he is not a witness of these terrible times—he would only have been flung into this terrible destruction, like the rest of us. Anyway we all hope it'll all end well.

Yours sincerely
Isaac Rosenberg

Extract from letter to Winifreda Seaton

15 Nov. 1917

From hospital

London may not be the place for poetry to keep healthy in, but Shakespeare did most of his work there, and Donne, Keats, Milton, Blake—I think nearly all our big poets. But, after all, that is a matter of personal likings or otherwise. Most of the French country I have seen has been devastated by war, torn up—even the woods look ghastly with their shell-shattered trees; our only recollections of warm and comfortable feelings are the rare times amongst human villages, which happened about twice in a year; but who can tell what one will like or do after the war? If the twentieth century is so awful, tell me what period you believe most enviable. Even Pater° points out the Renaissance was not an outburst—it was no simultaneous marked impulse of minds living in a certain period of time—but scattered and isolated.

To Joseph Leftwich

8 Dec. [1917]

22311 Pte. I. Rosenberg | 11th. K.O.R.L. |
Lines B.6. | 51, General Hospital | B.E.F. France

Dear Leftwich,

I am in hosp[ital] and have been here for about 2 months—lucky for me—I fancy—as I got out of this late stunt° by being here. My brother Dave on the Tanks got a bullet in his leg and is also in hosp—also my wilder brother in the S[outh].A[frican].H[eavy].A[rtillery]. is in hosp. And now your letter has been buffeted into hosp, and that it has reached me must be looked upon as one of the miracles of this war.

I know Isaacs,° who I like—but his poetry didn't appear to me much good—but then, when he showed it to me—I was on leave and poetry was quite out of my line then and possibly the poetry in them may have been too delicate and subtle for me to discover at the time. We never spoke about Whitman—'Drum Taps' stands unique as War Poetry in my mind.

I have written a few war poems but when I think of 'Drum Taps' mine are absurd. However I would get a pamphlet printed if I were sure of selling about 60 at 1s each—as I think mine may give some new aspects to people at home—and then one never knows whether you'll get a tap on the head or not: and if that happens—all you have written is lost, unless you have secured them by printing. Do you know when the Georgian B[ook].° will be out? I am only having about half a page in it—and it's only an extract from a poem—I don't think anybody will be much the wiser. What's the idea of my joining your J[ewish] affair,° it's no use to me out here, is it? Besides after the war, if things go well—I doubt whether I'd live in London. But you can put me down if you like.

I. Rosenberg

To Edward Marsh

Postmarked 26 Jan. 1918

My address is on the other side.
[Pte I Rosenberg 22311 | 4 Platoon A Coy |
11th K.O.R.L. | B.E.F.]

My dear Marsh

I have been in topsy turveydom since I last saw you and have not been able to write. Even now it is in the extremest difficulties that I'm writing this. I wanted to talk about the Georgian Book which I had sent over to me but have not had time to more than glance through. I liked J. C. Squire's poem° about the 'House' enormously and all his other poems. Turner's° are very beautiful and Sassoon° has power. Masefield seemed rather commonplace, but please don't take my jud[g]ment at anything because I have hardly looked at them. I am back in the trenches which are terrible now. We spend most of our time pulling each other out of the mud. I am not fit at all now and am more in the way than any use. You see I appear in excellent health and a doctor will make no distinction between health and strength. I am not strong. <What is happening to me now is more tragic than the 'passion play'. Christ never endured what I endure. It is breaking me completely.>° What has happened to your Life of Rupert Brooke. Is it out yet. I suppose you are kept very busy.

Yours sincerely
I Rosenberg

To Gordon Bottomley

Dated by GB: Field Post Office. 30 Jan. 1918

Dear Mr Bottomley

I have been in the trenches some time now and it is most awkward to get letters away—I had the Georgian Book sent me and though I had to send it back I had just time to gallop through it—and seeing yours made me very anxious to know what has been happening to you. There are some things in the G.B. that delight me as much as anything—J.C. Squire's 'House' is fine and one or two more things. Your 'Atlantis' gives the book a first class quality and it's a pity Abercrombie has nothing. My address is

Pte I Rosenberg 22311
4 Platoon A. Coy
11th K.O.R.L. B.E.F.

I'm writing this in the line and have no light or paper. There is a lot I'd like to write—[line deleted by censor] and I have Balzacean schemes suggested this time. I just write this to let you know I'm still a harassed mortal IR.

Extract from letter to Winifreda Seaton

4 Feb. 1918

We had a rough time in the trenches with the mud, but now we're out for a bit of a rest, and I will try and write longer letters. You must know by now what a rest behind the line means. I can call the evenings—that is, from tea to lights out—my own; but there is no chance whatever for seclusion or any hope of writing poetry now. Sometimes I give way and am appalled at the devastation this life seems to have made in my nature. It seems to have blunted me. I seem to be powerless to compel my will to any direction, and all I do is without energy and interest.

To Gordon Bottomley

17 Feb. 1918

Dear Mr Bottomley

I do not know when I begin a letter whether to plunge into gloomiest of Byronic misanthropy, (as indeed, my inclination pushes me to,) or be nice and placid and acquiescent about things. I know if I didn't explain myself properly I'd only appear weak and stupid, and as the situation does not give me the chance to explain myself, it must be left unexplained just yet, at least.

From your letter, your cause of complaint has been most real and that you have been able to write to me, is I hope, a true sign that it is all over. I am delighted that you are writing poetry again—it is too long since you've written. I liked 'New Year's Eve'. It perhaps had not the richness and exceptional effect of the others—but it had the qualities you aimed for—piercing and vital. I have been transferred to Pte I Rosenberg 22311 8 Platoon. B Coy. 1st Batt. K.O.R.L. B.E.F. My own Batt is broken up° and what was left of them mixed up with other Battalions. Just now we are out for a 'rest'. Poetry seems to have gone right out of me, I get no chance to even think of it. My 'Unicorn' is dead, and it will need a powerful Messiah to breathe life into its nostrils. I could more easily draw than write, but the weather is too cold for that, if I did get the time. Thank you for what you say about my 'Kolue' speech. If the war does not damage me completely I'll beat that yet.

Yours sincerely
Isaac Rosenberg.

To John Rodker

23 Feb. [1918]

Dear Rodker

I did not know you were a fixture or I'd have written direct to the Settlement.° I don't see the papers so your news is *news*. However we're expecting to go up the line soon, after some weeks rest. I'd like to read Elliott's work° but I hardly get a chance to read letters sent to me. If we get any time there is no seclusion and always interruptions. I am very glad you can read and if you write to my sister for Hueffer's book° I daresay she'll find it for you. I'll mention it in my next letter also. Address

Miss A. Rosenberg
87 Dempsey St
Stepney. E.
Mine is 22311 Pte I R
8 Platoon, B Coy. 1st K.O.R.L. B.E.F.

I suppose I could write a bit if I tried to work at a letter as an idea—but sitting down to it here after a day's dull stupefying labour—I feel stupefied. When will we go on with the things that endure?

Yours sincerely
Isaac Rosenberg

To Gordon Bottomley

24 Feb. 1918

Dear Mr Bottomley

I am still on rest; it may be only for a while. When I get up the line again it is goodbye to letter writing for a dreary time; unless one writes from hospital soon. I know a letter that is not expressive is hardly worth sending, but yet from the seat of war any kind of letter means a lot—if it only implies security.

I wanted to send some bits I wrote for the 'Unicorn' while I was in hospital and if I find them I'll enclose them. I tried to work on your suggestion and divided it into 4 acts, but since I left the hosp. all poetry has gone quite out of me. I seem even to forget words and I believe if I met anybody with ideas I'd be dumb. No drug could be more stupefying than our work—(to me anyway) and this goes on like that old torture of water trickling drop by drop unendlingly on one's helplessness.

 Pte I Rosenberg 22311.
 8 Platoon. B. Coy. 1st Batt. K.O.R.L. B.E.F. France.

I find I can't copy these bits from 'The Unicorn' so am sending one or two poor things,° but I aimed for something in them.

To John Rodker

[Early March 1918]
Dear Rodker

 I could not answer your last letter as immediately as I wished because of a lot of unexpected things. Things happen so suddenly here that really nothing is unexpected—but what I mean is quite a lot of changes came on top of each other and interfered with my good epistolary intentions. I hope you still keep the same good spirits of your last letter and that the work is not beyond your strength. My work is but somehow we blunder through. From hospital I went back to the line and we had a rough time with the mud. Balzac could give you the huge and terrible sensations of sinking in the mud. I was in the trenches a month when our Batt broke up and I am now in another Batt of our regiment. When you write again write to

 Pte I Rosenberg 22311
 8 Platoon. B. Coy
 1st Batt K.O.R.L.
 B.E.F.

Just now we're out for a rest and I hope the warmer weather sets in when we go up the line again. It is quite impossible to write or think of writing stuff now, so I can only hope for hospital or the end of the war if I want to write. In hospital I saw the Georgian Book. Turner is pretty good—but somehow I seem to have lost all sense of discrimination and everything seems good. My own is so fragmentary that I think it were better left out. I hear it is selling well. You have got an article on Trevelyan, I hear. He sent me his Comedy which I liked very much. I know little of his other work.

Yours sincerely
Isaac Rosenberg

To Gordon Bottomley

7 March 1918

Dear Mr Bottomley

I believe our interlude is nearly over and we may go up the line any moment now—so I answer your letter straightaway. If only this war were over our eyes would not be on death so much—it seems to underlie even our underthoughts. Yet when I have been as near to it as anybody could be, the idea has never crossed my mind—certainly not so much as when some lying doctor told me I had consumption. I like to think of myself as a poet, so what you say, though I know it to be extravagant, gives me immense pleasure.

Your six horse metaphor is a very kind and gratifying criticism and you may be sure I will keep it in mind. In the page for 'The Unicorn' they were only disconnected bits I'd selected from some poorer stuff so I am sorry for puzzling you.

I am trying to get transferred to the 'Judaens'.° I think they are now in Mesopotamia. Jacob Epstein whom I know is with the Judaens, and several other friends of mine. They also run a magazine. If I ever do get the chance to run up to Warrington, and it is not at all unlikely for the situation you've imaged out to happen very shortly, I'd jump at the chance. I don't think I've a chance of leave for a long long time, or I might go then. We hear a lot of this coming 'earthquake'° along the line; but whatever happens if I can, I will always write you, and keep you informed of my existence.

Yours sincerely
Isaac Rosenberg

8 Platoon B Coy 1st K.O.R.L. B.E.F. France.

Do you see Mr Trevelyan. I think I told you I'd read his Farce on the War and how deeply true it was. He has his [*sic*] the sentiments of most of us out here.

Above all I am most glad to in [*sic*] your note of hope and confidence—one of my great peacetime pleasures must be to read a new play of yours.

To Rosenberg's mother

[Early spring 1918]

Dear Mother
    Rec Parcel—everything in it champion—but really there is no need to send butter, eggs or Borsht, just now, at any rate. I suppose we get our food much easier than you—and in this village we get any amount of extra. I have not heard from Samuels so don't know whether he is Colonel of the Batt. I applied for a transfer about a month ago but I fancy it fell through. I shall apply again. Neither Mrs. Cohen or Löwy have written to me though I have written. You can let them have my new address if you care to. Did you come across any notices of my thing in the Georgian book? I don't know who the Sergeant was Annie saw—several are on leave now—they mostly live in the North of England though. I hope our Russian cousins are happy now. Trotsky, I imagine will look after the interests of his co-religionists°—Russia is like an amputated limb to our cause and America is the cork substitute:° I doubt whether she is more. 8 Platoon B Coy 1st Bat. K.O.R.L. B.E.F. I hope you manage to get things all right and comfortably. We hear such rotten tales about home. Love to all Isaac

Extract from letter to Winifreda Seaton

8 March 1918

    I do not feel that I have much to say, but I do know that unless I write now it will be a long time before you hear from me again, without something exceptional happens. It is not very cold now, but I dread the wet weather, which is keeping off while we are out, and, I fear, saving itself up for us. We will become like mummies—look warm and lifelike, but a touch and we crumble to pieces. Did I send you a little poem, 'The Burning of the Temple'? I thought it was poor, or rather, difficult in expression, but G. Bottomley thinks it fine. Was it clear to you? If I am lucky, and come off undamaged, I mean to put all my innermost experiences into the 'Unicorn'. I want it to symbol- ize the war and all the devastating forces let loose by an ambitious and unscrupulous will. Last summer I wrote pieces for it and had the whole of it planned out, but since then I've had no chance of working on it and it may have gone quite out of my mind.

To David Rosenberg

[March 1918]
Dear Dave

We've been very busy lately and I've not been able to answer your letters. I'm now back in reserves and know that even this poor scrawl will be better than nothing and you will understand it as but the vanguard of a host. I wanted to write a battle song for the Judaens but so far I can think of nothing noble and weighty enough. I wrote a slight poem which I will send in next letter.

My address now is
Pte I R 22311
6 Platoon B Coy
1st K.O.R.L. B.E.F.

I do hope you get your leave for Pasach° and the Stepney business will be over by then.

Best love
Isaac

To David Rosenberg

[March 1918]
Dear Dave

I had a letter from you yesterday but lost it before I could properly read it. So can't reply to the actual wording. Have you my new address

Pte I R 22311
8 Platoon B. Coy. 1st K.O.R.L. B.E.F.
I had the Georgian book sent out to me but was obliged to return it
when I went up the line—it was so bulky. I could have sent it on to
you but I never thought of it. Perhaps you may find one of your lot has
it. There is some good stuff in it but very little. Gordon Bottomley
stands head and shoulders above the rest.
I'm not saying this because he wrote me there were few pages in the
book as beautiful as mine. His 'Atlantis' in this Georgian Book is one
of the most beautiful of modern poems. There is a rotten poem by
Herbert Asquith° and some paltry stuff by very good poets. Masefield
is far from his best. 18 writers are included altogether. J.A. is having a
lark I see.

Best love
Isaac

To Edward Marsh

Postmarked 7 March 1918

My dear Marsh
I see my sister has been on the warpath again, and after your scalp in
her sisterly regard for me. They know my lackadaisical ways at home
and have their own methods of forcing me to act. I have now put in for
a transfer to the Jewish Batt—which I think is in Mesopotamia now.
I think I should be climatized to the heat after my S. African experi-
ence. I'll let you know if I get it. I am now in
8 Platoon B Coy
1st. K.O.R.L. B.E.F.
as our old Batt broke up.
I saw the G[eorgian].B[ook]. It does not match the first G.B. nor
indeed any of the others in my mind. But I put that down to the War
of course. Turner is very poetic. Masefield sentimentalises in too
Elizabethan a fashion. There is a vivid poem about Christ in the
Tower° I remember I liked very much. And of course G.B.'s 'Atlantis'
stands out. I saw the book about 3 months ago and not for long. I was

going into the trenches then. What have you done with your 'Life of R[upert].B[rooke].' Is it complete yet.

    I'm sending this letter to Ministry. Mun[itions]. because I sent a letter a month or so ago to Raymond Buildings and got no answer. If you are very busy do try and drop just a line so that I know you've rec my letter.

Yours sincerely

I Rosenberg

To Edward Marsh

28 March [1918] Postmarked 2 April 1918

My dear Marsh

    I think I wrote you I was about to go up the line again after our little rest. We are now in the trenches again and though I feel very sleepy, I just have a chance to answer your letter so I will while I may. It's really my being lucky enough to bag an inch of candle that incites me to this pitch of punctual epistolary. I must measure my letter by the light.

    First, this is my address

      22311 Pte I R.

      6 Platoon B Coy 1st K.O.R.L. B.E.F.

    We are very busy just now and poetry is right out of our scheme. I wrote one or two things in hospital about Xmas time but I don't remember whether I sent them to you or not. I'll send one, anyhow.

    During out little interlude of rest from the line I managed to do a bit of sketching—somebody had colours—and they weren't so bad, I don't think I have forgotten my art after all. I've heard nothing further about the J[ewish].B[attalion]. and of course feel annoyed—more because no reasons have been given me—but when we leave the trenches, I'll enquire further. I don't remember reading Freeman.° I wanted to write a battle song for the Judaens but can think of nothing strong and wonderful enough yet. Here's just a slight thing.

['Through these pale cold days']

    I've seen no poetry for ages now so you mustn't be too critical—My vocabulary small enough before is impoverished and bare

Yours sincerely

I Rosenberg

COMMENTARY

ABBREVIATIONS

1922	*Poems by Isaac Rosenberg.* Selected and edited by Gordon Bottomley, with an introductory memoir by Laurence Binyon. London, 1922
1937	*The Collected Works of Isaac Rosenberg: Poetry, Prose, Letters and Some Drawings.* Edited by Gordon Bottomley and Denys Harding. With a Foreword by Siegfried Sassoon. London, 1937
1949	*The Collected Poems of Isaac Rosenberg.* Edited by Gordon Bottomley and Denys Harding. With a Foreword by Siegfried Sassoon. London, 1949
1979	*The Collected Works of Isaac Rosenberg: Poetry, Prose, Letters, Paintings and Drawings.* With a Foreword by Siegfried Sassoon. Edited with an Introduction and Notes by Ian Parsons. London, 1979
2004	*The Poems and Plays of Isaac Rosenberg.* Edited by Vivien Noakes. Oxford, 2004
2007	*Isaac Rosenberg: Poetry Out of My Head and Heart. Unpublished Letters.* Edited by Jean Liddiard. London, 2007
A&L	*Art and Letters*
AR	Annie Rosenberg (later Annie Wynick)
BEF	British Expeditionary Force
BL	British Library
BL	Manuscripts and typescripts discovered in the British Library in 1995
IR	Isaac Rosenberg
DH	Denys Harding
GB	Gordon Bottomley
IWM	Imperial War Museum
JC	Joseph Cohen, *Journey to the Trenches: The Life of Isaac Rosenberg, 1890–1918.* London, 1975
JL	Jean Liddiard, *Isaac Rosenberg: The Half Used Life.* London, 1975
JMW	Jean Moorcroft Wilson, *Isaac Rosenberg: The Making of a Great War Poet. A New Life.* London, 2008
KORL	King's Own Royal Lancasters
Moses	*Moses: A Play* by Isaac Rosenberg. London, 1916
MS	Manuscript
N&D	*Night and Day* [London, 1912]
SAWC	*South African Women in Council: A Journal Of Interest For The Cultured Woman.* Cape Town, South Africa
TS	Typescript
Youth	*Youth* by Isaac Rosenberg. London, 1915

POEMS AND PLAYS

Notes have been kept to a minimum. Dates of composition, where known, and of publication are always given.

Rosenberg reworked much of his writing extensively. In order to keep these notes as uncluttered as possible, only the most important variants have been given; a full listing of these is to be found in *2004*. A collection of manuscripts discovered in the British Library in 1995 was withheld from the editor at the time of the preparation of *2004*. As a result of these, two poems—'The Jew' and 'In War'—have been redated and therefore moved from their positions in the earlier volume, and the first line of 'The Burning of the Temple' has been slightly, but significantly, altered. *BL* also contain a number of variants to some of the poems written by Rosenberg in France. The most important of these are given here.

Rosenberg was in the habit of reusing lines and phrases in different poems and in his plays. Since this is an important aspect of his way of working, cross-references to other poems and plays have been given; extensive cross-references to holograph drafts not published here can be found in *2004*.

I have given the dates of first publication. Where a poem was published more than once in IR's lifetime, or where it was published in a journal before the first collected edition of his poems in 1922, I have given these details also.

POEMS

1 *Ode to David's Harp*. Date of composition unknown, but the poem was written out on 26 Sept. 1905. Published *1937*.

JC says that after reading this poem in an earlier version, IR's sister Minnie wrote to the Librarian of the Whitechapel Library, Morley Dainow, asking if he could help Isaac. He responded by suggesting IR come to see him. Before the meeting IR sent him a copy of 'Ode to David's Harp', and other poems. Dainow was encouraging, but writing to IR in Sept. 1905, he cautioned him: 'I should not advise you to write so much. Only write when you feel inspired & then arises such poems as the "Harp of David" and the "Charge of the Light Brigade".' They met shortly afterwards, and the following month he wrote to IR's father, speaking of the pleasure he had had in meeting his son, but adding, 'I trust that you will use your influence over him, (which I think is profound) to emancipate him from the bonds of tyrannical orthodoxy.'

Writing to Laurence Binyon on 18 Dec. 1920, Dainow recalled: 'One day I was approached by a Jewish young lady who asked me whether I could help her young brother whose aim in life was to be a poet. The next day a fragile Jewish boy was brought to me by this lady. This boy was Isaac Rosenberg. | I took young Rosenberg for walks, and discovered him to be perfectly convinced that his vocation in life was that of a Poet and a Painter. He was then, I believe, between the ages of 10 and 12 years. I enjoyed being with the boy and was much impressed both by his confidence and his sensitivity. In return for my interest and time he sent me the "David's Harp".'

See Byron's 'Hebrew melodies', 'The Harp the Monarch Minstrel Swept'.

Title and content of poem. 'But the spirit of the Lord departed from Saul, and an evil spirit from the Lord troubled him. And Saul's servants said unto him, Behold now, an evil spirit from God troubleth thee. Let our lord now command thy servants, which are before thee, to seek out a man, who is a cunning player on an harp: and it shall come to pass, when the evil spirit from God is upon thee, that he shall play with his hand, and thou shalt be well. And Saul said unto his servants, Provide me now a man that can play well, and bring him to me. Then answered one of the servants, and said, Behold, I have seen a son of Jesse the Bethlehemite, that is cunning in playing, and a mighty valiant man, and a man of war, and prudent in matters, and a comely person, and the Lord is with him. Wherefore Saul sent messengers unto Jesse, and said, Send me David thy son, which is with the sheep [. . .] And it came to pass, when the evil spirit from God was upon Saul, that David took an harp, and played with his hand: so Saul was refreshed, and was well, and the evil spirit departed from him' (1 Samuel 16: 14–19, 23). 'And David and all the house of Israel played before the Lord on all manner of instruments made of fir wood, even on harps, and on psalteries, and on timbrels, and on cornets, and on cymbals' (2 Samuel 6: 5).

2 [*In art's lone paths I wander deep*]. Composed 1906. Published *JC* p. 201.

The poem was unknown until 1959 when it was found among the papers of Frank L. Emanuel (1866–1948). Emanuel, to whom IR had been introduced by J. H. Amschewitz (see note to the poem 'To J. H. Amschewitz'), was IR's guardian for the Jewish Board of Guardians during his apprenticeship with Hentschel. He invited IR to join 'The Limners', a group of artists and art teachers who met in his studio 'for criticism and chat', and to receive encouragement and support. He bought from IR his drawing of a barrister (Plate 3), but writing to Binyon in April 1921, he deplored the influence of the Slade on IR (see note to p. 247). His painting *Kensington Interior* (1912) is in the Tate.

3 *Zion.* Composed 1906 or 1907. The TS is inscribed by IR: '16 years old when I wrote this'. Published *1922*.

Title. The Jebusite city of Jerusalem, or City of David, was captured by David in about 1000 BC and became his capital. The name is used figuratively to denote the chosen People of God, the Israelites.

l. 19. Josiah had brought the people of Judah back to an observation of the Mosaic Covenant, but after his death Jehoiakim ruled as an irresponsible despot. Under his son, Jehoiachin, the city fell to the Babylonians, leading to its destruction by Nebuchadnezzar, king of Babylon, in 586 BC and the captivity and exile of the peoples of Judah.

Song of Immortality. Date of composition unknown. Published as ll. 230–49 of 'Night and Day' in *N&D*. In an undated letter [spring 1915] to Edward Marsh (see p. 267), IR described 'Song of Immortality' as 'absolutely Abercrombie's idea in the Hymn to Love, and it's one of my first poems'. IR met Edward (later Sir Edward) Marsh (1872–1953), on 10 Nov. 1913 at the Café Royal, where IR was a guest of Mark Gertler. He was an influential patron of the arts. He edited five volumes of *Georgian Poetry* between 1912 and 1922. Marsh was a career civil servant and Private Secretary to Winston Churchill during much of the First World War. A descendant of the murdered British Prime Minister Spencer Perceval (1828–90), he used his inherited share of the compensation money paid to Perceval's family to support the arts.
l. 12. *banks of Eterne* banks of eternity.

4 *Dawn Behind Night*. Composed 1909. Published *1937*.
l. 6. See 'In War' ll. 11–13.
l. 8. See '[Wan, fragile faces of joy!]' l. 5, 'Dead Man's Dump' l. 64.
l. 10. See 'The Cage' l. 3, 'Raphael' ll. 91–2.

5 *A Ballad of Whitechapel*. Date of composition unknown. Published *1922*.
Title. Whitechapel, in London's East End docklands, was for two centuries a point of arrival for immigrant families escaping persecution, and was notorious for its poverty. IR lived there with his family between 1907 and 1912.
l. 10. See '[In the heart of the forest]' l. 16.
l. 31 *unsmirched*: not in *OED*. Smirched: marked, soiled, made dirty.
l. 35. See Matthew 2: 11: 'and when they had opened their treasures, they presented unto him gifts; gold, and frankincense, and myrrh'; and 'A Ballad of Time, Life and Memory' l. 10.
ll. 37–44. See letter to Ruth Löwy [March 1912] on p. 238.
ll. 46–7. See 'As a Besieged City' l. 7.

7 *Death*. Date of composition unknown. Published *1937*.
For IR's thoughts on death, see the undated letter [Jan. or Feb. 1911] to Winifreda Seaton, on p. 228. JL suggests that IR met Miss Seaton, a middle-aged school-mistress, in his early 'teens. Both *JC* (p. 20) and *1979* say that they were introduced by J. H. Amschewitz.
ll. 1, 9. See 'Dead Man's Dump' ll. 14.
l. 5. See 'Dead Man's Dump' l. 31, 'August 1914' ll. 6–7.
l. 10. See '[Sacred, voluptuous hollows deep]' l. 21.

l. 11 *Lethe's wine*: the waters of oblivion, from the name of one of the
rivers of Hades where the souls of the dead must drink in order to
forget all that is past.

8 *A Ballad of Time, Life and Memory*. Composed before 2 Jan. 1911.
Published *1937*.
Joseph Leftwich (see note to 'Lines Written in an Album: To J.L.')
later recalled: 'The very next night [Mon. 2 Jan. 1911] Winsten and I
were promenading along our usual route (Rodker was attending a class),
when we met Rosenberg, whom I have not previously known. [...] At
once Rosenberg was speaking to us of poetry, and soon he stopped under
a lamp-post and pulled out a bundle of scraps of paper and read to us
some of his work. "In the Workshop" [...] was one of the poems he
then read to us, and another [...] was "Life, Time and Memory" ' (*The
Jewish Chronicle*, Supplement no. 167, Feb. 1936, p. i, Joseph Leftwich,
'Isaac Rosenberg').
l. 10. See 'A Ballad of Whitechapel' l. 35.
ll. 19–25. See Keats 'Ode on a Grecian Urn'.
l. 40. See 'The Amulet' l. 15, 'The Unicorn' l. 150.

9 *In the Workshop*. Composed before 2 Jan. 1911: see note to 'A Ballad of
Time Life and Memory'. Published *A Piece of Mosaic* (May 1912),
N&D as 152–7 of 'Night and Day'.
Originally an independent poem, it was later incorporated into 'Night
and Day'. Bernard Winehouse (*Notes and Queries*, vol. 23, no. 1, Jan.
1976, pp. 16–17) notes that the poem was in a booklet (*A Piece of Mosaic*)
prepared for a Palestine Bazaar held in London on 13 May 1912, below
the reproduction of a painting by IR entitled *The Wharf* 'in which three
brutalized faces appear against a background of cranes and warehouses'.
A copy has recently been discovered in the Hartley Library, University
of Southampton.

To J. H. Amschewitz. Composed Jan. 1911. Published *N&D*.
IR met the painter John H. Amschewitz (1882–1942) through his
mother from whom Amschewitz's mother bought embroidery. He was
eight years older than IR. Writing in 1937, Amschewitz recalled: 'He
could not have been more than about ten when his mother brought him
to me with his work. [...] At that time I was a struggling student
myself. I advised him as best I could and awkwardly purchased a
drawing with poem attached, for half a crown whereat he burst into
tears and rushed from my presence. [...] | It was in my studio that he
met most of the friends that figure in this book [*1937*] and who
influenced his life—the late Dr Eder, Miss Seaton [see note to
'Death'], whose literary knowledge and kindly criticism helped and
encouraged him, and Michael Sherbrooke [see note to 'To Michael
Sherbrooke on hearing his recitation of the "Raven". Poe'], the well-
known actor who gave recitals of his poetry and did his utmost to further

Rosenberg's interests. [. . .] One day he came into my studio. I could see
he was labouring under some mental excitement, and said: "Mr
Amschewitz, I have got a poem here,"—feeling in his pockets the
while—"I think it is a good idea"—(the search in his pockets getting
more frantic) and then disappointedly, "I must have forgotten it some-
where"—and then he collapsed, shaking with laughter—"Great Snakes!
but I have forgotten to write it!" ' (*The Zionist Record*, South Africa, 23
July 1937, p. 15). In a letter of 17 June [1912] Amschewitz had written
to a Mr Spielmann, enclosing a copy of *N&D* and saying: 'He seems to
have a soul far above the ordinary both as an artist & poet, and it
is wonderful when one remembers that his education has been that
of an east-end board school & incomplete at that—& that these poems
were written under the most grinding poverty—under which he still
lives.'

IR discusses Amschewitz's work in 'Romance at the Baillie Galleries:
'The Works of J. H. Amschewitz and the late H. Ospovat' on pp. 209–10.
A portrait of IR by Amschewitz was exhibited in the Baillie Galleries in
1912, in the 1936 London Portrait Society Exhibition (no. 46), and in the
1959 Leeds University exhibition 'Isaac Rosenberg, 1890–1918' (*Leeds*
p. 36). It hung for a while in Jews' College, London, and is now believed
to be owned by the Amschewitz family.

ll. 12–14. See Keats, 'When I have fears that I may cease to be' ll. 12–13:
[. . .] then on the shore | Of the wide world I stand alone.

10 [*In the heart of the forest*] Composed before 4 Feb. 1911. Published *1937*.
An illuminated fair copy dated 1911 was presented to J. H. Amschewitz.

JC (p. 38) notes that on Saturday, 4 Feb. 1911 IR called on Joseph
Leftwich, 'bringing with him an album belonging to Amschewitz's
sister. He was returning it to her, having added at her request a drawing
and a poem entitled "In the Heart of the Forest" '. Leftwich later
recalled: 'Once Rosenberg showed us an album belonging to Amsche-
witz's sister which he was taking back to her after adding to it a drawing
and a poem. He had left in the centre of the drawing a space shaped like a
tombstone into which he had written his poem. I remember nothing of it
now except that we separately found it reminiscent of "Hiawatha", and
that Rosenberg protested that he had not read "Hiawatha" ' (*The Jewish
Chronicle*, Supplement no. 167, Feb. 1936, p. i, Joseph Leftwich, 'Isaac
Rosenberg.').

l. 11. See '[Wistfully in pallid splendour]' l. 1.
l. 16. See 'A Ballad of Whitechapel' l. 10.

12 [*My days are but the tombs of buried hours*] Date of composition unknown.
Published (under the title 'My Days') *1922*.
l. 5. See Shakespeare, *King John*, III. i. 324: that bald sexton, Time.

[*The world rumbles by me—can I heed?*] Date of composition unknown.
Published *1937*.

l. 3. See Yeats, 'The Lover tells of the Rose in his Heart' ll. 4, 8: [...]
your image that blossoms a rose in the deeps of my heart.

l. 13. See 'Heart's First Word [I]' l. 10, 'Bacchanal' ll. 11–12, '[If you are
fire and I am fire]' l. 1.

l. 14. See '[So innocent you spread your net]' l. 5.

13 *Lines Written in an Album: To J.L.* Date of composition unknown.
Published *1937*.

J.L. is Joseph Leftwich (1892–1984), one of 'The Whitechapel Boys'
(see Chronological Summary of Isaac Rosenberg's Life, 1911). Leftwich
was a poet whose work included *Along the Years. Poems: 1911–1937*
(1937). In the Foreword to this (pp. xi–xii) he says: 'I began to write
verse in 1911, under the influence of my friend Isaac Rosenberg. Not
that he told me to write, or bothered much about what I wrote. He was
too self-absorbed to do that. [...] My other friend of that period, John
Rodker, had also been writing before we met Rosenberg in 1911, when
he became the fourth member of our group. Rosenberg had been writing
poetry for years, and we three immediately recognised his extraordinary
ability, and [...] Rodker, Winsten and I immediately recorded our
conviction that "Rosenberg is a genius".' Leftwich's poem to IR entitled
'Killed in Action' was first published in the magazine *Colour* in Oct.
1919, where it was wrongly attributed to IR, and was subsequently
reprinted by GB in *1922*. A diary that Leftwich kept in 1911 is a valuable
source of biographical material on IR.

l. 14. See 'Midsummer Frost' l. 27.

14 *To Mr & Mrs Löwy, on their Silver Wedding.* Composed 1911. Published
1937.

Mrs Henrietta Löwy introduced IR to Mrs Herbert Cohen who
supported his studies at the Slade.

Summer in Winter: Six Thoughts. Composed ?1911. Published *1937*.

l. 25. Ruth is Mrs Löwy's daughter; see note to p. 23, 'The Garden of Joy'.

16 *Fleet Street.* Date of composition unknown. Published *1937*.

Early in Jan. 1905, IR began work as an apprentice with Carl
Hentschel, Engravers, of Fleet Street, London E.4.

Twilight [I]. Date of composition unknown. Published *1937*.

ll. 3–4. See 'Far Away' ll. 1–2.

ll. 6–8. See 'The Mirror' ll. 3–4.

17 *Birthday Song.* Date of composition unknown. Published *1937*.

ll. 11–12 'The Dead Past' l. 8.

[*Lady, you are my God*]. Composed 1911 or 1912. Published *N&D*.

JC (p. 82) says that the poem was written by IR for the painter David
Bomberg (see note to p. 221), for Bomberg to give as a present to Sonia
Cohen whom they had met in the Whitechapel Library where she would go

after working in a nearby sweat-shop. IR did an oil painting of her. She later married John Rodker (see note to p. 298).

18 *Spiritual Isolation: Fragment.* Date of composition unknown. Published (1–28 only) *N&D*; complete *2004.* See 'Rudolph', p. 195.
l. 9 *withouten*: without *OED* arch.
l. 35. See 'Aspiration' l. 2, 'At Night' l. 17, 'The Burning of the Temple' l. 14.

19 [*God looked clear at me through her eyes*]. Date of composition unknown. Published *1937.*
l. 5. See 'Night and Day' ll. 174–5, 244.

20 *The Dead Past.* Date of composition unknown. Published *1937.*
l. 8. See 'Birthday Song' ll. 11–12.
[*O! in a world of men and women*]. Date of composition unknown. Published *N&D.*

21 *Love To Be.* Date of composition unknown. The second stanza was incorporated into the poem, 'Night and Day' (ll. 274–89), published in *N&D*; complete *1937.*
Title. See 'Night and Day' ll. 289–90.
l. 15. See 'Heart's First Word [I]' ll. 21–2.

22 *The Nun.* Date of composition unknown. Published *1922.*
l. 10. See Keats 'Ode on a Grecian Urn' l. 49: Beauty is truth, truth beauty.
Heart's First Word [I]. Date of composition unknown. Published (as 'Heart's First Word') *N&D*; *Colour*, vol. 2, no. 5, June 1915, p. 164.
l. 10. See 'Bacchanal' l. 12, '[If you are fire and I am fire]' l. 1, '[The world rumbles by me—can I heed?]' l. 13.
ll. 17–18. See '[Like some fair subtle poison is the cold white beauty you shed]' ll. 8–9.
ll. 21–2. See 'Love to Be' l. 15.

23 [*So innocent you spread your net*]. Date of composition unknown, but the poem was written out on 9 April 1912. Published *1937.*
ll. 1–2, 5. See Blake 'Song' [How sweet I roam'd from field to field] l. 11: He caught me in his silken net.
l. 5. See '[The world rumbles by me—can I heed?]' l. 14.
The Garden of Joy. Composed ?summer 1912. Published (15–28 only) *JL*, p. 79; complete *2004.*
    The poem was written for Ruth Löwy, the daughter of Mrs Henrietta Löwy. She was a student at the Slade with IR, and later married the publisher Victor Gollancz (1893–1967). *Joy* was the title of one of IR's paintings, for which Ruth Löwy modelled. In a fragment torn from an undated letter to her [July or Aug. 1912] (p. 241) IR wrote: 'I hope you have a good time when you are away—live in the garden of Joy so that

when you get back you will know what sort of expression to wear when I put you in my "garden of Joy".'

24 *In the Woods.* Date of composition unknown. Published (as ll. 186–200 of 'Night and Day') *N&D*, (as 'In the Park') *Youth, Moses.*

25 *In Kensington Gardens.* Date of composition unknown. Published (as ll. 174–85 of 'Night and Day') *N&D.*
    IR took Ruth Löwy for drawing lessons in Kensington Gardens, a place he also used as a subject for his own landscape painting.

Knowledge. Date of composition unknown. Published *1937.*
l. 5. See 'Returning, we hear the larks' ll. 15–16.

26 [*A woman's beauty is a strong tree's roots*]. Date of composition unknown. Published (as a fragment) *1937.*

In November. Date of composition unknown. Published *N&D.*

27 [*When I went forth as is my daily wont*]. Date of composition unknown, Published *N&D.*
l. 5 *chaunt:* chant
l. 8. See 'Night and Day' l. 127, 'Midsummer Frost ll. 13–29. *undulant* undulating.

The Key of the Gates of Heaven. Date of composition unknown. Published *1937.*

28 *The Cage.* Date of composition unknown. Published *1937.*
ll. 1, 12. See 'The Poet [1]' l. 13, '[A bird trilling its gay heart out]' ll. 1–4.
l. 3. See 'Dawn behind night' l. 10, 'Raphael' ll. 91–2.

Bacchanal. Date of composition unknown. Published *1937.*
l. 12. See 'Heart's First Word [I]' l. 10, '[If you are fire and I am fire]' l. 1, '[The world rumbles by me—can I heed?]' l. 13.

29 [*Now the spirit's song has withered*]. Date of composition unknown. Published *1937.*

30 [*O heart, home of high purposes*]. Date of composition unknown. Published *1937.*

To J. Kramer. Composed at the Slade between Oct. 1911 and March 1913. Published (as a fragment) *1937.*
    Jacob Kramer (1892–1962) was a fellow-student at the Slade. *JC* (p. 97) notes that with Morris Goldstein 'they often drew side by side. Not infrequently Rosenberg would pass them fragments of paper on which he had scrawled some verses'. On one occasion, when IR was being consistently bullied by another student, a Chilean called Alvaro Guevara, Kramer decided to step in and beat up Guevara, bringing a prompt end to the bullying. Goldstein had been a school-friend of IR, and studied with him at the Bolt Court Art School.

31 *Don Juan's Song.* Date of composition unknown. Published (ll. 1–7, 15–21 only) *1922*, (complete) *1937*.

You and I. Date of composition unknown. Published *1937*.
l. 8. See 'Raphael' l. 101.
l. 10. See 'If you are fire and I am fire' l. 1.

32 *As We Look.* Date of composition unknown. Published *1937*.

33 *Psyche's Lament.* Date of composition unknown. Published *1937*.

34 [*Like some fair subtle poison is the cold white beauty you shed*]. Date of composition unknown. Published *1937*.
ll. 8–9. See 'Heart's First Word [I]' ll. 17–18.

35 *Tess.* Date of composition unknown. Published *N&D*.
Thomas Hardy's *Tess of the D'Urbervilles: A Pure Woman* was published in 1891. Thomas Hardy (1840–1928), English novelist and poet. In 'On a Door Knocker' (see p. 191) IR wrote: In this age of romance we are bent so profoundly on romancing ourselves that we have little time to notice the romances of others. We read novels, true; but they are Hardy, Zola, Turgenif; dreadfully realistic, so as to get more zest from the romance of life, by contrast with this ugly realism.'

Aspiration. Date of composition unknown. Published *N&D*, *Youth*.
l. 1. See *Moses* ll. 31–2, 'Art' (p. 218). 'Art is now, as it were a volcano. [...] The roots of a dead universe are torn up by hands, feverish and consuming with an exuberant vitality—and amid dynamic threatenings we watch the hastening of the corroding doom.'
l. 6. See 'The Mirror' ll. 7–8.
l. 16 *enaureole* not in *OED*; an aureole is a halo of radiating light, hence to surround with a halo.

36 *Raphael.* Date of composition unknown. Published *1937*.
Raphael (1483–1520) was the High Renaissance painter whose classicism was revered by the European academic tradition. In 1508 he was summoned to Rome by Pope Julius II and spent the rest of his life there. It was in defiance of this tradition that the Pre-Raphaelite Brotherhood took its first stand in 1848. In his notes for a proposed article on 'The Pre-Raphaelite Exhibition' of winter 1911–12 (see p. 207), IR recalled the foundation of the Brotherhood, where one of those gathered spoke 'of the correct soulnessness of Raphael—"O, if he hadn't lived" then art had continued uninterrupted—of the crying need of a return to the men before Raphael'. IR's own sympathy was more with the PRB than with the Italian High Renaissance. See note to p. 206.
Annetta Raphael was a young immigrant who lived in Whitechapel, and a close friend of IR. She was a dressmaker by day, a part-time violin and piano teacher, who studied painting in the evenings. *JC* (pp. 47–8) speculates that Annetta, 'a few years older than Rosenberg, lonely, sensitive, and a little awkward, must be considered as the most likely

person to have initiated Rosenberg into sexual experience', and says that
when IR was killed Annetta suffered a nervous breakdown.

See Browning 'Andrea del Sarto'.

l. 33 *Limned*: painted.

l. 43 *Mighty Angelo*: Michelangelo (1475–1564), the Italian Renaissance
painter, sculptor, and poet.

l. 46 *Jove's Thunders*: Jove, or Jupiter, was the Roman god of thunder.

l. 71 *elatement*: elation. *mayhap* perhaps.

ll. 91–2. See 'Dawn Behind Night' l. 10, 'The Cage' l. 3.

l. 96 *effable*: that can be expressed or described in words.

l. 101. See 'You and I' l. 8.

39 *To Michael Sherbrooke on Hearing his Recitation of the 'Raven'. Poe.*
Composed ?March 1912. Published *Etudes Anglaises*, vol. 30, 1977,
pp. 74–5.

Edgar Allan Poe's melancholy poem 'The Raven' was published in
1845. IR met Sherbrooke (1874–1957) in Amschewitz's studio, early in
1912. He wrote about this meeting to Ruth Löwy in an undated letter
[March 1912] (p. 239), and about the reason for his quarrel with him in
an undated letter to Mrs Cohen [Dec. 1912] (p. 249). Sherbrooke, who
was of Polish descent, was the son of an East End Rabbi, originally called
Czerzik.

J. H. Amschewitz spoke of Sherbrooke giving recitals of IR's poetry
(South African lecture, reported in the *Zionist Record*, 27 Nov. 1936,
quoted *JL* p. 60). For more about the of portrait of Michael Sherbrooke
by Amschewitz, see IR's review 'Romance at the Baillie Galleries: The
Works of J. H. Amschewitz and the late H. Ospovat' on pp. 209–10.

Night and Day. The poem incorporates work written as far back as 1910.
Published in *N&D*.

In writing 'Night and Day' IR not only incorporated complete earlier
poems ('In the Workshop', 'Noon in the City', 'In the Park', 'Song of
Immortality') but also wrote separate short pieces conceived not as
complete poems but as the stages by which he arrived at a longer
piece. In a letter to Edward Marsh postmarked 15 May 1914 (p. 256),
he explains this method of writing: 'that is the only way I can write, in
scraps, and then join them together—I have the *one idea* in mind'.

See Milton 'L'Allegro' and 'Il Pensero', and Blake 'Songs of Innocence'.

ll. 18–20. See 'Dead Man's Dump' ll. 20–2.

l. 68. See 'The Mirror' l. 8.

l. 76. See 'At Night' ll. 13–14, 'Chagrin' ll. 21–2.

l. 84. See Keats 'Ode to a Nightingale' ll. 4 and 11: [. . .] and Lethe-
wards had sunk [. . .] | O, for a draught of vintage!

l. 127. See '[When I went forth as is my daily wont]' l. 8.

ll. 174–5, 244. See '[God looked clear at me through her eyes]' l. 5.

ll. 289–90. See 'Love To Be' title.

51 *To Nature.* Date of composition unknown. Published *1937.*

Dust Calleth to Dust. Composed ?1912. Published *Etudes Anglaises,* vol. 30, 1977, pp. 73–4.
l. 1. See Francis Thompson 'An Anthem of Earth' l. 259: In a little dust, in a little dust.

52 *My Songs.* Composed ?1912. Published *1937.*

To the Present. Composed ?1912. Published *1937.*

53 [*Have we sailed and have we wandered*]. Composed ?1912. Published *1937.*
ll. 5–8. See '[Wistfully in pallid splendour]' ll. 9–12.
l. 7. See 'Apparition' l. 3.

[*We are sad with a vague sweet sorrow*]. Composed ?autumn 1912. Published *1937.*

54 *Spring.* Composed ?autumn 1912. Published *1922.*

The Poet [I]. Composed ?autumn 1912. Published *1937.*
l. 13. See 'The Cage' ll. 1, 12, '[A bird trilling its gay heart out]' ll. 1–4.

55 [*O'er the celestial pathways the mortal and immortal strays*]. Composed ? late 1912. Published *1937.*

Peace. Composed late 1912. Published *1937.*

56 *Twilight [II].* Date of composition unknown. Published *1937.*

The Poet [II]. Composed ?1913. Published *1937.*

Creation. Date of composition unknown. Published (ll. 1–9 and ll. 11–44) *1922*; (ll. 1–9 and ll. 11–70) *1937*; ll. 71–80 (as a fragment) *1937.*
l. 81. See the Kabbalistic view of creation as an emanation, the coming into being of the universe through the unfolding of the essence of God in stages rather than *creatio ex nihilo.*

59 [*Even now your eyes are mixed in mine*]. Date of composition unknown. Published *1937.*
ll. 5–7. See 'Break of Day in the Trenches' ll. 9–11.

60 *A Question.* Date of composition unknown. Published *1922.*

A Careless Heart. Date of composition unknown. Published *1922.*

61 *Twilight [III].* Date of composition unknown. Published *1937.*

[*Invisible ancient enemy of mine*]. Date of composition unknown. Published *1937.*

62 *In Piccadilly.* Date of composition unknown. Published *Youth*; *A&L* vol. 2, no. 3, Summer 1919, p. 106. In IR's copy of *Youth*, he has crossed through this poem and the other two poems ('Love and Lust' and 'A Mood') that made up Part 2: 'The Cynics Lamp', and before sending a copy of the book to Sydney Schiff, IR tore out the page on which this section was printed, telling him in a letter of 4 June 1915: 'You will notice I've torn out a page in the book. The poems were very trivial and

I've improved the book by taking them out' (see p. 274). He apparently also removed the page before sending a copy to R. C. Trevelyan, explaining in an undated letter [last week of May 1916]: 'My reason for "castrating" my book before I sent it was simply that the poems were commonplace and you would not have said: "You do it like a navvy" but, "You do it like a bank clerk" ' (see p. 296).

Midsummer Frost. Drafted early in 1914. Published *Youth* (as 2 separate poems, 'Midsummer Frost [I]' and 'Midsummer Frost [II]') *1979*. For a full commentary on the misreading of this poem in *1979* see *2004* pp. 327–8.

IR sent a fair copy to Edward Marsh in May 1914. In reply, Marsh sent a detailed critique of the work (now lost), in particular of 'Midsummer Frost'. For the response to the criticism see the undated letter to Marsh [May or June 1914] on p. 258.

64 *Wedded [I]*.Possibly composed early in 1914. Published *1937*.
l. 10. See '[My soul is robbed by your most treacherous eyes] [I]' l. 12, [II] l. 14.

65 *Song*. Date of composition unknown. Published *1922*.

A Mood. Date of composition unknown. Published *Youth*. See note to 'In Piccadilly' above.

66 [*If you are fire and I am fire*]. Composed 1914. Published *Youth, A&L* vol. 2, no. 3, Summer 1919, p. 106.
l. 1. See '[The world rumbles by me—can I heed?]' l. 13, 'Heart's First Word [I] l. 10, 'Bacchanal' l. 12, 'You and I' l. 10.
See letter to Miss Molteno of [late April or May 1915], p. 272.

None Have Seen the Lord of the House. Date of composition unknown. Published *Youth*.

67 [*What if I wear your beauty as this present*]. Composed ?1914 in South Africa. Published *1937*.
[*Her fabled mouth love hath from fables made*]. Composed ?1914 in South Africa. Published *1937*.

68 [*A bird trilling its gay heart out*]. Composed ?1914 in South Africa. Published *1937*.
ll. 1–4. See 'The Cage' ll. 1, 12, 'The Poet [1]' l. 13.
Beauty [I]. Composed ?1914 in South Africa. Published *1937*.

69 *Of Any Old Man*. Composed ?1914 in South Africa. Published *1922*.
Dawn. Composed ?1914 in South Africa. Published *1922*.
l. 4 *threnody*: a song of lamentation.

70 *Subjectivity*. Drafted in the early summer of 1914 and completed some time in 1915. Published *1937*.
ll. 2–3. See Fragment XLIV '[The pigmy skies cover]' ll. 1–3.

ll. 17–18. See XLIV 'The Female God' l. 10.

71 *On Receiving News of the War: Cape Town.* Composed 1914, in South Africa. Published *1922.*

To Wilhelm II. Composed 1914, in South Africa. Published (as a fragment) *1937.*

For IR's thought on the German emperor, see his letter to Marsh (postmarked 8 Aug. 1914) on p. 261.

Title. Wilhelm II. Kaiser Wilhelm II (1859–1941), emperor of Germany during the Great War. He was forced into exile in Holland in 1918, bringing an end to the Hohenzollern dynasty and the German monarchy.

72 *The Female God.* Composed autumn 1914, in Cape Town. Published *1922.*
ll. 5–6. See 'Apparition' ll. 5–7
l. 10. See 'Subjectivity' ll. 17–18.
ll. 21–2. See 'Apparition' ll. 1–2.

73 *Beauty [II].* Possibly composed autumn 1914, in South Africa. Published *SAWC,* vol. 2, no. 3, Dec. 1914, p. 13
l. 10 *burning bush*: in Exodus 3: 2. A bush that burned without being consumed, a manifestation of God to mankind, his presence making the spot holy.
l. 11. See note to 'Returning, we hear the larks'on p. 388.

The Dead Heroes. Composed autumn 1914, in South Africa. Published *SAWC,* vol. 2, no. 3, Dec. 1914, p. 20; *Youth.*
l. 6. See Blake, *Milton,* Preface, ll. 9–11: Bring me my Bow of burning gold: | Bring me my Arrows of desire: | Bring me my Spear:

74 [*I have lived in the underworld too long*]. Composed late 1914, in South Africa. Published *1922.*

75 [*Under these skies, that take the hues*]. Composed late 1914, in South Africa. Published (as a fragment) *1937.*

[*Break in by subtler nearer ways*]. Composed late 1914, in South Africa. Published *Youth.*

On a Lady Singing. Composed late 1914, in South Africa. Published *1922.*

76 [*As a sword in the sun*]. Composed late 1914, in South Africa. Published (1–8 only) *1922*; complete *1979,* where the third stanza is given as a cancelled stanza.

[*Sacred, voluptuous hollows deep*]. Possibly composed between June 1914 and Feb. 1915, in South Africa. Published *1937.*
l. 19 *transplendent*: brilliantly translucent.
l. 21. See 'Death' l. 10.

77 *Love and Lust.* Composed between June 1914 and Feb. 1915, in South Africa. Published *Youth.*
See note to p. 62, 'In Piccadilly'.

At Sea-Point. Composed between June 1914 and Feb. 1915, in South Africa. Published *1937*.

Sea-Point is a beauty spot near Cape Town.

l. 1. See 'Break of Day in the Trenches' l. 1.

78 [*I know you golden*]. Possibly Composed between June 1914 and Feb. 1915, in South Africa. Published *1937*.

79 *The Mirror.* Possibly composed between June 1914 and Feb. 1915, in South Africa. Published *1937*.

ll. 1–2. See 'Dusk and the Mirror' ll. 35–6.

ll. 3–4. See 'Twilight [I]' ll. 6–8.

ll. 5–6. See 'Dead Man's Dump' ll. 27–8.

ll. 7–8. See 'Aspiration' l. 6.

l. 8. See 'Night and Day' l. 68.

The Exile. Possibly composed between June 1914 and Feb. 1915, in South Africa. Published *1937*.

80 [*A flea whose body shone like bead*]. Possibly composed between June 1914 and Feb. 1915, in South Africa. Published *1937*.

l. 5. See 'Break of Day in the Trenches' l. 7.

81 *Expression.* Composed late 1914 or early 1915. Published *Youth.*

[*Who loses the door that the wind*]. Composed late 1914 or early 1915. Published *1937*.

82 *God Made Blind.* Composed late 1914 or early 1915. Published *Youth.* See letter to Marsh [spring 1915] p. 264.

83 [*Summer's lips are aglow, afresh*]. Composed 1914 or 1915. Published *1937*.

[*O be these men and women*]. Composed 1914 or 1915. Published *1937*.

84 *Nocturne.* Composed 1914 or 1915. Published *1937*.

A Girl's Thoughts. Composed 1914 or 1915. Published *Youth*; *Colour*, vol. 2, no. 6, July 1915, p. 203.

85 *The Blind God.* Composed 1914 or 1915. Published *1922*.

[*Walk you in music light or night*]. Composed 1914 or 1915. Published *1937*.

At Night. Composed 1914 or 1915. Published *1922*. See note to p. 102 'Marching—as seen from the left file'.

l. 9. See 'Sleep [I]' l. 4.

ll. 13–14. See 'Night and Day' l. 76, 'Chagrin' ll. 21–2.

l. 17. See 'Aspiration' l. 2, 'The Burning of the Temple' l. 14.

86 *April Dawn.* Composed 1914 or 1915. Published *Youth.*

ll. 1–2. See '[My soul is robbed by your most treacherous eyes] [I]' l. 3.

87 *Wedded [II]*. Composed 1914 or 1915. Published *Youth*; *Colour*, vol. 3, no. 1, Aug. 1915, p. 7; *Moses*; *A&L* vol. 2, no. 3, Summer 1919, p. 107.

Chagrin. Composed 1914 or 1915. Published *Moses*.

ll. 1–5 *Absalom*: See 2 Samuel 13–19. Son of David who usurped his father's throne. Seeking to escape his enemies, his hair was entangled in the branches of an oak tree and he was slaughtered.

ll. 21–2. See 'At Night' ll. 13–14.

88 *The Cloister*. Composed 1914 or 1915. Published *Youth*.

[*My soul is robbed by your most treacherous eyes*] [*I*]. Date of composition unknown. Published *Youth*.

l. 13. See 'Wedded [I]' l. 10.

89 [*A warm thought flickers*]. Date of composition unknown. Published *1937*.

90 [*My soul is robbed by your most treacherous eyes*] [*II*]. Date of composition unknown. Published *Youth, 1937*.

l. 3. See 'April Dawn' l. 1.

l. 14. See 'Wedded [I]' l. 10.

Night. Date of composition unknown. Published *1937*.

91 *Apparition*. Date of composition unknown. Published *1937*.

ll. 1–2. See 'The Female God' ll. 21–2.

l. 3. '[Have we sailed and have we wandered]' l. 7, '[Wistfully is pallid splendour]' l. 11.

ll. 5–7. See 'The Female God' ll. 5–6.

92 [*Wistfully in pallid splendour*]. Date of composition unknown. Published *1937*.

l. 1. See 'In the Heart of the Forest' l. 11.

ll. 1–2. See 'Far Away' ll. 1–2, 'Twilight [I]' l. 4.

l. 2. See '[As a sword in the sun]' l. 10.

ll. 19–12. See '[Have we sailed and have we wandered]' ll. 5–8.

l. 11. See 'Apparition' l. 3.

Far Away. Date of composition unknown. Published *1937*.

ll. 1–2. See 'Twilight [I]' l. 4, '[Wistfully in pallid splendour]' ll. 1–2.

93 [*Glory of hueless skies*]. Date of composition unknown. Published *1937*.

Auguries. Date of composition unknown. Published *1937*.

ll. 5–6. See '[Past days are hieroglyphs]' ll. 1–5 and Fragment '[My days are scrawled upon a tree]' l. 1.

ll. 9–11. See '[I did not pluck at all]' l. 1.

94 [*I am the blood*]. Date of composition unknown. Published *1937*.

95 *Heart's First Word [II]*. Date of composition unknown. Published *Moses*; *A&L*, vol. 2, no. 3, Summer 1919, pp. 106–7.

As a Besieged City. Date of composition unknown. ?Summer 1915. Published *1937*.

l. 7. See ' Ballad of Whitechapel' ll. 46–7.

96 *The One Lost.* Composed *1914* and *1915*. Published (ll. 1–8 only) *Youth*; complete *1922*.
See l. 9 Francis Thompson 'The Hound of Heaven'.

[*Past days are hieroglyphs*]. Composed ?1915. Published *1937*.
ll. 1–5. See 'Auguries' l. 5–6.

97 *Torpor.* Possibly composed in 1915. Published *Moses* as ll. 105–23 of *Moses*; 1922.
     IR sent a copy of the poem to Sydney Schiff. Schiff gave careful thought to IR's work, and IR responded in a letter of thanks of 8 June 1915 (see p. 274) Schiff edited the summer 1919 edn of *A&L*, in which he published five of IR's poems and a memoir written by AR.
ll. 1–4. See 'Sleep [II]' ll. 17–20.

God. Possibly composed ?1915. Published (ll. 1–15) *Moses*; (ll. 1–18); *Rainbow*, n.d.
l. 2. See 'Sleep [I]' l. 13, 'Sleep [II]' l. 9.
ll. 11–12. See 'Sleep [II]' l. 7.
ll. 11–15. See *Moses* ll. 347–52.
l. 29. See *Moses* l. 143.

98 *Evening.* Possibly composed 1915. Published (ll. 6–9) *Moses*, 200–3; (as a fragment) *1937*; (1–5 only, as a fragment) *1979*.

99 [*I did not pluck at all*]. Possibly composed 1915. Published *Moses*; *A&L* vol. 2, no. 3, Summer 1919, pp. 107–8.
l. 1. See 'Auguries' ll. 9–11.

Sleep [I]. Possibly composed 1915. Published *Moses*.
l. 4. See 'At Night' l. 9.
ll. 5–6. See 'Sleep [II]' ll. 1–2.
ll. 12–17. See 'Sleep [II]' l. 9–13.
l. 13. See 'God' l. 2.

100 *Lusitania.* Composed summer 1915. Published *1937*.
     The British passenger liner *Lusitania* was sunk by a German torpedo on 7 May 1915 on a homeward voyage from New York. 1,198 people died, including 100 Americans. The Germans claimed, with justification, that the ship was carrying small-arms ammunition, although this was denied at the time. The killing of innocent civilians caused outrage, and was a contributing factor to America's later entry into the war.
l. 1. See 'Significance' l. 9.
l. 5. See Marlowe, *Faustus* ll. 1328–9: Was this the face that launch'd a thousand ships, | And burnt the topless towers of Ilium?

Dusk and the Mirror. Possibly composed summer 1915. Published *1937*.
l. 26 *plashless*: not in *OED*; *plash*: the noise made when any object strikes the surface of water so as to break it up or plunges into or through it.
ll. 35–6. 'The Mirror' ll. 1–2.

l. 39 *Narcissian augurs*: Narcissus, a nymph who fell in love with his image in a pool; he constantly strove to reach it, but as he did so the image broke up. An augur is one who foretells the future.

102 *Significance*. Possibly composed summer 1915. An eight-line holograph in the British Library, relating to ll. 9–12, was published in *Scrutiny* vol. 3, no. 4, March 1935, p. 353; full text *1937*.

l. 9. See 'Lusitania' l. 1.

Marching—as seen from the left file. Composed mid–late Dec. 1915 at Bury St Edmunds. Published *Moses; Poetry: A Magazine of Verse*, vol. 9, no. 3, Dec. 1916, p. 128.

This is the first poem known to have been written by IR after he enlisted at the end of Oct. 1915. Marsh had suggested that IR send a copy of *Youth* to Lascelles Abercrombie to whom Marsh had introduced him. IR responded to Marsh: 'I have sent on the poems to L.A. I sent this one as well which I like.' For Abercrombie's response to the poems, see IR's undated letters [early Dec. 1915] to Marsh on p. 283, and to Schiff [early Dec. 1915] on p. 284.

IR added extra lines to an early draft: see the undated letter to Marsh [postmarked 29 Jan. 1916] on p. 291. The fair copy sent to Abercrombie has not been traced, and I have found no record of what these extra lines were. They have not survived in MS or TS, nor do they appear in either *Moses* or *Poetry: A Magazine of Verse*, both of which were pub. in IR's lifetime; it is possible that they are part of the poem as it has survived.

Marsh's response to the poem was evidently not encouraging, for in an undated letter [postmarked 5 Jan. 1916], IR writes: 'I am sorry you didn't like that poem; I thought I had hit on something there' (see p. 290). He talks of the poem in an undated letter to Schiff (see p. 293).

IR sent a copy of *Moses* (in which this poem was published) to the American poet, Ezra Pound (1885–1972). IR's introduction to Pound may have been through either Marsh or Rodker. Rodker had discussed the American journal, *Poetry: A Magazine of Verse*, edited in Chicago by Harriet Monroe (1860–1936), with IR in Dec. 1915. In Jan. 1916 Rodker sent 'Marching', and one other poem, to Monroe, telling her: 'His poems are rare and remarkable gems and have won approval from most eminent men of letters in England. But I will not dilate on their quality—though the form is conventional, the matter is ultra-modern and I am sure it will appeal to you. Myself I am convinced—It is a great work.' Monroe decided to publish 'Marching', and wrote back to Rodker, asking him to contact IR as she had a query about punctuation, and wanted permission to take out a line. Rodker replied that he was unable to contact IR, but that there should be a full stop after 'hoofs of death' in l. 12, and that the line in parenthesis—(Who paws dynamic air now)—should be kept, adding 'It is very fine' (see *JC* pp. 134–5).

Pound, who was Foreign Correspondent of *Poetry*, had already sent Monroe some of IR's poetry (see note to p. 275 *sending my things to America*). However, he does not seem to have been over-enthusiastic about IR's work. In a postscript to a letter of 28 June 1915 to Monroe, he wrote: 'Don't bother about Rosenberg, send the stuff back to him direct unless it amuses you.' Monroe had asked Pound's advice in a letter which crossed with his earlier one, and he replied to her in an undated letter [received 20 Sept. 1915]: 'I think you may as well give this poor devil a show. Yeats called him to my attention last winter, but I have waited. I think you might do half a page review of his book, and that he is worth a page for verse. | "At night" seems good enough, if only for the sake of the phrase "the sun spreads wide like a tree". The S[a]vage Song [*Moses* ll. 164–75] is crammed with Blake, you might or might not use it to fill out the pages. I have sent him ba[c]k the rest of his mss. | He has something in him, horribly rough but then "Stepney East" [...]!'. Despite Pound's patronising tone, Monroe liked 'Marching—as seen from the left file', and a later poem 'Break of Day in the Trenches'— both of which appear to have been sent direct to Monroe by IR—enough to publish them in *Poetry* in Dec. 1916. Yeats was invited by GB to write an Introduction to *1937*, but he declined, saying that IR's verse was 'all windy rhetoric' (quoted *TLS*, 29 Aug. 1975, p. 958).

l. 10. *Mars* the Roman god of war.

103   *Sleep [II]*. Composed before March 1916. Published *1979*.
ll. 1–2. See 'Sleep [I]' ll. 5–6.
l. 7. See 'God' ll. 11–12.
l. 9. See 'God' l. 2.
ll. 9–13. See 'Sleep [I]' ll. 12–17.
ll. 17–20. See 'Torpor' ll. 1–4, *Moses* ll. 105–8.

104   *Spring 1916*. Possibly composed March 1916. Published *Moses*.
In an undated letter [27 May 1916] to Marsh, IR said: 'I'll write them at home to send you a copy of my poems [*Moses*], one called "Spring 1916", I particularly like, & I think you will'. (See p. 297.)

[*A worm fed on the heart of Corinth*]. Possibly composed May or June 1916 in England. Published *1937*.
ll. 1–2. Corinth, Babylon, and Rome were powerful cities which fell partly as a result of inner corruption. Corinth was proverbial for its loose living.
l. 3. Paris, the son of Priam, King of Troy, whose abduction of Helen led to the siege of Troy.

105   *The Troop Ship*. Composed in France, June 1916. Published *1922*.

In the Trenches. Composed in France, June or early July 1916. A poem with this title was enclosed in a letter to Bottomley postmarked 12 July

1916 (see p. 30); however, the text is that of 'Break of Day in the Trenches' (see below). Published (as part of a letter) *1937* pp. 352–3.

106 *Break of Day in the Trenches.*

Composed in France, June 1916. Published *Poetry: A Magazine of Verse,* vol. 9, no. 3, Dec. 1916, pp. 128–9. See note to 'In the Trenches' above.

Enclosed with a letter to GB postmarked 12 July 1916 in *BL*, was a holograph of 'Break of Day in the Trenches'. Entitled 'In the Trenches', it contains some significant and interesting variants which are given below.

On receiving a fair copy of this poem, GB wrote to IR: 'Thank you for the deeply interesting poems you send. I am glad to have them. [. . .] "In the Trenches" is the most completely good; it falls away a little at the end, but I like it ever so much.' In his next letter to IR he said: 'Your sister very kindly sent me the revision of your Rat poem. [. . .] I thought the end was greatly improved, and I felt it ran straight along quite clearly and in a good shape.' In an undated letter [late July 1916] to Trevelyan, IR wrote: 'I have asked my sister to send you a poem Bottomley liked— "Break of day in the trenches". Perhaps the end is not quite clear & wants working on'. (See p. 306.)

In his Foreword to the *1937* edn. (p. ix) Sassoon said: ' "Break of Day in the Trenches" has for me a poignant and nostalgic quality which eliminated critical analysis. Sensuous front-line existence is there, hateful and repellent, unforgettable and inescapable.'

l. 1. See 'At Sea-Point', l. 1.

l. 2 *Druid Time*: the priestly officers of pre-Roman Britain to whom sunrise was of particular significance.

l. 4 *sardonic*: in *BL*, IR first put 'uncanny' (cancelled).

l. 5 *the parapet's poppy*: *BL* has 'a poppy from the parapet'.

l. 7 *Droll rat*: *BL* has 'Queer rat' (cancelled), then 'Droll subterranean rat'. See '[A flea whose body shone like bead]' l. 5.

l. 9 *Now*: *BL* has 'For'; *this*, *BL* has 'an'.

ll. 9–10. Donne 'The Flea' l. 3: It sucked me first, and now sucks thee.

ll. 9–11. '[Even now your eyes are mixed in mine]' ll. 5–7.

l. 10 *You*: *BL* has 'And'.

l. 12 *sleeping green*: *BL* has 'poppy blooded field'.

Following l. 12 *BL* has an extra line: Our hands will touch through your feet.

l. 16 *Bonds to the*: *BL* has 'Helpless'.

ll. 20–6. In *BL* these lines read: At the hiss, the irrevocable swiftness, | The laconic earth buffet. | A shell! | Safe. Again Murder has overlooked us, | Only white with powder & chalk.

l. 22. Blake 'The Tyger', ll. 9–16: And what shoulder, and what art, | Could twist the sinews of thy heart? | And when thy heart began to beat, | What dread hand? and what dread feet? | What the hammer? What the

chain? | In what furnace was thy brain? | What the anvil? what dread
grasp | Dare its deadly terrors clasp?
ll. 23–4. Herbert 'Virtue', ll. 5–8: Sweet rose, whose hue angry and brave
| Bids the rash gazer wipe his eye: | Thy root is ever in its grave, | And
thou must die.

August 1914. Composed summer 1916 in France. Published *1937*.
ll. 6–7. See 'Death' l. 5, 'Dead Man's Dump' l. 31.

108 *The Dying Soldier.* Date of composition unknown. Written in France.
Published *1922*.

[*Wan, fragile faces of joy!*]. Date of composition unknown. Written in
France. Published *1922*.
l. 5. See 'Dawn Behind Night' l. 8, 'Dead Man's Dump' l. 64.

109 *Pozières.* Composed mid-Aug. 1916, in France. Published (as a frag-
ment, and as part of a letter) *1937*.
      For IR's thoughts on writing Pozières as a hymn, see the undated
letter to Bottomley, postmarked 17 Sept. 1916, on p. 318. The Battle of
Pozières Ridge on the Somme lasted from 23 July to 3 Sept. 1916.

The Immortals. Date of composition unknown. Written in France.
Published *1922*.
      See 'Louse Hunting'. It is not known which of these poems was
written first.
l. 15 *Balzebub*: Beelzebub, a god of the Philistines (2 Kings 1: 2), who is
referred to in Matthew 12: 24 as 'the prince of the devils'.

110 *Louse Hunting.* Composed between the summer of 1916 and Feb. 1917,
in France. Published *1922*.
      Because of the difficulty in reading what appears to be the only
surviving MS, edns. before *2004* differ in a number of places. All read
(1) 'and glistening' for 'aglisten' and omit (2) 'of fiends'; in (11) all
correct IR's 'sprung' to 'sprang' and (12) read 'verminous' in place of
'vermin' *1922* reads (14) 'This plunge' for 'The place', (17) 'baffled' for
'battled', (21) 'That' for 'hot'. All have (19) 'Pluck; for 'Dug' and (20)
'supreme' for 'the supreme'. In (22–3) for 'vermin | Charmed' *1922* has
'vermin willed | To charm'. In his note in *1937* p. 386, DH discussed the
variant of 1, and speaks of 'another manuscript—now lost', a possibility
that GB had put to him to explain the discrepancy in his earlier readings
(letter from GB to DH of 15 July 1936). However, the nature of the
misreadings and the subsequent correspondence suggest that DH
believed that GB worked from the existing MS, and that there
had not been another. The manuscript demonstrates most clearly the
conditions under which IR was writing at the front. It is written with a
soft pencil on bad quality paper which has been folded in four and
is muddy and torn, especially down the right-hand side. It exists

only in a very rough draft, and is the most difficult of his works to transcribe. No text can be final.

The first mention of the thoughts for this poem come in a letter to GB postmarked 23 July 1916: 'Last night we had a funny hunt for fleas. All stripped by candlelight, some Scots dancing over the candle burning the fleas, and the funniest, drollest and dirtiest songs and conversation ever imagined. Burns "Jolly Beggars" is nothing to it.' On 8 Aug. 1916, GB wrote to IR: 'I thought your Flea Hunt was a great subject; you must cherish it and carry it through. If I were you I should not tell too many poets about it, or certainly one of them will not be able to keep his hands off it. I find it difficult to resist it.' IR planned not only a poem but also a drawing of the subject; in a letter postmarked 17 Sept. 1916 (see p. 318), he told GB: 'I must draw the "Flea hunt" if I don't write it.' He made a sketch of the scene, which he sent to GB, for on 19 March 1917 GB wrote to thank him, saying: 'I was more than glad to have your letter, and the Rear Elevation of a Flea-Hunt. Or should one call it View of a Flea-Hunt from the South-West? I like it ever so much, and shall remind you of your intention to work it up when you are back again; the design is first-rate and has a good and novel balance; the man's vertical legs make it feel huge and inevitable like a prehistoric temple. And the quality of your colour interests me too. | I should call this a static Flea Hunt though, and I should like to see what you would make of the active Flea-Hunt which you first described, with the men jumping over candles and singeing the fleas. That would yield quite a different kind of composition, all moving and flowing lines, like a Witches' Sabbath of long slim bodies as if Botticelli had gone mad and designed a naked ballet for the Russian dancers. And it would be as much your own as the other, for it is all summarised in your letter of last Summer.' Neither the earlier letter nor the drawing appears to have survived, and IR apparently did not send a finished copy of the poem to GB, who worked from this draft when preparing the *1922* edn. See also the undated letter (postmarked 8 Feb. 1917) to Marsh on p. 327.

During the preparation for the *1937* edn. GB and DH conferred at some length about the confusions created by its condition. For example, referring to his readings of l. 14 and l. 17, GB wrote to DH: '"This plunge" I agree that your reading *may* be the right one, except that the "a" *is* a "u". I voted for "plunge" because he sent me at the same time a drawing in which 3 or 4 louse-hunters *were* plunging delightfully, vigorously, and making the word seem inevitable. | "Baffled" still seems to me a possibility in spite of the "tt" in littleness, just below; but in 1917 it seemed the inevitably right word which I should not have dared to change—it said so unerringly what everybody was feeling. I suppose it does not seem so cogent or irresistible now: but "battled" seems without significance, and just that kind of conventionally poetic

word that Rosenberg never did use. "Baffled" still has a stinging mean-
ing for me, even in retrospect: but I do not see how "arms" can be
"battled" when they are hung on a wall and out of use.' In his reply, DH
wrote: 'It's clear, I think, in "The place" or "This plunge": "This" is a
very natural reading if you take the "S" of "See" from the line below
and if the end stroke of "Soon" in the line above is seen, as it easily can
be, as the dot over the "i" (which is actually a closed "e"); again in
"place" the "a" is unclosed (but see also the "a" in "battled"—that is
rather open too) so that "u" is a reasonable interpretation, and the "h" of
"the" below combines with "c" to make a good "g"—all of this added to
the fact that some other line (perhaps an accidental stroke) has been
written over and adds to the confusion enough to reconcile you to the
omission of the "n" that "plunge" would require. | I'm afraid there can't
be much doubt about "battled" either if we take into account the
"bayonets" that preceded it and the clear form of "f" all through this
MS. I could show you a number of places (though few in these late
poems) where R did use an everyday word first and then "poeticize" it,
and I've come across "embattled" in one of his earlier fragments. There
is this point too—that if it were human "arms" it would most naturally
mean the shadows of the arms on the wall (since they weren't actually
killing the lice on the wall), and then it would be strange to say that they
<mixed> with the shadows on the wall. I take it that the shadows on the
wall were darting about amongst the bayonets—and that by candle-light
the shadows and the bayonets would be confused together.' GB
responded: 'No: it never struck me they were human arms.'
See 'The Immortals'. It is not known which of these poems was written
first.
l. 13. 'Night and Day' l. 204.

From France. Composed in France, probably in 1916. Published *1937*.
l. 9. Traditionally in the Jewish culture, passers-by place a stone on a
grave.

112 *The Destruction of Jerusalem by the Babylonian Hordes*. Composed in early
Nov. 1916. MS enclosed with a letter to Bottomley in *BL*, postmarked
12 Nov. (see p. 321), in which he says 'I wrote a little thing yesterday
which still needs working on'. Published *1922*.
     In a letter to IR of 26 Nov. 1916, GB wrote: 'I am deeply interested
in the lyrical ballad about the Babylonian Hordes which you have sent
me, and for which I send many thanks. I agree with you that it will
stand more working on, but in essence it is already a fine thing. I like
its vigour and directness; it gives me the comforting feeling that you
are learning to say what you want to say in a straighter, swifter, more
economic way than you did formerly. When this ballad is enriched and
ripened and tightened up in the joints a little it will be very very good
indeed'.

Title. Jerusalem feel to the Babylonians in 597 BC. The city was destroyed by Nebuchadnezzar, king of Babylon, in 586 BC leading to the captivity and exile of the peoples of Judah.

l. 9 *the Bull god*: the bull played a considerable part in Babylonian religion. Ishtar compelled her father, Anu, to create the bull of heaven, though the hero Gilgamesh tore off its skin and horns. Winged human-headed bulls served as tutelary gods.

l. 15. Solomon, King of Israel (d. *c.*930 BC) had many wives and several hundred concubines who, in his last years, led him astray.

l. 17. See 'Daughters of War' ll. 16–17.

l. 19. Solomon built the magnificent temple in Jerusalem (1 Kings 6: 37, 38).

l. 20 *gird*: a sharp blow, a spasm of pain.

113 *Returning, we hear the larks.* Composed 1917, in France. Published *1922*.
       For IR's thoughts on joy, see the undated prose piece entitled 'Joy' (p. 211). In 1912, IR did a charcoal and monochrome wash drawing entitled 'Hark, hark, the lark'.

l. 7. See Shelley, 'To a Skylark' ll. 59–60: All that ever was | Joyous, and clear, and fresh, thy music doth surpass.

ll. 8, 13, 15. See *The Amulet* ll. 186–8 and *The Unicorn* ll. 176–7.

ll. 10–12. See Shelley, 'To a Skylark' ll. 33–5: From rainbow clouds there flow not | Drops so bright to see | As from thy presence showers a rain of melody.

ll. 15–16. See 'Knowledge' l. 5.

Dead Man's Dump. Composed in its existing form by 14 May 1917. IR was transferred to the Royal Engineers in Jan. 1917, and part of his responsibility was taking wire up to the line at night. Published *1922*.
       In a letter postmarked 8 May 1917 IR told Marsh (see p. 331): 'I've written some lines suggested by going out wiring, or rather carrying wire up the line on limbers and running over dead bodies lying about. I don't think what I've written is very good but I think the substance is, and when I work on it I'll make it fine.' Marsh wrote back that he did not like IR's mixing rhyme with free verse, to which IR responded (letter postmarked 27 May 1917, see p. 332): 'I liked your criticism of "Dead man's dump". Mr Binyon has often sermonized lengthily over my working on two different principles in the same thing and I know how it spoils the unity of a poem. But if I couldn't before, I can now, I am sure, plead the absolute necessity of fixing an idea before it is lost, because of the situation it's conceived in. Regular rhythms I do not like much, but of course it depends on where the stress and accent are laid. I think there is nothing finer than the vigorous opening of Lycidas for music; yet it is regular. Now I think if Andrew Marvell had broken up his rhythms more he would have been considered a terrific poet.'

In a letter to GB postmarked 31 May 1917 (see p. 334), IR said: 'I wrote a poem about some dead Germans lying in a sunken road where we dumped our wire. I have asked my sister to send it on to you, though I think it commonplace'.

After receiving a copy of the poem, GB wrote to IR on 29 June 1917: 'I like "Dead Man's Dump" too [as well as 'Daughters of War']; it is more unequal, and in places it suggests that it has absorbed more raw material, "neat", than it can assimilate. But in places it gets beyond that more completely than any other war poetry I have seen, and now and then—as in the two sections beginning "What fierce imaginings"—you get the same astonishing and entrancing quality as in the other poem. This kind of quality is your high-water mark yet, so you must keep it up.'

l. 1 *limber*: the wheeled, detachable section of a gun carriage that is used for transporting material and supplies to the front line.

l. 3 *crown of thorns*: the mocking crown with which Christ was crowned King of the Jews before his crucifixion (Matthew 27: 29).

l. 14. See 'Death' ll. 1, 9.

ll. 18–20. See 'Night and Day' ll. 18–20.

ll. 21–5. See Francis Thompson, 'An Anthem of Earth' ll. 259–60, 262–3: In a little dust, in a little dust, | Earth, thou reclaim'st us [. . .] Thou dost this body, this enhavocked realm | Subject to ancient and ancestral shadows.

l. 24. See *Moses* ll. 102–3.

l. 25. In a holograph enclosed with a letter to GB postmarked 23 June 1917 in *BL*, IR has: 'Emptied of all that made the young lean Time | Eye with thief's eyes, shouldering his masters load | Of proud Godhead ancestralled essences'. See 'The Amulet' l. 153.

ll. 27–8. See 'The Mirror' ll. 5–6.

ll. 27–9. See Psalm 103, vv.15–16: As for man, his days are as grass: as a flower of the field, so he flourisheth. For the wind passeth over it, and it is gone; and the place thereof shall know it no more.

l. 31. See 'Death' l. 4, 'August 1914' ll. 6–7.

l. 34 *ichor*: in Greek mythology, the ethereal fluid that flows in the veins of the gods.

l. 56. See *The Amulet*, 'Tel's Song' l. 4.

l. 64. See 'Dawn Behind Night' l. 8, '[Wan, fragile faces of joy]' l. 5.

ll. 63–79. See Wilfred Wilson Gibson, 'Wheels' ll. 3–5, 7–8, 35–7, 67–8: He tumbled heavily, but all unheard | Amid the scurry of wheels that crashed and whirred | About his senseless head [. . .] | And as he lay | He heard again the wheels he'd heard all day[. . .] | And still within a hair's breath of his ear | The crunch and gride of wheels rings sharp and clear, | Huge lumbering wagons, crusted axle-deep [. . .] | and a roar | Of wheels and wheels and wheels for evermore [. . .]. This poem was published in *New Numbers*, vol. 1, no. 3, Aug. 1914.

ll. 76–9. See Blake, 'The Marriage of Heaven and Hell' Plate 7, l. 2: Drive your cart and your plough over the bones of the dead.

116 *Daughters of War. B*egun in about Oct. 1916 and completed some time after June 1917, in France. Published *1922.*

IR himself considered this his most important poem. On a typescript of 'Returning, we hear the larks', which he sent to Rodker, he scribbled: 'I will send you when I get it typed a poem I call Daughters of War, done in the grand style, but I think my best poem.'

The earliest mention of it is in a letter from GB of 21 Dec. 1916. In a lengthy critique of an early draft, GB wrote: 'I was more than pleased to have your new poem, and to see that all the present disabilities cannot stop the creative mind from working in you; for this poem is the real thing, and contains real poetry in an intensity which it is not granted to many people to reach. It has imperfections; but it contains more than one part of the new merit of which you speak, because in the best passages it attains a texture of a personal yet a high quality, and it nowhere fails in keeping up this texture completely. To produce a texture is not the purpose of art or its raison d'être, as the Imagist painters often think; yet they are so far right in that the achievement of a mysterious, inscrutable texture that justifies itself to a long-trained taste is the surest test as to whether a work of art has been achieved—as well as being the surest way in which the personal nature of the artist can find legitimate play while he is busied about his high impersonal business. It is the same in all great art—Milton or Whitman, Whistler Titian or the early Rossetti, Stravinsky or Mozart. | So I am sure your poem has elements of the best kind of beauty in it, because it has a remarkable, close-knit, firm, spare texture; and because the formation of the texture causes a feeling of music in the mind. | It is unequal: it gathers strength as it goes on, and it is at its best at the end, where it is simple as well as complex. At the beginning it is not sure-footed, it is not certain of its direction. The grand and impressive image of the tree-root, for instance, is only half dug out, and you rely on the good will of the reader to get it into its proper relationship. But when the poem finds its pace it steadies itself and goes straight to its intention, so that I feel as if you were the man who invented the Valkyries and the Amazons for the first time.'

Returning to the poem in a letter of 12 Feb. 1917, GB said: 'Your idea of doing a Judas Maccabaeus is first rate, and I hope you will keep tight hold of it until you find an opportunity to tackle it. It, and a whole host of the similar gorgeous subjects which are your birthright, have never been properly done in English literature, and I believe you have the power in you to make them your own and also to make memorable things of them. The fragment of The Daughters of War which you sent me has remarkable and exceptional qualities, and it would fit splendidly into a Judas Maccabaeus drama.'

In a letter to GB postmarked 31 May 1917 (see p. 334) IR wrote: 'I've made it into a little book for you, as I like the poem.' This 6-page presentation copy is written on scraps of paper—parts of envelopes, part of page torn from a receipt book, part of a serrated sheet torn from a notebook—with the outer cover made from the outside of a Utopia Writing Tablet. The pages are stitched together with thread, and inscribed on the outer cover is: 'Daughters | of | War.', and inside: 'For Gordon Bottomley | Isaac Rosenberg. | May 1917.| France'. See Fig. 6, p. 117.

On 29 June 1917, GB wrote to thank him for this, and for typed copies of the poem which AR had sent him: 'It is most kindly and delicately done of you to think of making me the book: I thank you for it and for your thoughtfulness with all my heart, and you can be sure I shall always keep it among my treasures. | The poem is certainly your finest; and it is *very* fine. I still am not quite sure that I quite understand every phrase of it, but I recognise that this need not be all the poem's fault; but what really matters is that its music and its movement are of the grandest kind, and all your own. It contains the rarest qualities: your hold on them is here and there somewhat uncertain, but you [have] them and you only need to get a steady grip of them to reach the highest places of poetry.'

GB was not alone in finding some parts of the poem difficult. IR wrote to Marsh about the problem of obscurity in a letter postmarked 30 July 1917 (see p. 341), and again in an undated letter [late July or Aug. 1917] (see p. 341), returning to the subject once more in a letter to GB postmarked 19 August 1917 (see p. 344).

For more on the composition of the poem, see the undated letter [postmarked 27 May 1917] to Marsh on p. 332. As with 'Dead Man's Dump', IR sent various drafts back to England to be typed, and then reworked them.

In the summer of 1917, hearing that an extract from 'Moses', '[Ah Koelue!]' had been selected to be included in Marsh's volume *Georgian Poetry, 1916–17*, IR was disappointed that 'Daughters of War' had not been chosen. Writing to him on 7 Aug. 1917, GB explained: 'I understand very well your wishing that "Daughters of War" could go in too. It is your most remarkable poem for vision and originality and texture of language, and to me it gives the most certain promise of a fine future if you cultivate your talent and bring it completely within your own control. | Yet I understand equally why Mr. Marsh demurs: I am probably a very bad and misleading guide for you, for I am always ready to meet a poet half-way when he says things I like in a way that I like; and I have only myself to please: but the public which Mr. Marsh, as editor, has to consider will not meet you half way, but will require you to go all the way; and in editing a composite volume there is a need to set and keep a standard of clarity, and to ensure that language has a certain definiteness of meaning for which an editor can make himself responsible.| If I were asked I could not deny that I thought "Daughters of War" obscure; I could not, in fact always explain to anybody what it means. But the feeling is so right, and the salient points are firm enough to enable me to leap from one to the next. But I might not be able to persuade Mr. Marsh that that was enough. | The opening was certainly one of the most baffling places, and I had to be content with its general gist; the fine and powerful image of "the root side of the tree of life" in particular did not explain itself completely, but its intention was so profoundly right that I had not the heart to tell you so, but just leapt at its significance. I think that the new version which you now send me is much clearer and more to the point, and you have improved it without sacrificing any essential detail; but I am still not certain whose "expiring voice" it is that "has ceased in the boughs". Is it connected with "dumb faces"? | The middle of the poem contains all the finest things, and it does not give me any trouble; but when I come to the section beginning "One whose great lifted face" I cannot get completely hold of the sense of "Whose new hearing drunk the sound | Where pictures, lutes and mountains mixed | With the loosed spirit of a thought." This is not completely developed, as photographers say. And the last section is the same; the suggestions are tremendous and stimulating to the imagination, but I cannot always follow them out, especially "My sisters have their males | Clean of the dust," etc. to the end. If you feel you can carry these parts through, you know I shall be glad to be your critic if you think I can be useful.'

ll. 1–14. For an alternative version of these lines in *BL*, see the letter to GB postmarked 3 Aug. 1917 on p. 342.

ll. 16–17. See 'The Destruction of Jerusalem by the Babylonian Hordes' l. 17.

l. 22 *Amazons* in Greek mythology, a race of sturdy women warriors. Any male progeny of their encounters with neighbouring tribes were either destroyed or sent away.

119   *The Jew*. Possibly composed summer 1917. Published *1922*.

   JC (p. 127) wrote that 'Among the first poems he composed in barracks was a short protest which he called "The Jew".' *JL* (p. 187) and *JMW* (1975, p. 150) both suggest that the poem was written during IR's early months in barracks in England. This conclusion probably came from IR's thoughts of being a private and a Jew in the British army contained in an undated letter [early Nov. 1915] to Schiff on p. 279. There is no evidence for this dating on the surviving holograph or TS in the IWM, indeed the holograph was written in indelible pencil which IR appears to have used only in France. In *BL*, a pencil holograph of the poem was enclosed with a letter to GB postmarked 11 July 1917. The paper on which it is written is torn from the lower half of p. 2 of the letter which talks of IR's Jewishness, and seems to match the paper of the IWM holograph. This letter may have prompted him to send a copy of a poem he had written earlier, but, in the absence of any further evidence, I think it is more likely—though by no means certain—that the poem was prompted by his thoughts on his Jewish heritage contained in this letter, and was written in the summer of 1917.

l. 5 *the bronze, the ruddy*: 'bronze skinned & ruddy,' *BL*.

Girl to Soldier on Leave. Composed in France in September or October 1917. Published *1922*.

l. 1 *Titan*: in Greek mythology, warriors of enormous size and strength who fought a prolonged struggle against Zeus, the supreme god of the ancient Greeks, who defeated them and expelled them from heaven. Leftwich recalled IR [*c*.1911] doing 'illustrations to his own poems and to other poems—a charcoal composition, for instance, illustrating a passage in Keats, depicting the Titans, some with masses of rock on their bodies, some strangling snakes' (*The Jewish Chronicle*, Supplement, no. 167, Feb. 1936, p. ii). This probably refers to Keats, 'Hyperion. A Fragment', Book II.

ll. 5–8, 17–20. Omitted in *BL* pencil holograph.

l. 6 *Prometheus*: in Greek mythology, one of the Titans who stole fire for mankind and was punished for this by being chained to Mount Caucasus. Each day an eagle preyed on his liver, and each night it was renewed until at last he was released.

l. 9. See 'Soldier: Twentieth Century' l. 14, '[Through these pale cold days]' l. 1.

l. 11 *Babel cities*: Genesis 11: 3–9. A city built of burned brick with a tower to reach to heaven, a symbol of man's ambition and presumption for which God punished him by making many tongues and scattering mankind across the face of the earth.

l. 12 *Pressed upon*: Bore down on, *BL*.

l. 13 *Weary gyves*: Vulturelike, *BL*.

ll. 13, 16, 20. *gyve*: a shackle or fetter.

l. 15 *Circe's swine*: in Greek mythology, a sorceress who turned Odysseus' companions into swine.

l. 17 *the Somme*: a region in north-western France that was the site of fierce fighting, particularly between July and November 1916.

120 *Soldier: Twentieth Century*. Possibly composed in the autumn 1917. Published *1922*.

l. 1 *Titan*: see note to 'Girl to Soldier of Leave' l. 1.

l. 5. See Fragment LXIX ll. 5–6, *The Unicorn* ll. 88–9.

l. 14 See 'Girl to Soldier on Leave' l. 9, '[Through these pale cold days]' l. 1.

121 *In War*. The first two stanzas were composed some time before 19 July 1916, in France. The complete poem was enclosed with a letter to Bottomley in *BL*, postmarked 22 Oct. 1917 (see p. 352). Published *1922*.

When IR sent the poem, GB who replied: 'Thank you for the deeply interesting poems you send. I am glad to have them. "Fret the nonchalant noon" has something very remarkable about it, but I think you can ripen it further.'

IR's two brothers, David and Elkon, served in the war, but neither was killed. In his letter to Bottomley, IR says 'It happened to one of our chaps, poor fellow—and I've tried to write it.'

123 *The Burning of the Temple.* Composed before March 1918 in France. Published *1922.*

For IR's thoughts on the clarity of this poem, see his letter to Miss Seaton of 8 March 1918 on p. 362. In *BL*, a TS of the poem was enclosed in a letter to GB postmarked 24 Feb. 1918. In this, in l. 1, IR has added in ink the letter 'i' to the word 'wrath' making it 'wraith'. This alteration has not been made to the only other surviving TS, on which the text of this poem has previously been based.

l. 1 *Solomon*: King of Israel (d. *c*.930 BC) who built the magnificent temple in Jerusalem (1 Kings 6: 37, 38) which was destroyed by the Babylonians in 586 BC.

l. 14. See 'Spiritual Isolation' l. 35, 'Aspiration l. 2, 'At Night' l. 17.

[*Through these pale cold days*]. Composed in March 1918 in France. Published *1937.*

This is the last of IR's poems to have survived; he was killed on 1 April.

l. 1. See 'Girl to Soldier on Leave' l. 9, 'Soldier: Twentieth Century' l. 14.

l. 3 *three thousand years*: Saul was named first King of Israel in *c*.1020 BC; he was succeeded by King David in *c*.100 BC.

l. 7 *Hebron*: a city in the Judean hills near Jerusalem that was one of the holy cities of Israel.

FRAGMENTS

124 I. Composed ?early in 1911. On a TS of 'On a Door Knocker'.

II. Composed in the spring or early summer of 1911. On notes for 'Rudolph'.

III. Composed ?in the summer of 1911.

125 IV, V. Dates of composition unknown. On a fair copy of 'Twilight [III]'.

126 VI. Composed in ?1911 or 1912. On a fair copy of 'Tess'.

VII. Composed before 1912. On a draft of 'In the Woods', with the pencil prose fragment: 'Lack of depth of profundity makes our age an age of sceptics'.

VIII, IX, X. Composed ?between Oct. 1911 and March 1913.

127 XI. Composed ?between Oct. 1911 and March 1913.

XII. Composed ?in 1912. On a TS of 'To The Present'

128   XIII. Date of composition unknown. On a fair copy of '[O! in a world of men and women]'.

XIV. Composed ?in the autumn of 1912. With pencil notes on youth (see p. 225).

128–30   XV, XVI, XVII, XVIII, XIX, XX, XXI, XII, XXIII. Composed ?in 1913.

130   XXIV. Composed ?in 1914. Written in *New Numbers*, vol. 1, no. 2, April 1914.

131   XXV. Composed ?in 1914. On a draft of 'Beauty [I]'.

XXVI. Composed in 1914 or 1915. On a sheet with drafts of 'The One Lost' and 'God Made Blind'.

132   XXVII. Composed in 1914–15. On a sheet with drafts of 'A Girl's Thoughts' and 'Subjectivity'.

XXVIII. Composed in 1914–15. On a sheet with drafts of 'Song' and *Moses*.

XXIX. Composed in 1914 or 1915.

132–5   XXX–XXXIX. Composed between late 1914 and Feb. 1915, in South Africa. XXX is on a sheet with drafts of '[Break in by subtler nearer ways]' and a 'fair copy of [I have lived in the underworld too long]'; XXXI is a draft of 'Love and Lust', XXXII, XXXIII and XXXIV are on a draft of 'Auguries'; XXXVII is on a fair copy of 'The Mirror'; XXXVIII is on the fly-leaf of *The Italian Futurist Painters*; XXXIX is on a draft of '[A flea whose body shone like bead]'.

135   XL. Composed in 1914 or 1915. On drafts of 'The Blind God'.

135–6   XLI, XLII, XLIII, XLIV. Composed in 1914–15. XLI and XLIII are on drafts of 'At Night'; XLIV is on a TS of 'At Night'.

138   XLV. Composed between 1914 and mid-1916.

XLVI XLVII. Composed in ?1914 or 1915. On a fragment from *Moses*.

XLVIII, XLIX. Composed pre ?1915. On a draft of 'Evening'.

139   L. Composed in the spring of 1915.

LI, LII. Composed in ?1915. On a draft of 'Chagrin'.

139–40   LII, LIV, LV. Composed in 1915.

140   LVI, LVII. Composed in 1915. On a draft of *Moses*.

LVIII. Composed ?in 1915.
Cf. 'Evening'.

141 LIX, LX, LXI. Composed in ?1915. On a fragment from *Moses*.

142 LXII. Composed in the summer of 1915. On drafts of 'Significance', 'Lusitania' and 'Dusk and the Mirror'.

LXIII. Composed in 1915. On a TS of 'As a Besieged City'.

LXIV. Composed in 1915 or 1916. On a draft of 'Emerson'.

143 LXV. Composed in 1915 or 1916. On a draft of *Moses*.

LXVI. Composed ?in March 1916. On a fair copy of 'Spring 1916'.

LXVII. Composed in 1915 or 1916.

LXVIII. Composed in 1916 or 1917. On the fly-leaf facing the title-page of IR's copy of *Moses*.

LXIX. Composed in 1917. On a draft of *The Unicorn*.
ll. 5–6. See 'Soldier: Twentieth Century' l. 5, *The Unicorn* ll. 88–9.

144 LXX. Composed in 1917. On another draft of *The Unicorn*.

LXXI. Date of composition unknown. The fragment is preceded by a prose paragraph: 'I said I have been having some fits of despondency lately; this is what they generally end in, some Byronic sublimity of plaintive caterwauling'. On a draft of 'Fleet Street'.

LXXII. Date of composition unknown. On a draft of '[A woman's beauty is a strong tree's roots]'.

145 LXXIII, LXXIV. Date of composition unknown. On a TS of 'The Key of the Gates of Heaven'.

LXXV, LXXVI. Date of composition unknown. On a fair copy of 'You and I'.

LXXVII. Date of composition unknown. *1937* notes that this is on a TS of 'Wedded', but does not specify if this is 'Wedded [I]' or 'Wedded [II]'.

146 LXXVIII. Date of composition unknown. On a draft of 'Apparition'.

146–54 LXXIX–CII. Dates of composition unknown.

PLAYS

155 *Moses: A Play* was published in May 1916. It was printed by The Paragon Printing Works, 8 Ocean Street, Stepney Green. London.

The earliest dated reference to the play is in a letter to Schiff of 4 June 1915 (see p. 273) in which IR wrote: 'I am also enclosing a sketch for a play, which may interest you', although there is a possible earlier reference in an undated letter of ?spring 1915 to Winifreda Seaton (see p. 266) in which he wrote 'Do write me exactly what you think of my play.' That he was ready to share his thoughts suggests that the play must have been in his mind for several weeks. The earliest MS for which there is a possible date is a pencil fragment on the verso of '[A flea whose body shone like bead]'. The dating for this poem is provisional, but pencil notes on the holograph link it to Rosenberg's time in South Africa. This suggests that he may have been thinking about the play before he left Cape Town in Feb. 1915.

Two versions of the play have survived. The earlier, dated 1915, is in one act; the second version has two acts. Rosenberg published the play before leaving for France to ensure that it was not lost or destroyed, but in letters to Ruth Löwy [Feb. or March 1917] (see p. 329), to Israel Zangwill [late May 1916] and to GB, postmarked 11 July 1917 (see below), he makes it clear that this was not to be its final version. As with so much of Rosenberg's work, what we have are drafts to which he intended to return after the war.

Writing to Trevelyan in a letter postmarked 15 June 1916 (see p. 298), IR explained that: 'Moses symbolises the fierce desire for virility and original action in contrast to slavery of the most abject kind.' Sending a copy of the play to Israel Zangwill in late May 1916 (see pp. 295–6), he said: 'I have not worked him out as a character quite in the way I wished, because I had to hurry to get it finished before I went out', and more than a year after its publication, he told GB, in a letter postmarked 11 July 1917 (see p. 338), that he 'meant to go on with Moses because I have made ambition to be the dominant point in his character which I've considered is very unfriendly to my ancestor. I did mean to contrast him with a Christ like man, which I may yet do'.

Moses. Moses (fl. *c.*14th–13th century BC) was the Hebrew prophet who was to lead the Jews out of Egypt into the Promised Land. As a baby he was placed in a basket of reeds beside the Nile, where he was discovered by the daughter of the Pharaoh (probably Rameses II, 1304–1237 BC), who adopted him. The play is based on the story of Exodus 2: 11–12: 'And it came to pass in those days, when Moses was grown, that he went out unto his brethren, and looked on their burdens: and he spied an Egyptian smiting an Hebrew, one of his brethren. And he looked this way and that way, and when he saw that there was no man, he slew the Egyptian, and hid him in the sand.'
Stage directions: Thebes: On the Nile in Upper Egypt, an important city in the Middle Kingdom (*c.*2040–1786 BC).
l. 6. See 'Dead Man's Dump' l. 24.

l. 6 *sixteenth pyramid*: the number appears to have no particular significance.

l. 13 *satraps*: subordinate rulers, often with imputation of tyranny or ostentation. *OED*

ll. 31–2. See 'Aspiration' l. 1.

l. 102. See 'Dead Man's Dump' l. 24.

ll. 105–23. See 'Torpor'.

ll. 105–8. See 'Sleep [II]' ll. 17–20.

l. 143. See 'God' l. 29.

ll. 199–202. See 'Evening' ll. 6–9.

l. 224 *Behemoth*: the Hebrew form of the Egyptian word for water-ox (Job 40:15); a huge, strong animal.

ll. 347–51. See 'God' ll. 11–15.

175　*The Amulet.* There is no surviving evidence to tell us when Rosenberg began work on *The Amulet*. The first mention is in a letter to GB, postmarked 12 July 1916 (see p. 301), in which he said: 'I had ideas for a play called "Adam and Lilith" before I came to France, but I must wait now'. On 4 Aug. 1916 (see p. 308), he told Marsh: 'I have a fine idea for a most gorgeous play, Adam and Lilith. If I could get a few months after the war to work and absorb myself completely into the thing, I'd write a great thing.' By the end of May 1917, he appears to have put together a draft where the hero is now Saul, but then realizes that it is still far from what he has in mind, writing to Marsh: 'I hope you have not yet got my poem "The Amulet" I've asked my sister to send you. If you get it please don't read it because it's the merest sketch and the best is yet to come.' He then tells Marsh something of the idea behind the play (see p. 333). *Introductory stage directions*: *helm*: helmet.

l. 11 *horn*: a wind instrument resembling an animal horn in shape.

l. 15. See 'A Ballad of Time, Life and Memory' l. 40.

ll. 22–37. The description of the loaded cart sunk in the mud and pulled free by mules is probably based on IR's experience of seeing similar sinking carts pulled by mules on the Western Front.

ll. 70–1. See '[Wan, fragile faces of joy!]' ll. 5–6.

l. 121. See 'Torpor' l. 19.

l. 139. See 'Midsummer Frost' l. 17.

l. 147 *chimera's eremite*: In Greek mythology, a chimera is a fabled fire-breathing monster with a lion's head, a goat's body and a serpent's tail; thus, a grotesque creature formed of the parts of various animals. An eremite is a religious recluse or hermit.

l. 150. See 'At Night' l. 1.

l. 153. See 'Dead Man's Dump' l. 25.

l. 183. See 'Heart's First Word [II]' l. 14.

ll. 186–8. See 'Returning, we hear the larks' ll. 15, 8, 13.

ll. 192–4. See 'Tel's Song' ll. 6–8.

l. 196. See 'Tel's Song' l. 5.

182 *The Unicorn*. During the summer of 1917 Rosenberg abandoned *The Amulet* and began work on *The Unicorn*, reusing many lines from the earlier play.

In a letter postmarked 30 July 1917 (see p. 340), he wrote to Marsh: 'I've asked my sister [. . .] not to send the Amulet because I've changed the idea completely and I think if I can work it out on the new lines it will be most clear and most extraordinary. It's called "The Unicorn" now. I am stuck in the most difficult part; I have to feel a set of unusual emotions which I simply can't feel yet. However if I keep on thinking about it it may come.' Writing to GB in a letter postmarked 11 July 1917 (see p. 338), he said: 'Perhaps you know my little poem "Wedded", well it is a commentary on that. But the woman is not subtle enough and the man is hardly yet suggested, and the third character is a sort of castrated neuter gender.' He lays out his plans more fully in a letter to GB postmarked 3 Aug. 1917 (see pp. 342–3): 'It's called "The Unicorn" now, it's about a decaying race who have never seen a woman; animals take the place of women, but they yearn for continuity. The chief's Unicorn breaks away and he goes in chase. The unicorn is found by boys outside a city and brought in and breaks away again. Saul who has seen the unicorn on his way to the city for the week's victuals, gives chase in his cart. A storm comes on, the mules break down, and by the lightning he sees the unicorn race by. A naked black like an apparition rises up and easily lifts the wheels from the rut and together the[y] ride to Saul's hut. There Lilith is in great consternation having seen the unicorn and knowing the legend of this race of men. The emotions of the black (the chief) are the really difficult part of my story. Afterwards a host of blacks like centaurs on horses and buffaloes come rushing up, the unicorn in front. On every horse is clasped a woman. Lilith faints Saul stabs himself, the chief places Lilith on the Unicorn, and they all race away.' This version was completed in the late summer of 1917.

While on leave in Sept. 1917, IR reminded GB that his ideas were still only forming, telling him (see p. 345): '"This Unicorn" as will be obvious, is just a basis, its final form will be very different, I hope.' A month later he told him (letter postmarked Oct. 1917, see p. 350): 'I want to open with the tower of skulls of the decaying men. An ancient hermaphrodite is about to die and tells the secret of their birth. Tel the chief the rider of the unicorn plans the raid [. . .] Now I should like to write my play in prose a good deal and where it becomes vehement, poetry.'

At the end of Feb. 1918 (in a letter of 24 Feb. 1918, see p. 359) he lamented to GB about his lack of progress with the play: 'I wanted to send some bits I wrote for the "Unicorn" while I was in hospital and if I find them I'll enclose them. I tried to work on your suggestion and divided it into 4 acts, but since I left the hosp. all the poetry has gone quite out of me.' He expressed his intentions for the finished play in a letter to Miss Seaton on 8 March 1918 (see pp. 361–2), saying: 'If I am lucky, and come off undamaged, I mean to put all my innermost experiences into the "Unicorn". I want it to symbolize the war and all the devastating forces let loose by an ambitious and unscrupulous will. Last summer I wrote pieces for it and had the whole of it planned out, but since then I've had no chance of working on it and it may have gone quite out of my mind.'

l. 31 *maenad*: A priestess or female votary of Bacchus. *OED*

ll. 88–9. See 'Soldier: Twentieth Century' l. 5, Fragment LXIX ll. 5–6.

l. 99 *chaunt*: chant.

l. 103. See 'At Night' ll. 7–8.

l. 144. See 'Tel's Song' l. 5.

l. 150. See 'A Ballad of Time, Life and Memory' l. 40.

ll. 157–8. See 'At Night' ll. 1–2, 'Tel's Song' ll. 6–8.

ll. 161–2. See 'Tel's Song' l. 9.

l. 176. See 'Returning, we hear the larks' l. 8.

l. 177. See 'Returning, we hear the larks' l. 13.

l. 233. See 'Tel's Song' l. 1.

189 *Tel's Song* relates to l. 232 of *The Unicorn*. IR did not incorporate the lines in the only draft copy of the play to have survived.

l. 4. See 'Dead Man's Dump' l. 56.

190 *The Tower of Skulls* relates to l. 210 of *The Unicorn*. IR did not incorporate the lines in the only draft copy of the play to have survived, but in a letter to DH of 15 April 1936, GB wrote: 'I hold for certain that "The Tower of Skulls" was a part of "The Unicorn"—for it came in its place in that complete version (I mean complete *pro tem*) which he showed to me and then destroyed.'

PROSE

Many of the prose pieces are no more than scrappy notes. Obvious drafts for more finished pieces have not been given, but individual notes that may be of interest are here, some of these as part of the Commentary. For example, IR jotted down his thoughts in preparation for his article 'Art', many of which were not included in the article. These are of value in adding to our understanding of his thoughts on painting, and so are given here. Where he has played with the idea of two words, and has not excised one of them, both are given, separated by a vertical line, e.g. 'charm|essence'.

191 *On a Door Knocker*. Written Feb. 1911. On Sunday 19 Feb. 1911, the Whitechapel Boys decided that they would all write pieces in prose which they would read to one another on Sunday 5 March. IR completed his piece by the following Wednesday, but when they gathered once

more to read, he discovered that only he and Leftwich had written pieces. Undeterred, the four decided to collaborate on a novel, a proposal that flickered for a while but came to nothing. *JC* (pp. 43 and 47) describes how they ate peanuts, and the evening ended with 'a riotous shell fight, littering the floor and rolling about with laughter'.

Hardy, Zola, Turgenif. Thomas Hardy (1840–1928), English novelist and poet. IR wrote a poem 'Tess' inspired by Hardy's novel *Tess of the d'Urbervilles*; Emile Zola (1840–1902), French writer and critic, leader of the naturalist school. He conceived a series of twenty novels, *Les Rougon-Macquart*, the history of a family in the reign of the Emperor Napoleon III (1852–70), of which the best known today is *Germinal* (1885); Ivan Sergeevish Turgenev (1818–83), Russian novelist whose works include *On the Eve* (1860) and *Fathers and Sons* (1862). Vladimir Nikolaitch Panshin is a character in his novel *A Nest of Gentlefolk* (1859).

193 *On Noses.* Date unknown.

194 *Rudolph.* Written April 1911. This was almost certainly inspired by a dinner party to which he had been invited by Lily Delissa Joseph, who had first seen IR when he was copying a painting in the National Gallery in March 1911. In his diary for 1911, Leftwich wrote: 'Is this a real happening at Mrs. Delissa Joseph's? Rosenberg says no—but I am not satisfied with his denial. The whole thing has the nature of fact, and not of an invented tale'.

would have preferred. Following this, in a draft of 'Rudolph', IR has these notes:
'In this garret, the old tragedy of poverty and genius, was rehearsed day after day
Is crucifixion necessary
Why must life be broken
To save mankind
Poverty married genius
They had numerous offspring, but all were blind or maimed or tinged with melancholia.
He brought a child, a laughing odd imp he called Whimsicality
But one fine day G[enius] divorced her husband. She had borne too long his insults and reproached, threats of suicide—and returned to her first husband the devil. He had always suspected her of bigamy although she had produced a certificate of her husband's death. But before her final desertion genius made the acquaintance of another genius, who was wedded to prosperity—and being invited to their table he succeeded in making her a harlot, and he unfaithful to his wife and she to her husband—they finally eloped.
He accused her of bigamy and invented the devil as her husband.

He brought a child Whims[icality] whose features were like his and asked her to look after it. She discovered his liaison with P[overty] and immediately divorced him'

195 *Van Eyck*. Jan van Eyck (*c*.1395–1441), Flemish painter.M

201 *patience was a crime*. Following this in the TS are the excised lines:
'Through a mutual friend he was introduced to a clever young poet, Leonard Harris, who had recently published some exuberant erotic poems a la Wilde & Swinburne, & Harris had invited him to supper without having seen him yet. Rudolph on receiving the invitation had no idea of what an invitation to a wealthy supper meant, or he would have sooner thought of dropping through a chimney pot than going. He expected just to have a chat with Harris at his bachelor chambers and regale. But when the bell rang for supper, to be introduced formally to each individual member of the family, to concentrate all his divine energies on what to do with the strange thing he surmised was a napkin; talk, while wondering whether the small fork ought to be used or the big one, & guiltily change it again when after glancing furtively to see what the others were doing, he discovered he was wrong; to feel the servant watching him in sublime contempt; yes, he could feel the superb pity in her voice when she asked him whether he wanted Claret or [
At home he always had his meals alone. He had never mixed with people there or elsewhere, consequently, the supper was an event to him. How had he acquitted himself. In the small talk of table, superficial wit might easily pass as genuine as long as it full-filled the purpose [   ] laugh . . . '

203 *Uncle's Impressions in the Woods at Night*. Written?1911–12.

204 *The Slade and its Relations to the Universe*. Written 1911 or 1912.
Additional notes on this piece, include: 'We have seen how planted by the impressionists & the desire to express & interpret life as it appealed to the emotion, to give a perception not a conception, the seed had taken root & finally flourished, grown into a tall stately tree beneath which all new movements take shelter.
As a cradle for ideas
A reaction against tradition'

the Slade. Founded in 1871 as part of University College, London, and noted for its emphasis on life study rather than the traditional drawing from the antique. The high quality of its teaching attracted many important young painters.

Gower St[reet]. The street in Bloomsbury where University College, London—of which the Slade is a part—is situated.

205 *The Slade and Modern Culture*. Written 1911 or 1912.

Whistler. James McNeill Whistler (1834–1903), American-born painter and engraver who worked all his adult life in Europe. In 1877 he was involved in a famous libel case with the painter and critic John Ruskin (1819–1900) who, on seeing Whistler's work *Nocturne in Black and Gold: the Falling Rocket* (1875), fulminated against him for 'flinging a pot of paint in the public's face'. Whistler, who won, was awarded only a farthing in damages and became bankrupt.

206 *The Pre-Raphaelite Exhibition: Notes for an Article.* Written late 1911 or early 1912. The exhibition, 'Works by English Pre-Raphaelite Painters', lent by Birmingham Corporation, was held at the Tate Gallery between 14 Dec. 1911 and 31 March 1912.

In 1848, a group of originally three (later increased to seven) formed a group calling itself the Pre-Raphaelite Brotherhood. Believing that painters should work direct from nature, and wishing to return to the clear, crystalline colours of medieval painting, they saw that the influence of Raphael in particular had perpetuated a soulless, mannered and academic approach; for, as Ruskin had expressed it in *Modern Painters* (1846), 'the mindless copyist studies Raffaelle, but not what Raffaelle studied'. Raffaello Sanzio, always known as Raphael (1483–1520), was an Italian High Renaissance painter who, with Michelangelo and Leonardo, is considered one of the giants of the Renaissance.

A[lfred] Stevens. (1818–75), English sculptor and painter. The exhibition, 'Works by Alfred Stevens', ran at the Tate from 5 Nov. 1911 to 31 March 1912.

M[ichel] Angelo. On the verso of the MS is a pencil drawing by IR of Adam from Michelangelo's *Creation of Man* on the Sistine Chapel ceiling.

207 *Millais.* John Everett Millais (1829–96), English painter. With Dante Gabriel Rossetti and William Holman Hunt, he was one of the founding members of the PRB. He was later President of the Royal Academy. Many people consider that, though his early work is powerful and exciting, the quality of his later work fell away.

Hughes. Arthur Hughes (1832–1915), English painter associated with the PRB.

One. Dante Gabriel Rossetti (1828–82), English Pre-Raphaelite painter and poet of Italian parentage.

Keats. John Keats (1795–1821), English poet, whose work was the inspiration for early PRB paintings.

Botticelli. Sandro Botticello (1445–1510), Italian early Renaissance painter from Florence. Perhaps his most famous work is *The Birth of Venus* (1482–6) now in the Uffizi.

Lorenzo and Isabel. 'Isabella; or, the Pot of Basil'. Millais' drawing was for his painting entitled 'Isabella' (1848–9).

Rossetti's pen-and-ink drawings for Tennyson. A series of drawings illustrating the work of Alfred Tennyson (1809–92), English Poet Laureate appointed in 1850.

Millais' 'Mariana at the Moated Grange'. Tennyson's poem entitled 'Mariana' which was influenced by Keats's 'Isabella; or, the Pot of Basil' ll. 233 ff.

208 *Velasquez painted and Rembrandt.* Diego Rodríguez de Silva y Velásquez (1599–1660), Spanish painter; Rembrandt (1606–69), Dutch painter and etcher.

The post-impr[essionists] The title given by the English art critic Roger Fry (1866–1934), to a group of Impressionist painters who, in their later work, moved beyond Impressionism, in particular the French painters Paul Cézanne (1839–1906), Paul Gaugin (1848–1903), and the Dutch-born Vincent Van Gogh (1853–90). Fry mounted immensely influential exhibitions of their work in London in 1910 and 1912.

Simeon Solomon. (1840–1905), Anglo-Jewish painter associated with the PRB, friend of Rossetti and Swinburne.

The Pre-Raphaelites and Imagination in Paint. Date unknown.

209 *Romance at the Baillie Galleries: The Works of J. H. Amschewitz and the late H. Ospovat.* Written in or before May 1912. Pub. *The Jewish Chronicle*, no. 2,251, 24 May 1912, p. 15.

H. Ospovat. Henry Ospovat (1877–1909), painter and illustrator of Russian origin, who settled and worked in London.

portrait of a young poet. A portrait of Rosenberg, painted in January 1911.

Roscius. Quintus Roscius Gallus (*c.*126–62 BC), Roman actor who particularly excelled in comedy.

210 *Fred Walker.* Frederick Walker (1840–75), English painter and illustrator.

211 *Joy.* Written in the summer of 1912. IR sent this to Ruth Löwy, whom he was using as a model for his painting of the same name which he worked on during the summer of 1912. (See a letter postmarked 15 July 1912 to Alice M. Wright on p. 240, and two undated letters to Ruth Löwy of [summer 1912], on pp. 241 and 243). See also 'Returning, we hear the larks'.

Emerson. Written in ?1915.

In a pencil scrap IR writes: 'This man paved the way for Whitman. His freedom, his daring, his inspiration, in Whitman's hands became a roadway right through humanity'.

212 *Art*. Written in the summer–autumn, 1914. Part I. Pub. *South African Women in Council*, vol. II, no. 3, Dec. 1914; Part II. *South African Women in Council*, vol. II, no. 4, Jan. 1915. The journal is advertised as being 'A journal of interest for the cultured woman'. Part II begins at: 'Then we have Michael Angelo'.

With his notes for 'Art' is a piece IR did not use, relating to the Futurists. This reads: 'exuberant vitality—hands that would span coinstaneously the ends of the world, avid to burn up the past, the useless ladders of civilization. | Theirs is an ideal of strength—the old the weak|useless must perish—our world is the beauty of battle of conflict, the triumph of speed, the annihilation of Space, the terribly beauty of the destruction. The leader of this futurist movement—Maronetti—is a remarkable personality, a great poet, who has compelled Europe to side with this excess of energy. It is foolish of me to try to explain what Maronetti does in his wonderful way.'

Further notes to this piece are:
'The revival
A concrete reality
Art does not assist moral valuations
Voluptuous iniquities
... freshness of appreciation to earnestly wrestle
    a higher plane of thought. Abstract ideas
    mere representation.
Nature is concentrated to an abstraction, the essence, it is a reality because it is complete.

Mere representation is unreal because it is a part|fragment, it does not take as it were the body of its new existence in its transmigration into Art.

Mere representation is unreal, is fragmentary. The bone taken from Adam remains a bone. To create is to apply pulsating, rhythmical principles to the part, a unity, another nature is created.

Passivity and detachment
Life becomes common and dull, the mind demands noble excitement.
We respond to colours, form is significant
Harsh and uncompromising.
Art that answers to the need of a lovely withdrawal from life
Music, partakers of the quality of dream from life
All ages have associated beauty with Art
Intensity, nobility of form
Inert, like arid

Vitality comes from genuine ides
vehemence of expression

Modern tendencies. Revival of form.
The Great masterpieces are not related to their age, the pictures as a rule that do reflect their age are quaint, even Velasquez, & in all prob. Degas will be. Michael Ang might have been a Greek. Botticelli Mantegna based themselves on classic art.
Innes in Landscape, perhaps the first English painter to paint far abstractly
After the idealisation of Turner   Chinese and Montegna
Art is symbolic   Select a portion.
Nature is   and applying rhythmical principles a unity, another nature is created
John's first mast[er] Rubens that facile superficial designer, not profound. Already at the Slade he had distinguished in understanding form. Form is the clear expression of the artist's idea of nature, by ingenious lines instinct with meaning his red hot expression'

214 *Blake's*. William Blake (1757–1827), English poet, painter, engraver, and mystic.

215 *Italian Primitives*. Painters of the pre- and early Renaissance, such as Cimabue (1240–1302), Giotto (c.1267–1337), Fra Angelica (1387–1455), Uccello (1397–1475), Piero della Francesca (c.1412–92), Mantegna (1431–1506), Botticelli (1445–1510), and Filipo Lippi (c.1457–1504).

Giotto. Giotto di Bondone (c.1267–1337), Florentine painter, particularly noted for his frescoes, and acknowledged as the greatest painter of the pre-Renaissance.

Leonardo Da Vinci. (1452–1519), Italian painter, sculptor, architect, scientist, engineer, and poet. A polymath of genius, he is considered to have been one of the greatest intellects ever to have lived.

216 *chiaroscuro*. The use of light and dark in a painting, particularly as applied to form.

the Venetians. The early sixteenth century Renaissance painters Giovanni Bellini (c.1430–1516), Giorgione (c.1478–1510), and Titian (c.1477–1576), who transformed the traditional approach to painting by their scale, composition, interest in light and colour, and handling of the new medium of oil paint.

Ingres. Jean Auguste Dominique Ingres (1780–1867), French painter, particularly noted as a draughtsman.

Degas. Edgar Degas (1834–1917), French Impressionist painter.

217 *Monet, Pissarro—and the other French Impressionists.* Claude Monet (1840–1926) French painter and one of the founders of Impressionism; Camille Pissarro (1830–1903), French Impressionist painter particularly noted for his dappled landscapes. The French Impressionists were a loosely bound group of painters, working between 1867 and 1886, who believed in working direct from nature, placing a particular emphasis on the changing quality of light and colour. Realizing that the eye combines colour in a painting as it does in nature, they used primary colours which they laid on in bold, individual strokes.

Futurist. A group of Italian, and later international, poets and painters who turned their back on the past and extolled the virtues of modern, mechanized life. In 1909 their manifesto was published by the Italian writer Filippo Tommaso Marinetti (1876–1944) in which he praised love of danger, speed and violence, glorifying war which he described as 'the world's only hygiene'. Central to their beliefs was the idea that no work without an aggressive character could be a masterpiece. Together with Cubism, Futurism was a major influence on the English Vorticist movement. See note to p. 212.

218 *Gioconda.* The portrait, better known as the Mona Lisa, by Leonardo which hangs in the Louvre.

Albrecht Dürer. (1471–1528), German painter and engraver, particularly noted for his draughtsmanship and depiction of the minute details of nature.

Gainsborough. Thomas Gainsborough (1727–88), English painter and early exponent of landscape painting.

Turner and Constable. Joseph Mallord William Turner (1775–1851), English painter who was particularly interested in the effects of light, considered by many, though not IR, to be the greatest English painter; John Constable (1776–1837), English landscape painter.

Augustus John. (1878–1961), English painter, who had studied at the Slade (1894–9), particularly praised for his draughtsmanship.

219 *Legros.* Alphonse Legros (1837–1911), French-born painter who in 1876 became an influential Professor of Fine Art at the Slade. He was particularly interested in the developments of modern French art.

Flaxman. John Flaxman (1755–1826), English sculptor and engraver who was appointed the Royal Academy of Arts' first Professor of Sculpture in 1810. Only two years older than Blake, he was a friend rather than teacher.

Leighton, Watts. Frederic, Lord Leighton (1830–96), English painter, particularly of Orientalist scenes, he was appointed President of the

Royal Academy in 1878 and was the only British painter to have been given a peerage; George Frederick Watts (1817–1904), English painter and sculptor, associated with the Aesthetic Movement.

Rubens, Vandyke, Watteau. Peter Paul Rubens (1577–1640), Flemish Baroque painter; Anthony Van Dyck (1599–1641), Flemish-born painter, and student of Rubens, Van Dyck settled in England in 1632 where he became painter to the Court of Charles I; Antoine Watteau (1684–1721), French Rococo painter.

220 *Dickens' slime and slush.* Charles Dickens (1812–70), English novelist.

Baudelaire published 'The Flowers of Evil', Swinburne his ballads, and Meredith 'Modern Love'. Charles Baudelaire (1821–67). His most famous work was *Les Fleurs du Mal* (1857), as a result of which not only the author, but also the printer and publisher, were found guilty of obscenity and blasphemy. As a result of its translation into German, he has been described as one of the founding fathers of modern German poetry; Algernon Charles Swinburne (1837–1909), English poet. George Meredith (1828–1909) English poet.

Manet. Edouard Manet (1832–83), French painter, generally regarded as the founder of Impressionism.

Puvis de Chavannes. Peter Puvis de Chavannes (1824–98), French painter and co-founder of the Société National des Beaux-Arts in Paris in 1862.

Wilson Steer, Professor Brown, Sargent, Walter Sickert, Henry Tonks. Philip Wilson Steer (1860–1942), English painter; Frederick Brown (1851–1941), English painter, Professor of Fine Art at the Slade from 1882 to 1917; John Singer Sargent (1856–1925), English painter, particularly of portraits now described as 'Swagger'; Walter Sickert (1860–1942), English painter and one of the leaders of the Camden Town Group, renowned for his paintings of domestic and music hall interiors; Henry Tonks (1862–1937), English painter. He trained as a doctor, studying drawing in his spare time, and was invited by Frederick Brown to join the staff of the Slade, becoming Professor of Fine Art in 1917.

Clausen. George Clausen (1852–1944), English painter of Dutch parentage. He was a founder member of the New English Art Club, and in 1906 became Professor of Painting at the Royal Academy. One of his most famous paintings is *Youth Mourning* painted in 1916 in response to the losses on the Western Front. It hangs now in the Imperial War Museum.

Vermeer and Van Hooch, William Rothenstein, Orpen and Walter Russell. Johannes Vermeer (?1632–75), Flemish painter, particularly of finely detailed domestic interiors; Pieter de Hooch (1629–84), Flemish painter, particularly of domestic interiors, said to have influenced Vermeer; William Rothenstein (1872–1945), English painter, he was Principal of the Royal College of Art from 1920 to 1935, and an official war artist in both world wars; William Orpen (1878–1931), Irish painter and Great War artist; Walter Westley Russell (1867–1949), English painter and illustrator.

Henry Lamb. (1883–1960), English painter and member of the Camden Town Group. He was an official War Artist, 1916–18.

Innes. James Dickson Innes (1887–1914), Welsh landscape painter of Scottish parentage.

Mark Gertler. (1891–1939), English painter of East End Jewish immigrant parents from Poland, Gertler was a friend of IR from Whitechapel, and a fellow student at the Slade. A pacifist and conscientious objector, his 1916 painting, *The Merry-Go-Round*, now in the Tate Gallery, is thought by many to be the most important painting to have come out of the Great War.

John Currie. (1884–1914), English painter and fellow student of IR at the Slade.

221 *David Bomberg.* (1890–1957), English painter. Born in Birmingham, he grew up in Whitechapel, where IR met him at the Whitechapel Library. He was a fellow student of IR at the Slade. His painting of IR, entitled 'Head of a Poet', was awarded the Henry Tonks Prize for 1913. It was sold for $10 in the John Quinn Collection Sale at the American Art Association in New York in Feb. 1927, and has since disappeared.

Roberts. William Roberts (1895–1980), English painter, founder member of the Vorticist Group and official Great War artist.

Stanley Spencer. (1891–1959), English painter and fellow student of IR at the Slade. In 1915 he enlisted in the RAMC and was sent out to Salonika, transferring to the infantry in 1917. In 1918 he was asked to paint a picture 'under such title as "A Religious Service at the Front" or any subjects in or about Salonika', but it was not until after the Armistice that he worked on 'Travoys arriving with wounded at a dressing station at Smol, Macedonia (September 1916)', his most celebrated war picture. After the war he painted a series of important murals for the Sandham Memorial Chapel at Burghclere in Hampshire. Depicting everyday scenes from military life, they culminated with an altarpiece entitled 'Resurrection of the Soldiers'. He was again a war artist in the Second World War. See also note to p. 248.

[*"Realism and Imagination in Paint"*. In a letter to Laurence Binyon of 18 Nov. 1919, Winifreda Seaton says that she is enclosing a short prose essay on "Realism and Imagination in Paint" which IR had sent to her with a letter. This essay does not appear to have survived.]

We are not affected by Art in the same way as life. Date unknown.

After 'the connection would be difficult to trace', one MS draft has a final sentence: 'The artist intuitively apprehends them, transfers it dramatically, disguised, and renamed objectives. Some artists take a delight in showing their ingenuity this way, but as a rule, what is gained is loss.'

Elsewhere, on a scrap, IR notes: 'Art affects us. | The senses respond to colours. Form has a more significant interest for the mind.'

222 *Vitality is a necessary consequence*. Date unknown.

An artist who depends on his art. Date unknown.

Art to be great. Written in ?1913.

The ultimate end of all the arts should be beauty. Date unknown.

This was written as an addendum to another piece which is now lost. At the top of the holograph is the note: Insert after 'beauty being its aim & ends'.

We have hints, suggestions. Date unknown.

223 *An age that believes in Blake and tolerates Tennyson*. Written ?between June 1914 and Feb. 1915.

Pope. Alexander Pope (1688–1744), English neoclassical poet and satirist.

'Crossing the Bar'. Written in ?1913.

224 *Hidden in air, in nature, are unexplored powers*. Date unknown.

Luther. Martin Luther (1483–1546), German theologian. In Oct. 1517, he nailed his Ninety-five Theses, critical of aspects of the Church's teaching, especially the selling of indulgences, to the door of the castle church in Wittenberg, setting in motion the Reformation.

Darwin. Charles Darwin (1809–82), English naturalist and author of the *Origin of Species by Means of Natural Selection* (1859), which set out his theory of evolution.

Marlowe. Christopher Marlowe (1564–93), English poet and dramatist. His play *Tamburlaine the Great* (1587), based on the story of the Mongol conqueror Tamberlane (1336–1405), depicts a Scythian shepherd who, in Part I, shows the Renaissance qualities of courage, freedom, and bold defiance, but in Part II is destroyed by his cruelty and lust for power.

Nietzsche. Frederick Nietzsche (1844–1900), German philosopher and creator of the theory of the superman.

the last vivid word. Date unknown.

Speech\Language is the mask. Date unknown.

Lack of depth. Probably written in 1911 or 1912.

We never excuse the absolute want of spirit. Written in ?1913.

Very few people say what they mean
On the same page are the notes:
  The sustained seriousness demanded [. . .]
  He knew no people—he did not talk—bought women only wish left him
  As he stood over her an irresistible feeling to crush her in his arms.
  She was proud, talked of intellectual women.
  He would not see her again—it was not fair to his feelings—if he dared not make love

225 *Poor people are born in troubles.* Written in ?1915.

Youth is still childhood. Written ?autumn 1912.

Sometimes in listening to a man. Written ?1915.

Conversation on trial of car. Written in ?1913.

'How are you getting on with the picture?' Written in?1913.

If there must be a quarrel. Written ?between June 1915 and Feb. 1915. Edward Roworth (1880–1964), South African painter.

226 *LSW. I beg to state.* Written in May or June 1916.
      This altercation relates to an incident that occurred when IR was travelling from Frimley, near Aldershot, to Waterloo in mid-May 1916.

LSW. London and South West Railway Company.

2/7. Two shillings and seven pence.

LETTERS

227 *Winifreda Seaton.* IR was introduced to Miss Winifreda Seaton, a middle-aged school mistress, by Amschewitz in, or shortly before, 1910. She encouraged his interest in poetry, introducing him to the work of Donne. His letters to her now appear to be lost, but those that were published in *1922*, many only as extracts, show a stimulating and lively correspondence.

this fiendish mangling-machine. From Jan. 1905 until Jan. 1911 IR was apprenticed to Carl Hentschel, a Fleet Street engraver, work that he hated.

228 *the——shop.* See note above.

229 *Byron.* Lord Byron (1788–1814), English poet and hero of the Greek War of Independence.

Donne. John Donne (1572–1631), English Metaphysical poet, a volume of whose poems IR took into the army with him. In a letter to Laurence Binyon of 18 Nov. 1919, Miss Seaton says: '[IR] grew to care for Donne almost as much as I do [. . .] and I remember a note of his beginning "You cruel girl, what have you done with my Donne?", when I kept an old and rather curious copy he picked up somewhere, and was in the habit of looking into every day.' It is impossible to know the sequence of IR's responses to Donne in his letters to Miss Seaton.

My Hood. Thomas Hood (1799–1845), the English poet and humorist whose most famous composition was 'The Song of the Shirt'.

230 *his poem to Donne.* Ben Jonson (1573–1637), English playwright and poet. His poem is entitled 'To John Donne'.

231 *Whitechapel Gallery.* The Whitechapel Art Gallery, opened in 1901, was founded by the social reformer, Revd Samuel Augustus Barnett, vicar of St Jude's church, Whitechapel, who wished to 'bring great art to the people of the East End of London' by exhibiting old masters alongside contemporary work. The gallery was financed by the philanthropist and newspaper magnate John Passsmore Edwards, who was also responsible for the earlier, adjoining Whitechapel Library, an important meeting place for the young intelligentsia of the East End, including IR. Opened in 1892, it became known as 'the university of the ghetto'. In 1937, the Whitechapel hosted a Memorial Exhibition for IR, opened by Sir Edward Marsh. The paintings to which IR refers here were in the 'Shakespeare Memorial and Theatrical Exhibition' which was opened by Sir Herbert Tree on 11 Oct. 1910.

Re[y]nolds and Hogarths. There is Hogarth's Peg Woffington. Joshua Reynolds (1723–92), portrait painter and first President of the Royal Academy of Arts on its foundation in 1768. William Hogarth (1697–1764), painter and engraver. Margaret (Peg) Woffington (1720?–60) was the actress, particularly of Shakespearean parts, who acted opposite David Garrick (1717–79).

Dr Eder. Dr David Eder, a psychiatrist and cousin of Israel Zangwill, to whom IR was introduced by the painter John H. Amschewitz.

232 *Crashaw.* Richard Crashaw (1612–49), English metaphysical poet.

'Kubla Khan'... Verlaine. 'Kubla Khan', the poem by the English poet, Samuel Taylor Coleridge (1772–1834); 'The Mistress of Vision', 'Dream-Tryst': poems by the English poet Francis Thompson (1859–1907), whose work IR particularly admired; Edgar Allan Poe (1809–49), American poet and short-story writer. His most famous poem 'The Raven', was published in 1845. In ?March 1912, IR wrote a poem 'To Michael Sherbrooke on Hearing his Recitation of the "Raven". Poe'; Paul Verlaine (1844–96), French poet who was associated with the early Symbolists, a group of French poets who were writing in the last three decades of the nineteenth century. They sought, by suggestion and evocation rather than objective description, to counter the influence of the realist school of writing, finding their truth in the inner life.

Sterne says. Laurence Sterne (1713–68), English novelist, author of *Tristram Shandy* and *A Sentimental Journey.*

233 *Flint's poems.* Frank Stewart Flint (1885–1960), English poet, authority on contemporary French poetry and a contributor to Ezra Pound's 1914 anthology *Des Imagistes.* His first volume of poetry was *The Net of Stars*, published in 1909, from which these poems come. The theme of the stanza from which IR quotes is joy.

234 *a painting to 'La Belle dame Sans Merci'.* Based on the poem by Keats.

Israel Zangwill. Israel Zangwill (1864–1926), Anglo-Jewish writer and political activist, particularly noted as a writer about East End life, including his novel *Children of the Ghetto* (1892). When IR was dismissed by Hentschel, Zangwill wrote to ask if he would be prepared to re-employ him, enclosing one of IR's pencil drawings as 'proof of the artistic powers of the sketcher'. He told Hentschel that IR was finding it difficult to get work and his family depended on him. 'He has sent me a batch of compositions in prose and verse, besides his sketch, all showing artistic faculty, so that he ought to be more valuable in your work than the average apprentice.' For the full text of the letter see *JMW*, p. 108. Although he showed little interest in IR while he was alive, in 1922 he wrote to Joseph Leftwich: 'I wonder now that Rosenberg was not brought more to my attention, though I fancy my brother Mark once showed me a little printed volume by which I was very much struck' (quoted in *JMW*, p. 407 n. 57).

236 *English Review.* Quality literary journal founded in Dec. 1908 by Ford Maddox Hueffer (1873–1939), an English novelist of German parentage who changed his name to Ford Maddox Ford.

Austin Harrison (1873–1928), editor of the *English Review* between 1910 and 1923.

your encouraging reply to my poetical efforts. Probably a copy of *Night and Day*. Laurence Binyon (1869–1943), poet and author of 'To the Fallen', wrote the Introductory Memoir to the first edition of IR's poems published in 1922. Binyon's letter with its encouraging reply has not survived, but in his memoir Binyon writes: 'It was impossible not to be struck by something unusual in the quality of the poems. Thoughts and emotions of no common nature struggle for expression, and at times there gushed forth a pure song which haunted the memory.' Binyon recalled that IR first wrote to him some time in 1912. He was Assistant Keeper of Prints and Drawings at the British Museum, where IR went to meet him. See also note to p. 299.

'Beata Beatrix'. The painting 'Beata Beatrix' (*c*.1864–70), symbolizing the death of Dante's Beatrice. Rossetti conceived the painting as a memorial to his wife, Elizabeth Siddall, who died in 1862. It hangs in the Tate Gallery, London.

Lippi Lippi. Fra Fillipo Lippi (1406–69), Florentine painter of the Quattrocentro.

237 *Francis Thompson*. See note at *'Kubla Khan'* on p. 413.

238 *I could write Art articles*. In 1906–11 Binyon had been art critic on the *Saturday Review*.

Mr Picciotto. Cyril M. Picciotto, whose book on mysticism, *Via Mystica*, was published in 1912. His wife was first cousin to Ruth Löwy. With C. M. Kohan, he edited the booklet, *A Piece of Mosaic*, privately printed for a Palestine Bazaar in London on 13 May 1912, in which IR published ll. 152–7 of 'Night and Day'.

the poem I sent you. 'A Ballad of Whitechapel'. The lines he mentions are 37–44.

sent me into ecstasies. This complaint is echoed in his ironic comments on the printer of *Moses*. See postcard to Marsh postmarked 19 May 1916, p. 294.

239 *Michael Sherbrooke*. See note to poem 'To Michael Sherbrooke on hearing his recitation of the "Raven". Poe' on p. 375.

Pre-Raphaelite show at the Tate. See 'The Pre-Raphaelite Exhibition: Notes for an Article' on pp. 206–8.

Miss Wright. Alice M. Wright was IR's teacher at Birkbeck. As well as teaching him painting, she encouraged his love of poetry, inviting him to her house where she and her sister, Lilian, discussed his work and gave him copies of Blake and Shelley. In 1908 Alice Wright published *English Nature Poems: an anthology*.

NOTES TO PAGES 240-7 415

240 *Birkbeck.* Birkbeck College is part of the University of London, specializing in part-time degrees. Rosenberg was a student there from 1905. See 'Chronology'.

'Joy'. See note to poem 'Returning, we hear the larks'. The painting was exhibited at the IR Memorial Exhibition at the Whitechapel in 1937, when it was bought for one hundred guineas; its present whereabouts are not known.

your poem. 'The Mirror'.

242 *the speech by Beatrice about death.* In *The Cenci, A Tragedy in Five Acts* (1820), V. iv. 48–74, by Percy Bysshe Shelley (1792–1822).

243 *copies of my poems. Night and Day*, published in the spring or early summer of 1912.

244 *When Milton writes on his blindness.* John Milton (1608–74), English poet, 'On His Blindness', Sonnet XIX.

?26 Sept. 1912. DH in *1937* (p. 333) gives this as a probable date, but does not say why.

245 *a poem I wrote.* DH notes in *1937* (p. 336) that two poems were enclosed: '[We are sad with a vague sweet sorrow]' and 'Spring'.

confusion about paying the Slade fees. Mrs Herbert Cohen was financing Rosenberg's studies at the Slade. Before the 1912–13 session she sent him a cheque which was five shillings short. Rosenberg did not immediately send this on to the college, who, to her immense irritation, contacted Mrs Cohen to find out why the fees had not been paid. Rosenberg, meanwhile, had written to her asking for the extra money. The letter containing the request was smudged, a sloppiness that further angered her.

247 *Newbolt.* Henry Newbolt (1862–1938), English poet, particularly of patriotic poems.

fair to Bomberg. This relates to an incident when Brown had criticized Bomberg's work, and Bomberg had struck him with a palette.

when you see my work?. Something of what Mrs Cohen may have had in mind is reflected in a letter to Binyon, dated 28 April 1921, from the painter Frank Emanuel: 'I always regretted that (with the sole desire of helping him) certain of his friends decided to send him to the Slade School—at this time enveloped in an extremely nasty and unhealthy "atmosphere". The art produced there was morbid, artificial and unclean and the influence has not even yet dissipated itself. The influence was bad for any young artist and doubly so for the already socialistic East End boys, who really required honest fresh air and sunshine let into their work and their lives to make their lives and their achievements healthier and happier. At the Slade stage scenery was preferred to nature, ugliness, sordidness and disease was preferred in it models—to beauty and health and cleanliness.'

248   *The 'Nativity' took the prize.* 'John Donne arriving in Heaven' by Stanley Spencer (1891–1959), a nativity scene set in Cookham, depicting divine events unfolding within contemporary life. The painting was exhibited between 5 Oct. and 31 Dec. that year in Roger Fry's Second Post-Impressionist Exhibition at the Grafton Galleries, and hangs now in the Fitzwilliam Museum in Cambridge.

The Pro. Professor Henry Tonks. See note to p. 220.

New English. The New English Art Club was founded in 1885 as an alternative and challenge to the Royal Academy. IR's drawing entitled 'Sanguine Drawing' was accepted for the winter exhibition, which opened at the end of Nov., and sold for £4.

Hampstead Rd. In 1912 IR moved out of his family home into rooms in north London. To begin with, in mid-July, he moved to 32 Carlingford Road, Hampstead. In Oct. or Nov., unable to afford the rent, he returned home. At some point he moved briefly to Hampstead Road. This is close to Euston mainline railway station; the railway lines run beneath it at one point. By Dec., he had found more satisfactory rooms at St George's Square, Regents Park.

MacEvoy. Ambrose McEvoy (1878–1927), painter who trained at the Slade and was elected to the New English Art Club in 1900. He was on the selection committee in 1912.

249   *the committee.* The Education Aid Society, also known as The Jewish Education Aid Society, which functioned between 1896 and 1948, giving grants to Jewish students. They approved IR's application, guaranteeing his fees at the Slade until March 1914. Ernest Lesser was the secretary of the Society, which supported a number of requests from IR, including paying his fare to South Africa in June 1914.

Quarrelling. See prose fragment on pp. 225–6.

the £4 I shall get for my drawing. See note to the *New English* above.

250   *I enclose another poem.* *1937* notes (p. 338) that this is '[O'er the celestial pathways the mortal and immortal strays]'.

the last one. *1937* notes (p. 338) that this is 'The Poet'.

251   *I shall be living in Fitzroy St.* IR did not move to Fitzrovia. See also note to p. 313.

on the other side. *1937* notes (p. 339) that this is a copy of 'Peace'.

this competition. The Prix de Rome, In order to qualify for consideration, candidates had to be British subjects. IR's uncertainty about this arose because of his parentage; however, he was born in England and was a British subject. The Prix de Rome was an annual competition in which the winners received £200 per annum and free study at the British School in Rome.

252 *send them to Exhibitions.* IR is talking of sending them in to independent exhibitions, but, before that, all the paintings submitted for the Prix de Rome were exhibited at the Imperial Institute Galleries in Exhibition Row, South Kensington.

the Society. The Jewish Educational Aid Society.

somewhere on the South Coast. At the end of Feb. 1914 IR spent a week in the seaside resort of Bournemouth.

should have done so. In fact, in 1913 the Slade student Colin Gill (1892–1940), won the Prix de Rome. At the outbreak of war he volunteered and went to France in the Royal Artillery. In 1916 he was transferred to the Royal Engineers as a camouflage officer, and became an official war artist in 1918. In a letter to Marsh of [Aug. 1916], IR made enquiries about the possibility of working on camouflage.

253 *F. Thompson's 'Dream tryst'.* See note to p. 232.

a small book of contemporary Belgian poetry. Contemporary Belgian Poetry, selected and translated by Jethro Bithell (1911). Maurice Maeterlinck (1862–1949), Belgian poet and dramatist, and winner, in 1911, of the Nobel Prize for Literature, influenced by both the Pre-Raphaelites and the French Symbolists. *Emile Verhaeern* (1855–1916), Belgian poet who was one of the founders of the Symbolist movement. A pacifist before the war, he wrote passionately about Belgium's plight after the invasion, including a poem 'Germany, Exterminator of Races'.

The Blakes at the Tate. The exhibition, 'Works by William Blake', was at the Tate Gallery between 15 Oct. 1913 and 18 Jan. 1914.

254 *I will go to Africa.* Rosenberg's sister, Minnie, had married Wolf Horvitch in Aug. 1913 and moved to Cape Town, South Africa with her husband. His father's older brother, Peretz Rosenberg, was a well-known rabbi in Cape Town and Johannesburg.

E[ducation].A[id].S[ociety]. See note to p. 249 (*the committee*).

a relation in Cape Town. See note above (*I will go to Africa*).

Whitechapel show. On 8 May 1914 an exhibition opened at the Whitechapel Art Gallery entitled 'Twentieth Century Art: A Review of Modern Movements'. Aimed at showing 'the progress of art' since

Impressionism, it included a specifically Jewish section, curated by David Bomberg. IR exhibited *Portrait of the Artist's Father*, *The Murder of Lorenzo*, *Head of a Girl*, *The Judgement of Paris*, and *Portrait*.

255 *my drawing printed in your book*. At the suggestion of Stanley Spencer, since February Marsh had been contemplating producing a book entitled *Georgian Drawings*, a companion to *Georgian Poetry*. It would contain fifty reproductions by twenty unknown artists, many of them IR's contemporaries at the Slade. It was to be published by subscription, but, partly as a result of the outbreak of war, it failed to obtain enough subscribers, and it never appeared.

one must either do cubism. Cubism was a school of art that began in Paris in 1907, and was characterized by the flattening and reduction of objects and figures to basic geometric forms. Its most important exponents were the Spanish painter Pablo Picasso (1881–1973) and the French painter Georges Braques (1882–1963).

256 *the lines I lately wrote*. The poem is no longer with the letter, but it is probably 'Midsummer Frost'.

Mrs Löwy. See note to 'To Mr and Mrs Löwy, on their Silver Wedding' on p. 371.

257 *the restaurant*. The Café Royal in Regent Street, London where Marsh regularly lunched.

the book. *Georgian Poetry 1911–1912*, published in Dec. 1912.

the Queen's Song of Flecker. James Elroy Flecker (1884–1915), English poet and dramatist. His hugely popular *Collected Poems* were published in 1916, but he is perhaps best known for his play *Hassan* (1922). 'The Queen's Song' was first published in *Forty-Two Poems* in 1911.

'The end of the world' by Bottomley. Gordon Bottomley (1874–1948), English poet and dramatist, was one of the leading Georgian poets. He first became aware of IR's work when he was sent copies of *Youth* and *Moses* by Lascelles Abercrombie in 1916, and became one of IR's most loyal supporters, editing the first collection of his poems in 1922, and collaborating with D. W. Harding in edition *1937*. His letters and encouragement were of immense importance to IR. They never met; ill health prevented him travelling far from his home, 'The Sheiling', Silverdale, Lancashire. 'The End of the World', was first published in *Chambers of Imagery: Second Series* in 1912.

258 *my poem*. 'Midsummer Frost'. Line 3 originally read 'How, like a sad thought buried in light woven words'.

259 *your friend.* See note to Stanley below.

Stanley. JMW (p. 213) suggests that this is Sir Herbert Stanley, who had gone to South Africa in 1910 as secretary to the Governor General, Viscount Gladstone. Marsh had given IR an introduction to Stanley, who had paid IR £15 for the portrait of his daughters.

260 *a series of lectures on modern art.* See pp. 212–21. These were published in *South African Women in Council: A Journal Of Interest For The Cultured Woman* (Cape Town), in two parts, in vol. 2, no. 3, Dec. 1914 and vol. 2, no. 4, Jan. 1915.

the Futurists. See note to pp. 217–18. The Futurists shared nothing with the early twentieth-century Royal Academy, the kind of institution that was anathema to them.

Paul Cézanne (1839–1906), French Post-Impressionist painter; *Vincent Van Gogh* (1853–90), Dutch-born member of the Post-Impressionist Movement. At the end of the letter, IR has written the word 'Epstein', intending to speak about him also. *Jacob Epstein* (1880–1959), was an American-born sculptor, the son of Polish Jewish immigrants, who worked mainly in England. For details of the other artists, see note to 'Art' on pp. 406–9. For Picasso see note to p. 225.

printing it in a local paper. See note to *a series of lectures on modern art* above.

261 *Tennyson's 'Battle in the Air'.* From 'Locksley Hall' ll. 119–28.

an exploring expedition to the North Pole. IR is probably referring to the expedition of Ernest Shackleton (1874–1922), who had left England for the South Pole on 1 Aug. 1914.

hotter places than this. In Oct. 1914 Rupert Brooke (1887–1915) had taken part, with the Royal Naval Division, in the ill-fated Antwerp expedition.

262 *Duncan Grant's dance.* Duncan Grant (1885–1978), Scottish painter and member of the Bloomsbury Group. His painting *Dancers* (1910–11) is now in the Tate.

Cokeham. Stanley Spencer who lived and painted in the riverside village of Cookham in Berkshire had the nickname 'Cookham'. See note to p. 248. His brother was the artist Gilbert Spencer (1892–1979) who had studied at the Slade, and, like Stanley, was a Royal Academician. I have been unable to discover the reason for his good fortune.

the last thing. JC (p. 109) reads this as 'the best thing'.

Sir John Molteno. (1814–96), first Prime Minister of Cape Colony.

264 *a dear friend of hers.* Olive Schreiner (1855–1920), South African writer and author of *The Story of an African Farm* (1883); the 'dear friend' is Miss Molteno, daughter of Sir John Molteno.

Lascelles Abercrombie. See note to *New Numbers* below.

the poem I like best. 'God Made Blind'.

265 *the 'Georgian book'. Georgian Poetry 1911–1912.*

New Numbers. Poetry magazine edited by Wilfrid Wilson Gibson (1878–1962) and Lascelles Abercrombie (1881–1938), in the Gloucestershire village of Dymock; there were four numbers, published in Feb., April, Aug., and Dec. 1914. The group, now known as the Dymock Poets, also comprised John Drinkwater (1882–1937), Rupert Brooke (1887–1915), Edward Thomas (1878–1917), and the American poet Robert Frost (1874–1963). Abercrombie's play *The Olympians* was published in the Feb. 1914 number.

Chambers of Imagery. Chambers of Imagery: First Series (1907), *Second Series* (1912).

266 *L. Douglas' sonnets.* Lord Alfred Douglas (1870–1945), whose *Sonnets* were published in 1900.

Goethe. Johann Wolfgang von Goethe (1749–1832), German poet, playwright, and novelist.

your London poem. A scrap in Miss Seaton's writing, among the Horwitch papers in IWM reads:

LONDON

Let but thy wicked men from out thee go,
        And the fools that crowd thee so—
    Even thou, who dost thy millions boast,
A village less than Islington will grow,
        A solitude almost.

my play. IR's first play, *Moses,* was not published until the summer of 1916, but there is evidence that he was working on it before leaving Cape Town in Feb. 1915 (see note to p. 155).

267 *Youth.* Published in 1915. See Appendix.

268 *Mr Shiff.* IR spelt his name both Shiff and Schiff; the latter is correct. Sydney Schiff (1868–1944) was a writer, translator, and publisher, using the pen name Stephen Hudson. IR met him through Gertler. He was generous to struggling young artists and writers, sending IR both money and artists' materials, and maintaining a correspondence with him until his death.

Alice Meynell. Alice Meynell (1847–1922), English poet and essayist.

269 *giving me this chance to print.* Marsh had financed the printing of *Youth*.

270 *Meredith's 'Lark ascending'.* 'The Lark Ascending' by George Meredith (1828–1909) was published in *Poems and Lyrics of the Joy of Earth* (1883). The first line should read: 'And every face to watch him raised'.

271 *I am so sorry.* Marsh's close friend Rupert Brooke died from blood poisoning on 23 April 1915, on his way to the Dardanelles.

Emerson's poems. Ralph Waldo Emerson (1803–82), American poet for whose work IR had a particular respect. See his essay 'Emerson' on pp. 211–12.

disturb you at such a time with pictures. Desperate for money, IR had turned up unannounced at Raymond Buildings, bringing with him some pictures he hoped Marsh might buy.

273 *poem on death.* 'The Soldier'.

poem on the nativity. 'The Masque of the Magi'.

274 *some people killed.* London suffered its first air attack at the end of May 1915.

I've torn out a page in the book. IR removed pages 11 and 12 containing the section 'The Cynics Lamp' because he considered the poems below standard; these were 'Love and Lust', 'In Piccadilly', and 'A Mood'.

Clutton Brock. Arthur Clutton Brock (1868–1924), critic, essayist, and journalist.

275 *Gertler has a remarkable painting at N[ew].E[nglish].* This was either a portrait of the Hon. Dorothy Brett, a fellow student at the Slade, or a double portrait of a man and wife, entitled *Rabbi and Rabbitzen*, a work on paper.

B. Shaw. George Bernard Shaw (1856–1950). Irish-born playwright.

Gaudier's work. Henri Gaudier-Brzeska (1891–1915). French sculptor who came to England in 1911 and became part of the Vorticist movement with Ezra Pound and Wyndham Lewis. At the outbreak of war he returned to fight in the French army, and was killed on 5 June 1915.

sending my things to America. Ezra Pound sent copies of 'At Night', 'Savage Song' [*Moses* ll. 165–76], and possibly other poems, to Harriet Monroe, editor of the American journal *Poetry: A Magazine of Verse* in the early summer of 1915 (see note to poem 'Marching—as seen from the left file'). In a letter received by Monroe on 20 Sept. 1915, Pound mentions these two poems, and also suggests that they give *Youth* a review. It is not known if IR ever sent a completed letter to Pound.

276 *evening school*. In the autumn of 1915 IR briefly attended evening classes in block-making.

278 *Reply to*. The letter is written on headed YMCA writing-paper; the words in italics are printed. A number of IR's letters were written on this paper; where this is so in the letters that follow, only IR's own writing is given in the heading.

joined the Bantaams. Formed after the outbreak of war in 1914, the Bantam Battalions were made up of men who failed to reach the required physical standard for the British Army. To qualify, they had to be not less than 5 feet and not more than 5 feet 3 inches tall. The 12th (Service) Battalion (East Anglia), to which IR was sent, had been formed in July 1915; in Nov. of that year it was attached to the 121st Brigade, 40th Division.

Falstaff's scarecrows. Shakespeare. *1 Henry IV*, IV. ii: 'If I'm not ashamed of my soldiers, I am a soused gurnet [...] No eye hath seen such scarecrows.'

279 *Can you tell me anything of Gertler*. Gertler was a pacifist and, after the introduction of conscription in Dec. 1915, a conscientious objector. Called before a tribunal, he was granted exemption from military service on medical grounds.

280 *your present*. On 8 Nov., Schiff had sent IR 10 shillings, as he did on 8 Dec.

Browne's 'Religion De Medici'. Sir Thomas Browne (1605–82), English writer and Scholar. His *Religio Medici* was published in 1643.

281 *an invalid in the blue uniform*. Wounded soldiers undergoing medical treatment wore a uniform of blue suit, white shirt, and red tie.

282 *a short drama. Moses*.

283 *the author of Erebus. Lyrics: by the Author of 'Erebus'*, was published in 1906. The author was Evangeline Ryves, whose book *Erebus: A Book of Verse* had been published anonymously in 1903. In his reply, GB suggests that IR may be thinking of *Eremus: a poem* (1894) by Stephen Phillips (1864–1915). See also letter to GB postmarked 31 May 1917 on p. 334.

284 *I sent pictures to the New English*. IR had three pictures accepted: two paintings, 'Grey and Red' and 'The Family of Adam'; and one drawing.

Winston Churchill's change. Marsh had been Private Secretary to Winston Churchill (1874–1965) as First Lord of the Admiralty. Churchill was the moving voice behind the decision to open up a second front by forcing the Dardanelles, but in May 1915, following the failure of the naval attacks and the landing of the expeditionary force, the First Sea Lord, Admiral Lord Fisher, resigned. Churchill was removed from the Admiralty and the War Council, and was appointed Chancellor of the Duchy of Lancaster. In Oct. the decision was made to abandon the Gallipoli peninsular, and the following month Churchill resigned from parliament and went to the Western Front.

285 *a photo*. Probably the same as that reproduced on p. 290.

286 *the busiest man in England*. After Churchill's resignation, Marsh joined the staff of 10 Downing Street as an Assistant Secretary in charge of Civil List pensions.

289 *12th South Lancashires*. The 12th (Service) Battalion, which had been formed as a bantam battalion in June 1915, was attached to the 120th Brigade, 40th Division in Jan. 1916. On 2 March 1916 it was absorbed into the 11th Battalion, the King's Own (Royal Lancaster Regiment), another bantam battalion, since it was found that many of the men who had enlisted were not fit enough to cope with army life. It was disbanded in France on 7 Feb. 1918.

290 *this conscription business*. Conscription was introduced into the British army in Jan. 1916.

that poem. Probably 'Marching—as seen from the left file'.

292 *my two latest poems*. Possibly 'Sleep [III]' and 'Spring 1916'.

293 *most of the men being unfit*. See note to *12th South Lancashires* above.

294 *11th (S) Batt. K.O.R.L.* See note to *12th South Lancashires* above.

a play & some small poems. Moses.

Raymond B[uildings]. Marsh lived in No. 4, Raymond Buildings, Gray's Inn.

The printer is superb. The printer of *Moses* had made many mistakes, in places altering the sense of what IR had written. These were corrected at proof stage. This wry comment about introduced errors echoes a similar statement about the typist who helped him to prepare *Youth*. See the letter to Ruth Löwy of [March 1912] on p. 238.

295 *the Coloured Countries*. A reference to the campaigns in the Middle East.

Trevelyan the poet (brother of the socialist M.P.). R. C. Trevelyan (1872–1951), poet, playwright and translator. The MP was Charles Trevelyan (1870–1958), the anti-war campaigner and co-founder of the Union of Democratic Control. It was Trevelyan who first drew IR to Bottomley's attention in 1916 by sending him copies of *Youth* and *Moses*.

Moses. On 12 June, Zangwill wrote to AR, after receiving a copy of *Moses*: 'Will you kindly thank your brother for the little volume of poems he sent me. I enclose P.O. for 2/6 towards the cost of printing them. | You can tell him from me that I think there are a good many beautiful and powerful lines, but that I hope his experiences of war will give his next book the clarity and simplicity which is somewhat lacking in this.' For IR's first contact with Zangwill, see the letter on p. 234.

298 *R is in prison.* IR met John Rodker (1895–1955) in 1911: with Simon Weinstein (later Stephen Winsten, 1893–1991) and Joseph Leftowitz (see note to 'Lines Written in an Album' on p. 371), the four formed a group calling themselves the Whitechapel Boys. Later well-known as a novelist, translator, and publisher, particularly of important Modernist work, during the war Rodker was a conscientious objector. To escape imprisonment, he found refuge with R. C. Trevelyan, but he later served a prison sentence in Dartmoor.

299 *your second Georgian book. Georgian Poetry 1913–1915* (1916). Bottomley's play was *King Lear's Wife.*

Is Binyon in London or in France? Binyon was too old for military service, but in 1915 and 1916 he spent time as an orderly in a military hospital in France. In 1917 the Red Cross asked him to prepare a report on the work of British volunteers with the French wounded and refugees.

300 *My sister sent me your letter.* On 5 June, Trevelyan wrote to IR: 'Dear Mr Rosenberg, I am very grateful to you for sending me copies of your Moses. I am sending your sister the money for them, and asking her to send me any other poems you may have printed, if such there are. I gave a copy of Moses to Bottomley, and also the copy of Youth you sent for him. He has been very unwell this last week, so he has not yet been able to write to you; but he is getting better, and intends to write to you. It is a long time since I have read any new thing that has interested and impressed me so much as your Moses and several of your short poems. It quite reminds me of the time when I first read Abercrombie's Interludes. There are some really first-rate things in Moses; and the main idea too seems to me a really fine and dramatic one. I shall have to read it again several times, as parts do not yet seem quite clear to me, and I am not sure yet whose fault it is, mine or the language. I like a number of the poems, "In the Park", "Wedded", "If you are fire", "Lady, you are my God", "Expression", and others too. Your best phrases and ideas had something very real and compelling about them. Bottomley also admires your work very much: but he will write to you himself. I wish you all good luck, and I hope you may some day meet. Yours sincerely R. C. Trevelyan.'

the image in the first stanza. The first stanza reads: 'Nimrod was a hunter, striding | A belated mastodon; | Forests where he took his riding | Lay like corn when night came on.'

what you say in your letter. On 4 July 1916, Bottomley had written to IR: 'I have received your deeply interesting books ['Youth'] [Bottomley wrote 'Faith'] & "Moses" from my friend Mr Trevelyan, and I feel sincerely gratified to learn from him that you cared to send them to me and that it has pleased you to learn that I value your poetry [...]

'I have read both your books with delight. There is no doubt there was never a more real poet in the world than you are: to have such a gift as yours is a great responsibility, for you are called on to develope it to the highest advantage, and to learn as time goes on to separate with increasing sureness of touch the pure gold from its flux. Most men have to learn to obey their superiors, but poets have no superiors, so they have the harder task of learning to obey the light that is within them, and, among dazzling and contradictory illuminations, to make sure which is the eternal light.

'Many things in "Youth" are of a fine quality—fine in a remarkable and unusual way. "April Dawn" and "If you are fire and I am fire" are first-rate, and "The One Lost" is even better—it has utterance of the really great, simple kind. I like nearly as much "In the Park", "Wedded", "The Dead Heroes" and "Expression". In another way I like the quality you get in "Midsummer Frost"; but you get it at the expense of definition, and the beautiful suggestions it raises do not make their full effect because they do not make the reader feel quite as sure as you are that you have your team well in hand and are sure of the way you are going.

'I cannot tell the deep pleasure with which I read "Moses". It is a prodigious advance: I understand you have done it lately under distracting conditions, and this seems to me the best promise that you are going on to do other fine things. It is not only that it has so much of the sureness of direction of which I have just been speaking, but it has the large fine movement, the ample sweep which is the first requisite of great poetry, and which has lately dropped out of sight in the hands of exquisite lyricists who try to make us believe there is a great virtue in being short of breath. Such speeches as "Had you embalmed your beauty" and "I am sick of priests and forms", and most of "The royal paunch of Pharaoh" speech are the very top of poetry, and no one ever did better: but I value still more the instinct for large organisation which holds the whole together: In the same book the separate expansion of the God passage and "Sleep" have the same fine qualities.

'I shall look with keen interest for what you do next: there is nothing you cannot do when you have once made firm your hold on the qualities already within your reach. There is a great field still almost untouched in The Old Testament stories; the right way of handling them has scarcely been found yet in English Poetry, but I believe you have it within your means if you care to go on with it.

'I hope you will let me hear of your future productions and publications, and that you will go on with your real work whatever may be the claims of your apparent work that must also be satisfied; in the meantime I send you my sincere hopes for your good fortune, and I shall always be your sincere well-wisher.

Gordon Bottomley.'

JC (p. 150) says that IR 'was so proud of the letter that after memorizing its contents, he sent it home for the pleasure his family would take in it and for its safekeeping'. The letter was indeed safely kept, and its having been sent home, away from the trenches, accounts for its unusually good condition.

In response to IR's suggestions that Bottomley may have been pulling his leg, Bottomley wrote on 19 July: 'You can be quite sure I was not pulling your leg. I have an idea that praise does not hurt a sincere artist, and that to dwell on reservations with regard to his work often conveys a feeling of doubt at a point when the real necessity is to recognise a real gift, a serious talent.

'However if it will comfort you and bring you an assurance of my good faith, I shall try to say all the disagreeable things I can about your work. Your writing is at times too incomprehensible; it is not enough to know yourself what you mean, you must make sure of shewing other people what you mean; and you can never make sure of their coming to meet you unless you put yourself imaginatively in their place and go part of the way to meet them. They have a right to ask this of you, because poetry is fundamentally the exercise of the imagination.

'I really meant this when I spoke in my last letter of the poet's responsibility, and of his need to obey his inward illumination completely.

'But I should never think of demanding that you should immediately cease to be incomprehensible; if you manage that in twenty years all will be well. Poetry is the use of language in its quintessence, and the final test of poetry's success is to have achieved a texture of words as beautiful as the texture of a Rodin bronze or a Titian painting. When a good poet is still at his beginning stage he finds it takes him all his time to develope this sense of words keenly and to raise their texture sufficiently above the merely useful texture of every-day speech, so that he finds he has not always enough power of attention to think of clarifying his meaning too. But it is one of the rewards of long devotion that with practice his sense of his material becomes instinctive; then he naturally feels the responsibility of clarity is there too, and realises that his appeal cannot be completely successful without it. At this moment I feel you rely too much on individual words for producing the sense of beauty; I think you will soon find that you will get this better by the phrasing of passages rather than by the placing of individual words. I can say this to you because I also once relied too much on beautiful and remarkable words and found them rather a blind alley. When you are back in England again I will send you an early book of mine which everyone told me was incomprehensible and promising: that will deliver me completely into your hands for my criticism'.

Marsh did not agree with Bottomley's first assessment of *Moses*, telling him: 'I wrote him a piece of my mind about Moses, which seems to me really magnificent in parts, especially the speech beginning "Ah Koelue" which I think absolutely one of the finest things ever written—but as a whole it's surely quite ridiculously bad. I hope you mix plenty of powder with your jam. I do want him to renounce the lawless and grotesque manner in which he usually writes and to pay a little attention to form and tradition.' He followed this up in a second letter: 'I wrote to [Rosenberg] with the utmost brutality, telling him it was an outrage on humanity that the man who could write the Koelue speech should imbed it in such a farrago. I wouldn't have been such a beast but that I wanted to counteract the praise he'd had from you! [...] he seems to me entirely without architectonics—both the shaping instinct and the reserve of power that carries a thing through' (quoted in *JC* pp. 150–1).

In response to this, on 26 Nov. 1916, Bottomley wrote to IR: 'Mr Marsh tells me that I am too indulgent to you, so I look to you to justify me by making sure all the time that you have got your thoughts and feelings into as sharp a focus as the astronomer must get his stars before he can make sure of them.'

302 *Dear Sonia.* IR had met Sonia Cohen in 1911 in Whitechapel. She later married John Rodker.

303 *Miss Asquith.* Violet Asquith (1887–1969), daughter of the Prime Minister and later, as Lady Violet Bonham Carter, first woman President of the Liberal Party Organization.

304 *your book. Rhythmic Waves*, published under the pseudonym J. C. Churt. The poems dealing with the war can scarcely have appealed to IR, in particular 'The Battlefield' which began with the fiction, 'On the broad field of battle I stood', and ended with the lines: 'Into the Life the dead then passed, | Radiant with gladness. | Oh, happy dead!'.

The Poetry Review. The magazine of the Poetry Society, first published under the editorship of Harold Monro, in 1912.

Walt Whitman. (1819–92), American poet and author of *Drum Taps* (1865), from which this poem comes.

Yeats. William Butler Yeats (1865–1939), Irish poet and playwright. See note to 'Marching—as seen from the left file' on p. 383.

Noyes. Alfred Noyes (1880–1958), traditionalist, anti-modernist English poet, particularly of narrative verse and ballads relating to English history.

a Jewish play with Judas Macabeas for hero. This play was never written.

305 *The poem 'In the Trenches'*. In fact, 'Break of Day in the Trenches', which was a reworking of the earlier poem 'In the Trenches'.

a funny hunt for fleas. This seems to have been the starting point for the poem about searching for other vermin in 'Louse Hunting'.

King Lear's Wife. Play by Gordon Bottomley published in *Georgian Poetry 1913–1915*.

Nimrod poem. 'Babylonian Lyric' in *Chambers of Imagery: Second Series* (1912).

306 *Abercrombie's 'Hymn to Love'*. Published in *Emblems of Love* (1912).

307 *a trench poem of mine*. 'Break of Day in the Trenches'.

any of his plays to send me. In response to this letter, Schiff sent him, on 30 July, a copy of *Georgian Poetry 1913–1915*.

Trevor Blackmore's work. Trevor Ramsey Villiers Blakemore (*c*.1880–1953) was a poet and the author of a study of the painter Herbert Schmalz (1911). He also wrote an article, 'Rudyard Kipling: The Poet of Reality', in *The Poetical Gazette: The Official Journal of the Poetry Society*, no. 19, April 1912, which is among IR's papers.

I am glad Bomberg has done something definite at last. Bomberg went to France in June 1916. The following year he was transferred to a Canadian regiment as a war artist. He had married, in March 1916, Alice Mayes.

a poem I wrote in the trenches. 'Break of Day in the Trenches'.

309 *Trevor Blakemore's letter*. This does not appear to have survived.

John Drinkwater. English playwright and poet who was one of the Dymock Poets (see note to *New Numbers* on p. 420).

the new one. In 1913, Sydney Schiff (see note to p. 268) published a novel, *Concessions*, under his own name, and several more books under the pseudonym Stephen Hudson. His 1916 book was *War Time Silhouettes*.

those terrific conceptions of Balzac, and one I read of Stendhal's. Hardy I think is a better poet than novelist. Honoré de Balzac (1799–1850), French novelist, most famous for his series of novels *La Comédie Humaine*, which included *Eugénie Grandet* and *Le Père Goriot. Stendhal* (1783– 1842), pseudonym of the French novelist Marie-Henri Beyle, whose most famous works were *The Red and the Black* and *The Charterhouse of Parma. Thomas Hardy*: see note to p. 35.

311 *Rothenstein.* William Rothenstein (1872–1945), English painter of Ger- man Jewish descent. He studied at the Slade, and was an official war artist during the war.

enough for me. This sentence is crossed through, possibly by IR, or else by the censor.

312 *Strakers Stationery. JMW* (p. 254) says that Strakers was the stationer's shop below Rodker's flat.

Wells' Biblical play. Charles Jeremiah Wells (1800–79) wrote *Joseph and his Brethren: a dramatic poem* (1824) under the pseudonym H. L. Howard. The original article in *Fortnightly Review* had been published in 1875. IR had been reminded of the book in a postscript to Bottomley's letter to him of 4 July 1916, in which he wrote: 'I wonder if you know the play "Joseph & His Brethren", written a hundred years ago by Keats' friend C. J. Wells? It is very unequal, but I think you would find something to like in the scene between Joseph and Potiphar's Wife.' Bottomley sent a copy of the play to IR in France on 7 Sept. 1916, and in the accompanying letter said: 'I was interested to learn that you had made its acquaintance through Swinburne's essay, and I did the same myself twenty years ago. I wonder how you came across the essay? Perhaps it has been reprinted'. In 1908 the play had been reissued under Wells' own name, with the Swinburne article as an introduction, but IR had found it in the original *Fortnightly* (see letter to GB post- marked 17 Sept. 1916 on p. 318).

those small Tangera Greek figures in Chambers of Imagery. In *Chambers of Imagery: Second Series* (1912), there is a poem entitled 'Tanagret'; it must be this to which IR is referring. In a letter to him of 7 Sept. 1917, Bottomley wrote: 'If you like my Tanagra poem you must certainly remind me to send you on your return my large early book which I promised you: I think you might find among its eccentricities lengths of poetry here and there which make something of the same appeal'. After the opening stanzas which describe Faustine's beauty, Swinburne's poem, which was first published in 1862, is very different in feel.

It tells chillingly of an evil, Faustian woman, whereas Bottomley's is a gentle poem to a dead lover. Tanagra, in Boeotia in Greece, is noted for its classical terracotta figures.

313 *It is all Café Royal poetry now.* IR appears to be drawing a comparison between the more indirect and sometimes florid aspects of some late nineteenth century French poetry, and the immediacy of expression and simplicity of vocabulary that were the aim of the Georgians. The Café Royal is probably the Parisian gathering place, symbolic of the so-called café society, rather than the bohemian gathering place in Regent Street frequented by Edward Marsh and his circle of poets.

our own Heine. Heinrich Heine (1797–1856), German Jewish poet who spent much of his life in France, best known for his lyric poems, including the ballad 'Die Lorelei' (1827).

Rabelais. François Rabelais (?1494–1553), French humanist scholar and writer, author of the series of five novels, *Gargantua and Pantagruel*, boisterously satirical works in the Gallic comic tradition.

Butler. Probably Samuel Butler (1835–1902), English satirist and novelist, author of *Erewhon* and *The Way of All Flesh.*

Artist [R]ifles. The Artists' Rifles were established in 1859 as a volunteer corps which drew particularly on men who made their living in the arts. During the First World War it operated both as a fighting unit and as an Officer Training Corps whose members, once commissioned, went on to serve in other regiments.

Fitzroy Street flea. Fitzroy Street gave its name to Fitzrovia, a part of London north of Oxford Street and west of Bloomsbury particularly associated with the arts, including Harold Monro's Poetry Bookshop. In 1905 Sickert had taken a studio at 8 Fitzroy Street, and in 1907 the Fitzroy Street Group of painters, a precursor of the Camden Group, began to meet and exhibit their work at no. 19.

one I wrote about our armies. Possibly 'Pozières'. This was the aberration of a particular censor, since both before and after this letter IR had no problem with the censorship of his poetry.

'Nation'. Founded in 1907 as a liberal newspaper, *Nation* published high quality poetry and criticism. During the war it became increasingly left wing, campaigning for a negotiated peace. Its editor was the radical journalist H. W. Massingham (1860–1924), a supporter of the Union of Democratic Control (see note to p. 295).

314 *S[olomon].* J. Solomon (1860–1927), English Jewish painter, particularly of mythological, biblical, and genre subjects. IR met Solomon through Amschewitz, who urged him to endorse IR's application for

funds through the Jewish Educational Aid Society so that IR could study at the Slade. Solomon declined to recommend him, but his sister, Lily Delissa Joseph, was one of those who gave IR early encouragement in his painting (see Chronology 1911). Early in the war he realized the need for camouflage. In 1916 he was sent to France, initially working with the French and then setting up a British camouflage unit.

this little thing. Probably 'Pozières'.

Abercrombie's comedy. The End of the World, first published in *New Numbers,* vol. 1, no. 2, April 1914, and then in *Georgian Poetry, 1913–1915.* The play, set in the kitchen of a public house, has such characters as Huff the Farmer and Warp the Molecatcher, and slang, e.g. 'You fleering grinning louts, | I'll give it you now'. Bottomley described it as 'a rare and enchanting work by a great poet, and fills me with admiration'. It has the same title as a poem by Bottomley (see note to p. 257).

315 *Adam and Eve.* The drawing (see Plate 7), which was probably done in 1912 or 1913, is now in the Tullie Museum and Art Gallery in Carlisle.

Miss Pulley. Miss Pulley rented rooms in the building which also housed Harold Monro's Poetry Bookshop. One of these she let to Sonia Cohen, and IR visited her there.

317 *Lawrence.* D. H. Lawrence (1885–1930), English novelist and poet.

Westminster Gazette. A newspaper published between 1892 and 1928. The poem was reprinted in the *Westminster Gazette* on Monday, 4 Aug. 1916, having been awarded the prize in a competition in the *Saturday Review.* Headed 'A Song for Camp Concerts', it was signed 'Etien. BEF France'.
Me and Bill and Ginger | Sailed away to France; | Said goodbye to Farver, | Landed back at Harver; | Didn't have a chance | To parlez-vous at Harver or go upon the spree, | But started touring Flanders—| George, and Bill, and me. || Since that time we've travelled—| Ginger, me, and Bill—| Seen what's left of Wipers, | Dodged the German snipers | Under Vimy Hill, | Rested in the valley where Somme goes down to sea, | And strafed the Boche at Montauban—| Ginger, Bill, and me. || When the war is over, | When we've done with guns, | We three mean to go, Sir, | Where we do not know, Sir, | But far from any Huns, | And run a farm or something as cosy as can be, | And no more France or Flanders | For Ginger, Bill, and me!

Somme Cinemas. An hour-long film about the opening stages of the Battle of the Somme was released in British cinemas at the end of Aug. 1916.

Chesterton on Zangwill. G. K. Chesterton (1874–1936), English writer. Chesterton was a friend of Zangwill (see note to p. 234) who, in 1911, had published *Appreciations and Criticisms of the Works of Charles Dickens*, in the Introduction of which he discussed the character Aaron in *Our Mutual Friend*: 'In a moral sense there is no doubt at all that Dickens introduced the Jew with a philanthropic idea of doing justice to Judaism, which he had been told he had affronted by the great gargoyle of Fagin [. . .] It is certainly unfortunate for the Hebrew cause that the bad Jew should be so very much more convincing than the good one [. . .] There is nothing about [old Aaron] that in any way suggests the nobler sort of Jew, such a man as Spinoza or Mr Zangwill [. . .] To describe the high visionary and mystic Jew like Spinoza or Zangwill is a great and delicate task in which even Dickens might have failed'. Zangwill's *The War for the World* was published in 1916; IR may be referring to a review of this by Chesterton which I have been unable to trace.

318 *the rejected masterpiece.* 'Pozières' had been returned by *Nation*.

Joseph. See note to p. 312. IR sent a field postcard to GB dated 13 Sept. and postmarked 16 Sept. 1916 acknowledging receipt of his letter of 6th and noting: 'Letter follows at first opportunity'.

Fortnightly. Fortnightly Review, a high quality and influential literary magazine founded in 1865.

your fine louse song. 'The Elder Woman's Songs' from *King Lear's Wife*. The song begins: 'A louse crept out of my lady's shift'. Writing to IR on 7 Sept. 1916, Bottomley thanked IR for proposing to give him *Adam and Eve*, but added: 'I must not let you present me with your Flea-Hunt also: in the first place because you ought to do it yourself, and secondly because I am so universally reprobated for my louse in Kg. Lear's Wife that my reputation would not survive a flea as well.'

Keatings. Proprietary brand of insect powder that was advertised as destroying bugs, fleas, moths, and beetles.

319 *printed by you.* The poem was published in Chicago in Harriet Monroe's *Poetry: A Magazine of Verse* in Dec. 1916. The poems he enclosed were 'Break of Day in the Trenches' and 'The Troop Ship'. See note to p. 102.

My Lilith. Principal character in IR's plays *The Amulet* and *The Unicorn*.

320 *Flaubert's 'Salambo'.* Gustav Flaubert (1821–80), French novelist, whose most famous novel is *Madame Bovary*. *Salammbô* was published in 1856.

a book of yours had appeared. In 1916 Binyon published a volume of poems entitled *The Anvil*. Dedicated *Aux Camarades Français*, it derives from his observations on the Western Front, particularly with the French. See note to p. 299.

321 *Yom Tov.* Jewish festival.

Minnie. IR's eldest sister, who became Minnie Horvitch, with whom IR stayed in South Africa.

home for the winter now. IR's father, Dovber, or Barnett (1859/60–1936), was an itinerant pedlar who did not work in the winter months.

322 *your annual. An Annual of New Poetry 1917.* This contained poems by Gordon Bottomley, W. H. Davies (1871–1940), John Drinkwater, Edward Eastway (Edward Thomas), Robert Frost, Wilfrid Wilson Gibson, T. Surge Moore, and R. C. Trevelyan (see note to *New Numbers* on p. 265).

Moore's Sicilian Idyll. The first scene of T. Surge Moore's 'A Sicilian Idyll' was published in *Georgian Poetry 1911–1912* (1912). To *An Annual of New Poetry: 1917* he contributed a long poem entitled 'Micah'.

Judith. Both poems were published in Abercrombie's volume *Emblems of Love* (1912).

323 *Gibson's new book 'Battle'.* Gibson's collection *Battle* was published in 1915. Gibson did not serve in France, but his descriptions of trench life are immediate and compelling.

'The Sheiling'. Bottomley's home in Silverdale, near Carnforth, Lancashire.

324 *the poem I spoke about.* 'Daughters of War'.

Signed R S Oglethorpe. The censored lines are not poetry; the draft of 'Daughter of War' was signed and approved by the same officer. This contrasts with IR's complaint in his letter to Marsh of [Aug. 1916] (see p. 313) that 'I have been forbidden to send poems home, as the censor won't be bothered with going through such rubbish'. The final page, or pages, of the letter are missing.

325 *changes in the government.* Herbert Asquith (1852–1928) was the Liberal Prime Minister at the outbreak of war. In May 1915 he formed a coalition government. Mounting criticism of the conduct of the war, and the high rate of casualties, led to his resignation in Dec. 1916. He was succeeded by David Lloyd George (1863–1945), who initially declined to put Churchill into his Cabinet. However, in July 1917, he appointed Churchill Minister of Munitions, and Edward Marsh became once more his Private Secretary.

326 *My sister wrote me she would be writing to you.* After IR had told his family that he had influenza, Ann wrote to Marsh to ask if he could arrange for him to be moved from the front because of their anxieties about his health: 'Make up any tale, but do see what can be done at once. What to

do with my mother, I really don't know, as she is worried to death'. Having heard from IR, in a letter that appears to be lost, Marsh had already written to a friend of his at the War Office, A. J. Creedy, who replied: 'I am sorry for the Hebrew bard, but as you can imagine it is not easy to do anything from the W.O. as he is within the jurisdiction of G.H.Q.' Instead, he suggested that Marsh write privately to IR's adjutant 'telling him what you know of R and what you think of his budding genius, and ask him whether R is really fit for trench work and not more suitable for some clerical job'. IR's commanding officer, Captain O. G. Normoy, replied to Marsh that IR had been medically examined and was fit, but that he would keep an eye on the situation and make changes if these seemed necessary. Meanwhile, the examining doctor had recommended that he be temporarily reassigned to less demanding work, and he had been moved behind the lines to a Works Battalion.

327 *I wrote a poem some while ago which Bottomley liked so.* 'The Destruction of Jerusalem by the Babylonian Hordes'. For GB's response, see the note to this poem on p. 387.

Colonial Office. After the fall of Asquith's government (see note to p. 325 on *changes in the government*) Marsh was demoted and sent to the Colonial Office as a clerk in the West African Department. He took up gardening (see letters to Marsh postmarked 10 Oct. 1916 on p. 319) and concentrated on his literary interests.

Daumier or Goya. Honoré Daumier (1808–79), French painter, lithographer, and sculptor, particularly noted for his bitingly satirical cartoons which highlighted corruption and injustice; Francisco José de Goya y Lucientes (1746–1828), Spanish painter and etcher whose visionary and uncompromising attacks on political and social abuses included a series of etchings entitled *The Disasters of War* (1863).

329 *'Ah Kolue' speech. Moses* ll. 176–98. Edward Marsh reprinted this in *Georgian Poetry 1916–1917* (1917).

G.B. has urged me to write Jewish Plays. In a letter of 12 Feb. 1917, Bottomley wrote: 'Your idea of doing a Judas Maccabeus is first rate, and I hope you will keep tight hold of it until you find an opportunity to tackle it. It, and a whole host of the similar gorgeous subjects which are your birthright, have never been properly done in English literature, and I believe you have the power in you to make them your own and also to make memorable things of them.'

Gilbert Cannan has written a novel called 'Mendel'. Gilbert Cannan (1884–1955). Subtitled *A Story of Youth* and published in 1916, the novel is based on the love affair between Gertler and Dora Carrington (1893–1932), the painter associated with the Bloomsbury Group.

Trevelyan's 'Annual'. An Annual of New Poetry (1917).

330   *Sturge Moore is a poet I like very much though I only know his 'Sycillian idyll' in GB.* T. Surge Moore (1870–1944), English poet. His poem 'A Sicilian Idyll' was published in *A Sicilian Idyll, and Judith* (1911), and in *Georgian Poetry 1911–12* (1912). 'GB' is Georgian Book.

Mr Trevelyan's Play. 'The Pearl Tree', published in *An Annual of New Poetry*, and described by Bottomley as 'a charming, delicate Hindu play'.

the lively happenings of late sound very promising. Early in 1917 the tide of battle had turned in the Middle East, and on 11 March Baghdad had fallen to the British army.

331   *some lines suggested by going out wiring.* 'Dead Man's Dump'.

332   *Lycidas.* Elegiac poem to his friend, Edward King, who was drowned, written in 1637 by Milton.

I forget the name of the poem. 'To his Coy Mistress' by Andrew Marvell (1621–78).

a much finer poem. 'Daughters of War'.

333   *?Postmarked 29 May 1917. 1937* gives no information about dating for this letter; *1979* says [Postmarked 29 May 1917]; the original, in the Berg, has no envelope attached.

334   *Erebus.* See note to p. 283.

I've made it into a little book for you. See note to 'Daughters of War' on p. 391.

335   *Dave doing and Elkon.* IR's brothers.

Peretz's boys. IR's cousins, the sons of his father's brother Peretz Rosenberg (see note to p. 354).

337   *'Within your Roman House'.* Entitled 'To——, with a Play';——was Edward Thomas. The poems he is discussing were published in *An Annual of New Poetry: 1917.*

'All Souls'. 'All Souls, 1914'.

338   *Abercrombie is a shell inspector.* Writing to IR on 29 June 1917, Bottomley had said of Abercrombie's wartime employment: 'It is weariful and grievous to me that good poets should be so wastefully used, and all because the German nation has gone out of its mind and given itself over to wicked folly.'

Matthew Arnold (1822–88), English poet and critic, author of 'The Scholar Gypsy' and 'Dover Beach', was a school inspector for thirty-five years, a task he often found monotonous and did not particularly enjoy.

340 *your memoir*. A memoir of Rupert Brooke first published in *The Collected Poems of Rupert Brooke: With a Memoir* in July 1918.

343 *Ray*. IR's youngest sister, Rachel, later Mrs Lyons.

a little book compiled by the Chief Rabbi of Jewish interest. A Book of Jewish Thoughts for Jewish Sailors and Soldiers selected and arranged by the Chief Rabbi (Dr J. H. Hertz), 1917. There are in fact two pieces by Heine, 'The Book of Books' and 'Moses', and one piece by Disraeli (1804–81), entitled 'The Jews of York (1190)'. IR was rather unfair to Hertz, who printed seven pieces of his own work, occupying fewer than ten of the 176 pages which include work from nearly eighty authors, as well as sacred texts.

344 *Dear Mr Bottomley. 1922* p. 42 and *1979* p. 257, gave this letter as written to Edward Marsh, and suggested a possible date as June 1917. In fact, it was written to Gordon Bottomley, and is postmarked 19 Aug. 1917.

347 *Mr Trevelyan sent me his comedy. The Pterodamozels: an operatic fable*, privately printed by Trevelyan at the Pelican Press in Nov. 1916.

349 *taken sick*. All Rosenberg's biographers have said that his two months' stay in hospital was due to influenza. However, the 51st General Hospital at Etaples was one of a number of hospitals on the Western Front that treated only soldiers suffering from venereal disease.

In the undated fragment LXXVIII (p. 146), which is on the same sheet of paper as the poem 'Apparition', almost certainly written before Rosenberg went into the army, and undoubtedly before he went to France in 1916, there are the two lines, 'Where syphil[is] has placed its corroding finger | The damned disease will never die'. This might suggest some earlier contact with the disease.

During the war, 400,000 cases of VD were reported among British soldiers, most of whom had become infected during leave; in October 1917, 1,935 other ranks were admitted to the 51st General Hospital. The period from infection to the appearance of symptoms was anything from two days to three months. In the 51st, the treatment, which typically lasted up to sixty days, consisted of a series of injections of two drugs, Arsenobenzol or '606' which had been discovered in Germany in 1909 and hailed as a miracle cure, and a later version called Neoslavarsan or '919'. They could have highly unpleasant side effects due to the toxic effects of the arsenic and mercury. These were not only physical—vomiting, abdominal pain, diarrhoea, headaches—but also psychological, inducing in patients a 'general malaise'. In addition to the toxic effect of the injections, the official medical history of the First World

War reported that the prolonged lack of activity in hospital for those undergoing treatment 'led to a noticeable deterioration in their mental condition'. These factors would account for the sudden decline in Rosenberg's morale from the autumn of 1917, and his increasing sense of helplessness, exacerbated by the knowledge that any soldier reporting sick with VD was denied home leave for a year. At the end of the treatment most soldiers went straight back into active service; only those with complications went on for further treatment or convalescence. In November, Rosenberg was one of 1,332 other ranks to be discharged from the hospital back into the line.
See *A History of the Great War: Medical Services: Diseases of the War*, vol. 2, pp. 118–59, and the official diary of the 51st General Hospital in the National Archives.

a small poem I'll enclose. 'Girl to Soldier on Leave'.

350 *your suggestions.* The letter containing these suggestions has not survived, and the only extant full version of the play is a TS which IR had prepared for GB following cuts he had made. In correspondence with Denys Harding in preparation for *1937*, now in the University of Bristol Library, GB said: 'If the version before the latest one (mine) were to turn up, you would find it much more of a play, and with so much more kinship with "Moses" than with anything else that I think you would feel bound to put together. But I suspect he destroyed it in the trenches when he had put together his latest revision for me.' In a later letter he explained: 'the previous stage was much fuller, and the version represented by my typescript represents a severe pruning of that—following my criticism of its starting too many hares at once. This pruning was only done in the last weeks of Rosenberg's life. Now, of course, I would give a good deal for that earlier fuller version which I criticized: for he pruned it too much, and the lost version would give us a better idea of his intentions than we have now.'

Browning—say in Pippa Passes. Robert Browning (1812–89), English poet. 'Pippa Passes' was a dramatic poem published in *Bells and Pomegranates* (1841–6).

351 *Lucretius. Lucretius on Death: Being a translation of Book III, lines 930–1094 of De Rerum Natura* translated by Trevelyan and published in 1917. Titus Lucretius Carus (*c.*94–*c.*55 BC) was a Roman poet and philosopher.

352 *a poem I've just written.* 'In War'. This letter in *BL* alters the previously suggested date of this poem.

a poem of Verharen. See note to p. 253. The poem is 'The Sovran Rhythm'.

The hymn to the Setting Sun. The title is 'Ode to the Setting Sun'.

353 ——'s *letters.* Bottomley's letters. See pp. 425-7.

Tennyson thought Burns' love-songs important, but the 'Cottar's S[aturday]. N[ight].' poor. Wordsworth thought the opposite. Robert Burns (1759-96) Scottish poet, author of 'The Cottar's Saturday Night'; William Wordsworth (1770-1850), English Romantic poet.

354 *Sturge Moore...Wells.* For Moore see note to p. 330. H. G. Wells (1866-1946), English novelist and science fiction writer whose works included *The War of the Worlds* (1898) and *The War in the Air* (1908). *Mr Britling Sees it Through* (1916) was a novel about the First World War.

355 *Pater.* Walter Pater (1839-94). English writer, whose book *Studies in the History of the Renaissance* (1873) was immensely influential.

this late stunt. The Battle of Cambrai, 20 Nov.–early Dec. 1917.

Isaacs. Jacob Isaacs (1896-1973), scholar and critic.

The Georgian Book. Georgian Poetry 1916-17 (1917).

your J[ewish] affair. The Jewish Association of Arts and Sciences, for which Leftwich had nominated IR. This letter was written, in part, on the back of the nomination form, in which, under 'Address', IR had erased his home address and replaced it with 'The Chatty Chateau, British Armies', under 'Occupation' he had given 'Picture maker', and under 'Active Interests he had put 'Live Stock', a wry comment on the time he spent delousing; chats were lice.

356 *J. C. Squire's poem.* J. C. Squire (1884-1958), English writer and Georgian poet whose three poems in *Georgian Poetry 1916-1917* were taken from his work *The Lily of Malud and Other Poems* (1917). They were 'A House', 'To a Bull-dog', and 'The Lily of Malud'.

Turner's. W. J. Turner (1889-1946), Australian-born Georgian poet. The poems were taken from *The Hunter and other Poems* (*1916*), and were 'Romance', 'Ecstasy', 'Magic', 'The Hunter', 'The Sky-sent Death', and 'The Caves of Auvergne'.

Sassoon. Siegfried Sassoon (1886-1967), English poet. The poems from *The Old Huntsman* (1917) were 'A Letter Home', 'The Kiss', 'The Dragon and the Undying', 'To Victory', 'They', 'In the Pink', 'Haunted', and 'The Death-Bed'. *John Masefield* (1878-1967), English poet.

What is happening...It is breaking me completely. These lines were excised by the censor.

358 *My own Batt is broken up.* Because of a crisis in manpower, on 10 Jan. 1918, on the orders of the Cabinet Committee and against fierce opposition from the Army Council, the British army was reorganized. Divisions were reduced from twelve to nine battalions, and brigades from four to three battalions.

the Settlement. A penal settlement for conscientious objectors.

Elliott's work. T. S. Eliot (1888–1965). Hugely influential Modernist English poet and playwright of American birth who, in 1917, published his first volume, *The Love Song of J. Alfred Prufrock.*

Hueffer's book. The Good Soldier (1915). See note to p. 236.

359 *I am sending one or two poor things.* The letter does not have a valediction, but finishes at the bottom of a page of Church Army Recreation Hut writing paper. A second sheet has a pencil holograph of 'The Tower of S[k]ulls' inscribed by IR 'From The Unicorn', written on the same printed writing paper: there may have been no final page. Also enclosed with the letter were TSS of 'Returning, we hear the larks', 'The Burning of the Temple', and the first three stanzas of 'The Dying Soldier'. In the first line of 'The Burning of the Temple', IR has added, in pencil, an 'i' into the word 'wrath' making it 'wraith'.

360 *transferred to the 'Judaens'.* Five battalions of the Royal Fusiliers (38th–42nd Judaean) were formed in England in Jan. 1918 from Jewish volunteers. Three served abroad in Palestine and Egypt; two remained at home as training battalions.

this coming 'earthquake'. The Germans launched a ferocious attack on the British army on 21 March 1918. Bringing in troops released from fighting on the Eastern Front, and timed to start before the arrival of the Americans in any numbers, it had been known and talked about for several weeks. The following two weeks (during which IR was killed) brought the Germans to within a few miles of Paris and the point of breakthrough. But the Allies rallied, and the British, encouraged by Haig's famous 'Backs to the Wall' communiqué, held on to the strategic railhead at Amiens. On 4 April the German attack was discontinued.

361 *his co-religionists.* Leon Trotsky (1879–1940) was Jewish.

Russia is like an amputated limb to our cause and America is the cork substitute. Following the Russian Revolution of Oct. 1917, on 8 Nov. the Bolshevik government published peace proposals. The Treaty of Brest Litovsk, bringing an end to the war between Germany and Russia, was signed on 3 March 1918. Meanwhile, America had declared war on Germany on 6 April 1917, but it was not until early 1918 that US forces—the 'Doughboys'—began to arrive in France in significant numbers.

362 *Pasach.* Pasach or Paschu is the Jewish festival of Passover.

363 *a rotten poem by Herbert Asquith.* Entitled 'The Volunteer', it was a poem more typical of 1914 than 1917. Herbert Asquith (1881–1947) was the son of the British Prime Minister, also Herbert Asquith (1852–1928).

   a vivid poem about Christ in the Tower. 'The Tower' by Robert Nichols (1893–1944), English poet.

364 *Freeman.* John Freeman (1880–1929), English poet who had seven poems in *Georgian Poetry 1916–1917.*

APPENDIX
CONTENTS OF VOLUMES PUBLISHED BY ROSENBERG

Night and Day

Grey paper wrappers. NIGHT | AND | DAY. | By ISAAC ROSENBERG [Printed by Israel Narodiczky]. [London, 1912.]

> Night and Day.
> Aspiration.
> To J. M. Amschewitz.
> Heart's First Word [I].
> [When I went forth as is my daily wont].
> In November.
> [Lady, you are my God].
> Spiritual Isolation – fragment [ll.1–28].
> Tess.
> [O! in a world of men and women].

Youth

Grey paper wrappers. Youth | BY | ISAAC ROSENBERG. | LONDON, 1915 | I. Narodiczky, 48, Mile End Road, E.

1. FAITH AND FEAR
   > Aspiration.
   > In The Park ('Night and Day', ll. 186–200, 209–21).
   > *Desire Sings Of Immortality (listed in contents as 'Song of
   >   Immortality') ('Night and Day' ll. 230–49).
   > Noon In The City ('Night and Day' ll. 126–49).
   > None Have Seen The Lord Of The House.
   > A Girl's Thoughts.
   > Wedded ([II]).
   > Midsummer Frost.

2. THE CYNICS LAMP
   > Love And Lust.
   > In Piccadilly.
   > A Mood.

3. CHANGE AND SUNFIRE
April Dawn.
[If you are fire and I am fire].
[Dim-watery-lights, gleaming on gibbering faces] ('Night and
    Day' ll. 152–7).
[Break in my subtler nearer ways].
[Lady, you are my God].
The One Lost. (ll. 1–8).
*[My soul is robbed by your most treacherous eyes] [(II)].
God Made Blind.
*The Dead Heroes.
*The Cloister.
*Expression.

Poems marked with an asterisk were omitted from IR's initial scheme for
Youth; in this scheme he intended "Tess' to follow 'A Mood' in Part 2.

Moses: A Play

Burgundy cloth-covered board or yellow paper wrappers. MOSES | A PLAY. |
BY | ISAAC ROSENBERG. | London, 1916. | Printed by The Paragon
Printing Works, | 8, Ocean Street, Stepney Green, E.

Spring 1916.
MOSES.
God.
[I did not pluck at all].
Chagrin.
In The Park ('Night and Day' ll. 186–200, 209–20, 230–49. These lines
    run on to form a single poem, with the parenthesis (*Desire sings of
    immortality.*) following l. 220.
Wedded [(II)].
Marching – as seen from the left file.
Sleep.
Heart's First Word.

INDEX OF TITLES AND FIRST LINES

*indicates the title by which the poem was previously known.

SUBJECT INDEX